The Hanukkah Anthology

Publication of this book was made possible
by a gift from
SANDY AND SUSAN CHANDLER FRANK.
It is lovingly dedicated to the memory of
MOSES FRANK
who spent his life teaching
and to his granddaughter
ALEXANDRA CHANDLER FRANK
who is beginning her life learning.

PHILIP GOODMAN

The Hanukkah Anthology

The Jewish Publication Society

Philadelphia   Jerusalem
5752/1992

Library of Congress Catalog Card Information
The Hanukkah Anthology. Philip Goodman, comp.
  1976, 1992.
Cloth, ISBN 0–8276–0080–1   Paper, ISBN 0–8276–0401–7
1. Hanukkah.   2. Hanukkah–Literary collections.   I. Goodman, Philip, 1911–
BM695.H3H37   296.4'35'08   75-44637

The editor herewith expresses his sincere appreciation to the following publishers and authors who have kindly granted permission to use the material indicated from their published works.

Acum Ltd., Tel Aviv: *"Mi Yemalel?"* by Menashe Ravina and *"Hanukkah, Hag Yafeh Kol Kakh"* by Levin Kipnis.

American Friends of the Hebrew University, New York: "The Miracle of Hanukkah" by Judah L. Magnes, 1946.

American–Israel Publishing Co., Ltd., Tel Aviv: "Hanukkah among Eastern Jews," reprinted from *One People: The Story of the Eastern Jews* by Devora and Menahem Hacohen by permission of Sabra Books. Copyright © 1969 by American–Israel Publishing Co., Ltd.

Ch. Ben Arza & Co., Jerusalem: "The Eight-Day Miracle" from *The Book of Our Heritage*, vol. 1, by Eliyahu Kitov. Copyright © 1968 by 'A' Publishers and Eliyahu Kitov.

Barton's Candy Corporation, Brooklyn, N.Y.: "Five," reprinted by permission of Barton's Candy Corporation.

Behrman House Inc., New York: "The Miracle" from *Poems for Young Israel* by Philip M. Raskin, 1925. Reprinted by permission of Behrman House Inc.

Bloch Publishing Co., New York: "Hanukkah Lights" from *Collected Poems of Philip M. Raskin*, 1951; "The Tale of Hanukkah Retold by This Gay Minstrel's Pen of Gold" from *A Jewish Child's Garden of Verses* by Abraham Burstein, 1940. Reprinted by permission of Bloch Publishing Co.

Board of Jewish Education, New York: "Hanukkah in Nazi-Occupied Belgium" from *Young Moshe's Diary* by Moshe Flinker, 1971; "The Story of Hanukkah" by Deborah Pessin and "My Dreidel" by Hayyim Nahman Bialik from *Jewish Life and Customs: Unit Four: Hanukkah* ed. by Ben M. Edidin, 1942; "The Great Hanukkah Strike" by Bami from *More World Over Stories* ed. by Ezekiel Schloss and Morris Epstein, 1968; "One Hanukkah in Helm" by Yaacov Luria from *World Over*, vol. 22, no. 5 (December 2, 1960); "Reuben Lights a Torch" by Sol Klein from *World Over*, vol. 8, no. 4 (December 13, 1946); "A Dreidel for Tuvi" by Morris Epstein from *World Over*, vol. 14, no. 3 (November 28, 1952); "A Menorah in Tel Aviv" by Ya'akov from *The New World Over Story Book* ed. by Ezekiel Schloss and Morris Epstein, 1968; "Dances for Hanukkah" from *Folk Dances for Jewish Festivals* by Dvora Lapson, 1961, and *Jewish Dances the Year Round* by Dvora Lapson, 1957.

Brandeis University, Waltham, Mass.: "Hanukkah in the Soviet Union" from *The Jewish Religion in The Soviet Union* by Joshua Rothenberg, Philip W. Lown Graduate Center for Contemporary Jewish Studies and Ktav Publishing House, 1971.

Branden Press, Inc., Boston: "Hanukkah Candles" by Zalman Shneour and "A Hanukkah Top" by Nahum D. Karpivner from *Gems of Hebrew Verse: Poems for Young People*, trans. by Harry H. Fein. Copyright 1940 by Bruce Humphries, Inc. Used by permission of Branden Press, Inc.

E. J. Brill, Leiden: excerpts from *The Book of Judith*, ed. by Solomon Zeitlin, trans. by Morton S. Enslin, E. J. Brill, Leiden, for Dropsie University, Philadelphia, 1972.

Mrs. Ruth F. Brin, Minneapolis: "An Interpretation of Hanukkah" from *Interpreta-*

tions for the Weekly Torah Reading by Ruth F. Brin, Lerner Publications Co., Minneapolis, 1965.

Canadian Young Judaea, Toronto: "The Last Hour" by David Frishman, trans. by Abraham M. Klein, from *The Judaean*, vol. 2, no. 3 (December 1928).

CCAR Journal, New York: "The Festival of Hanukkah" by Ruby Fogel Levkoff from *CCAR Journal*, vol. 19, no. 4 (Autumn 1972).

Central Conference of American Rabbis, New York: "Kindle the Taper," music by Jacob Singer, and "Rock of Ages," trans. by Gustav Gottheil and M. Jastrow, from *Union Hymnal*, 3d edition, Central Conference of American Rabbis, 1932.

Columbia University Press, New York: "Marranism and Hanukkah" from *From Spanish Court to Italian Ghetto: Isaac Cardoso: A Study in Marranism and Jewish Apologetics* by Yosef Hayim Yerushalmi, 1971.

Harry Coopersmith, Santa Barbara: "O Hanukkah" and "Who Can Retell?" from *The New Jewish Song Book*, ed. by Harry Coopersmith, Behrman House, New York, 1965. Copyright © 1965 by Harry Coopersmith.

Crown Publishers, Inc., New York: "Hanukkah Money" taken from *The Old Country* by Sholom Aleichem, translated by Julius and Frances Butwin. © 1946 by Crown Publishers, Inc. Used by permission of Crown Publishers, Inc.; "The Battle of Modin" and "His Pride Was Too Much," taken from *My Glorious Brothers* by Howard Fast. Copyright 1948 by Howard Fast. Used by permission of Crown Publishers, Inc., and Howard Fast.

Doubleday & Company Inc., New York: "The Little Hanukkah Lamp" by Isaac Loeb Peretz, trans. by Nathan Ausubel, from *A Treasury of Jewish Humor*, ed. by Nathan Ausubel. Copyright © 1951 by Nathan Ausubel. Reprinted by permission of Doubleday & Company.

Farrar, Straus & Giroux, Inc., New York: "The Eternal Light" from *The Birthday of the World* by Moshe Davis and Victor Ratner, Farrar, Straus & Giroux, Inc., New York, 1959. Copyright © 1959 by The Jewish Theological Seminary of America. Reprinted with permission of Farrar, Straus & Giroux, Inc., Dr. Moshe Davis, and Mrs. Victor Ratner.

Rabbi Roland B. Gittelsohn, Boston: "The Menorah or the Tree?" by Roland B. Gittelsohn from *The Best of Ten Years in the Jewish Digest*, ed. by Bernard Postal and David H. White, Houston, 1965.

Samuel E. Goldfarb, Mercer Island, Washington: "Hear the Voice of Israel's Elders," "*Hanukkah*," and "*Oy Ir Kleine Likhtelekh*" from *The Jewish Songster*: Part 1, ed. by Israel Goldfarb and Samuel E. Goldfarb, Brooklyn, N.Y., 1925; "My Dreidel" from *The Jewish Home Institute: Chanuko: Third Week*, Bureau of Jewish Education, New York.

Hadassah Zionist Youth Commission, New York: "It Happened on Hanukkah" by Natan Alterman, translated by Steve Friedman, from *The Young Judaean*, vol. 49, no. 3 (December 1960).

Rev. Joseph Halpern, Ramat Gan, Israel: "A Syrian Diary" by Joseph Halpern from *Storytime: A Jewish Children's Story-Book* by Arthur Saul Super and Joseph Halpern, 1946.

Harper & Row, Publishers, Inc., New York: excerpts from *The First Book of Maccabees*, An English Translation by Sidney Tedesche. Copyright 1950 by Harper & Row, Publishers, Inc; excerpts from *The Second Book of Maccabees*, An English Translation by Sidney Tedesche. Edited by Solomon Zeitlin. Copyright 1954 by Harper & Row, Publishers, Inc. Reprinted by permission of the publisher.

Hartmore House, Bridgeport: "In Darkness Candles" from *The Fire Waits: Prayers and Poems for the Sabbath and Festivals* by Michael I. Hecht, 1972. Reprinted with permission of Hartmore House.

Harvard University Press, Cambridge: "Festival of Lights" from *Josephus: Jewish Antiquities*, vol. 7, trans. by Ralph Marcus (The Loeb Classical Library), Harvard University Press, Cambridge, 1943.

Hebrew Publishing Co., New York: "The Scroll of the Hasmoneans" from *Ha-Siddur ha-Shalem: Daily Prayer Book*, trans. and annotated by Philip Birnbaum, 1949.

Reprinted by permission of Hebrew Publishing Co.; "Hanukkah and the Rebirth of Israel" from *A People That Dwells Alone* by Yaacov Herzog, edited by Misha Louvish, Sanhedrin Press, 1975. Copyright 1975 by Pnina Herzog.

Ihud Habonim, Tel Aviv: "Jerusalem Candles" by Menashe from *Hamekasher Anthology*, 1956.

Jewish Life (published by Union of Orthodox Jewish Congregations of America), New York: "The Hanukkah Menorah" by Daniel Persky from *Jewish Life*, vol. 14, no. 2 (December 1946).

Jewish National Fund, Youth and Education Department, New York: "Hanukkah and the Redemption of the Land" by Joseph G. Klausner from *Chanukah Highlights: A Handbook for Teachers and Youth Leaders*, ed. by Misha Louvish, Jerusalem, 1959.

Jewish Publication Society of America, Philadelphia: "Hanukkah and Its History" by Solomon Grayzel, music for "Blessings on Kindling the Hanukkah Lights," "*Hanerot Hallalu*," and "*Maoz Tzur*" from *Hanukkah: The Feast of Lights*, ed. by Emily Solis-Cohen, Jr. Copyright © 1937, 1965; "Theodor Herzl's 'The Menorah' " from *Theodor Herzl: A Biography* by Alex Bein. Copyright © 1940; "Hanukkah in a Lithuanian Ghetto" from *Worlds That Passed* by A. S. Sachs. Copyright © 1928, 1956; "An Israeli Boy in Moscow" from *Between Hammer and Sickle* by Arie L. Eliav (Ben Ami). Copyright © 1967, 1969; "The Dolls' Hanukkah" from *What the Moon Brought* by Sadie Rose Weilerstein. Copyright © 1942, 1970; "The Magic Top" from *The Breakfast of the Birds and Other Stories* by Judah Steinberg. Copyright © 1917, 1945; selections from *The Holy Scriptures according to the Masoretic Text*. Copyright © 1917, 1955; selections from *The Book of Psalms: A New Translation according to the Traditional Hebrew Text*. Copyright © 1972; a selection from *The Legends of the Jews* by Louis Ginzberg. Copyright © 1911; "Recipes for Hanukkah" from *Jewish Cooking around the World: Gourmet and Holiday Recipes* by Hanna Goodman. Copyright © 1973. All books copyrighted by the Jewish Publication Society of America.

Jewish Reconstructionist Foundation, New York: "The Extra Flame" by Curt Leviant from *The Reconstructionist*, vol. 22, no. 15 (November 30, 1956).

The Jewish Spectator, New York: "The National Significance of the Maccabean Legacy" by Solomon Rappaport, *The Jewish Spectator*, vol. 17, no. 11 (December 1952); "The Living Menorah" by Avigdor Hameiri, *The Jewish Spectator*, vol. 12, no. 2 (December 1946).

The Jewish Week and The American Examiner, New York: "The Challenge of December" by Emanuel Rackman from *The Jewish Week and The American Examiner*, December 9, 1971; "Lights Are Kindled in Bergen-Belsen" by Philip Alstat from *The Jewish Week and The American Examiner*, November 30–December 6, 1972.

Johns Hopkins University Press, Baltimore: "Lights in the Frankfort Judengasse" by Heinrich Heine from *Judaic Lore in Heine* by Israel Tabak, 1948.

Rabbi Leo Jung, New York: "The Immortality of Israel" from *Crumbs and Characters* by Leo Jung, Night and Day Press, New York, 1942.

Kinderbuch Publications, New York: "The Pan of Oil" by Chaver Paver from *Yiddish Stories for Young People*, ed. by Itche Goldberg, 1966.

Alfred A. Knopf, Inc., New York: "The Hebraic and the Hellenic Views of Life" from *A History of the Jews*, 2d edition, by Abram Leon Sachar. Copyright 1930, 1940 and renewed 1958, 1968 by Alfred A. Knopf, Inc. Reprinted by permission of the publisher.

Ktav Publishing House, New York: "Bee-utiful Candles" from *The Pitzel Holiday Book* by Leonard Jaffe. Copyright © 1962; "The Old Dreidel" from *My Holiday Story Book* by Morris Epstein. Copyright © 1958.

Chaim Lewis, Johannesburg: "To Soviet Jewry: A Hanukkah Invocation" from *Shadow in the Sun* by Chaim Lewis, Juta & Company, Cape Town, 1972.

Macmillan Publishing Co., New York: "Hanukkah Celebration in the Warsaw Ghetto" from *Scroll of Agony: The Warsaw Diary of Chaim A. Kaplan*, translated and edited by Abraham I. Katsh. Copyright © Abraham I. Katsh, 1965.

Harold Matson Company, Inc., New York: "Hanukkah Today" from *This Is My God: The Jewish Way of Life* by Herman Wouk, Doubleday & Co., Garden City, N.Y., 1959.

Copyright 1959, 1970, 1973 by the Abe Wouk Foundation, Inc. Reprinted by permission of the Harold Matson Company, Inc.

McGraw-Hill Ryerson Limited, Scarborough, Ontario: "Mattathias" and "Candle Lights" from *The Collected Poems of A. M. Klein*, edited by Miriam Waddington, 1974. Reprinted by permission of McGraw-Hill Ryerson Limited.

William Morrow & Co., Inc., New York: "The Meaning of Hanukkah" by Theodor H. Gaster. Copyright © 1952, 1953 by Theodor H. Gaster. Reprinted by permission of William Morrow & Co., Inc.

National Jewish Welfare Board, New York: "With American Soldiers in World War II" from *GI Holy Days* by Zelda Popkin.

New Directions Publishing Corp., New York: "Meditation on Hanukkah" from *By the Waters of Manhattan* by Charles Reznikoff. Copyright 1949 by Charles Reznikoff. Reprinted by permission of New Directions Publishing Corporation and San Francisco Review.

Dr. Chaim Potok, Jerusalem, Israel: "Miracles for a Broken Planet" by Chaim Potok from *McCall's*, vol. 100, no. 3 (December 1972).

Random House, Inc., New York: "Judaism and Hellenism" from "The Biblical Age" by Yehezkel Kaufmann, trans. by Moshe Greenberg, from *Great Ages and Ideas of the Jewish People*, edited by Leo W. Schwarz. Copyright © 1956 by Random House, Inc. Reprinted by permission of the publisher.

Mrs. Rahel Rivlin, Jerusalem, Israel: "With Sephardic Children and Teachers in Jerusalem" by Joseph J. Rivlin from *"Hagigat Yeladim be-Hanukkah,"* *Tziyyon*, vol. 2, nos. 8–10 (1931).

The Philip H. & A. S. W. Rosenbach Foundation, Philadelphia: "Mighty, Praised beyond Compare" from *When Love Passed By and Other Verses* by Solomon Solis-Cohen, The Rosenbach Co., Philadelphia, 1929.

Schocken Books Inc., New York: "Kindling the Lights in Vitebsk, Russia," reprinted by permission of Schocken Books Inc. from *Burning Lights* by Bella and Marc Chagall. Copyright © 1946 by Marc Chagall.

Mrs. Leo W. Schwarz, New York: "The Graves of the Maccabees" by David Shimonowitz from *A Golden Treasury of Jewish Literature*, ed. by Leo W. Schwarz, Holt, Rinehart & Winston, New York, 1937.

Charles Scribner's Sons, New York: "A Hanukkah Party in Riga," reprinted by permission of Charles Scribner's Sons from *Like a Song, Like a Dream* by Alla Rusinek. Copyright © 1973 Jessie Zel Lurie Assoc.

Shengold Publishers, New York: "A Hanukkah Candle in Auschwitz" from *Sparks of Glory* by Moshe Prager. Copyright © 1974 by Moshe Prager. Reprinted by permission of Shengold Publishers.

The Soncino Press Limited, London, England: selections from *The Babylonian Talmud*, trans. under the editorship of Isidore Epstein, 1935–50; selection from *Lamentations Rabbah*, trans. by A. Cohen, vol. 7 of *Midrash Rabbah*, trans. under the editorship of H. Freedman and Maurice Simon, 1939–51; "A Single Spark" from *Judaism Eternal: Selected Essays* by Samson Raphael Hirsch, trans. by I. Grunfeld, 1956. Reprinted by permission of The Soncino Press. All rights reserved by The Soncino Press Limited.

Dr. A. Alan Steinbach, Hollywood, Florida: "Eight Golden Hanukkah Lights" from *Spiritual Cameos: Reflections and Meditations on the Holy Days and Festivals*, Gertz Bros., New York.

Tradition, New York: "Electric Substitutes for Hanukkah Lights" from "Survey of Recent Halakhic Periodical Literature" by J. David Bleich, *Tradition*, vol. 13, no. 2 (Fall 1972), published by Rabbinical Council of America.

Union of American Hebrew Congregations, New York: "Seven Sacrifices" from *The Unconquered* by Joseph Gaer. Copyright © 1932 by Union of American Hebrew Congregations; "For Hanukkah" from *Far Over the Sea* by Hayyim Nahman Bialik. Copyright © 1939 by Union of American Hebrew Congregations; "Eight Are the Lights" from *Within Thy Hand: My Poem Book of Prayers* by Ilo Orleans. Copyright © 1961 by Union of American Hebrew Congregations; "Judah Maccabeus to His Soldiers" from *Jewish Festivals in the Religious School* by Elma Ehrlich Levinger. Copyright © 1923 by Union of American Hebrew Congregations; "Hanukkah in a Monastery" by Isaac Neuman from *American Judaism*, vol. 13, no. 2 (Winter 1963–64).

United Synagogue Commission on Jewish Education, New York: "*Hanerot Hallalu*" from *The Songs We Sing*, ed. by Harry Coopersmith, 1950; "*Al ha-Nissim*" from *More of the Songs We Sing*, ed. by Harry Coopersmith, 1971. Copyright by the United Synagogue of America.

Vallentine, Mitchell & Co. Ltd, London: "Hanukkah Festival in London's White-chapel" from *East End Story* by A. B. Levy, Vallentine, Mitchell & Co. Ltd., London.

Dr. Meyer W. Weisgal, Rehovot, Israel: "The Festival of the Maccabees in Svislovitz" from *Childhood in Exile* by Shmarya Levin, 1929.

Women's League for Conservative Judaism, New York: "Hanukkah in Old Venice" from *Join Us for the Holidays* by Lillian S. Abramson. Copyright © 1958; "My Trendle" and "What's in My Pocket?" from *The Singing Way: Poems for Jewish Children* by Sadie Rose Weilerstein. Copyright © 1946.

Yale University Press, Inc., New Haven: excerpts from *Pesikta Rabbati: Discourses for Feasts, Fasts and Special Sabbaths*, trans. by William G. Braude. Copyright © 1968 by Yale University Press Inc.; excerpts from *The Code of Maimonides: Book 3: The Book of Seasons*, trans. by Solomon Gandz and Hyman Klein. Copyright © 1961 by Yale University Press, Inc.

YIVO Institute for Jewish Research, New York: "Hanukkah 1942 in the Vilna Ghetto" from "Diary of the Vilna Ghetto" by Herman Kruk, *YIVO Annual of Jewish Social Science*, vol. 13 (1965).

Credits for the illustrations are included in the list of illustrations that follows the contents.

TO

Solomon Grayzel

AND

A. Alan Steinbach

מכל מלמדי השכלתי

PREFACE

The Hanukkah Anthology is a successor to *Hanukkah: The Feast of Lights* by Emily Solis-Cohen, Jr., published in 1937 by The Jewish Publication Society under the auspices of Dr. Solomon Grayzel, the noted historian and editor of JPS. The 1937 volume was the first in the Society's Sabbath and Jewish Holiday Series and set the pattern for the others that followed. It was widely used over the years and was reprinted nine times. Dr. Grayzel was also editor of the Society when I prepared *The Purim Anthology* (1949) and *The Passover Anthology* (1961), and I welcome this opportunity to reiterate my sincerest appreciation to him for his constant and helpful guidance, the benefit of his erudition, and the interest and care he evinced in these books, from the initial outline to the final production. I am further grateful to him for permission to reprint his scholarly and lucid article "Hanukkah and Its History" in this anthology.

I want to extend my thanks for their courtesies and assistance to Dr. I. Edward Kiev of revered memory, late librarian of the Hebrew Union

College–Jewish Institute of Religion, New York, and Mrs. Sylvia Landress, librarian of the Zionist Archives and Library, and their staffs; Mrs. Deborah Brodie, children's book editor, Hebrew Publishing Co.; Dr. Herbert Parzen, author of *Architects of Conservative Judaism* and other scholarly works; Rabbi Irving Rubin of Congregation Kesher Israel, West Chester, Pennsylvania; Max Zeldner, formerly head of Department of Foreign Languages, William Howard Taft High School, Bronx, N. Y.; and Dr. Samuel D. Freeman, consultant in adult programming, National Jewish Welfare Board.

I am especially indebted to the following persons who have contributed orginal articles to this volume: Dr. Joseph Gutmann, recognized authority on Jewish art and professor of art history at Wayne State University, Detroit, Michigan, for his article "Hanukkah in Art" and his guidance in the selection of illustrations; Cantor Paul Kavon, director of the Department of Music of the United Synagogue of America, for compiling and editing "Music for Hanukkah"; Dr. Jacob Kabakoff, professor of Hebrew at Lehman College of the City University of New York, for "Hanukkah in Israel"; Solomon Feffer, chairman of the Department of Hebraic Studies at Rutgers University, Newark, New Jersey, for "Hanukkah Customs among Sephardic Jews," as well as for the translation of articles; and Seymour Warsaw, art director of the National Jewish Welfare Board for the illustrations in the arts and crafts section. The unsigned articles and translations for which no English source is cited were done by me.

Maier Deshell, editor of The Jewish Publication Society of America, and David C. Gross and Bernard I. Levinson, former and present executive vice-presidents of the Society, encouraged and stimulated me to prepare *The Hanukkah Anthology*. The Society's associate editor, Mrs. Kay Powell, carefully examined the manuscript and the proofs and helped me avoid stylistic and typographical errors. Mrs. Adrianne Onderdonk Dudden is responsible for the beautiful design of the book.

Dr. Sidney B. Hoenig, scholarly author and professor of Jewish history at Yeshiva University, generously reviewed the manuscript of this book and gave me the benefit of his profound knowledge and keen judgment, for which I am most grateful. He also wrote the fascinating chapter "Hanukkah Oddities."

Dr. A. Alan Steinbach, distinguished poet, literary critic, and editor of *Jewish Book Annual* and *Jewish Bookland*, meticulously read the typescript, offered numerous constructive criticisms, and greatly improved the literary style. He also translated the medieval poem "Shabbat and

Hanukkah Dispute before Me." His unfailing devotion to my work has been of inestimable value. I shall always cherish the warm friendship he has shown me.

Without the wholehearted cooperation of Hanna, my devoted wife and inspiring helpmate, I could not have completed this book or my preceding ones. Words do not suffice to express to her my everlasting gratitude.

Philip Goodman

New York City
Kislev 25, 5735 [1975]

INTRODUCTION

Hanukkah, also called the Festival of Lights, occurs on the twenty-fifth day of the winter month of Kislev. Lasting for eight days, the holiday commemorates the historic victory of the Maccabees over the forces of the Syrian tyrant Antiochus in the second century B.C.E. Hanukkah, which means "dedication," celebrates the reclamation of the Jerusalem Temple after years of pagan desecration. It also celebrates the liberation of the Jewish people from Hellenistic domination.

The triumph of the outnumbered and poorly equipped Jewish resistance over Antiochus's vastly superior army was indeed a military miracle. But rabbinic tradition points to a different sort of miracle that happened at this moment in Jewish history: According to the Talmud, when the victorious Jews came to rededicate the desecrated Temple, they found only one day's supply of pure olive oil for the Temple menorah. But, miraculously, the oil burned for eight full days, until a new supply could be obtained. Through the centuries, and even more so since the establishment of the state of Israel, Hanukkah has served as a symbol of national liberation and the triumphant Jewish spirit.

Because of its association with power and nationalism, the Rabbis tried to de-emphasize the military aspect of Hanukkah. The name Judah Maccabee does not appear at all in the Talmud. The celebration of the holiday includes no proscriptions against work and no special synagogue service. But, influenced by the American celebration of Christmas, Hanukkah has in contemporary times assumed the status of a major holiday, in which gift-giving has become central. In Israel, recent historical events, notably the Holocaust and the wars against the British and the Arabs, have likewise imparted increased significance to this festival, making it a popular national celebration.

Many customs have evolved around this holiday. The oldest involves lighting a menorah or *hanukkiah,* a nine-branched candelabrum (eight plus the *shammes*), adding one light (oil or candle) each night. One traditionally eats foods fried in oil to commemorate the miracle of the oil. It is also customary to eat dairy foods in honor of Judith, the Jewish heroine who saved Jerusalem from an Assyrian siege: Judith fed the enemy general Holofernes cheese to make him thirsty, and then, when he became drunk, cut off his head. It was said that her bravery later inspired Judah Maccabee.

One of the most popular customs of this holiday is gambling for nuts or pennies by spinning a special top called a *dreidl.* In Europe, it was traditional to give children coins, called Hanukkah *gelt,* to reward Torah study. In modern Israel, runners participate in a torchlight marathon from Modin, where the Maccabean revolt began, to Jerusalem, where it triumphed.

Because of Judith's association with Hanukkah, this holiday has traditionally been regarded as especially sacred to women, who perform no household duties while the candles burn. The new month that begins during the festival is sometimes called "the New Moon of the Daughters," a time for girls and brides to receive gifts.

Anthropologists tell us that both Christmas and Hanukkah probably originate in ancient celebrations of the winter solstice. Like the sunlight that begins to increase after this moment of seasonal transition, so, too, the candles of the menorah increase in brightness each night. The single cruse of oil that lasted for eight days instead of one symbolizes the enduring Jewish spirit, which has continued to shine through so many periods of darkness.

The twenty-one sections of *The Hanukkah Anthology* provide valuable resource materials for teachers, rabbis, parents, students, and newcomers to Judaism. The first six sections—"Hanukkah and Its History," "Hanukkah in the Bible," "Hanukkah in Postbiblical Writings," "Hanukkah in Talmud and Midrash," "The Medieval Scroll of the Hasmoneans," and "Hanukkah in Jewish Law"—present traditional texts for study and historical background. Three other sections—"Hanukkah in Many Lands," "Hanukkah Oddities," and "Hanukkah Sidelights"—provide fascinating background information highlighting folklore and customs typical of Hanukkah celebrations throughout the world. "The Hanukkah Cuisine," "Home Service for Hanukkah," "Hanukkah Programs and Activities," "Dances for Hanukkah," and "Music for Hanukkah" supply liturgical selections, lecture and discussion topics, games, songs, recipes, crafts, customs, and activities that can greatly enhance the enjoyment and understanding of this festival by both children and adults. Joseph Gutmann's article "Hanukkah in Art" demonstrates the rich aesthetic heritage inspired by this holiday. The volume also includes numerous illustrations and photographs that depict scenes and artifacts representative of the ways in which this holiday has been traditionally observed.

One of the unique features of this anthology is the abundant selection of both secular and religious literature on the themes of Hanukkah. These include Henry Wadsworth Longfellow's drama, *Judah Maccabeus;* essays by writers such as Samson Raphael Hirsch, Grace Aguilar, Herman Wouk, and Yehezkel Kaufmann; short stories by I. L. Peretz, Sholom Aleichem, and Howard Fast; and poems by Emma Lazarus, Saul Tchernichovsky, and Charles Reznikoff.

Parents and teachers will find in this anthology two sections especially designed for children—one containing classic stories by American, Israeli, and Yiddish writers, and a second presenting a number of poems suitable for a variety of ages, including several by Hayyim Nahman Bialik. In addition, some of the recipes from "The Hanukkah Cuisine" can also be adapted for classroom or home use.

The Talmud records an interesting debate between two of the greatest teachers of the rabbinic period, Hillel and Shammai, concerning the lighting of the Hanukkah lights. Hillel argued that one should begin by lighting one candle, and adding one candle each night to symbolize the increase of holiness as the festival reaches its fulfillment. Shammai, on the other hand, advocated beginning with all eight candles illuminated, decreasing the number until only one remained on the last night. As in most cases, tradition sided with Hillel, maintaining that one should always increase holiness rather than lessen it. But the Rabbis did not wholly dismiss Shammai's proposal in siding with his rival. Rather, they reasoned that in messianic times Jews would exchange Hillel's practice for Shammai's.

Why? Perhaps the Rabbis understood that human beings are not yet ready to diminish light in favor of darkness. Each Hanukkah, as we approach the longest night of the year, we need to bolster our spirits by kindling more and more light with our own hands. In our imperfect world, we lack the pure faith symbolized by that single cruse of oil that centuries ago defied the laws of nature to sanctify the House of God.

Such faith will be possible, however, in messianic times—the miraculous will then become commonplace. According to the midrash, at the End of Days, the moon will regain its original brightness rivalling that of the sun; darkness will thus disappear from the earth. All human beings will sit in peace under their vines and fig trees, and none shall make them afraid. And then Sammai's way of lighting the menorah will make perfect sense.

Ellen Frankel

Philadelphia
1992 / 5752

CONTENTS

3 Hanukkah in Postbiblical Writings 32

4 Hanukkah in Talmud and Midrash 66

11 Hanukkah in Poetry 205

12 Hanukkah in the Short Story 223

15 *The Hanukkah Cuisine* 290

16 *Children's Stories for Hanukkah* 298

17   *Children's Poems for Hanukkah*   *359*

18   *Home Service for Hanukkah*   *379*

19   *Hanukkah Programs and Activities*   *385*

ILLUSTRATIONS

The Hanukkah
Anthology

I HANUKKAH AND ITS HISTORY

SOLOMON GRAYZEL

The First Hanukkah: 165 B. C. E.

The last outpost marched through the gates; the heavy wooden doors were swung shut, and the iron bolts moved into their sockets. Erect and gloomy, the captain of the small band of Syrian soldiers stood in the narrow court awaiting the report of his returning outpost. Its corporal saluted: "Just outside the walls of the city." He went on. Without moving, the captain again calculated the chance of holding out until the Syrian army, defeated in the field, would reorganize and come to his aid. The Acra fortress was none too strong, his trained soldiers none too many. As to these self-despising Jews . . . His eyes wandered to where, silent, frightened, the bolder among them stood huddled in a corner. What good were

3

they who were the cause of this trouble? Smart uniforms, smooth tongues, loud protestations of loyalty. Better in games of skill than any of his soldiers, on the field of battle, could they do a tenth as well as those uncouth farmers who were now approaching Jerusalem? That army of farmers and their leader, Judah, by what power were they able to defeat a Syrian host? . . . Their mysterious God? . . . The captain knew a moment of fear.

Before the walls of the city, Judah the Maccabee and his army halted. The great moment had come; Jerusalem was before them. No resistance was to be expected to their entrance into the city. The Syrian garrison was small; even with the support of the somewhat larger number of Hellenist Jews, the best the invader could hope to do would be to defend the Acra, and perhaps make an occasional sortie. To the attack, therefore! His own followers knew Judah's plan: it was to take the Acra by assault, and thus cleanse the city entirely of all foreigners and apostates. The command was to move forward. With an exultant shout the Judeans crossed the ruined wall. As it began its march through the city, the army of Judah sang.

Silent streets, deserted houses! Is this Jerusalem, the joyous, the populous city? In the poorer section, into which the army first entered, the streets were covered with weeds. The inhabitants had been dispersed long ago by the invading Syrians. Some had remained to become martyrs. Some of the army, themselves fugitives, recalled Eleazar, the aged scribe, and Hannah and her seven sons. The singing began to subside; the army was saddened. Onward they marched, through wider streets, by handsomer houses. Here, too, a stillness as of the grave. The residents had but recently fled; this time before the conquering Jews. Here and there, in front of a home, stood a low, carved stone table. Angry mutterings now began to rise from among the army. They knew these stone tables; these were altars, altars upon which Jews had offered sacrifices to pagan gods. The marchers cursed them and called for vengeance.

To reach the Acra it was necessary to pass close to the Temple. No word of command was spoken, yet officers and men gravitated toward the center of holiness. They came close; they stopped. They saw dilapidated walls, doors torn from their hinges and hanging awry, curtains in tatters, grass, weeds. Over all hung a deathly stillness, and in the center, above a gold altar, the statue of a god—a dead god in a dead sanctuary. There could be no further talk of an attack upon the Acra. Against his better judgment Judah yielded. He did not even argue.

The Temple became a beehive of activity. Fighters became builders. Feverishly they worked to repair the walls, the doors, the curtains. They gathered all the utensils and put them aside, for these had been desecrated. The idol was taken out of the Temple area and stepped upon by thousands of feet until it was ground into a fine dust. But what to do with the altar? Upon it sacrifices had been performed by pious priests; its stones were therefore sacred even though defiled. It was taken apart, stone by stone, and put away into a corner. Pious hands built a new altar. Pious hands prepared bread for the table inside the hall. Pious hands prepared new utensils.

For weeks this activity went on. No one thought any longer of fighting against the Acra. Judah barely persuaded the men to take turns watching the fortress, lest the foe within break out and undo the work that had been done. Finally all was ready; all, that is, except the menorah, the sacred candelabrum for whose replacement no material was at hand. A celebration was in order. But for what day should it be set? A happy thought occurred to someone. The twenty-fifth of Kislev was but a few days off, and it marked the third anniversary of the desecration of the Temple. Indeed, what could be more fitting than that the rededication should take place on that day?

The day came, and it was celebrated gloriously. Priests were found in the army, and they performed the sacrifices. As some of these soldier-priests entered the chambers they discovered some old and obviously long-unused iron spikes. They attached small torches to them and made a menorah—a rough, soldier-menorah, but in a proper setting. Palm branches were held by hands that had held swords. Hallelujah was sung by throats that had shouted a battle cry. A new poem was recited by the Levites:

"I extol You, O Lord, for You have lifted me up, and not let my enemies rejoice over me."

Not far off, the Syrian captain stood on the watchtower of the Acra, relieved and puzzled.

That was the first Hanukkah.

The Origin of Hanukkah

How did Hanukkah come to be and how does it fit into the history of the Jewish people? Who are the men mentioned in the story, and why is it so important that we still remember it after twenty centuries? This is a much longer story. To tell it we must go back some centuries before the event, and follow the changes among the Jewish people in relation to the transformation of the Near East. For the story of Hanukkah reveals why they alone—and none of the petty nations who were their jealous neighbors, none of the great empires that contended for dominion over them—survived as a conscious and historic group.

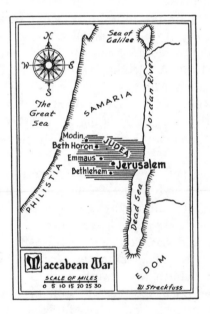

Alexander the Great will be the focal point for the first part of our story, since his coming to the East marks a definite era in the history of that part of the world. The touch of his conquering sword awakened Asia. New administrative methods, new men, new ideas replaced the lethargic system of the unwieldly, loosely bound, though benevolent, Persian Empire. The Eastern world was ready for this change, and not even a generation of warfare, which followed upon the conqueror's death while his generals were dividing the spoils of the conquest, did anything to hinder the spread of Greek civilization. The very soil responded to the new manner of life and, because of the modernization of the methods of agriculture, began to produce more abundantly. Commerce began to flourish because of the intimate connection between East and West. The population of the Asiatic lands bordering on the Mediterranean increased rapidly.

In the territory under Greek influence lived a little nation, small in area and in population. Before the advent of Alexander to the East the Greeks had hardly heard of this people. The name the Greeks gave to its land was Philistia, after the Philistines, who lived upon the coast. Nonetheless, vague rumors had reached the Greeks of a people dwelling inland who were devoted to agriculture and to an invisible celestial God, whose law of life its scribes were expounding. Travelers brought word to Greece of this "nation of philosophers who worship the sky."

Two centuries before the arrival of Alexander, the Jews, this inland people, having returned from Babylonian exile, had reconstituted their nation under the milder overlordship of the Persian king. They rebuilt the Temple in the city of Jerusalem, and, failing to reestablish the Davidic dynasty, they lived under the rule of the high priest of the House of Aaron, who combined autonomous secular power with his religious functions. Comparatively little is known about the history of the Jews during these two centuries. Their neighbors, the Philistines, Ammonites, and Samaritans, had tried to hamper the establishment of the nation, but the militant tactics of Nehemiah and the spiritual activity of Ezra repulsed their plots and set the small nation on the road to mental and physical independence.

Though we know practically nothing of what happened after these two leaders had done their life's work, it is clear that the age which followed their activity was highly productive spiritually. It was then that the prophetic books are said to have received the form in which we now have them. It was then that the small community was finally weaned away from those idolatrous practices against which the prophets had inveighed and which continued to characterize the religion of the peoples about them. Above all, it was then that the class of teachers known as scribes, *soferim*, was active, and so thorough was their teaching that when the avalanche of Greek civilization was sweeping everything before it, the Jewish mode of life was strong enough to offer successful resistance.

In fact, for a full century after the coming of Alexander, Judea continued to be unaffected by Greek ways. Their neighbors had succumbed easily. The cities in the district once known as Philistia, as well as those of Ammon, Moab, and Edom, had given up the very gods in whose names they had fought the Hebrews of Bible days; they had identified these gods with one or another of the gods of Olympus, adopted Greek dress and even Greek speech, and thus disappeared as entities from the pages of history. The Jews, to be sure, were also affected by the Greeks, but not in the same way. When the new Egyptian city of Alexandria was built, many Jews were taken there, and soon they became an important segment of that city's population and contributed greatly to its commercial development.

The Syrian emperors, in their turn, took many Jews out of Babylonia and settled them in the newly constituted cities of their empire. These Jews naturally learned Greek ways of dress and speech and other externals of Greek civilization. In the matter of religion, however, which played a central part in the constitution of the Greek city, the Jews held aloof, though this complicated their life and led to friction with their neighbors. But in Judea proper, small and somewhat isolated from the world's great highways, the inhabitants were not subjected to such external influences, and therefore continued in the even tenor of their ways.

But a situation soon developed that made the continuance of such isolation impossible. It has ever been the fate of Palestine to be a bone of contention between whatever power controlled Egypt and whatever power controlled Syria. Soon after the death of Alexander, Judea fell to Egypt and the Ptolemy family that ruled over it. In the last quarter of the third century B. C. E. the rulers of Syria, descendants of Seleucus, one of Alexander's generals, began to reassert their claim to the land. They did, in fact, cast an avid eye upon Egypt, and the district of Lower Syria, of which Judea was a part, was the first step in the realization of their ambitions to be Alexander's successors. In the year 198 B. C. E. Judea was finally incorporated into the Syrian state, and the Seleucid kings were faced with the problem of making that incorporation permanent.

How did the Jews themselves feel about this change in their overlord? When a nation attains international importance it is natural for the preferences of its people to be divided on the basis of public and private interests. United in religion, Jews the world over felt a sympathy for each other. Those of the Diaspora, that is, of the lands outside Palestine, were accustomed to sending their annual contribution for the support of the holy Temple in Jerusalem. Small as the individual contributions were, they added up to vast sums. On the other hand, the Jews of Judea could not but feel flattered or outraged according to the treatment meted out to their fellow Jews in Diaspora lands. Initially, the Ptolemies of Egypt were favorably disposed to the Jews of Alexandria, but for reasons we need not go into here, their policy underwent a change at the very time when the Syrian Empire sought to win Judean sympathy for itself. What is more, the high priest may have realized that, since the majority of the Jews of that day lived in Asia and under Syrian power, it was more to the advantage of the Temple for Jerusalem to be connected politically with this majority than with the comparatively smaller population then residing in Egypt. By and large, therefore, it would seem that the Jews of Judea were satisfied with the change of rule. They little dreamed what troubles it would bring upon them within the short space of thirty years.

It is well to bear in mind that the Jewish victories that are celebrated on Hanukkah were not only of political and religious importance, but of social significance as well. A social transformation was taking place within Jewish life that, in a very real sense, formed the basis for the religious and political uprising of the Maccabees. The beginnings of this social change were small. While Judea was still under Egyptian rule, a certain Jew of noble ancestry and related to the high priest, Joseph ben Tobias, took advantage of the anti-Egyptian inclinations of the high priest and of the Egyptian king's need for money to have himself appointed chief tax collector for the entire province of Syria. Supported by an Egyptian army he filled the hearts of the Jews and pagans of Palestine with fear, and his own pockets with money. In the loose administration of the time, being a tax collector meant more than collecting taxes; it was tantamount to economic dictatorship. Joseph and his sons, generally known as the Tobiades, along with the officials he appointed, achieved two objectives: they caused Jews to be disliked by the gentiles, and they established Jerusalem as a commercial center with themselves and their henchmen as a powerful aristocracy. Thereafter Jerusalem was no longer on a bypath in the Greek world; Judea's isolation was ended.

The Jewish theocracy was now turned into an oligarchy. The priests had until now constituted the aristocratic element of the population. Their duties were in the Temple, and their income was from the Temple treasury. Organized into a *gerousia*, an advisory council to the high priest, they were the chief authority of the autonomous state. Now, as a result of commerce, a class was added to the Judean population whose claim to power rested on its wealth. Like the Tobiades, this wealthy class either became identical with the ruling powers or identified itself with them.

Commerce and wealth brought these people in touch with Hellenistic attitudes and manner of life. Individual material success was the order of the day. The common people during the period when the Tobiades were rising to power have left no documents from which their feelings about the changed order could be gauged. But in the wise words of Ben Sira, who wrote the book Ecclesiasticus, now a part of the collection known as the Apocrypha, some modern scholars see a reflection of the situation that then obtained. Thus in chapter 13, verses 18–20, Ben Sira says: "What agreement is there between the hyena and the dog? And what peace between the rich and the poor? As the wild ass is the lion's prey in the wilderness, so the rich eat up the poor. As the proud hate humility, so doth the rich abhor the poor." Again and again he returns to this subject. A class struggle was on the horizon.

For the most part, however, the Jews were a peasant people, while wealth was centered in the cities. They must have heard of the ways of the wealthy, though their actual contact with them, while painful, could not have been frequent. Something in addition to economic pressure was needed to change social cleavage into actual revolt. This something soon appeared in the form of the hellenization of the upper stratum of Jerusalem society, a change so thorough as to shock the conservative and loyal population.

Their economic ambitions drove the Tobiades and their followers further on the road to hellenization. In order to increase their commercial opportunities it seemed necessary to place Jerusalem on an equal plane with other ambitious cities. Privileges of self-government were needed, none of which could be obtained unless Jerusalem adopted a thoroughly Greek constitution. No doubt a great deal of social prestige went hand in hand with these economic advantages. But all this could be done only after the conservative element of the population had been either won over or cowed, and especially after the actual rule over the land, lodged in the high priest, had been obtained by the elements favorable to the "reform."

Scandalized as the pious elements of the Jewish population, in and out of Jerusalem, were by the gymnasia that were now built in the city, by the new manners and the new Greek-style clothes affected by the young bloods of the aristocracy, and by the neglect on the part of the young priests of their sacred duties in the Temple, they still had no power to make their objection heard.

The hellenizing Jews then proceeded with the second part of their plan, namely, to capture the high priesthood. But this was a hereditary office, and not even a priest could succeed to it unless he was in the direct line of descent. Nevertheless, they thought they could effect a change by means of political maneuvering, for most of the Tobiades had made peace with the powers that were in the land. Onias III, the high priest of that day, on the other hand, was not only out of sympathy with the plans of the Tobiades, he was not even sympathetic to the rule of the Syrian power, as his forefathers had been, and would have liked to return Judea to the rule of Egypt. He recognized the advantages of a Western over an Eastern alliance. To undermine the authority of the high priest, the hellenizers told the Syrian king about large sums of money in the Temple treasury, especially about the fact that some of this money belonged to a man who was pro-Egyptian. At once a royal official was dispatched to Jerusalem. Legend has since embellished the details of his visit. He is supposed to have forced entrance into the Temple and to have been met there by a fiery horseman with two assistants, who beat him so much that he had to be carried out unconscious. Legend or no legend, the fact is that Heliodorus, the official in question, left Jerusalem and the Temple treasury intact.

Thus the first attempt to dislodge Onias III failed, but the idea that the Temple in Jerusalem had money lodged in the mind of the Syrian king. Antiochus IV, surnamed Epiphanes, which means "God Manifest," was now on the throne. He was a peculiar person —so queer, in fact, that some of his subjects called him "Epimanes," i.e., "the Madman." But there was nothing at all queer about his policy; it was characteristic of the age as well as of the man. He saw a chance for the realization of the old Syrian dream of conquering Egypt. That required money, and the loyalty, at least, if not the active cooperation of the border lands. To him the hellenizers turned once more with a proposal that they would pay liberally for a change in the high priesthood—especially since the loyalty of Onias was questionable—and for a Greek constitution for Jerusalem. The suggestion was that Onias be replaced by his younger brother, who was more amenable to hellenizing aims. That was done. Jason (Joshua), brother of Onias, became the high priest, and Jerusalem received a new name [Antioch, after the Syrian king?], to symbolize its new standing as a thoroughly Greek city.

If the conservative elements of the population were horrified by these changes—that the high priesthood should be bought and that a pagan power should have a hand in the appointment to it; that Jerusalem should bear a Greek name, and that Temple funds should be spent for the introduction of Greek customs—they were destined to be still more horrified by the next act in the drama. For about three years Jason remained high priest and was so subservient to the hellenizing influences that no fault could be found with him. But this very subservience made them look upon him as a tool. If the high-priestly office could be bought for money, why not buy it for one of their own leaders? Menelaus was the grecianized name of a man who had such ambitions. His Hebrew name may have been Honiah, i.e., Onias, and though in all likelihood he was a priest, he certainly was not in the traditional line of succession to the office. By promising a huge sum of money to Antiochus he received the appointment. Then began a civil war within the city of Jerusalem between the adherents of Jason, who with all his faults could at least lay claim to being of the legitimate line, and the extreme hellenizers, for whom Jewish tradition no longer possessed any sacredness at all.

Menelaus won. A reign of terror began in Jerusalem, which could be justified before the Syrian authorities only on the ground that the enemies of Menelaus were the enemies of Antiochus. Yet Antiochus' interest in Menelaus was purely financial. Threatened with removal unless he paid what he had promised, he had his brother steal and dispose of some of the sacred vessels in the Temple. This was sacrilege, a crime that horrified even the pagans. To protest against this the ex-high priest, Onias, came out of hiding. Menelaus, however, hired an assassin to dispose of him.

Menelaus could be secure only as long as Syrian arms could be called upon to uphold him. It was abundantly clear that even the population of Jerusalem, accustomed as it was to hellenizing efforts, did not consider him their representative, but the tool of the Syrian power and of a coterie of rich men. When a rumor spread that Antiochus had been killed on an Egyptian expedition, Jason reappeared upon the scene. Around him the populace of Jerusalem rallied, and Menelaus had to flee for his life. Unfortunately Antiochus was not dead, but only enraged that he had been cheated of the fruits of his victory over Egypt by the arrogant power of Rome. When he heard what had happened in Jerusalem, he ordered his appointee reinstated, and, in order to eliminate the "nonsensical" opposition of the Jewish masses once for all, he banned their customs and traditions. Circumcision and adherence to the dietary laws were forbidden. Upon the Temple altar Antiochus placed the statue of Zeus, so that sacrifices might be brought to the god whose manifestation on earth he considered himself to be.

Surely Antiochus did not realize what he was doing. He thought that he was merely hastening a process, about whose outcome he had no doubt. The other peoples, neighbors of the Jews, had succumbed quickly and easily to the lure of the hellenistic life. As far as he could see, the presumably "intelligent" Jew had readily yielded. If the masses of this obdurate people refused to yield, he was there to force them. Moreover, Antiochus considered the high priest his appointed official; he could not appreciate the Jewish attitude, which looked upon the high priest as the elect of God. Whether the hellenizing Jews realized the situation is a matter more open to doubt. Most of them appear to have welcomed the abolition of all that set Jews apart from non-Jews; their slogan was "Let us be like the rest of the nations!" They had imbibed the spirit of Greek individualism; personal life and success was their ideal. As far as they were concerned, the experiment of Jewish nationhood was over. They were willing to live under the high priesthood of Menelaus, and in the shadow of the Temple in which the celestial God was identified with Zeus, just as hellenized Tyre identified its Melkart with Heracles, and Askelon its Astarte with Aphrodite.

The last days of the Jewish people seemed to have arrived. Groups of Syrian soldiers went from town to town and from village to village, enforcing the new decrees. The unorganized peasantry had no means of resistance. The best they could do was to flee to the hills of Judea and to hide until the turbulent period was over. It is about this phase that the stories of heroism and martyrdom, such as that of Hannah and her seven sons and of old Eleazar, are told.

It was but natural that the bands of fugitives should begin to think of organized opposition. It may be that even before the final blow fell the pious opponents of hellenization came to be known as Hasidim.* Against them the decree of Antiochus was aimed, and from among them organized resistance could be expected. Their piety was their strength; it was also their weakness. They refused to fight on the Sabbath, even in self-defense. The story has come down about a band of a thousand who permitted themselves to be destroyed rather than desecrate the day of rest. Under such circumstances even organized resistance was useless.

One band of fugitive Hasidim soon came to stand out above the others. It was led by a family of priests from the little town of Modin, a short distance from Jerusalem. Whether because of an ancestor named Hasmon or for some other reason, they were known as Hasmoneans. The fact that they were priests gave them prestige. The old father, Mattathias, had incurred the enmity of the Syrians by refusing to participate in a heathen sacrifice, and by leading his five sons in an attack upon the Syrian troops that had come to enforce the decree against Judaism. With their townsmen who were Hasidim, they took to the hills and then pursued guerrilla tactics of attacking small bands of soldiers and hellenized Jews. There was one thing that distinguished them from all similar bands: they adopted the view that for purposes of self-defense fighting on the Sabbath was permissible. This, along with the unmistakable signs of military ability shown by one of the sons, Judah, very quickly attracted other Hasidim, so that at last the Jewish people had a miniature army in the field.

Judah the Maccabee stands out as among the few great military leaders whom the Jewish people produced. His name soon began to strike terror in the hearts of his enemies. The unexpected had happened; the Jews were in organized revolt.

The hellenized Jews, against whom the Hasidim had first directed their attacks, sent insistent calls for help to Antiochus. They claimed that ultimately the struggle was directed against the royal policy of cultural unification and that the king therefore had to assume the task of suppressing the Maccabean bands. As a result, the Syrian forces of the district began to bestir themselves. It is not likely that Antiochus himself, or any of his more important officials, would as

*They have no relation to the Hasidic movement started by R. Israel in the eighteenth century.

yet have taken much note of this rebellion of a poorly armed peasant population. It was obviously the task of the local authorities to quell what seemed to be a minor insurrection against royal authority. In this task, however, they found enthusiastic support among the gentile neighbors of Judea.

It has only been recently that attention has been called to this phase of the Maccabean struggle. It is here that we have an indication that back of the religious and political causes for the rebellion was one of wider significance, namely, the movement of the Jewish

1. Oil lamp with menorah design. Pottery. Eretz Israel. Third or fourth century.

population. The small territory upon which the Second Jewish Commonwealth was built after the return from the Babylonian exile was bound to become insufficient. At that very time, however, new Greek colonies and the spurt in the general population of the Syrian Empire brought new pagan powers on every side of the small Jewish state. Although the Jews could not forget that historically all that land was theirs, they did not, to be sure, lay claim to it at this time. Nevertheless, as their overflow population sought new homes in Alexandria, in Asia Minor, and in the Greek isles, it was natural for many to settle in cities and lands nearer home: in Galilee, on the Phoenician coast, and across the Jordan. To the religious differences, and to the enmity aroused by the Tobiades, was now added economic friction with Jewish competitors. Still, as long as an autonomous Jewish state was in existence and its leaders in good standing with the Syrian court, the pagans could not give vent to their hostility. Clearly it was to their advantage to have the Jewish state destroyed or at least weakened. That is why they responded so eagerly to the call for aid on the part of the local authorities in putting down the Jewish insurrection. They did not wait for the Jews to be definitely defeated, but at once began to harass and attack those who lived in their midst.

The first Syrian force that went to meet Judah was under the leadership of Apollonius, presumably the military governor of the district of Samaria. His force must have been small, and Judah easily overcame it. Apollonius was killed, and thereafter Judah used his captured sword in battle. Then came Seron, another official of the Palestinian district, with a larger force. Judah met him at Beth Horon, a few miles to the northwest of Jerusalem, and defeated him in a surprise attack. Only then did the Syrian authorities realize that a real effort would have to be made, and they dispatched two generals, Nicanor and Gorgias, with a large force, to overwhelm the Jewish rebels. It was in this battle that Judah showed himself to be a consummate strategist. Moreover, he knew the roads of hilly Judea, and his smaller army was much more mobile than the large force that opposed him. Taking advantage of a temporary division of the enemy, he attacked each army in turn, and put them to flight with great slaughter. The booty provided the Jewish army with ample supplies; for the first time the soldiers under Judah could be said to be properly equipped. In all these battles auxiliary forces from among the neighboring peoples participated as soldiers or came in the capacity of merchant camp followers, ready to buy slaves from among the anticipated Jewish captives.

In spite of these three victories Judah's chances for success were still slender. So tremendous was the Syrian superiority in resources that the Jewish rebellion would have been squelched easily, had not difficulties arisen for Syria in other directions. If we define "miracle" as an unexpected coincidence, the Hanukkah miracle occurred at this point. Chance worked in favor of the Jews, so that at the moment when the Syrian court should have been planning to send a large force to dispose of the rebellion in the border province near Egypt, it was compelled to go forth on an expedition in Parthia. Antiochus no doubt thought that he could afford to wait to settle the score with the Jews. For about a year there was a lull in the fighting against Judah and his army.

The Maccabean forces used the respite to advantage. The inadequate force that defended Jerusalem could not withstand the army of Hasidim. In triumph and exultation Judah led his band into the sacred city. The hellenizers scattered before him or shut themselves up in the fortress that Antiochus had built near the Temple. The destruction that had desolated the city during the three years of civil war saddened the conquerors, who proceeded to remove every trace of pagan occupation. Three years after its defilement the Temple was cleansed, the statue of Zeus was removed, and the altar upon which pagan sacrifices had been made was replaced. Once more the lights were kindled in the house of God, and pious priests officiated in it. For eight days the Jews celebrated the Feast of Dedication, the Feast of Hanukkah.

It is well to remember that the celebration of Hanukkah does not mark the end of the Maccabean War but the end of religious oppression, that is, the reestablishment of Jewish worship—destined not to be interrupted by the Syrians thereafter.

Judah continued the struggle. He further utilized his respite from Syrian attacks to wreak vengeance upon those neighboring cities whose gentile population had shown itself hostile to the Jews. Expeditions were sent to Galilee, across the Jordan, and to the cities on the coast. The first two expeditions were successful. Perhaps Judah would have liked to annex the conquered territory to Judea, but with another invasion from Syria still threatening he did not dare. Nor would the Hasidim who constituted his fighting force have been willing to have their battles for their faith turned into a war of annexation. That was left for Judah's Hasmonean successors to accomplish. He contented himself with showing the pagans that the Jews were not helpless and with transporting some of the most dangerously situated Jews back into Jewish territory.

Now the danger from the north became real. Lysias, whom Antiochus Epiphanes had left as regent of his western kingdom and as his son's guardian while he went off to Parthia, bestirred himself to settle matters in Judea. With a large force he descended upon Jerusalem, and Judah was not equal to meeting him in battle. After a spirited battle during which one of his brothers lost his life, Judah was confined within Jerusalem, and his army began to suffer the hardships of a long and painful siege. Once more, however, Providence intervened to the advantage of the Jewish cause. Antiochus died in the course of his Parthian campaign, and, fortunately for the Jews, just before his death he appointed another general as guardian of his young heir, Antiochus V. On hearing this report, Lysias was anxious to leave Jerusalem and hurry north to meet his rival. Thus when the outlook was blackest for the Jews, their enemy suggested a cessation of hostilities. The terms of peace offered the Jews gave them back their former status: freedom of faith, practice, and worship, with no efforts at hellenization by force. The one right that Lysias reserved for the Syrian crown was the right to appoint the high priest. The new appointee was not Menelaus, who was so obnoxious to the Jews, but a man named Alkimus, or Eljakim, who evidently belonged to the moderate hellenizers.

These terms were highly satisfactory to the vast majority of the Hasidic party. They had fought the war because their religious scruples had been outraged, and now that the Syrians promised not to interfere, they were willing to lay down the sword and return to the plow. Judah, however, saw the situation in a more realistic light. He did not trust the Syrians and even less the hellenizing Jews, from among whom the new high priest was chosen. He aimed at complete independence, and his resolution was fortified when Alkimus, supported by Syrian soldiers, had some sixty of the popular party executed as soon as he came to power. Nowhere is any direct reason offered for this act. Presumably Alkimus wanted to strengthen himself with the pro-Syrian group, or he may have resented the demands of the popular party for a share in the government. The result was that Judah's forces, reduced to a small number because of the peace and in hiding, once more began to grow. Alkimus thereupon clamored for a return of the Syrian force.

Syrian general Nicanor appeared with a fair-sized army and a host of elephants, but Judah defeated him. Nicanor was killed, and the Jews set the day down as a minor holiday—the Thirteenth of Adar. Shortly thereafter, however, a larger force appeared, and the position of Judah was clearly hopeless. With but eight hundred followers around him, he spurned the advice to run away. He fought his last fight and fell upon the field of battle.

Judah's death ended the Maccabean War. A few of his followers, under the leadership of his two remaining brothers, Jonathan and Simon, escaped across the Jordan and awaited a favorable opportunity to complete the work of Judah. The opportunity was not slow in coming, but the details of this event are beyond the purview of this story. Religious freedom had been attained, but that was not all they had fought for. For the time being the old group of wealthy men and priestly aristocrats was still in the saddle. They had learned to be more wary in the hellenization of the Jews, but they had not yet learned that Judaism had vitality beyond their strength to extinguish. Behind them still stood the power of Syria, ever willing to take a hand in internal Jewish affairs. Around them lived the gentiles, whose cities were like dikes trying to stem the expansion of a people that needed more room. The aristocrats and hellenizers did not realize that the common people had learned their own power and would not again permit others to ride roughshod over them. Before their very eyes the Syrian Empire was disintegrating. One by one its outlying provinces were falling away, while dynastic dissension weakened it from within. In the distance stood the rising power of Rome, watching this process with great satisfaction. In fact, Judah the Maccabee and later his brother Jonathan made alliances with Rome against the power of Syria. Above all, the common people among the Jews had gained the consciousness that their own point of view and their own civilization should and could be preserved.

Judah died in 160 B.C.E. In 152 B.C.E. Jonathan, his brother, became high priest and autonomous ruler of Judea. In 135 B.C.E. Simon, the last of the brothers, was appointed hereditary ruler and high priest by a popular assembly representative of all the people. The Hasmonean Era had begun, and the Hasmonean kings began to extend their dominion.

This religious and national victory is celebrated on Hanukkah.

The History of the Festival

Holidays may also be playthings of fate; of this Hanukkah is an example. In a very real sense, as we have seen, it contains features that make it comparable to both Passover and Purim. Like the former it marks a time when Jewish life was preserved from the danger of being absorbed by a different culture; like the latter it celebrates a deliverance from the hands of one who plotted the annihilation of the Jewish group. Yet no seder takes place on Hanukkah, nor is the synagogue service materially prolonged. The story of Mordecai donning sackcloth has been included in the Bible canon, whereas Judah's girding of the sword has not. Small candles are lit and small gifts are distributed. Work is permitted as usual. Is this discrimination intentional? Has the long memory of the Jewish people failed in this solitary instance? The truth of the matter is that the history of Hanukkah as a holiday reflects the history of the Jewish group.

Jewish tradition associates the origin of Hanukkah with something that happened before the Maccabean dedication of the Temple. One of the main sources for our knowledge of the Maccabean Age, 2 Maccabees, happily preserved in the so-called Apocrypha, tells in its first chapter why the twenty-fifth of Kislev was chosen for the dedication. The story goes that when the exiles returned from Babylon and rebuilt the Temple, the fires on the altar were miraculously kindled by a liquid fire that had been hidden away at the destruction of the First Temple. In commemoration of this miracle—so the story seems to imply, though the author of 2 Maccabees does not say so explicitly—fires would be kindled by the Jews. Now, the day upon which this miracle was supposed to have taken place was the twenty-fifth of Kislev, and it was, therefore, a sort of strengthening of an ancient holiday when the Maccabees chose that same day to rededicate the Temple they had restored.

How much of this story about hidden fire can really be believed? The author of 2 Maccabees was trying to persuade the Jews of Egypt to observe the holiday of Hanukkah. That, as a matter of fact, is why he wrote the book. For a variety of reasons the Egyptian Jews had no interest in Hanukkah. Their ancestors had not been threatened by Antiochus.* What is more, the head of Judaism in the land of

---

*It is well to keep in mind that Antiochus' original decree against Judaism was directed at the province of Judea and did not affect even the Syrian Diaspora. It is

Egypt was a descendant of the Onias who was high priest when all the trouble started. Consequently, he must have regarded himself as the rightful claimant to the office in Jerusalem which the Hasmoneans occupied after the victory against the Syrians. It was not to be expected, therefore, that Egyptian Jews should find any interest in a holiday established by, and in memory of, the Maccabeans. Naturally the author of a book that urged Hanukkah upon the Jews of Egypt was likely to look for other, non-Maccabean arguments to prove the sacredness of the day. Close at hand he found an old tradition. Was it based on fact or was it purely fancy? He did not know; but it was useful, and he seized upon it to drive home his point.

As a matter of fact, the same book offers another much more plausible reason for the original celebration of those days. It calls Hanukkah a "second Sukkot," and offers the explanation that when Judah's pious followers had finally cleansed the Temple, they recalled that in the stress of the last campaign they had been prevented from observing Sukkot. This omission they then proceeded to rectify: "Therefore they bare branches and fair boughs, and palms also, and sang psalms unto Him that had given them good success in cleansing His place." Presumably they also dwelt in booths. That, too, may be why Hanukkah is celebrated for eight days; it equals the number of days of Sukkot. As to the lights, they may have been no more than mere concomitants of the celebration. After all, it is quite natural for people to kindle lights in connection with a holiday. We do so to this day.

There is still another theory. When the Syrians were masters of the city, it was common practice for them and renegade Jews to have small private altars outside the home upon which a family sacrifice would be offered in honor of a pagan god. The Hasidim destroyed these altars, and as a sort of counterbalance they instituted a ritual of lighting candles in honor of Israel's God. These were to be placed at the entrance to a house, where the pagan altars had stood, or at least were to be visible from the street.

First Maccabees, as well as 2 Maccabees, states that after the first Hanukkah was over the Jews of that day decided to establish the holiday as an annual event. It has been generally assumed that 1

---

easy to see, however, that had Judea been hellenized, the Diaspora Jews would not have long survived as Jews.

Maccabees was written some time between 135 and 105 B.C.E. If that is so, we may go a step further and assume that down to about the year 125 B.C.E., roughly, the holiday was still observed. But there is strong reason to believe that it soon was no longer prevalent. How else is one to explain the curious facts that in the literature of the subsequent age Hanukkah is very rarely mentioned and that sages like the schools of Shammai and Hillel discuss whether a Jew is to start with one light and add one each succeeding night, or with eight lights and subtract one? Had the holiday been well known among the people, so elementary a question would have been long settled.

The conclusion seems inevitable that for a period of one hundred years Hanukkah was practically dormant. It may be that the Jews of Palestine continued to kindle lights. If they did so, it was because of an ancient tradition about a miracle when the Temple was rebuilt long before the Maccabees. But of the last-named, their victories, their martyrs, and their holidays, the memories were vague indeed.

What might account for the dormancy of a holiday so promisingly launched? The answer generally given is based upon the political and religious differences that developed among the Jews after the Judean state had become independent. The complete autonomy for which Judah the Maccabee had fought and died was finally achieved by his brother Jonathan. He was master of Judea, and was freely acclaimed as high priest by the party of the Hasidim. A few years later Jonathan too lost his life in defense of his country. Thereupon a solemn convocation of the Jews met in a Great Assembly and elected Simon, the last remaining brother of Judah, to be hereditary ruler and high priest. For seven years Simon ruled. The nation was loyal to him, and he was loyal to the traditions for which he had fought in former days. Simon's son was readily accepted as his successor, for the days of comradeship and glory were still fresh in the people's minds, and they loved the Hasmonean for his family as well as for himself. Each anniversary of Hanukkah must have been reunion time for the old soldiers. Proudly they recounted their experiences and pledged renewed loyalty to the cause for which they had fought. But the generation of original Hasidim was passing away. New men and new problems brought the era of goodwill to an end.

If in their piety and naïveté the Hasidim had dreamed that with the expulsion of the Syrians an age of peace and brotherhood would reign within Judea, they must have become disillusioned very quickly. The progressive disintegration of the Syrian Empire was making Judean independence ever more secure. Economic prosperity was also increasing. What is more, those ancient enemies the hellenistic cities, rivals in culture and in trade, were now lying defenseless. They invited conquest by the ambitious Hasmonean kings. But the increase of wealth and political dominion brought back the very conditions that had motivated the rebellion against the Syrians. The common people again became dissatisfied. They had no interest in wars of conquest, and they resented the un-Jewish modes of life of their Hasmonean king and his court. A breach was inevitable.

It began during the reign of Simon's immediate successor, his son John Hyrcanus. This discussion is not concerned with the parties that came into being. It is sufficient to note that in consequence of such a situation Hanukkah as a holiday was bound to suffer. Even under ordinary circumstances the fervor of the observance of those days would die down with the death of the original generation. Had the Hasmoneans continued to be popular, the holiday would probably have been encouraged among the people as a tribute to the dynasty. But quite the contrary was the case. The common people no longer saw any reason for thanking God for the Hasmonean tyrants. They certainly did not feel the need for celebrating a second Sukkot.

It is surprising, therefore, not that Hanukkah was well-nigh forgotten, but that one hundred years later it was revitalized. The reason for this restoration must be sought in the changed conditions among the Jewish people. Due to internal dissension and civil wars, Judea again lost its independence. Now it was the Roman eagle, greedy for power, that sank its talons into the Jewish state. Rome deprived Judea of practically all it had conquered, and gave independence to the pagan cities. By the grace of Rome the weakest of the Hasmonean descendants ruled as a sort of tribal prince. But his every movement was guarded by the family of the Idumean convert to Judaism, Antipater, who was completely subservient to the Roman power. There were still a few Hasmoneans alive, and they tried again and again to regain their throne and the people's independence. As in the days of the Maccabees, groups of Jewish patriots began to roam the country. The Romans and their hirelings, Antipater and his sons, called them bandits. But those "bandits" were very popular with the common people, who looked upon

them as rebels against Rome. If only among the remaining Hasmoneans another Maccabee would arise to bring the great deliverance!

That was the period, it would seem, when 2 Maccabees was written. The Judeans had begun to recall the Maccabean Era; it was
desirable to get the Diaspora Jews to join in Judean hopes for
throwing off the Roman yoke. But to undertake such propaganda
openly might have been too dangerous. Hence only the purely
religious connotation of the holiday was emphasized. It was represented as the day of miracles not only during the liberation from
Syria, but also when the Second Temple was rebuilt.

The movement to regain Jewish independence failed. One by one
the last remnants of the Hasmonean house fell under the hand of
Herod. But the hope did not die out that God would again send a
leader as He had sent Mattathias and his sons. Thus, the idea of
Hanukkah was cautiously revived, and soon thereafter the schools
of Hillel and Shammai were obliged to take cognizance of the popular custom and to regulate it by law. Perhaps they too would have
preferred to make it a really important festival. But by that time
Herod was ruling with a heavy hand, and any such revival of a
holiday of independence would surely have been construed by him
for what it really would have been: an expression of hope for the
downfall of Rome. Nor could the teachers of the day fall back upon
the excuse that Hanukkah had been ordained by God, for the Maccabean story had been written too late to be included among the
Jewish sacred books. Therefore, while they spoke much about
Purim, all that they could do with regard to Hanukkah was to validate the current custom—the kindling of the lights.

Years passed and legends began to grow around the Maccabean
story. Josephus, who wrote around 100 C.E., was the last to tell the
story in fair historic form. But his books were not for the Jews, nor
were they long read by them. The two books of the Maccabees, not
being included in the sacred collection of Jewish literature, also
dropped out of sight among the Jews. All that was left was a vague
memory and a Feast of Lights. It was a situation that called for
embellishments of the story, and these soon developed. Thus
emerged the story of the miracle of the cruse of oil that was expected to last for one day but burned for eight, and all the accumulated legends contained in the Scroll of Antiochus, a booklet
composed centuries later. Hence also the story, which has even

crept into the prayers, that Judah's father, the aged Mattathias, had been a high priest. In some way, moreover, Hanukkah became linked with the Jewish woman's devotion to her people; no doubt the story of Hannah contributed to this. The Jews always recognized to what extent their survival has been due to the loyalty of Jewish women.

In general, legends, too, are historical events. They are not the history of the events that they take as their basis, but they are the historical material for an understanding of the mind, the hopes, the attitude to life of the people who create them and of those who believe them. The more the possibility of a physical restoration receded into the background, the more the purely religious interpretation of the holiday came to the fore. It was then that the old name, Feast of Lights, was replaced by the name Hanukkah—Feast of Dedication. The former was the only name by which Josephus knew the holiday. But soon Hanukkah assumed a significance greater than the celebration of a military victory, greater even than the hope of regaining independence. The Temple, representing religious life, the altar, portraying self-sacrifice, the menorah, standing for law and study, were considered more important, and the Maccabees were remembered because they saved and rededicated these religious objects. Hanukkah, then, came to represent the survival of Jewish culture and the continuance of Jewish life, a symbol of the unswerving obedience of the Jew to God and to the Torah.

As a religious holiday Hanukkah was sometimes the cause of trouble for the Jews. In talmudic days in Babylonia the Jews lived among a people to whom fire was sacred. There were periods of persecution when the Jews suffered for their use of lights to celebrate Hanukkah, and the rabbis of the day had to legislate exactly where the Hanukkah lights might or might not be placed, and even under what circumstances they might be extinguished. On the whole, however, it has been a holiday of merriment and lightheartedness. New customs began to develop in its celebration; songs were written in honor of the festival, and the Hanukkah lamp became a characteristic symbol in the Jewish home. Hanukkah became a season of joy and thanksgiving.

In our own day the meaning of Hanukkah is again undergoing a change. Influences, both Jewish and environmental, have been helping to strengthen the ceremonies connected with it, and to render its message more eloquent. But whatever the transformations it is still destined to undergo, Hanukkah will continue to serve, as it has served for two thousand years, to keep alive the eternal hope that God will not forsake His people and that right must triumph over might.[1]

2 HANUKKAH IN THE BIBLE

Although the biblical Book of Daniel predicts future events, it has been canonized in *Ketuvim* (Writings) rather than in *Neviim* (Prophets).[1] According to tradition, Daniel, who lived in the sixth century B.C.E., was an interpreter of symbolic visions and dreams. The most notable of his visions presaged the revolt of the Hasmoneans against Antiochus IV Epiphanes four centuries later. Daniel's vision reveals the rise and fall of a brutal despot and the ultimate triumph, through divine intervention, of those loyal to their religion. The prediction of this revolt and its successful conclusion may well have encouraged the Hasmoneans to rise up against the tyrant.[2] Modern biblical commentators maintain that the Book of Daniel was composed during the period of religious persecution by Antiochus IV Epiphanes. Hence the author only hinted at the anonymous characters in the book, which was read clandestinely. It served as an antidote to the oppressions and gave inner strength, encouragement, and hope to the Jews.

27

Psalm 30 was recited both at the dedication of the Second Temple and at its rededication by the Maccabees. In some editions of the prayer book, the psalm is included in the Hanukkah candlelighting ceremony. Its title, "A psalm of David. A song for the dedication of the Temple," renders it most appropriate for such an occasion. While the text specifies an individual who was delivered from danger and recovered from illness, the psalm also applies to Jewish national life.[3]

iiiiiii
=
A Vision of the Maccabean Revolt

And the king of the north [Antiochus the Great] shall come, and cast up a mound, and take a well-fortified city; and the arms of the south [armed forces of Egypt] shall not withstand; and as for his chosen people, there shall be no strength in them to withstand. But he [Antiochus] that cometh against him [Ptolemy] shall do according to his own will, and none shall stand before him; and he shall stand in the beauteous land [Judea], and in his hand shall be extermination. And he shall set his face to come with the strength of his whole kingdom, but shall make an agreement with him; and he shall give him the daughter of women [Antiochus' daughter, Cleopatra], to destroy it; but it shall not stand, neither be for him. After this shall he set his face unto the isles, and shall take many; but a captain shall cause the reproach offered by him to cease; yea, he shall cause his own reproach to return upon him. Then he shall turn his face toward the strongholds of his own land; but he shall stumble and fall, and shall not be found.

Then shall stand up in his place one [Seleucus IV] that shall cause an exactor to pass through the glory of the kingdom; but within a few days he shall be destroyed, neither in anger, nor in battle.

And in his place shall stand up a contemptible person [Antiochus IV Epiphanes], upon whom had not been conferred the majesty of the kingdom; but he shall come in time of security, and shall obtain the kingdom by blandishments. And the arms of the flood shall be swept away from before him, and shall be broken; yea, also the prince of the covenant [Onias III, the high priest]. And after the league made with him he shall work deceitfully; and he shall come up and become strong, with a little nation.

In time of security shall he come even upon the fattest places of the province; and he shall do that which his fathers have not done, nor his fathers' fathers: he shall scatter among them prey, and spoil, and substance; yea, he shall devise his devices against fortresses, but only until the time.

And he [Antiochus] shall stir up his power and his courage against the king of the south [Ptolemy IV of Egypt] with a great army; and the king of the south shall stir himself up to battle with a very great and mighty army; but he shall not stand, for they shall devise devices against him. Yea, they that eat of his food shall destroy him, and his army shall be swept away; and many shall fall down slain. And as for both these kings, their hearts shall be to do mischief, and they shall speak lies at one table; but it shall not prosper, for the end re-

2. *Hanukkah lamp. Bronze.*
Germany [*?*]. *Fourteenth century* [*?*].

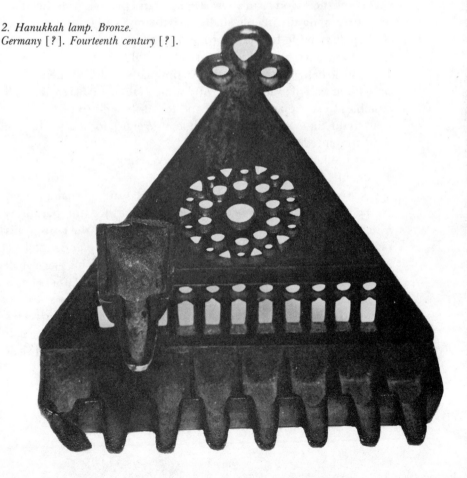

maineth yet for the time appointed. And he [Antiochus] shall return to his own land with great substance; and his heart shall be against the holy covenant [having desecrated the Temple and killed many Jews en route]; and he shall do his pleasure, and return to his own land.

At the time appointed he shall return, and come into the south; but it shall not be in the latter time as it was in the former. For ships of Kittim shall come against him, and he shall be cowed, and he shall return, and have indignation against the holy covenant, and shall do his pleasure; and he shall return, and have regard unto them [hellenizing Jews] that forsake the holy covenant. And arms shall stand up on his part, and they shall profane the sanctuary [in Jerusalem], even the stronghold [Temple fortifications], and shall take away the the continual burnt offering, and they shall set up the detestable thing [idol] that causeth appalment. And such as do wickedly against the covenant shall be corrupted by blandishments; but the people that know their God shall show strength, and prevail. And they that are wise among the people shall cause the many to understand; yet they shall stumble by the sword and by flame, by captivity and by spoil, many days. Now when they shall stumble, they shall be helped with a little help [by the Maccabees]; but many shall join themselves unto them with blandishments. And some of them that are wise shall stumble, to refine among them, and to purify, and to make white, even to the time of the end [of Antiochus' reign]; for it is yet for the time appointed.

And the king [Antiochus] shall do according to his will; and he shall exalt himself, and magnify himself above every god, and shall speak strange things against the God of gods; and he shall prosper till the indignation [of Israel's God] be accomplished; for that which is determined shall be done. Neither shall he regard the gods of his fathers; and neither the desire of women, nor any god, shall he regard; for he shall magnify himself above all. But in his place shall he honor the god of strongholds; and a god whom his fathers knew not shall he honor with gold, and silver, and with precious stones, and costly things. And he shall deal with the strongest fortresses with the help of a foreign god; whom he shall acknowledge, shall increase glory; and he shall cause them to rule over many, and shall divide the land for a price.

Daniel 11.15–39[4]

iiiiiiii
=

A Song for the Dedication of the Temple

A psalm of David.
A song for the dedication of the Temple.

I extol You, O LORD,
  for You have lifted me up,
  and not let my enemies rejoice over me.
O LORD, my God,
  I cried out to You,
  and You healed me.
O LORD, You brought me up from Sheol,
  preserved me from going down into the Pit.

O you faithful of the LORD, sing to Him,
  and praise His holy name.
For He is angry but a moment,
  and when He is pleased there is life.
One may lie down weeping at nightfall;
  but at dawn there are shouts of joy.

When I was untroubled,
  I thought, "I shall never be shaken,"
  for You, O LORD, when You were pleased,
  made [me] firm as a mighty mountain.
When You hid Your face,
  I was terrified.
I called to You, O LORD;
  to my LORD I made appeal.
"What is to be gained from my death,
  from my descent into the Pit?
Can dust praise You?
Can it declare Your faithfulness?
Hear, O LORD, and have mercy on me;
  O LORD, be my help!"

You turned my lament into dancing,
  You undid my sackcloth and girded me with joy,
  that [my] whole being might sing hymns to You endlessly;
  O LORD my God, I will praise You forever.

Psalm 30[5]

3 HANUKKAH IN POSTBIBLICAL WRITINGS

Outstanding among the Jewish postbiblical literary works are 1 and 2 Maccabees and Judith. These are included in the Apocrypha, the collection of writings omitted from the canon of the Hebrew Bible.

First and Second Maccabees, particularly the former, are the basic sources for the origin of the Hanukkah festival. They present the historical account of the first triumphant conquest of the spirit over tyranny—the desperate Jewish struggle for religious freedom and civil independence against ruthless Hellenist despots. Central in both books are Judah the Maccabee and the events in the Hasmonean revolt. First Maccabees, whose author is unknown, chronicles the Hasmonean lineage from the accession of Antiochus IV Epiphanes (175 B.C.E.) to the reign of John Hyrcanus (136–5 B.C.E.), when it was redacted. Although originally written in Hebrew, it survived in a Greek translation in the Septuagint. Second Maccabees is a condensed version of a book composed in Greek by Jason of Cyrene, a Hellenistic Jew, probably in the first century C.E. It records cases of religious martyrdom; for example, that of Eleazar and the mother of the seven sons elsewhere referred to as Hannah.

The Book of Judith recounts the story of a beautiful and heroic widow who risked her life to save her town beleaguered by enemy forces. In this literary masterpiece, probably written sometime between the second century B.C.E. and the first century C.E., the narrator emphasizes Judith's fervent piety. She believed with unremitting faith that God would grant a miraculous victory if her people adhered devoutly to their Jewish heritage. In midrashim and in a *piyyut* Judith is alluded to as a member of the Maccabean family; hence this Apocryphal book is linked to Hanukkah. Rabbi Samuel ben Meir (c. 1085–1174) maintained that the miracle of Hanukkah was effected through Judith (*Tosefot Megillah* 4a). On Hanukkah, Jewish women serve cheese dishes to commemorate Judith's scrupulous observance of the dietary laws by eating only dairy food while in the enemy camp.

The controversial Jewish historian Flavius Josephus (c. 38 C.E.– c. 100 C.E.), in his *Jewish Antiquities,* used 1 Maccabees (chapters 1–13) as his source for the history of the period. However, he altered and elaborated the text in many instances, adding what he considered to be lacking.

Megillat Taanit, a chronicle of festive national days when it is forbidden to fast, was written in the last days of the Second Temple by Hananiah ben Hezekiah ben Goren. The medieval scholia on this text includes the account, incorporated in the Talmud, of the miracle of the cruse of oil when the Temple was rededicated by the Maccabees.

iiiiiiii
=

Hellenism in Judea

When Seleucus died and Antiochus, called Epiphanes, succeeded to the kingdom, Jason, brother of Onias, supplanted his brother in the high priesthood; he promised the king in his petition three hundred and sixty talents of silver and eighty talents from some other source of revenue. In addition to this he promised to pay another hundred and fifty if he might be given permission to set up a gymnasium and ephebeum and to register the Jerusalemites as Antiocheans. The king assented to this, and he took office. Immediately he started out to convert his countrymen to the Greek way of life. He set aside the established royal laws favorable to the Jews, which had been obtained through John, father of Eupolemus, when he went as ambassador to the Romans to establish a friendly alliance. He broke down the lawful manners of life, and introduced new customs forbidden by the law. He took delight in establishing a gymnasium right under the citadel itself, and induced the finest of the young men to wear the petasus hat. To such heights did the passion for adopting Greek customs develop and the fad for imitating foreign manners advance, because of the ever-growing abominable wickedness of Jason, no high priest he, that no longer were the priests interested in the service of the altar. Despising the Temple and neglecting the sacrifices, they would hasten to participate in the unlawful exercises of the palaestra as soon as the summons came for the discus-throwing. They valued as nothing the customs their fathers honored, and coveted only Greek honors as worthy of attainment. Because of this, dire calamity fell upon them, for those very people whose customs they had zealously admired and wished to imitate in every detail became their enemies and persecuted them. After all, to sin against the laws of God is no light matter, but this, opportune time will soon show.

2 Maccabees 4.7–17[1]

iiiiiiii
=

The Persecutions of Antiochus

And it came to pass after Alexander of Macedon, son of Philip, who came from the land of Chittim, had completely defeated Darius, king of the Persians and the Medes, that he succeeded him as the first ruler over the Greek Empire. He waged many wars, conquered strongholds, and slew kings of the earth. He ranged to the ends of the earth and took spoil from a multitude of nations. When the land was at peace before him, he became arrogant, and his heart was

שהיה יום החמשה מלו
וזח
ושבת, ושבית, עזות

הנסים ועל הפרקן ועל ה
הגבורות ועל הבשעית
ועל המלחמות שעשיה
לאבותינו בימים ההם ובזו
ובזמן זה בימי בקריה
בן יוחנן כהן גדול וחשם

וכשמעואר ובבי כשעבמייה עליהם בלכות יון הרשעיה ועל עבד
ישראל להשכיחם מתיריהך וללעבימייה מחוקי רצונך ואקה ברחמיך
הרבים עברית להב בעקה צריכם רבה אה ריבם דנת אבדינם נקבית
אלהקובהבה ביסרקובבורים ביד חלשיםדרבים ביד מעטים וסמאים
בידי מהורים ורשעים ביד צדרקים וזדים ביד עשקי תורתיך מלך
עשיה שם גדול וקדוש בעולמבך ולעמבדי ישראך עשית כשתעה גו
גדולה גפורקן כהיום הגה ואחר מד באו בביך לרביר ביתיך ומבאו אה
היכלך וטהרה אלהקיךשך והלקיקו גרות בחברות הקדשיך ותבעו ו
שמבנה ימי חנובבה אלו להרדות ולהלל לשמברך הגדול ' ועל מלם '

למרים '''

הנסיב ועל הפרקן ועל ה ג
הגבורה ועל הבשעה '
ועל הבבריוה לחבבזה שעשיה
לאבזהינו בימים ההם ובו '
ובזמן זה בימי מרדבי '
ואכהר בשושן הבירה בש ן
כשעבמד עליהם הבן הרשע ובקש להרשמיד להרוג ולאבד אכ כל
היהדהרם בצער ועד זקן טת ונשים ביום אחד משלשה לחדש '
שנב עשר הוא חרש אדר ושללם לבוו ואקה ברחביך הרבים הברת

רלהעב נטיש לוה/ ביהב שוה
סלחות שוישבהם שורק
וחקתה'ב מחהות וחקביד
וייהך וחהוהלנהוה תנובשם /
וסהו וזמן להאב דיעיר ל
לבדיה כאבר חרם שיבה '
לטבות ב פרוסהרכ
סבי ליוש במרשכ נריסם ב

בפמש נטהם לקהוה נמבי ' וה
וזרך על חהבם בשהיר למנהת
חמת פסך וחלבם וחמות ער
שערבה שלוי ל"ך בנולהול '
ומ וני לטהיריי מו שליו ושהוזן
לשהוזעך הלהבויר שמבליה גה
היתב לה ביום הממה לתך ט
מהובגל זיהם עני ישהוי ש
שיש בהם ען עיו נשבם זהד

חהי עמי עמש יה'ב לזהב כי דידהכל כי דירזה נהבן רחק עשה יהה תשבהשה בהוש ' אלהמן מיו ילל שמן וחמ זאל ה ולהלהבי ימב וחזוה דל
ריאמנ ' עהיו דיוומי ורמשי נתבשהב בתביסית לאך טבלוי וההוהז ' ולש שוחב מהה לה שלוי להתקבטש נבני יבעבוב שהבכל חהי
לכד ' מיור' מביר' מילוה הק כדי עבד עמד נמבש שליו להתקבששט בני יעמב טך ' ולהזלם לוו היה וחקבזי להחרי ימבשו ק
כהם' יין שבהמגן המובר מבנק של יחד למבנהי בגה ' נגהמבד ירש יש שמחיון מבדי יחד מזל מבן לבב א '
ע דרין למך ' מהחזוך ל'וחה מבבד לעבמחד הידוע מהדיל בגל מש שבו ' מהטכב שריכ בהזהבלימין מני מל'חד בעמטה ובי ' ין
מהך הסמכל' ל מחרזמבד לעמברמד ומבבה שוה יהז בהמביון מני ' ומחוחנו נטם מהחזבלהעי מני 'ומבודרים וזה לקביז הזנ א
החהזיב' וריום דמטה לשמהגזין למי שלוי לזו מזוע לוזהרי ' חזם ' יש לו מזה ' הכם יקהז וכהב בג ' יקהז הזהב כ ירמו ' ירל ' למד כ

3. Kindling the lights. **Mahzor** *in Miscellany. Ferrara [?], Italy. Circa 1470.*

uplifted. He levied a very powerful army and ruled over countries and rulers of the heathen, who paid him tribute. Soon afterwards he fell ill and realized that he was about to die. He summoned his illustrious retainers, who had been reared with him from his youth, and divided his kingdom among them while he was still living. Alexander had reigned twelve years before he died, and his retainers took over, each in his own territory. They all donned crowns after he died, as did their sons after them, for many years, and they did much evil on the earth. From them there came forth a sinful shoot, Antiochus Epiphanes, son of King Antiochus, who had been a hostage in Rome. He became king in the one hundred and thirty-seventh year [of the Seleucid Era] of the Greek kingdom.

At that time there came forth from Israel certain lawless men who persuaded many, saying: "Let us go and make a treaty with the heathen around us, because ever since we separated from them, many evils have come upon us."

The plan seemed good in their eyes, and some of the people went eagerly to the king, who gave them permission to perform the rites of the heathen. They built a gymnasium in Jerusalem in accordance with the custom of the heathen. They also subjected themselves to uncircumcision and stood aloof from the sacred Law. Thus they joined the heathen, and sold themselves to do evil.

When, in the judgment of Antiochus, his kingdom was well established, he seized upon the idea of becoming king of the land of Egypt, so that he might rule over the two kingdoms. He invaded Egypt with a heavy force, with chariots, elephants, and cavalry, together with a great fleet. He waged war against Ptolemy, king of Egypt. Ptolemy turned back from before him and fled, while many were slain. They captured the fortified cities in the land of Egypt; and he despoiled the land of Egypt.

After smiting Egypt, in the one hundred and forty-third year, Antiochus turned back, went up against Israel, and entered Jerusalem with a great army. He entered the Temple in his arrogance and took the golden altar, the lamp for the light and all its equipment, the table of the shewbread, the cups, the bowls and the golden censers, the curtain, the crowns; and the golden adornment on the front of the sanctuary he stripped off entirely. He seized the silver, the gold, and the precious vessels; he also took the hidden treasures which he found. Taking them all he carried them away to his own country. He massacred people and spoke most arrogantly.

And great was the sadness in Israel, everywhere;
Both rulers and elders groaned;
Maidens and young men languished,
The beauty of the women was altered.
Every bridegroom took up lamentation,
And she that sat in a bridal chamber mourned.
Shaken was the earth over those who dwelt therein,
And the whole house of Jacob was clothed with shame.

After two years the king sent the officer of the Mysians to the cities of Judah and entered Jerusalem with a strong force. He spoke peaceful words to them craftily, and they trusted him. Then he fell suddenly upon the city and dealt it a great blow, destroying many people of Israel. He despoiled the city, burnt it with fire, and razed its houses and its surrounding walls. They led the women and children captive and took possession of the cattle. They fortified the city of David with a high and strong wall with mighty towers, and it became their citadel. They put sinful people therein, men who were transgressors against the law; and they entrenched themselves in it. They stored up arms and provisions, and after collecting together the spoils of Jerusalem, they laid them up there. They became a great menace, for it served as an ambuscade against the sanctuary, an evil adversary against Israel continually.

They shed innocent blood around the altar,
    And polluted the sanctuary.
Because of them the inhabitants of Jerusalem fled,
    She became a dwelling place of foreigners,
    And foreign she became to her own brood,
    And her children forsook her.
Her sanctuary was laid waste like a wilderness,
    Her feasts were turned into sadness,
    Her Sabbaths into a reproach,
    Her honor into contempt.
As great as had been her glory,
    By so much was her dishonor increased.
    And her high renown was turned into sadness.

Then the king ordered all in his kingdom to become one people, and that everyone should forsake his own laws. All the heathen acquiesced in the decree of the king. Even many from Israel consented to his worship and sacrificed to idols and profaned the Sabbath. The king also sent letters by messengers to Jerusalem and the cities of Judah, commanding them to follow customs foreign to the land, to withhold burnt offerings and sacrifices, and drink offerings from the sanctuary, to profane the Sabbaths and festivals, to pollute the sanctuary and the holy ones, to build high places, and sacred groves and idols, to sacrifice swine's flesh and unclean cattle, to leave their sons uncircumcised, and to defile themselves with every kind of uncleanness and profanation, so that they might forget the Law and change all the ordinances. Whoever would not obey the order of the king was to die.

In this manner he wrote to all his kingdom, and appointed over-seers over the people and enjoined the cities of Judah to offer sacrifices in each and every city. Many of the people, who were ready to forsake the Law, joined them and did evil in the land, and forced Israel into all the secret hiding places of fugitives.

On the twenty-fifth day of Kislev in the one hundred and forty-sixth year, he erected an abomination of desolation upon the altar, and in the surrounding cities of Judah they erected altars. They burned incense also at the doors of the houses and in the streets. The Books of the Law which they found, they tore into pieces and burned. Wherever a book of the covenant was found in anyone's possession, or if anyone respected the Law, the decree of the king imposed the sentence of death upon him. Month after month they dealt brutally with every Israelite who was found in the cities. On the twenty-fifth of the month they offered sacrifices upon the altar which was set on the altar of burnt offering. In accordance with the decree, they put to death the women who had circumcised their children, hanging the newborn babies around their necks; and they also put to death their families as well as those who had circumcised them. Nevertheless, many in Israel were firmly resolved in their hearts not to eat unclean food. They preferred to die rather than be defiled by food or break the holy covenant, and they did die. Great was the wrath that came upon Israel.

1 Maccabees 1²

iiiiiiii

The Revolt of Mattathias

At that time Mattathias, son of Johanan, son of Simon, a priest of the family of Joarib, moved away from Jerusalem, and settled in

Modin. He had five sons: Johanan surnamed Gaddi, Simon called Thassi, Judah called Maccabee, Eleazar called Auaran, and Jonathan called Apphus. When he saw the blasphemous things that were taking place in Judah and Jerusalem, he said:

> Wretched am I, why was I born to behold,
>> The dissolution of my people and the destruction of the
>> Holy City,
> To sit idly by while it is given into the hand of its enemies,
>> The sanctuary into the hand of foreigners?
> Her people have become as a man without honor,
>> Her glorious treasures captured, taken away;
> Her infants have been killed in her streets,
>> Her young men, by the sword of the enemy.
> What nation has not shared,
>> And what kingdom has not seized her spoil?
> All her adornment has been taken away,
>> Instead of a free woman, she has become a slave.
> Yea, behold, our sanctuary and our beauty,
>> And our glory have been laid waste!
> The heathen have profaned them.
> Why then should life continue for us?

Mattathias and his son stored their clothes, put on sackcloth, and mourned bitterly.

Then the king's officers who were compelling the people to renounce God came to the town of Modin, to force them to sacrifice. Many Israelites came forward to them; even Mattathias and his sons were there. The officers of the king said to Mattathias: "You are a leader, a prominent and great man in this town. You are firmly supported with sons and brothers. Come forward first, and carry out the order of the king, as all the heathen, the men of Judah, and those left in Jerusalem have done; then you and your sons will be counted among the friends of the king. You and your sons will be honored with silver and gold and many gifts."

Mattathias answered and replied in a loud voice: "Though all the heathen within the bounds of the royal domain obey him, and each one forsake the worship of his fathers, and show preference for his commands, yet will I, my sons, and my brothers walk in the covenant of our fathers. Far be it from us to forsake the Law and the testaments. We will not listen to the decree of the king by going astray from our worship, either to the right or to the left."

When he stopped speaking these words, a Jew came forward in sight of all to sacrifice upon the altar in Modin, in accordance with the decree of the king. When Mattathias saw him, he was filled with zeal, and his soul was stirred up. He brought courage to decision, and running up he slew him upon the altar. The king's man who was enforcing the sacrifice he also killed at the same opportune time, and pulled down the altar. Thus he showed his zeal for the Law, as Phineas had done toward Zimri, son of Salom. Then Mattathias shouted out in a loud voice in the town, saying: "Let everyone who is zealous for the Law, and would maintain the covenant, follow me."

He and his sons fled to the mountains and left whatever they possessed in the town.

Many who sought justice and judgment went down into the wilderness, to settle there, with their sons, their wives, and their cattle, because misfortunes had fallen hard upon them. Then news reached the king's officers and the forces in Jerusalem, the city of David, that men who had rejected the command of the king had gone down to the hiding places in the wilderness. Many pursued them, overtook them, encamped against them, and organized an attack against them on the Sabbath day. They said to them: "This is enough! Come out and obey the command of the king, and you will live." But they answered: "We will not come forth, nor will we obey the command of the king to profane the Sabbath day." Then they attacked them. They did not defend themselves nor did they hurl a stone against them, nor block up the hiding places, saying: "Let all of us die in our innocence; may heaven and earth testify in our behalf that you destroy us against all justice." They attacked them on the Sabbath, and they, their wives, their children, and their cattle died, to the number of a thousand souls.

When Mattathias and his friends heard this, they mourned greatly over them, each one saying to the other: "If all of us do as our brothers have done, and do not fight against the heathen for our lives and our laws, they will soon destroy us from off the earth." They then made the following decision: "If any man attack us in battle on the Sabbath day, let us oppose him, that we may not all die as our brothers did in the hiding places."

At that time a company of Hasidim joined them, an exceedingly forceful group of Israel, each one offering himself willingly in defense of the Law. All the refugees from misfortune joined them and came to reinforce them. They mustered an army and smote sinners in their anger and lawless men in their wrath, while the rest fled to the heathen to save themselves. Mattathias and his friends went about, and tore down the altars, and circumcised by force as many of the uncircumcised children as they found in the borders of Israel. They pursued the contemptuous ones, and the work prospered in their hands. Thus they rescued the Law from the hand of the heathen and the kings, and gave no occasion for triumph to the sinner.

When the days drew near for Mattathias to die, he said to his sons: "Now arrogance and reproach have become strong. This is a time of destruction and anger. My children, be zealous for the Law, and give your lives in behalf of the testament of our fathers. Be mindful of the deeds of our fathers, which they performed in their generations, that you may receive great glory and eternal renown. Was not Abraham found faithful in time of trial, and it was accounted to him for righteousness? Joseph, in the time of his distress, kept the commandment and became lord of Egypt. Phineas, our ancestor, in preserving his zeal received the promise of eternal priesthood. Joshua for fulfilling a command became a judge in Israel. Caleb for bearing witness in the congregation obtained an inheritance in the land. David because of his mercy inherited the throne of an everlasting kingdom. Elijah because of his great love for the Law was taken up into heaven. Hananiah, Azariah, and Mishael, because they had faith, were rescued from fire. Daniel because of his innocence was saved from the mouth of the lions. Consider how, throughout each generation, none who put their trust in Him will lack strength. Of the words of a sinful man be not afraid, because his glory shall become dung and worms. Today he may be exalted, but tomorrow he will nowhere be found, because he has returned to his dust, and memory of him will have perished. As for you, my children, be strong and courageous in behalf of the Law, for through it you will be glorified. Behold Simon your brother; I know that he is a man of wise counsel. Obey him always; he will be a father to you. Judah Maccabee, strong in might from his youth, will be the leader of the army and will fight the people's war. As for you, gather about you all who observe the Law, and avenge fully the wrong done to your people. Requite the heathen measure for measure, and obey the ordinance of the Law."

Then he blessed them and was gathered to his fathers. He died in the one hundred and forty-sixth year, and he was buried in Modin, and all Israel made great lamentation for him.

1 Maccabees 2³

iiiiiiii

Judah the Maccabee Becomes the Leader

Then Judah, his son, who was called Maccabee, arose in his
  stead,
And all his brothers helped him,
As well as all those who were adherents of his father,
And gladly they fought Israel's war.
He spread his people's glory far and wide,
He donned a breastplate like a giant,
And girded on his weapons of war.
He organized battles, protecting his camp with the sword;
He was like a lion in his deeds,
Like a lion's whelp roaring for its prey.
He sought out and pursued those who broke the Law
And exterminated those who troubled his people.
Lawbreakers cowered for fear of him,
All workers of iniquity were thrown into confusion,
And deliverance was accomplished by his hand.
He angered many kings,
But gladdened Jacob by his deeds;
So forever will his memory be for a blessing.
He went about among the cities of Judah,
And from it he utterly destroyed the godless ones;
Thus he turned away wrath from Israel.
To the ends of the earth he was renowned,
And he brought together those who were ready to perish.

Apollonius mustered the heathen, with a large force from Samaria, to wage war against Israel. When Judah learned this he went out to meet him and struck him down and killed him. Many were killed, and the rest fled. Then they took their spoils. Judah took the sword of Apollonius and fought with it all his life.

When Seron, the general of the Syrian army, heard that Judah had mustered a levy and a company of faithful men about him, along with others accustomed to going out to war, he said: "I will make a name for myself and be renowned in the kingdom. I will make war on Judah and those who are with him, who set at naught the command of the king."

He went up again with a strong expedition of godless men to help him take revenge on the Israelites. He approached as far as the ascent of Beth Horon, where Judah with only a few men went out to meet him. When his men saw the expedition coming to meet them, they said to Judah: "How can we, so few in number, be able to fight against so great a multitude? Then too, we are faint, for we have had nothing to eat today."

Judah replied: "It is an easy thing for many to be hemmed in by the hands of a few. There is no difference in the sight of heaven to save by many or by few. Victory in battle does not depend on the size of an army, but rather on strength that comes from heaven. They are advancing against us, full of violence and lawlessness, to destroy us, our wives and our children, and to plunder us. We are fighting for our lives and our Laws. He Himself will shatter them before us; but as for you, be not afraid of them."

When he stopped speaking, he drove at them suddenly, and Seron and his expedition were crushed before him. They pursued him down the descent from Beth Horon as far as the plain, and about eight hundred men were slain, while the rest fled to the land of the Philistines. Then began the fear and dread of Judah and his brothers to fall upon the heathen around them. His fame reached even to the king, and the heathen told about the military prowess of Judah.

When King Antiochus heard this, he was enraged, so he gathered together all the forces of his kingdom, a very strong expedition. He opened his treasury, gave a year's pay to his soldiers, and charged them to be prepared for every emergency. He saw, however, that the money in his treasury had run short. The revenues of the country were small because of the dissension and calamity that he had caused in the land by removing the laws which had existed from earliest days. He was cautious also lest he might not have enough, as had happened once or twice, for the expenses and the presents which he had given before with extravagance, surpassing in this the kings who came before him. He was at a loss as to what to do, but finally decided to go to Persia, to take the revenues of the countries, and to levy a large sum of money. He left Lysias, a prominent man of royal lineage, over the king's affairs from the river Euphrates to the borders of Egypt, and entrusted him to rear Antiochus, his son, until his return. He handed over to him half of his forces and the elephants. He gave him orders about everything that he wanted him to do, especially about the inhabitants of Judea and Jerusalem, against whom he was ordered to send an army to uproot and destroy the strength of Israel and the remnant of Jerusalem, to efface their memory from the place, to settle strangers in all their borders, and to parcel out their land by lot.

The king then took half of the forces that were left and set out from Antioch, his royal city, in the one hundred and forty-seventh year, crossed the Euphrates River and made his way to the upper countries.

4. *Kindling the lights.*
Woodcut. From Sefer Minhagim,
Amsterdam, 1723.

Meanwhile Lysias selected Ptolemy the son of Dorymenes, and Nicanor and Gorgias, able men of the friends of the king, and sent with them forty thousand infantry and seven thousand cavalry, to go to Judah and to destroy it according to the command of the king. They started off with their entire army, and came and pitched camp near Emmaus in the plain country. The merchants of the country heard news of them, and took a great sum of silver and gold and fetters, and came to the camp to buy the Israelites as slaves. An army from Syria and from the land of the Philistines joined them.

When Judah and his brothers saw that misfortunes were increasing, and armies were encamping on their borders, aware of what the king had said when he ordered his men to destroy the people completely, they said to one another: "Let us repair the evil fortune of our people and fight for our people and the sanctuary." The congregation gathered together to be ready for war, and to pray and to seek mercy and compassion.

> Jerusalem was uninhabited like a wilderness;
>   None of her offspring went in or went out.
> The sanctuary was trodden down,
>   And sons of foreigners were in the citadel.
> It became a solitary lodge for the heathen.
>   Joy was removed from Jacob,
> And flute and harp ceased.

They gathered together and went to Mizpeh, opposite Jerusalem, because Israel formerly had a place of prayer in Mizpeh. On that day they fasted, and donned sackcloth, put ashes on their head, and tore their garments. They spread out the scroll of the Law, upon which the heathen had drawn likenesses of their idols. They brought the priestly garments and the firstfruits and the tithes. They shaved the Nazirites, who had fulfilled their days, and cried to heaven with a loud voice, saying: "What shall we do with these men, and where shall we take them away, now that Thy Temple is trodden down and profaned, and Thy priests are in sadness and humiliation? See how the heathen have come together against us to destroy us. Thou knowest what they scheme against us. How shall we be able to stand our ground before them, unless Thou helpest us?" Then they sounded the trumpets and shouted with a loud voice.

After this Judah appointed officers over the people, captains, lieutenants, and sergeants. He ordered those who were building houses, or were betrothed to women or planting vineyards or were timid, to return each one to his own home in accordance with the Law. Then the army moved and encamped to the south of Emmaus. Judah said: "Gird yourselves and acquit yourselves like brave men. Be ready early in the morning to fight these heathen who have gathered against us to destroy us and our sanctuary, because it is better for us to die in battle than to look upon the tragedies of our nation and our sanctuary. But whatever be the will in heaven, thus shall He do."

1 Maccabees 3[4]

iiiiiii
=

Victories of the Maccabees

Gorgias meanwhile took five thousand men and a thousand select horsemen, and his expedition marched out by night so that it might fall upon the encampment of Judah and smite them suddenly. Men from the citadel served him as guides. When Judah heard of this, he and his valiant men started out to attack the army of the king in Emmaus, while the forces were still scattered from the camp. When Gorgias entered the camp of Judah in the night and found no one, he hunted for them in the mountains, because he said: "These fellows are fleeing from us."

As soon as it was daybreak, Judah was seen in the plain with three thousand men, although they had neither such armor nor swords as they would have wished. They saw the strongly parapeted camp of the heathen, with horsemen who were experienced in war surrounding it. Judah said to the men who were with him: "Do not fear their number, and do not be afraid of their attack. Remember how our fathers were saved at the Red Sea, when Pharaoh pursued them with a host. Now, then, let us cry to heaven to see if He will have mercy upon us, and will be mindful of the testament of the fathers, and will destroy this camp before us today, that all the heathen may know that there is One who will redeem and save Israel."

The heathen raised their eyes and saw them coming against them. They came out of the camp to battle. Judah's men sounded the trumpets and joined battle. The heathen were crushed and fled to the plain, while all those who were in the rear fell by the sword. They pursued them as far as Gazara and the plains of Judea and Ashdod and Jamnia, and about three thousand men were slain.

When Judah and his army returned from pursuing them, he said to his men: "Do not be greedy for spoil, because there is a battle before us. Gorgias and his army are near us, in the mountain. Take your stand now against our enemy, and join battle with them, and after that take the spoil without fear."

Before Judah had completed these words, a detachment was seen emerging from the mountain, and saw that their side had been routed and that they were burning the camp, for the smoke that was seen made plain what had taken place. When they perceived this, they were greatly frightened, and seeing also the army of Judah in the plain ready for attack, they all fled into the land of the Philistines. Judah thereupon turned back to plunder the camp, and they took much gold and silver, blue, purple and chrysolite, and great riches. On their return they sang a song of thanksgiving and gave thanks to heaven: "For He is good, for His mercy endureth forever." And Israel had a great deliverance on that day.

Those of the foreigners who were saved came and told Lysias everything that had happened. When he heard it he was confused and discouraged, because what he had wished to happen to Israel had not taken place, nor had that which the king charged him with come about.

In the following year he gathered together sixty thousand picked men and five thousand horsemen to fight against them. They entered Idumea, and encamped at Beth Sura, where Judah met them with ten thousand men. When he saw how strong the expedition was, he prayed and said: "Blessed art Thou, O Savior of Israel, who staved off the charge of the mighty man by the hand of Thy servant David, and didst deliver the camp of the Philistines into the hands of Jonathan son of Saul, and his armor-bearer. In the same way hem in this camp by the hand of Thy people Israel, and let them be put to shame in spite of their army and their horsemen. Make them cowardly. Melt the boldness of their strength. Let them quake at their destruction. Cast them down with the sword of those that love Thee, and let all who know Thy Name praise Thee with hymns."

Then they fell upon each other, and there fell of the army of Lysias about five thousand men, and they fell from before them. When Lysias saw the growing rout of his army, and in turn the increasing boldness of Judah, and how ready they were either to live or to die nobly, he marched away to Antioch. There he levied mercenary troops in greater numbers so that he might come back again against Judea.

1 Maccabees 4.1–35[5]

iiiiiiii

The Dedication of the Sanctuary

Judah and his brothers said: "Now that our enemies are crushed, let us go up to purify and dedicate the sanctuary."

The entire army gathered together and went up to Mount Zion. They saw the sanctuary desolated and the altar profaned, the gates burned up, and weeds growing in the courts as in a forest or as on one of the mountains, and the priests' chambers torn down. They tore their garments and made great lamentation, and put ashes on their heads, and fell on their faces on the ground, blew solemn blasts upon the trumpets, and cried out to heaven. Judah appointed certain men to fight against the garrison in the citadel, until he could cleanse the sanctuary. He selected priests without blemish, whose delight was in the Law, and they purified the sanctuary, carrying out the stones that had defiled it into an unclean place. They took counsel as to what they should do about the altar of burnt offering, which had been defiled. A good plan occurred to them, namely, to tear it down, lest it become a reproach to them, because the heathen had defiled it. So they pulled down the altar, and put away the stones in the Temple mount, in a suitable place, until a prophet should come to decide what to do with them. They took whole stones, according to the Law, and constructed a new altar like the former one. They built the sanctuary and the interior of the Temple, and hallowed the courts, and made new holy vessels, and brought the candlestick, the altar of incense, and the table into the Temple. They burned incense on the altar and lit the lights on the candlesticks so that they would shed light in the Temple. They put loaves of bread upon the table, hung up the curtains, and finished all the work which they had undertaken.

They also adorned the front of the Temple with golden crowns and small shields, and rededicated the gates and the priests' chambers, and fitted them with doors. Thus there was great joy among the people, and the reproach caused by the heathen was removed. Judah and his brothers and the entire congregation of Israel decreed that the days of the dedication of the altar should be kept with gladness and joy at their due season, year after year, for eight days from the twenty-fifth of the month of Kislev.

1 Maccabees 4.36–51, 57–59[6]

iiiiiii
=

Festival of Lights
FLAVIUS JOSEPHUS

Judah assembled the people and said that after the many victories that God had given them, they ought to go up to Jerusalem and purify the Temple and offer the customary sacrifices. . . .

And when he had carefully purified it, he brought in new vessels, such as a lampstand, table, and altar, which were made of gold, and hung curtains from the doors, and replaced the doors themselves; he also pulled down the altar, and built a new one of various stones which had been hewn with iron. And on the twenty-fifth of the month Chasleu [Kislev], which the Macedonians call Apellaios, they kindled the lights on the lampstand and burned incense on the altar and set out the loaves on the table and offered whole burnt offerings upon the new altar. These things, as it chanced, took place on the same day on which, three years before, their holy service had been transformed into an impure and profane form of worship. For the Temple, after being made desolate by Antiochus, had remained so for three years; it was in the hundred and forty-fifth year that these things befell the Temple, on the twenty-fifth of the month Apellaios, in the hundred and fifty-third Olympiad. And the Temple was renovated on the same day, the twenty-fifth of the month of Apellaios, in the hundred and forty-eighth year, in the hundred and fifty-fourth Olympiad [165 B.C.E.]. Now the desolation of the Temple came about in accordance with the prophecy of Daniel, which had been made four hundred and eight years before; for he had revealed that the Macedonians would destroy it.

And so Judah together with his fellow citizens celebrated the restoration of sacrifices in the Temple for eight days, omitting no form of pleasure, but feasting them on costly and splendid sacrifices, and while honoring God with songs of praise and the playing of harps, at the same time delighted them. So much pleasure did they find in the renewal of their customs, and in unexpectedly obtaining the right to have their own service after so long a time, that they made a law that their descendants should celebrate the restoration of the Temple service for eight days. And from that time to the present we observe this festival, which we call the Festival of Lights, giving this name to it, I think, from the fact that the right to worship appeared to us at a time when we hardly dared hope for it. Then Judah erected walls round the city, and, having built high towers against the incursions of the enemy, he placed guards in them; and he also fortified the city of Beth Sura in order that he might use it as a fortress in any emergency caused by the enemy.

Jewish Antiquities 12.7.6–7[7]

They celebrated it for eight days with rejoicing in the manner of the Feast of Tabernacles, mindful of how but a little while before at the festival of Tabernacles they had been wandering about like wild beasts in the mountains and caves. That is why, bearing thyrsi and graceful branches and also palm leaves, they offered up hymns to Him who had given them success in purifying His own place of worship. They decreed by edict and confirmed by vote that the entire nation of the Jews should celebrate these days every year.

2 Maccabees 10.6–8[8]

On the twenty-fifth thereof [Kislev] is the day of Hanukkah. For eight days mourning is forbidden.

Scholia: When the Greeks entered the Temple, they defiled all the oils that were there. When the House of the Hasmoneans prevailed and won a victory over them, they searched and found only one cruse [of oil] with the seal of the high priest that was not defiled. It had only [enough oil] to burn for one day. A miracle happened, and there was light from it for eight days. In the following year they established eight festival days.

Megillat Taanit 9

iiiiiiii
=

The Martyrdom of Eleazar

Eleazar, one of the foremost scribes, a man well advanced in years and of most noble countenance, was compelled to open his mouth in an attempt to force him to eat swine's flesh. He welcomed death with glory rather than life with pollution, and of his own free will went to the rack. Spitting out the food, he became an example of what men should do who are steadfast enough to forfeit life itself rather than eat what is not right for them to taste, in spite of a natural urge to live. Those who were in charge of the forbidden sacrifice, because they had known the man for such a long time before, took him aside and urged him privately to bring meat, prepared by himself, which would be proper for him to use, and to pretend that he was eating the meat of the sacrifice ordered by the king. Thus he might be saved from death and on account of his old friendship for them he might obtain courteous treatment. He, however, high-minded as always, . . . declared himself in no uncertain terms, saying that they should rather quickly send him forth to Hades:

"It is not suitable to my age to pretend, lest many of the youth think that Eleazar in his ninetieth year has changed to heathenism. They, because of my pretense and for the sake of this short span of life, will be led astray through me, and I shall come to a stained and dishonored old age. Even if for the present I were to escape the punishment of men, nevertheless I could not escape, either living or dead, the vengeance of the Almighty. Therefore by departing this life courageously now, I shall show myself worthy of my old age, and to young men I shall have left a noble example of how to die happily and nobly in behalf of our revered and holy laws."

After saying this he immediately went to the rack. . . . As he was dying under the blows, he said with his last sigh: "The Lord in His sacred knowledge is aware that though I could escape death I now endure terrible suffering in my body under these floggings; yet within my soul I suffer this gladly, because of my reverence for Him." In this way he died, leaving in his death an example of nobility and memorial of valor, not only to the young but also to the great majority of his nation.

2 Maccabees 6.18–31[9]

iiiiiiii
=

The Seven Brothers and Their Mother

It happened also that seven brothers, with their mother, were arrested and tortured with whips and scorpions by the king, to compel them to partake of swine meat forbidden by the Law. One of them made himself their spokesman, and said: "What do you intend to ask and to learn from us? It is certain that we are ready to die rather than transgress the laws of our fathers."

The king in his rage ordered that pans and caldrons be heated red hot. They were heated at once, and he ordered that the tongue of the spokesman should be cut out, that they should scalp him in the Scythian manner and cut off his extremities, while the rest of his brothers and his mother were looking on. When he had been reduced to a completely useless hulk, he ordered them to bring him, while he was still breathing, to the fire, and to fry him in the pan. As the vapor from the pan grew more dense, the children with their mother encouraged each other to die nobly, saying:

"The Lord God is watching, and in very truth will have compassion on us, just as Moses declared in his song, which bears testimony against them to their very face, saying: 'And He will have compassion upon His servants.' "

When the first one had died in this way, they brought the second to be mocked. Then they tore off his scalp with the hair and asked him:

"Will you eat, or else have your body dismembered limb from limb?"

He, however, replied in the mother tongue, and said: "Never."

For this reason he too underwent the same order of torture. But with his last breath, he said:

"You accursed wretch, you may release us from our present existence, but the King of the universe will raise us up to everlasting life because we have died for His laws."

After him the third one was brought to be mocked. When he was ordered to put out his tongue, he did so quickly. He courageously stretched forth his hands, then nobly said:

"From heaven have I had these, yet because of God's laws I count them as nothing, for from Him I hope to have them back again."

5. *Hanukkah lamp. Bronze.*
Aschaffenburg, Germany. 1706.

The result of this was that the king himself and his men were struck with admiration by the spirit of the young man because he minimized his sufferings.

When he too had died, they mutilated and tortured the fourth one in the same manner. As he was dying he said:

"Better is it for people to be done to death by men if they have the hopeful expectation that they will again be raised up by God, but as for you, there will be no resurrection to life."

Next they brought up the fifth and treated him shamefully. As he looked at the king he said:

"Because you, a finite mortal, have authority among men, you may work your will; but do not think that God has abandoned our people. You will see how His overwhelming power will torment you and your offspring."

After him they brought on the sixth. As he was about to die, he said:

"Do not vainly deceive yourself. We suffer these things because of ourselves, because we sinned against our own God. That is why these astounding things have come upon us. But do not think that you will go free in thus daring to wage war against God."

Their mother was truly wonderful and is worthy of blessed memory. Though she saw her seven sons die in the space of a single day, she bore it bravely because of her faith in the Lord. She encouraged each one of them in their mother tongue, filled as she was with a noble spirit. She stirred up her womanly nature with manlike courage, and said to them:

"How you ever appeared in my womb, I do not know. It was not I who graced you with breath and life, nor was it I who arranged in order within each of you the combination of elements. It was the Creator of the world, who formed the generation of man and devised the origin of all things, and He will give life back to you in mercy, even as you now take no thought for yourselves on account of His laws."

Antiochus then thought that he was being treated contemptuously and suspected the reproachful tone of her voice. As the youngest son was still alive he appealed to him not only by words but also by oaths, [saying] that he would make him both rich and enviable if he would leave the ways of his fathers; that he would consider him as a friend, and would put him in an office of trust. When the young man paid no attention to him at all, the king summoned the mother and urged her to advise the lad to save himself. After he had exhorted her for quite a while, she undertook to persuade her son. She leaned over him, and jeering at the king, she spoke in the mother tongue as follows:

"My son, have pity on me, who carried you in my womb for nine months. For three years I nursed you, reared you, brought you to this stage of your life, and sustained you. I beg of you, my child, to look up to heaven and earth and see all that is therein, and know that God did not make them out of things that were already in existence. In the same manner the human race came into being. Do not be afraid of this executioner, but show yourself worthy of your brothers. Accept death, that in God's mercy I may receive you back again along with your brothers."

While she was still speaking, the young man said: "What are you waiting for? I will not obey the king's command, but I will obey the command of the Law that was given to our fathers through Moses. But you, who have shown yourself to be the contriver of every evil against the Hebrews, shall not escape the hands of God. We are really suffering for our own sins. Although our living God, in order to punish and discipline us, is angry at us for a little while, He will again be reconciled with His servants. You profane wretch, vilest of all men, be not vainly buoyed up by your insolent, uncertain hopes, raising your hand against His servants. You have not yet escaped the judgment of the Almighty, all-seeing God. Indeed, our brothers, after enduring brief trouble, are under God's covenant for everlasting life; while you under God's judgment will receive just punishment for your arrogance. I, like my brothers, surrender body and soul for our paternal laws, invoking God speedily to be merciful to our nation, and to make you acknowledge through affliction and torment that He alone is God, while it has devolved upon me and my brothers to stay the wrath of the Almighty, which has justly been brought against the whole of our nation."

With this the king became furious, and dealt with him worse than with the others, bitterly resenting his sarcasm. He then died in purity, believing implicitly in God. Finally, after her sons, the mother also died.

Let this then be enough about eating of idolatrous sacrifices and inhuman tortures.

2 Maccabees 7*[10]

---

*The spirit of loyalty to the monotheistic faith as exemplified in this account was reiterated in talmudic and midrashic literature through variations of the narrative. For parallel accounts in the tractate Gittin and *Lamentations Rabbah,* see the next chapter, "Hanukkah in Talmud and Midrash."

iiiiiii
=

The Story of Judith

Judith Proposes to Save Her People

And the children of Israel who dwelt in Judea heard of all that Holofernes, the chief captain of Nabouchodonosor king of the Assyrians, had done unto the nations, and how he had sacked all their shrines and had given them over to destruction; and they were in great fear of him and were terrified for Jerusalem and the Temple of their God. . . .

And the children of Israel raised their cry to their God, because their spirit had grown faint, because all their enemies had compassed them about, and it was impossible to escape from their midst. And all the army of Asshur remained encamped around them, their foot soldiers and chariots and horsemen, for thirty-four days. And all their vessels of water utterly failed all those who dwelt in Bethulia, and their cisterns were going dry, and they did not have enough water to drink their fill for a single day, for by measure were they giving them to drink. And their babies lost heart, and the women and the young men fainted from thirst and were falling prone in the streets of the city and in the ways through the gates, and there was no might left in them.

And all the people assembled against Ozias and the rulers of the city, the young men and the women and the little children, and cried out with a loud voice and said, in the presence of all the elders: "May God judge between you and us because you have done us great wrong by not speaking words of peace with the children of Asshur. And now we have no helper, but God hath sold us into their hands to be brought low before them in thirst and great destruction. And now call them and hand over the whole city for spoils to the people of Holofernes and to all his army. For better is it for us to be made their booty. For we shall be their slaves, and our lives will be spared, and we shall not see the death of our babes before our very eyes, and our wives and children gasping out their lives." . . .

And Ozias said to them: "Courage, brethren, let us hold out for five days more, in which our God will turn His mercy toward us, for He will not utterly forsake us. But if these days pass and no succor

come upon us, I will do according to your words." And he dispersed
the people, each to his own post, and they departed to the walls and
the towers of their city. . . .

And in those days Judith heard thereof. . . . And her husband was
Manasseh of her tribe and her family. And he had died in the days
of the barley harvest. . . . And Judith had been living as a widow in
her house for three years and four months. And she had made for
herself a tent on the roof of her house and put sackcloth on her
loins, and the garments of her widowhood were upon her. And she
was wont to fast all the days of her widowhood, save on the day
before the Sabbath and the Sabbath and the day before the New
Moon and the day of the New Moon and the feasts and days of joy
of the House of Israel. And she was exceedingly fair of form and
lovely to behold; and Manasseh her husband had left her gold and
silver and manservants and maidservants and cattle and fields, and
she had remained thereon. And there was none who brought
against her an evil report, because she feared God exceedingly.

And she heard the wicked words of the people against the magis-
trate because they had waxed faint of heart at the lack of water, and
Judith heard all the words of reply which Ozias had said to them,
how he had sworn to them that he would hand over the city to the
Assyrians after five days. And sending her favorite slave girl, who
was over all her possessions, she summoned Chabris and Charmis,
the elders of the city, and they came to her, and she said unto them:
"Hearken to me, I pray you, ye rulers of those who dwell in Bethulia,
because your word which you spake before the people on this day
is not right, and you have established this oath which you spoke
betwixt God and you and have promised to hand over the city to our
enemies if God does not turn within those days to aid you. Pray tell
me, who are you who have made trial of God this day and stand in
the stead of God among the sons of men? . . . Nay, nay, brethren;
stop provoking your God to anger. Because if He be unwilling to
succor us within these five days, He hath the power, within any
number of days which He chooses, to shelter us or even to destroy
us in the face of our enemies." . . .

And Ozias said to her: "All that thou hast said hast thou spoken
in good heart, and there is none who will gainsay thy words; because
today is not the first day that thy wisdom hath been manifest. . . .
But the people were exceedingly thirsty, and they forced us to do
as we spake to them and to take upon ourselves an oath which we

will not violate. And now, pray for us, because thou art a devout woman, and God will send rain to fill our cisterns and we shall faint no more." And Judith said to them: "Hearken unto me, and I will do a thing which will go down through endless generations among the children of our people. As for you men, ye shall stand at the gate this night, and I shall go forth, I and my favorite, and within the days after which ye said ye would hand over the city to our foes, God will look with favor on Israel, by my hand. But ye are not to inquire about my act, for I shall not tell it to you until those things which I shall do have been accomplished." And Ozias and the magistrates said to her: "Go in peace, and may God go before thee to take vengeance on our foes." And turning back from the tent they went to their stations.

Then Judith fell upon her face and put ashes on her head and laid bare the sackcloth which she had put on, and at the moment when that evening's incense offering was being carried into the house of God in Jerusalem, Judith cried with a loud voice to God and said: "Yea, verily, God of my father and God of the inheritance of Israel, Ruler of the heaven and the earth, Creator of the waters, King of all Thy creation, hearken Thou to my supplication; and make my word and deceit for the wound and bruise of those who have purposed hard things against Thy covenant and Thy hallowed house and the crest of Zion and the house of Thy sons' possession. And make every nation and every tribe to know full well that Thou art God, the God of all power and might, and that there is none other shielding the people of Israel save Thee."

Judith 4.1–2, 7.19–27, 30—8.15, 8.28—9.1, 9.12–14[11]

Judith in the Camp of Holofernes

And it came to pass that when she had ceased crying unto the God of Israel and had finished all these words, she arose from where she lay prostrate and called her maid and went down into the house where she was wont to stay during the Sabbaths and her feast days; and she laid aside the sackcloth which she had put on, and divested herself of her widow's garb, and washed her body all over with water, and anointed herself with costly ointment, and vamped up the hair of her head, and put upon it a tire, and clad herself in her gayest attire, with which she had been wont to be garbed in the days while Manasseh her husband was alive, and she took sandals for her feet, and put on anklets and bracelets and rings and her earrings and all her finery, and adorned herself gaily so as to beguile the eyes of as many as should behold her. And she gave to her maid a leathern bottle of wine and a cruse of oil, and filled a pouch with barley groats and a cake of figs and loaves of fine bread, and she carefully wrapped all her dishes and put them upon her. And they went forth to the gate of the city of Bethulia and found standing at it Ozias and the elders of the city, Chabris and Charmis. When they saw her and that her face was altered and her apparel changed, they marveled very greatly at her beauty and said to her: "May the God of our fathers cause thee to find favor and to accomplish thy purposes that the sons of Israel may be filled with pride and Jerusalem exalted." And she worshiped God and said to them: "Give orders to open for me the gate of the city, and I shall go forth for the accomplishment of

6. *Hanukkah lamp. Silver. Amsterdam, Holland. 1719.*

those matters whereof ye spake with me"; and they gave orders to the young men to open for her even as she had spoken. And they did so. And Judith went forth, she and her handmaid with her. . . .

And they went straight on in the vale, and an outpost of the Assyrians met her. And they arrested her and demanded: "Of what folk art thou, and whence hast thou come and whither dost thou go?" And she said: "A daughter of the Hebrews am I, and am fleeing from them because they are about to be given to you for fodder. And I am on my way to the presence of Holofernes, the chief captain of your army, to tell to him words of truth, and I will show him a way whereby he shall go and master all the hill country, and there shall not be lost of his men one person or one life." When the men heard her words and remarked her face—her beauty was in their eyes exceeding great—they said to her: "Thou hast saved thy life by hastening to come down to the presence of our lord. And now draw nigh to his tent, and some of us will accompany thee until they deliver thee into his hands. But now, if thou standest before him, have no fear in thy heart, but announce to him as thou hast said, and he will treat thee well." And they chose a hundred of their number and set them as escorts for her and her maid, and they led her to the tent of Holofernes. And there arose a great concourse in the whole camp, for her presence was noised about from tent to tent. And when they came up, they stood around her as she stood outside the tent of Holofernes, until she had been announced to him. . . . And Holofernes was resting on his bed, under the canopy which was woven of purple and gold and emerald and precious stones. And they gave word to him about her, and he went out to the fore part of the tent, with silver lamps going before him. When Judith came before him and his attendants, they all marveled at the fairness of her face. And falling upon her face she did obeisance to him, and his slaves raised her up.

And Holofernes said to her: "Be of good cheer, woman; have no fear in thy heart, because I am not one to harm anyone who has seen fit to serve Nabouchodonosor, the king of all the earth. And now, as for thy people who dwell in the hill country, if they had not made light of me, I would not have lifted my spear against them. But it is they who have brought all this upon themselves. And now, tell me for what reason thou hast fled from them and come to us. For thou art come into safety. Be of good cheer, this night thou shalt live and henceforth, for there is none who will harm thee; rather, all will treat thee well, as is the case with the slaves of my lord, King Nabouchodonosor." And Judith said to him: "Receive the words of thy slave, and let thy handmaid speak before thee, and I will tell my lord nothing false this night. And if thou wilt follow out the words of thy handmaid, God will accomplish with thee a deed to the full, and my lord wilt not fall short of his design. . . . For we have heard of thy wisdom and the wonderful feats of clever cunning of thy brain, and report has come to all the earth that thou alone art good in all the kingdom and able in knowledge and wondrous in the arts of war. And now, as to the matter of which Achior spake in thy council, we have heard his words because the men of Bethulia spared him, and he made known to them all that he had spoken in thy presence. Wherefore, my sovereign lord, do not disregard his words, but store it in thy heart because it is true; for our people is not to be chastened, sword will not prevail against them, if they do not sin against their God. And now that my lord be not thwarted and fail to achieve his goal, death will fall upon them, for a sin has laid hold of them, whereby they will enrage their God whenever they do amiss. When their supply of food had completely failed them and all their water had become scant, they determined to resort to their cattle and decided to spend all that God had commanded them in His laws not to eat. And the firstfruits of wheat and the tithes of wine and oil, which they had consecrated and set aside for the priests who stand in Jerusalem before the face of our God, which things it is not proper for any of the people even to touch with their hands, them they have decided to consume. And to Jerusalem, because even they who dwell there have done these deeds, have they sent messengers to bring back to them permission from the council. And it shall be that when the word reaches them and they so do, on that very day will they be given over to thee for destruction. Wherefore I thy slave, having learned all this, fled from before them, and God has sent me to do things with thee at which the whole earth will be astounded, as many as shall hear of them, because your slave is God-fearing and worships the God of heaven night and day; and now I will remain with thee, my lord, and thy slave shall go forth each night into the valley, and I shall pray to God, and He will tell me when they have committed these deeds of sin. And I will come and bring thee word, and thou shalt go forth with all thine army, and there is no one of them who will withstand thee. And I will guide thee through the midst of Judea until thou comest before Jerusalem, and I will set thy seat in her midst, and thou shalt drive them like sheep who have no shepherd, and before thee shall no dog dare to growl with his tongue; because these things were told me according to my foreknowledge and were reported to me, and I have been sent to announce them to thee."

And her words were pleasing in the eyes of Holofernes and of all who attended him, and they marveled at her wisdom and said: "There is not such a woman from one end of the earth to the other, for fairness of face and understanding of words." And Holofernes said to her: "God hath done well in sending thee before the people that might be in our hands but destruction for those who made light of my lord. And now, thou art pretty of face and able of speech. If thou doest as thou hast spoken, thy God shall be my God, and thou shalt sit in the house of King Nabouchodonosor and shalt be of note throughout the whole earth."

And he gave the command to conduct her where his silver plate was kept and gave the order to spread before her some of his own dainties and of his own wine to drink. And Judith said: "I shall not eat them lest it be an offense, but provision will be made from the things which have come with me." Holofernes said to her: "But if the things with you fail, where will we get things like them to give thee, for there is none of thy race with us?" And Judith said to him: "As thy soul liveth, my lord, thy handmaid will not use up the things with me until God by my hand accomplishes what He hath purposed." And the servants of Holofernes led her to the tent, and she slept until midnight; and toward the morning watch she arose. And she sent word to Holofernes: "Please let my lord give orders to permit thy handmaid to go forth for prayer." And Holofernes bade his bodyguard not to hinder her. And she abode in the camp three days. And each night she went forth to the vale of Bethulia and bathed in the camp at the spring of water. And when she had come out of the water, she was wont to beseech the God of Israel to make straight her way for the elevation of the children of His people. And coming in clean, she was wont to stay in the tent until she partook of her food toward evening.

And it came to pass on the fourth day that Holofernes made a feast for his slaves only, and he did not include in the invitation any of those on duty. And he said to Bagoas, the eunuch who was in charge of all his possessions: "Come, now, go and persuade the

Hebrew woman, who is with thee, to come to us and eat and drink with us, for lo, we will be put to shame if we let such a woman go without having intercourse with her, because if we do not force her, she will laugh us to scorn." And Bagoas went out from before Holofernes and came to her and said: "Let not this fair maid, I pray, hesitate to come to my lord to be honored in his presence, and thou shalt drink wine and make merry with us and become this day as a daughter of the children of Asshur who attend in the house of Nabouchodonosor." And Judith said to him: "And who am I to say nay to my lord? Because all which will be pleasing in his eyes will I hasten to do, and this will be a source of joy to me till the day of my death." And arising, she arrayed herself in her apparel and all her woman's finery, and her slave girl came forward and strewed on the ground for her before Holofernes the lambskins which she had received from Bagoas for her daily use, that she might recline on them as she ate. And Judith came in and reclined, and the heart of Holofernes was delighted to ecstasy at her, and his soul reeled, and he was exceedingly eager to lie with her; and he had been biding his time to deceive her from the day when he had first seen her. And Holofernes said to her: "Drink, I pray thee, and make merry with us." And Judith said: "Indeed yes, my lord, I will drink, because my life hath been exalted today to a height beyond that of all the days since my birth." And taking, she ate and drank before him what her slave had prepared. And Holofernes was enraptured with her and drank exceeding much wine, more than he had ever drunk in one day since he was born.

But when the hour had become late, his slaves made haste to withdraw. And Bagoas closed the tent from without and excluded the attendants from the presence of his lord, and they went off to bed, for all were weary since the party had lasted so long. And Judith was left alone in the tent, and Holofernes was prone on his bed, for he was fair swimming in wine. And Judith had bidden her slave girl to stand outside her chamber and to await her departure even as she did every day, for she had said that she would go out for her prayers. And she had spoken to Bagoas in the same wise. And all had gone away, and no one was left in the chamber, small or great. And taking her stand by his bed, Judith said in her heart: "God of all power, look down with favor in this hour upon the works of my hand for the exaltation of Jerusalem; because now is the time to come to the aid of Thine inheritance and to carry out my designs for the shattering of the enemies who have risen up against us." And going to the bedpost which was at Holofernes' head, she took down from it his sword, and nearing the bed she seized hold of the hair of his head and said: "Give me strength this day, God of Israel." And with all her might she smote him twice in the neck and took his head from him. And she rolled his body from the couch and took the canopy from the poles; and a moment later she went out and gave Holofernes's head to her maidservant, and she put it in her pouch of victuals. And the two went forth together according to their wont for prayer. And having traversed the camp they compassed that valley and went up the mountain of Bethulia and came to its gates.

Judith 10.1–18, 21—11.6, 11.8—13.10[12]

The Triumphant Return of Judith

And Judith called out from afar to those on guard at the gates: "Open, open the gate, I beg you! God, our God, is with us, to show yet again His strength in Israel and His might against the enemies, even as He hath done this day." And it came to pass that when the men of her city heard her voice they hastened to go down to the gate of their city, and summoned the elders of the city. And all, both great and small, ran together because it seemed incredible that she had come, and they opened the gate and welcomed them, and having lit a fire for light, they circled them around. Then she said to them with a loud voice: "Praise God, give praise; praise God who hath not withdrawn His mercy from the House of Israel but hath shattered our enemies this night by my hand." And drawing out from the pouch the head, she showed it and said: "Behold, the head of Holofernes, the chief captain of the army of Asshur, and behold, the canopy under which he lay in his drunken stupor. And God smote him down by the hand of a female. And as God liveth, who watched over me on the way I went, (I swear to you) my face deceived him to his undoing, and he wrought no deed of sin with me to defile or cause me shame." And all the people were exceeding amazed and bowed down and worshiped God and said with one accord: "Blessed art Thou, our God, who hath brought to naught this day the enemies of Thy people." . . .

And Judith said to them: "Hearken to me, I pray thee, brethren, and take this head and hang it on the battlement of your wall. And it shall be, as soon as morning dawns and the sun comes forth upon the earth, that ye shall take up your weapons of war, each of you, and ye shall go forth, every able man of you, from the city and shall give them a leader as though you were about to descend upon the plain against the outpost of the children of Asshur, and ye shall not descend. And these fellows will take up their arms and go to their camp and will arouse the generals of the army of Asshur; and they will rush to the tent of Holofernes and will not find him; and fear will fall upon them, and they will flee from before you." . . .

When the children of Israel heard, all with one accord fell upon them and set to cutting them to pieces as far as Choba. In like manner, both those from Jerusalem and from all the hill country came, for men had told them what had taken place in the camp of their enemies. And those in Gilead and those in Galilee outflanked them with great losses until they passed Damascus and its borders. And the rest of those who dwelt in Bethulia fell upon the camp of Asshur and despoiled them and became exceeding wealthy. When the children of Israel returned from the slaughter, they took possession of what was left, and the towns and villages in the hill country and in the plain got hold of much spoils, for the amount was exceedingly great.

And Joakim the high priest and the council of the children of Israel who dwelt in Jerusalem came to behold the good deeds which God had wrought for Israel and to see Judith and to hail her.

Judith 13.11–17, 14.1–3, 15.5–8[13]

4 HANUKKAH IN TALMUD AND MIDRASH

The inexhaustible mine of the Talmud from which the Jewish people extracted spiritual and educational ores has inspired and guided them for many centuries. Redacted in the fifth century, this monumental work has been a vital source that nourished the Jews in their long torturous sojourn in the Diaspora.

While there are talmudic tractates that deal in name or in theme with Rosh Hashanah, Purim, and other holy days as they are based on canonized biblical sources, there is no tractate titled "Hanukkah," as this festival has no official canonized text. Aside from occasional scattered references in the Talmud, only a few pages in the tractate Shabbat are devoted to Hanukkah. However, laws pertaining to the Festival of Lights are found in Soferim (Scribes), a minor tractate omitted from the talmudic canon.

The extensive midrashic literature, created over a long time span, aims to adduce ethical and spiritual teachings from the Scriptures. *Pesikta Rabbati* (Large Section), probably redacted in Palestine in the seventh century, includes homilies and discourses drawn from early sources for the festivals, fast days, and special Sabbaths. *Midrash Rabbah* (Great Midrash), the most imposing of these collections, is the product of many hands over a period of many centuries up to the twelfth. The selection in this chapter from *Or Zarua* (Light Is Sown), by Rabbi Isaac ben Moses of Vienna, who lived in the thirteenth century, is quoted from a midrash.

ïïïïïïï
=

The Woman and Her Seven Sons

It is for Your sake that we are slain all day long, that we are thought of as sheep to be slaughtered (Psalms 44.23). Rab Judah said that this refers to the woman and her seven sons. They brought the first before the emperor and said to him, Serve the idol. He said to them: It is written in the Law, *I the Lord am your God* (Exodus 20.2). So they led him away and killed him. They then brought the second before the emperor and said to him, Serve the idol. He replied: It is written in the Torah, *You shall have no other gods beside Me* (ibid. 3). So they led him away and killed him. They then brought the next and said to him, Serve the idol. He replied: It is written in the Torah, *Whoever sacrifices to a god other than the Lord above shall be proscribed"* (ibid. 22.19). So they led him away and killed him. They then brought the next before the emperor saying, Serve the idol. He replied: It is written in the Torah, *You shall not bow down to them* (ibid. 20.5). So they led him away and killed him. They then brought another and said to him, Serve the idol. He replied: It is written in the Torah, *Hear, O Israel, the Lord is our God, the Lord is One* (Deuteronomy 6.4). So they led him away and killed him. They then brought the next and said to him, Serve the idol. He replied: It is written in the Torah, *Know therefore this day and keep in mind that the Lord alone is God in heaven above and on the earth beneath; there is no other* (ibid. 4.39). So they led him away and killed him. They brought the next and said to him, Serve the idol. He replied: It is written in the Torah, *You have affirmed this day that the Lord is your God. . . . And the Lord has affirmed this day that you are, as He promised you, His treasured people* (ibid. 26.17–18); we have long ago sworn to the Holy One, blessed be He, that we will not exchange Him for any other god, and He also has sworn to us that He will not change us for any other people. The emperor said: I will throw down my seal before you and you can stoop down and pick it up, so that they will say of you that you have conformed to the desire of the king. He replied: Fie on thee, Caesar, fie on thee, Caesar; if thine own honor is so important, how much more the honor of the Holy One, blessed be He! They were leading him away to kill him when his mother said: Give him to me that I may kiss him a little. She said to him: My son, go and say to your father Abraham, Thou didst bind one [son to the] altar, but I have bound seven altars. Then she also went up onto a roof and threw herself down and was killed. A voice thereupon came forth from heaven saying: *A happy mother of children* (Psalms 113.9).

Gittin 57b[1]

It is related of Miriam, the daughter of Tanhum, that she was taken captive with her seven sons. [Here the account of the death of six of the sons is substantially the same as in the selection above. Then the encounter of the emperor and the youngest son continues.] The emperor said to him: "Your brothers had had their fill of years of life and had experienced happiness; but you are young, you have had no fill of years and life and have not yet experienced happiness. Prostrate yourself before the image and I will bestow favors upon you." He replied: "It is written in our Torah, *The Lord will reign for ever and ever* (Exodus 15.18), and it is said, *The Lord is King forever and ever; the nations will perish from His land* (Psalms 10.16). You are of no account and so are His enemies. A human being lives today and is dead tomorrow, rich today and poor tomorrow; but the Holy One, blessed be He, lives and endures for all eternity." The emperor said to him: "See, your brothers are slain before you. Behold, I will throw my ring to the ground in front of the image; pick it up so that all may know that you have obeyed my command." He answered: "Woe unto you, O emperor! If you are afraid of human beings who are the same as yourself, shall I not fear the supreme King of kings, the Holy One, blessed be He, the God of the universe!" He asked him: "Has, then, the universe a God?" He replied: "Shame on you, O emperor! Do you, then, behold a world without a Master!" He asked: "Has your God a mouth?" He answered: "In connection with your gods it is written, *They have mouths,*

7. *Hanukkah lamp with bucket to catch the drippings. Silver.*
By Jacob Marsh. London, England. 1747–48.

but cannot speak (ibid. 115.5); in connection with our God it is written, *By the word of the Lord the heavens were made"* (ibid. 33.6). "Has your God eyes?" He answered: "In connection with your gods it is written, *Eyes [have they], but cannot see* (ibid. 115.5); in connection with our God it is written, *The eyes of the Lord, that run to and fro through the whole earth"* (Zechariah 4.10). "Has your God ears?" He answered: "In connection with your gods it is written, *They have ears, but cannot hear* (Psalms 115.5); in connection with our God it is written, *And the Lord hearkened, and heard"* (Malachi 3.16). "Has your God a nose?" He answered: "In connection with your gods it is written, *Noses [have they], but cannot smell* (Psalms 115.6); in connection with our God it is written, *The Lord smelled the pleasing odor"* (Genesis 8.21). "Has your God hands?" He answered: "In connection with your gods it is written, *They have hands, but cannot touch* (Psalms 115.7); in connection with our God it is written, *My own hand founded the earth"* (Isaiah 48.13). "Has your God feet?" He answered: "In connection with your gods it is written, *Feet [have they], but cannot walk* (Psalms 115.7); in connection with our God it is written, *And His feet shall stand in that day upon the Mount of Olives"* (Zechariah 14.4). "Has your God a throat?" He answered: "In connection with your gods it is written, *They can make no sound in their throat* (Psalms 115.7); in connection with our God it is written, *And sound goeth out of His mouth"* (Job 37.2). The emperor asked: "If there are all these attributes in your God, why does He not deliver you out of my hand in the same manner that He rescued Hananiah, Mishael, and Azariah from the hands of Nebuchadnezzar?" He answered: "Hananiah, Mishael, and Azariah were worthy men, and King Nebuchadnezzar was deserving that a miracle should be performed through him. You, however, are undeserving; and as for ourselves, our lives are forfeit to heaven. If you do not slay us, the Omnipresent has numerous executioners. There are many bears, wolves, serpents, leopards, and scorpions to attack and kill us; but in the end the Holy One, blessed be He, will avenge our blood on you." The emperor immediately ordered him to be put to death.

The child's mother said to him: "By the life of your head, O emperor, give me my son that I may embrace and kiss him." They gave him to her, and she bared her breasts and suckled him. She said to the king: "By the life of your head, O emperor, put me to death first and then slay him." He answered her, "I cannot agree to that because it is written in your Torah: *No animal from the herd or from the flock shall be slaughtered on the same day with its young* (Leviticus 22.28).

She retorted: "You unutterable fool! Have you already fulfilled all the commandments save only this one!" He immediately ordered him to be slain. The mother threw herself upon the child and embraced and kissed him. She said to him: "My son, go to the patriarch Abraham and tell him, 'Thus said my mother, Do not preen yourself [on your righteousness], saying I built an altar and offered up my son, Isaac. Behold, our mother built seven altars and offered up seven sons in one day. Yours was only a test, but mine was in earnest.' " While she was embracing and kissing him, the emperor gave an order and they killed him in her arms. When he had been slain, the sages calculated the age of that child and found that he was two years, six months, and six and a half hours old. At that time all the peoples of the world cried out: "What does their God do for them that they are all the time slain for His sake!" And concerning them it is written, *It is for Your sake that we are slain all day long* (Psalms 44.23). After a few days the woman became demented and fell from a roof and died, to fulfill what is said, *She that hath borne seven languisheth* (Jeremiah 15.9). A *bat kol* issued forth and proclaimed, *A happy mother of children* (Psalms 113.9); and the Holy Spirit cried out: "For these things I weep."

Lamentations Rabbah 1.16.50[2]

iiiiiiii
=

The Reason for Hanukkah

What is [the reason for] Hanukkah? For our Rabbis taught: On the twenty-fifth of Kislev [commence] the days of Hanukkah, which are eight on which a lamentation for the dead and fasting are forbidden. For when the Greeks entered the Temple, they defiled all the oils therein, and when the Hasmonean dynasty prevailed against and defeated them, they made search and found only one cruse of oil which lay with the seal of the high priest, but which contained sufficient for one day's lighting only; yet a miracle was wrought therein and they lit [the lamp] therewith for eight days. The following year these [days] were appointed a festival with [the recital of] Hallel and thanksgiving.

Shabbat 21b

iiiiiii
=

Kindling the Lights

Our Rabbis taught: The precept of Hanukkah [demands] one light for a man and his household; the zealous [kindle] a light for each member [of the household]; and the extremely zealous—Beth Shammai maintain: On the first day eight lights are lit and thereafter they are gradually reduced [by one each day]; but Beth Hillel say: On the first day one is lit and thereafter they are progressively increased. Ulla said: In the West [Palestine] two *amoraim*, R. Jose b. Abin and R. Jose b. Zebida, differ therein: one maintains, the reason of Beth Shammai is that it shall correspond to the days still to come, and that of Beth Hillel is that it shall correspond to the days that are gone; but another maintains, Beth Shammai's reason is that it shall correspond to the bullocks of the Festival [of Tabernacles], whilst Beth Hillel's reason is that we promote in [matters of] sanctity but do not reduce.

Shabbat 21b

And why are lamps kindled during Hanukkah? At the time that the sons of the Hasmonean, the high priest, triumphed over the kingdom of Greece, upon entering the Temple they found there eight rods of iron which they grooved out and then kindled wicks in the oil which they poured into the grooves.

Pesikta Rabbati 2.1[3]

Let our Master instruct us: If a Hanukkah lamp has some oil left over in it, what is to be done with the oil? In keeping with the tradition of the *amoraim*, our Masters taught as follows: If a Hanukkah lamp has oil left over in it after the first day, one adds oil to the lamp and lights it on the second day. If oil is left over after the second day, one adds more oil to the lamp and lights it on the third day; and so on for the successive days. But if on the eighth day some oil is still left, one makes a fire of the oil and burns it by itself. Why so? Because the oil was set aside for a religious purpose, hence it is forbidden to make use of it [for any other purpose].

Pesikta Rabbati 3.1[4]

Let our Master teach us: Is a man permitted to kindle from a Hanukkah lamp a lamp which is to be used for a secular purpose?

8. *Hanukkah lamp. Silver chased with biblical scene,*
Elijah and the ravens. By John Ruslen. London. 1709.

In keeping with the tradition of the *amoraim*, as R. Aha stated in the
name of Rab, our Masters taught as follows: From a Hanukkah lamp
it is forbidden to kindle a lamp which will be used for a secular
purpose; but to kindle one Hanukkah lamp from another Hanukkah
lamp is permitted.

From what usage is the inference drawn that it is permitted to
kindle one Hanukkah lamp from another? From a usage—so taught
R. Jacob ben Abba in the name of R. Aha—sanctioned in the tending
of the lampstand in the Temple where the holy of holies was, for our
Masters [of the Mishnah] taught as follows: "Whenever the priest

found that the lampstand's two easternmost lamps had gone out, he would clear away their ash, then rekindle them from the lamps which were still burning" (Tamid 3.9). Now if, when one of the lamps upon the lampstand in the innermost part of the Temple was found extinguished, usage permitted rekindling that lamp from a companion, all the more it follows that it is permitted to kindle one Hanukkah lamp from another Hanukkah lamp.

Pesikta Rabbati 8.1[5]

What are the regulations respecting Hanukkah? The Rabbis said: On the twenty-fifth of Kislev the Hanukkah lamp is kindled, and it is forbidden to use an old lamp [if it is an earthen lamp, because the burnt oil renders it unsightly]; but if a person has only an old lamp, he must thoroughly heat it in fire [to burn away the old oil], nor may the Hanukkah lamp be moved from its place before it is extinguished.

The commandment to kindle it extends from sunset until the last person has left the street [as then it no longer serves as a public demonstration]. . . .

It is a religious precept to place the Hanukkah lamp by the door which is near the public domain, in such a manner that the mezuzah should be on the right hand and the Hanukkah lamp on the left, to fulfill what is stated, *How fair you are, how beautiful* (Songs of Songs 7.7)—*how fair* with the mezuzah and *how beautiful* with the Hanukkah lamp. The number of lights [for each night] is in accordance with the ruling of the school of Hillel [i.e., one light on the first night, two on the second, and so on], because in sacred matters one should proceed to a higher grade but not descend to a lower one [and also because the number of lights should] correspond to the days of the festival as they pass.

In what manner are the benedictions said? On the first day, the person who kindles [the lamp] says three benedictions while the onlooker says two. The person who kindles says: "Blessed art Thou, O Lord . . . who hast sanctified us by Thy commandments and hast given us command to kindle the light of Hanukkah." Then [after the three benedictions] he says: "We kindle these lights on account of the deliverances and the miracles and the wonders which Thou didst work for our fathers, by means of Thy holy priests. During all the eight days of Hanukkah these lights are sacred, and it is not permitted to make any profane use of them but we are only to look at them, in order that we may give thanks unto Thy Name for Thy wonders, Thy miracles, and Thy deliverances." [The third benediction is] "Blessed art Thou, O Lord . . . who hast kept us in life." [Before this] he says: "Who wroughtest miracles for our fathers."

Soferim 20.3–6

R. Jeremiah ruled, He who sees the Hanukkah light [while he himself did not light one in his own home] must recite the benediction. What benediction does one recite? Rab Judah answered, On the first day he who kindles the light must recite three benedictions and he who sees it must recite two [omitting the first benediction "to kindle the light"]; henceforth he who kindles the lights recites [the first] two benedictions and he who sees them only [the second] one. What is the [first] benediction? "Blessed [art Thou, O Lord our God, King of the universe] who hast sanctified us by Thy commandments, and commanded us to kindle the light of Hanukkah." But [since it is not mentioned in the Bible] where did He command us? [The commandment is deduced from the verse], *You must not deviate* [Deuteronomy 17.11; even from that which the Rabbis instituted]. R. Nahman b. Isaac replied, [Deduction is made from the verse,] *Ask your father, he will inform you* (ibid. 32.7). Which [benediction] does one omit [after the first day]? The [third] benediction on the season ["Who has kept us alive, etc."]. Might it not be suggested that one omits the [second] benediction concerning the miracle? The miracle occurs every day [and therefore cannot be omitted].

Sukkah 46a

R. Joshua b. Levi said: The [precept of the] Hanukkah lamp is obligatory upon women, for they too were concerned in the miracle.

Shabbat 23a

R. Joshua b. Levi said: All oils are fit for the Hanukkah lamp, but olive oil is the best. Abaye observed: At first the Master [Rabbah] used to seek poppy-seed oil, saying, The light of this is more lasting; but when he heard this [dictum] of R. Joshua b. Levi he was particular for olive oil, saying, This yields a clearer light.

Shabbat 23a

Raba said: It is obvious to me [that if one must choose between] the house light and the Hanukkah light [if one cannot afford both], the former is preferable, on account [of the importance] of the peace of the home; [between] the house light and [wine for] the

Sanctification of the Day, the house light is preferable, on account of the peace of the home. Raba propounded: What [if the choice lies between] the Hanukkah lamp and the Sanctification of the Day: is the latter more important, because it is permanent [as it occurs every week], or perhaps the Hanukkah lamp is preferable, on account of advertising the miracle? After propounding, he himself solved it: The Hanukkah lamp is preferable, on account of advertising the miracle.

Shabbat 23b

Rab Judah said in R. Assi's name: One must not count money by the Hanukkah light. . . . It is that precepts may not appear disdainful to him.

Shabbat 22a

iiiiiii
=

Thanksgiving and Hallel

In the thanksgiving benediction we include [on Hanukkah] "and thanks for the wonders and salvation of Thy priests which Thou hast wrought in the days of Mattathias, son of Johanan, high priest, and the Hasmoneans his sons. So also, O Lord our God and God of our fathers, perform for us miracles and wonders, and we will give thanks unto Thy Name forever. Blessed art Thou, O Lord, who art all-good." The miracles [of the days] of Mordecai and Esther are also mentioned [on Purim] in the thanksgiving benediction. Both miracles are likewise mentioned in the Grace after Meals.

The whole Hallel is recited during all the eight days of Hanukkah. . . .

On eighteen days and one night the individual reads the whole Hallel and they are: the eight days of Hanukkah, the eight days of Tabernacles, the Festival of Solemn Assembly, the first festival day of Passover and the night preceding it. In the Diaspora [the whole Hallel is read on] twenty-one days and two nights. The most proper way of performing the commandment is to read the Hallel psalms on the two nights [of Passover] in the Diaspora in the synagogue, to say the benediction over them, and to recite them melodiously to fulfill what is stated, *Let us extol His Name together* (Psalms 34.3). When, however, one reads [the Hallel] at home [during the seder], there is no need to say the benediction because it has already been said in the congregational service.

Soferim 20.8–9

Why is the Hallel read? Because [one of the psalms included in the Hallel] declares *The Lord is God; he has given us light* (Psalms 118.27). Then why is it not read on Purim, when, as Scripture records, [the right was granted to the Jews] *to assemble and fight for their lives; if any people or province attacks them, they may destroy, massacre, and exterminate its armed forces* (Esther 8.11)? If the Hallel is read on Hanukkah, why should it not also be read on Purim? Because the Hallel is not read except on the overthrow of a kingdom, and since the kingdom of Ahasuerus continued, therefore the Hallel is not read. But as for the kingdom of Greece which the Holy One, blessed be He, did destroy, the Jews proceeded to give voice to the Hallel, a hymn of praise, saying: In times past we were servants to Pharaoh, servants to Greece; but now we are servants to the Holy One, blessed be He: *O servants of the Lord, give praise* (Psalms 113:1).

Pesikta Rabbati 2.1[6]

Let our Master instruct us [in regard to the following]: Inasmuch as *Musaf* is not said on weekdays in Hanukkah, when a worshiper is saying either the *Musaf* that falls [on the Sabbath in Hanukkah] or the *Musaf* for the New Moon [of Tevet] that falls in Hanukkah, is he required to say the words that mention Hanukkah?

In keeping with tradition of the *amoraim*, as R. Simon cited it in the name of R. Joshua, our Masters taught as follows: Even though *Musaf* is not ordinarily said during Hanukkah except on the Sabbath, nevertheless, when the New Moon falls in Hanukkah, one is required to say the words that mention Hanukkah in the *Musaf* for the New Moon. So, too, on a Sabbath falling in Hanukkah, even though *Musaf* is not said during Hanukkah except on the Sabbath, nevertheless, one is required to say in the Sabbath *Musaf* the words that mention Hanukkah. And in what part of the *Musaf* is one to say the words that mention Hanukkah? In the Thanksgiving for God's mercies.

Pesikta Rabbati 4.1[7]

iiiiiii
=

Fasting Prohibited

On the occasion a fast was decreed in Lydda on Hanukkah and R. Eliezer went down there and bathed and R. Joshua had his hair cut [though bathing and haircutting were prohibited on fast days]. They said to the residents, Go and fast in atonement for having fasted [on Hanukkah]!

Rosh Hashanah 18b

iiiiiii
=

The Hanukkah Lights Will Shine Forever

Aaron was distinguished not only by being selected to dedicate the sanctuary through the lighting of the candles, God ordered Moses to communicate to his brother the following revelation: "The sanctuary will on another occasion also be dedicated by the lighting of candles, and then it will be done by thy descendants, the Hasmoneans, for whom I will perform miracles and to whom I will grant grace. Hence there is greater glory destined for thee than for all the other princes of the tribes, for their offerings to the sanctuary shall be employed only so long as it endures, but the lights of the Hanukkah festival will shine forever."

Or Zarua 1.139[8]

iiiiiii
=

The Seven Hanukkahs

Seven events are marked by Hanukkah—by a rite of dedication: The dedication at the creation of the world, in connection with which it is written *The heaven and the earth were finished* (Genesis 2.1), for, like the word "finished" in the verse *Thus was finished all the work of the*

Tabernacle (Exodus 39.32), here also the word *finished* can indicate
nothing other than an occasion marked by a rite of dedication; the
dedication carried out by Moses, as set forth in the passage beginning with the words *On the day Moses finished setting up the Tabernacle*
(Numbers 7.1); the dedication of the First Temple, of which it is
written *A psalm of David. A song for the dedication of the temple* (Psalms
30.1); the dedication of the Second Temple, as is said *And they offered
at the dedication of this house of God* (Ezra 6.17); the dedication of the
wall [enclosing the city], of which it is said *At the dedication of the wall
of Jerusalem they sought the Levites out . . . to bring them to Jerusalem, to keep
the dedication with gladness* (Nehemiah 12.27); the dedication which we
are now considering, the Hanukkah instituted by the Hasmonean
family; and finally the dedication of the world-to-come, which also
is to be celebrated with the light of lamps, as is written *And the light
of the moon shall become like the light of the sun, and the light of the sun shall
become sevenfold, etc.* (Isaiah 30.26).

Pesikta Rabbati 2.6[9]

5 THE MEDIEVAL SCROLL OF THE HASMONEANS

The Scroll of the Hasmoneans, also known as the Scroll of Antiochus, recounts the triumph of Mattathias and his sons over the truculent Syrian despot Antiochus, who was intent on exterminating them. It is largely a legendary account, bearing only meager resemblance to the historical facts in 1 Maccabees; indeed, there are obvious discrepancies between the two works. Originally written in Aramaic, the scroll was known to Saadia Gaon, who lived in the tenth century.

The Scroll of the Hasmoneans was apparently intended for reading in the synagogue during Hanukkah, to invest it with the same status as Purim, when the Scroll of Esther is read. Included in some prayer books, the Scroll of the Hasmoneans was read on the Sabbath of Hanukkah in a number of Jewish communities, notably in Yemen, in Italy, and in Ghardaia in the Sahara.[1]

In most modern Jewish prayer books this scroll is omitted. An exception is *Ha-Siddur ha-Shalem: Daily Prayer Book*, translated by

Philip Birnbaum (New York, 1949), in which the Hebrew and English translation appear.

iiiiiiii
=

The Scroll of the Hasmoneans

The Greek monarch Antiochus was a powerful ruler; all the kings heeded him. He subdued many provinces and mighty sovereigns; he destroyed their castles, burned their palaces, and imprisoned their men. Since the reign of Alexander there had never been a king like him beyond the Euphrates. He erected a large city on the seacoast to serve as his royal residence, and called it Antioch after his own name. Opposite it his governor Bagris founded another city and called it City of Bagris, after himself. Such are their names to this day.

In the twenty-third year of his reign, the two hundred and thirteenth year after the Temple had been rebuilt, Antiochus determined to march on Jerusalem. He said to his officers: "You are aware that the Jews of Jerusalem are in our midst. They neither offer sacrifices to our gods nor observe our laws; they abandon the king's laws to practice their own. They hope moreover for the day when kings and tyrants shall be crushed, saying: 'Oh, that our own king might reign over us, that we might rule the sea and the land, so that the entire world would be ours.' It is indeed a disgrace for the royal government to let them remain on the face of the earth. Come now, let us attack them and abolish the covenant made with them: Sabbath, New Moon festivals, and circumcision." The proposal pleased his officers and all his host.

Immediately King Antiochus dispatched his governor, Nicanor, with a large body of troops. He came to the Jewish city of Jerusalem and massacred many people; he set up a heathen altar in the Temple, concerning which the God of Israel had said to His faithful prophets: "There will I establish My residence forever." In that very place they slaughtered a swine and brought its blood into the holy court. When Johanan ben Mattathias heard of this deed, he was filled with rage and his face changed color. In his heart he drew a

top: 9. *Hanukkah lamp. Silver. Frankfort, Germany. Eighteenth century.*
above: 10. *Hanukkah lamp. Silver, partly gilt. Augsburg, Germany. Early eighteenth century.*

plan of action. Whereupon he made himself a dagger, two spans long and one span wide, and concealed it under his clothes. He came to Jerusalem and stood at the royal gate, calling to the gate-keepers: "I am Johanan ben Mattathias; I have come to appear before Nicanor." The guards informed Nicanor that the high priest of the Jews was standing at the door. "Let him enter!" Nicanor said.

Johanan was admitted to Nicanor, who said: "You are one of the rebels who rebel against the king and do not care for the welfare of his government!" Johanan replied: "My lord, I have come to you; whatever you demand I will do." "If you wish to do as I please," said Nicanor, "then take a swine and sacrifice it upon the altar. You shall wear royal clothes and ride the king's own horse; you shall be counted among the king's close friends." To this, Johanan answered: "My lord, I am afraid of the Israelites; if they hear that I have done such a thing they will stone me. Let everyone leave your presence, so as not to inform them." Immediately Nicanor ordered everybody out.

At that moment Johanan ben Mattathias raised his eyes to heaven and prayed: "My God and God of my fathers Abraham, Isaac, and Jacob, do not hand me over to this heathen; for if he kills me, he will boast in the temple of Dagon that his god has handed me over to him." He advanced three steps toward Nicanor, thrust the dagger into his heart, and flung him fatally wounded into the court of the Temple. "My God," Johanan prayed, "do not count it a sin that I killed this heathen in the sanctuary; punish thus all the foes who came with him to persecute Judea and Jerusalem." On that day Johanan set out and fought the enemy, inflicting heavy slaughter on them. The number of those who were slain by him on that day totaled seven thousand. Upon returning, he erected a column with the inscription: "Maccabee, Destroyer of Tyrants."

When King Antiochus heard that his governor, Nicanor, had been slain, he was bitterly distressed. He sent for wicked Bagris, the deceiver of his people, and told him: "Do you not know, have you not heard, what the Israelites did to me? They massacred my troops and ransacked my camps! Can you now be sure of your wealth? Will your homes remain yours? Come, let us move against them and abolish the covenant which their God made with them: Sabbath, New Moon festivals, and circumcision." Thereupon wicked Bagris and his hosts invaded Jerusalem, murdering the population and proclaiming an absolute decree against the Sabbath, New Moon festivals, and circumcision. So drastic was the king's edict that when a man was discovered to have circumcised his son, he and his wife were hanged along with the child. A woman gave birth to a son after her husband's death and had him circumcised when he was eight days old. With the child in her arms, she went up on top of the wall of Jerusalem and cried out: "We say to you, wicked Bagris: This covenant of our fathers which you intend to destroy shall never cease from us nor from our children's children." She cast her son down to the ground and flung herself after him so that they died together. Many Israelites of that period did the same, refusing to renounce the covenant of their fathers.

Some of the Jews said to one another: "Come, let us keep the Sabbath in a cave lest we violate it." When they were betrayed to Bagris, he dispatched armed men who sat down at the entrance of the cave and said: "You Jews, surrender to us! Eat of our bread, drink of our wine, and do what we do!" But the Jews said to one another: "We remember what we were commanded on Mount Sinai: 'Six days you shall labor and do all your work; on the seventh day you shall rest.' It is better for us to die than to desecrate the Sabbath." When the Jews failed to come out, wood was brought and set on fire at the entrance of the cave. About a thousand men and women died there. Later the five sons of Mattathias, Johanan and his four brothers, set out and routed the hostile forces, whom they drove to the coast; for they trusted in the God of heaven.

Wicked Bagris, accompanied by those who had escaped the sword, boarded a ship and fled to King Antiochus. "O king," he said, "you have issued a decree abolishing the Sabbath, New Moon festivals, and circumcision in Judea, and now there is complete rebellion there. The five sons of Mattathias cannot be defeated unless they are attacked by all the combined forces; they are stronger than lions, swifter than eagles, braver than bears. Be pleased to accept my advice, and do not fight them with this small army lest you be disgraced in the sight of all the kings. Send letters to all your royal provinces; let all the army officers without exception come with armored elephants." This pleased King Antiochus. He sent letters to all his royal domains, and the chieftains of various clans arrived with armored elephants. Wicked Bagris invaded Jerusalem for the second time. He broke through the wall, shattered the gateway, made thirteen breaches in the Temple, and ground the stones to dust. He thought to himself: "This time they shall not defeat me; my army is numerous, my hand is mighty." However, the God of heaven did not think so.

The five sons of Mattathias went to Mizpeh in Gilead, where the House of Israel had been saved in the days of Samuel the prophet. They fasted, sat in ashes, and prayed to the God of heaven for mercy; then a good plan came to their mind. These were their names: Judah, the firstborn; Simon, the second; Johanan, the third; Jonathan, the fourth, Eleazar, the fifth. Their father blessed them, saying: "Judah my son, I compare you to Judah the son of Jacob who was likened to a lion. Simon my son, I compare you to Simon the son of Jacob who slew the men of Shechem. Johanan my son, I compare you to Abner the son of Ner, general of Israel's army. Jonathan my son, I compare you to Jonathan the son of Saul who defeated the Philistines. Eleazar my son, I compare you to Phinehas the son of Eleazar, who was zealous for his God and rescued the Israelites." Soon afterwards the five sons of Mattathias attacked the pagan forces, inflicting severe losses upon them. One of the brothers, Judah, was killed.

When the sons of Mattathias discovered that Judah had been slain, they returned to their father, who asked: "Why did you come back?" They replied: "Our brother Judah, who alone equaled all of us, has been killed." "I will join you in the battle against the heathen," Mattathias said, "lest they destroy the House of Israel; why be so dismayed over your brother?" He joined his sons that same day and waged war against the enemy. The God of heaven delivered into their hands all swordsmen and archers, army officers and high officials. None of these survived. Others were compelled to seek refuge in the coastal cities. In attacking the elephants, Eleazar was engulfed in their dung. His brothers searched for him among the living and the dead and could not find him. Eventually, however, they did find him.

The Jews rejoiced over the defeat of their enemies, some of whom were burned while others were hanged on the gallows. Wicked Bagris was included among those who were burned to death. When King Antiochus heard that his governor, Bagris, and the army officers had been killed, he boarded a ship and fled to the coastal cities. Wherever he came the people rebelled and called him "The Fugitive," so he drowned himself in the sea.

The Hasmoneans entered the sanctuary, rebuilt the gates, closed the breaches, and cleansed the Temple court from the slain and the impurities. They looked for pure olive oil to light the menorah, and found only one bottle with the seal of the high priest so that they were sure of its purity. Though its quantity seemed sufficient only for one day's lighting, it lasted for eight days, owing to the blessing of the God of heaven who had established His Name there. Hence, the Hasmoneans and all the Jews alike instituted these eight days as a time of feasting and rejoicing, like any festival prescribed in the Torah, and of kindling lights to commemorate the victories God had given them. Mourning and fasting are forbidden on Hanukkah, except in the case of an individual's vow which must be discharged. Nevertheless, the Hasmoneans did not prohibit work on this holiday.

From that time on the Greek government was stripped of its renown. The Hasmoneans and their descendants ruled for two hundred and six years, until the destruction of the Temple.

And so the Jews everywhere observe this festival for eight days, beginning on the twenty-fifth of Kislev. These days, instituted by priests, Levites, and sages of Temple times, shall be celebrated by their descendants forever.

Translated by Philip Birnbaum[2]

6 ḤAΠUKKAH IΠ JEWISH LAW

The vast corpus of Jewish law embodied in many sources was systematized by Moses ben Maimon (1135–1204), popularly known as Maimonides or Rambam, in his *Mishneh Torah* (Second Torah). This work received serious consideration in practically every relevant discussion of Jewish law. Some three centuries after Maimonides, Joseph Karo (1488–1575), recognized as the last great codifier of rabbinical Judaism, compiled the *Shulhan Arukh* (Prepared Table). Moses Isserles (c. 1515–72) introduced changes and emendations to Karo's text, which is still accepted as the authoritative basis for traditional Jewish practice. The *Kitzur Shulhan Arukh* (Abridged Prepared Table), a condensed and popular version of Karo's and Isserles's monumental work, was prepared by Solomon Ganzfried (c. 1800–86).

Selections from the *Mishneh Torah* and *Kitzur Shulhan Arukh* that follow treat with the laws and customs pertaining to the recital of Hallel on Hanukkah, the kindling of the lights, and other aspects of the festival.

ꟷꟷꟷꟷ

Laws Relating to Hallel
MOSES MAIMONIDES

The day on which the Israelites were victorious over their enemies
and destroyed them was the twenty-fifth day of Kislev. When they
reentered the Temple, they found within its precincts only one
cruse of ritually pure oil, enough to burn for but a single day. Yet
they kept alight with it the required number of lamps for eight
days, until they could press olives and produce new ritually pure
oil.

Consequently, the sages of that generation ruled that the eight
days beginning with the twenty-fifth of Kislev should be days of
rejoicing on which the Hallel is to be recited, and that on each one
of the eight nights lamps should be lit at eventide over the doors
of the houses, to serve as manifestation and revelation of the miracle. These days are known as Hanukkah. Funeral eulogies and
fasting are forbidden on them, just as they are on Purim, and the
lighting of lamps on them is a commandment based on the authority of the scribes, analogous to the commandment to read the
Megillah.

On each of these days, the whole of the Hallel should be recited,
and both individuals and congregations should preface it with the
following benediction: "Blessed art Thou, O Lord our God, King
of the universe, who has sanctified us with His commandments and
has commanded us to recite the Hallel in full." Note that although
the recitation of the Hallel is a commandment based only on the
authority of the scribes, the phrase "who has sanctified us with His
commandments" is included in this benediction, just as it is included in the benediction before reading the Megillah or depositing
an *eruv*. For a benediction so phrased should be recited over any act
based on the authority of the scribes where the keynote is certainty.
It is only where the principal reason for performing an act based on
the authority of the scribes is to allow for a doubt—as is the case
with the tithing of *demai* produce, for example—that no such benediction is to be recited.

Mishneh Torah, Laws of the Megillah and Hanukkah 3.2–3, 5[1]

11. Hanukkah lamp. Tin. Maingegend. 1756.

Laws Governing the Hanukkah Lamps
MOSES MAIMONIDES

How many lamps should be lighted on Hanukkah? According to
the commandment each house should light one lamp, whether
the household consists of many persons or of only one. A more
zealous way of fulfilling this commandment is to light as many
lamps as there are members of the household, one lamp for
each member, man or woman. A still more zealous way, indeed
the best possible one, is to light a lamp for each person on the

first night, and add one more lamp per person each night thereafter.

Thus, if a household consists of ten members, on the first night it should light ten lamps, on the second twenty lamps, on the third thirty lamps, and so on, so that on the eighth night it would light eighty lamps.

However, the prevailing custom in all our cities in Spain is to light one lamp for all the members of a household on the first night, and to add another lamp on each succeeding night, so that on the eighth night eight lamps are lit; this is the case whether a household consists of many persons or of only one.

Hanukkah lamps may not be lit before sunset, but only at sunset —neither later nor earlier. If one forgets or deliberately fails to light the lamp at sunset, he may light it up to the time when people cease to walk about in the streets. How much time does this amount to? About half an hour, or a little more. Once this time has passed, however, one may not light the lamp on that night at all. Enough oil should be placed in the lamp to make it burn until the time when people cease to walk about in the street. If one lights the lamp and it goes out after awhile, he need not relight it. If it is still burning after people have ceased to walk about in the street, and one wishes to extinguish it or remove it, he may do so.

Any kind of oil and wick may be used in the Hanukkah lamp— even oil which does not flow easily through the wick, and a wick to which the flame does not adhere properly. Even on the Sabbath which falls during Hanukkah, it is permissible to burn in the Hanukkah lamp oils and wicks that may not be burnt in the Sabbath lamp. The reason for this is that no use may be made of the light of the Hanukkah lamp, either on a Sabbath or on a weekday.

In times of peril, one may place the Hanukkah lamp inside his house—it is even enough to place it on the table. There must be, however, another lamp in the house to provide illumination. If there is a hearth fire burning, no other lamp is necessary, but if the householder is a person of distinction, who would not normally make use of the light of a hearth fire, another lamp is still required.

A Hanukkah lamp lit by a deaf mute, an imbecile, a minor, or a heathen is invalid; it must be lit by one who is in duty bound to light a Hanukkah lamp. If one lights the lamp indoors, and then takes the lighted lamp out and places it over the door of his house, it too is invalid; it must be lit at its proper place. If one stands outside the door holding the lamp in his hand, he has not fulfilled his duty, because an observer would think that he is holding it for his own convenience. If a lantern has been burning all day long during the Sabbath, it should be extinguished immediately after the Sabbath, the benediction should be recited, and the lantern should be relit; for it is the lighting of the lamp which constitutes the fulfillment of the commandment, not the act of setting it up outside the house.

If a courtyard has two doors on different sides, two Hanukkah lamps are required, lest the passersby on the side where there is no lamp should think that the courtyard did not put out a Hanukkah lamp at all. If the two doors are on the same side of the courtyard, a lamp burning at one of them is sufficient.

If a wayfarer knows that a lamp will be lit on his behalf at his home, he need not have one lighted for himself at the place where he is staying. If he has no home to light a lamp in his behalf, he should have one lighted for himself at the place where he is staying and should make a contribution toward the cost of the oil. If his present residence is a separate house, he should light a lamp at this house, even if one is lit on his behalf at his own home, because of what passersby might think otherwise.

The commandment to light the Hanukkah lamp is an exceedingly precious one, and one should be particularly careful to fulfill it, in order to make known the miracle, and to offer additional praise and thanksgiving to God for the wonders which He had wrought for us. Even if one has no food to eat except what he receives from charity, he should beg—or sell his garment to buy—oil and lamps, and light them.

If such a poor man needs oil for both a Sabbath lamp and a Hanukkah lamp, or oil for a Sabbath lamp and wine for the Sanctification benediction, the Sabbath lamp should have priority, for the sake of peace in the household [since the household members would be discomfited by sitting in darkness], seeing that even a divine Name might be erased to make peace between husband and wife. Great indeed is peace, forasmuch as the purpose for which the whole of the Law was given is to bring peace upon the world, as it is said, *Her ways are ways of pleasantness, and all her paths are peace* (Proverbs 3.17).

Mishneh Torah, Laws of the Megillah and Hanukkah 4.1–3, 5–6, 8–12, 14[2]

iiiiiii
=

Laws Concerning Hanukkah
SOLOMON GANZFRIED

One should recount to his household the miracles that were performed for our forefathers in those days [of the Maccabees]. . . .

One should generously dispense charity during Hanukkah; these days are appropriate for rectifying flaws in one's character through charity, especially when given to maintain the poor engaged in the study of the Torah.

Fasting is not allowed during Hanukkah, but on the day previous to and following Hanukkah a eulogy may be delivered and fasting is permitted.

Work is permitted on Hanukkah; however, women refrain from work during the entire time the lights are burning, and they should not be deterred [from this obligation]. The reason women are more scrupulous is because of the harsh decree affecting the daughters of Israel [during the Maccabean period]; for example, a virgin about to be married was required to have sexual intercourse with the monarch. Furthermore, the miracle was effected by a very beautiful woman, the daughter of Johanan the high priest. When the monarch demanded that she lie with him, she replied that she would acquiesce. Then she fed him cheese dishes until he became thirsty. He then drank wine, became drunk, and fell asleep; whereupon she severed his head and brought it to Jerusalem. When the enemy general saw that their king was dead, he and the army fled. Therefore, it is customary to eat dairy dishes on Hanukkah in remembrance of the miracle achieved by milk.

All oils are proper for the Hanukkah lights; however, olive oil is preferable since the miracle in the Temple was accomplished with olive oil. If it is not available, one may select any other clean and clear oil, or wax candles can be used as their light is clear. . . .

A clay lamp lit on one night becomes old, and should not be used on the second night because it is unsightly. Therefore, one should use a beautiful metal menorah. If it is within one's means, he should purchase a silver candelabrum to show deference for the precept.

It is a common custom among those who are most scrupulous that every member of the household kindles one light on the first night, two on the second, and adding progressively until eight lights are lit on the eighth night. Each one should be careful to set his lights in a special place in order to recognize how many lamps are lit. They should not be kindled in a place where other lights are lit throughout the year, so that the Hanukkah lamps will be explicitly identifiable.

It is a precept to light the Hanukkah lamp at the entrance [of the house] near the street to commemorate the miracle; thus it was done in the time of the Talmud. However, since we now live among non-Jews we light inside the house. If there is a window facing the street one kindles the lamps there; if not, they are lit near the entrance. . . .

The lights should be in an even row; neither higher nor lower. There should be a separation between the lights so that the flames will not merge and flare up. Wax candles should be separated from each other so that their heat will not cause the wax to drip and spoil the candles. . . .

The time of kindling is when the stars appear and not later. It is forbidden to initiate any action, even to study the Torah, before the lighting. Only if one has not recited the evening service, he should first pray and then light. Before lighting the menorah, one should assemble all the members of the household to make a public event. Sufficient oil should be provided to burn for at least a half hour. If one did not light immediately [when the stars appear], he may kindle and pronounce the benedictions as long as his family is still awake. Once the household is asleep, there is no longer [the possibility of] proclaiming the miracle, therefore he should light without pronouncing the benedictions. . . .

The order of kindling, according to our custom, is as follows: on the first night one lights the lamp on the extreme right; on the second, a lamp is added to its left, and each night thereafter another is added to the left. The last one added is lit first and the lighting continues from left to right.

During the time prescribed for the precept [of kindling the Hanukkah lights], that is, for a half hour, it is forbidden to derive benefit from their illumination. Therefore, it is customary to place near the candles the *shammash* candle with which they were lit; thus if he makes use of the light, it will be that of the *shammash*. The *shammash* should be placed on a slightly higher level than the other lights, so it is clear that it is not counted as one of them.

Lights are lit in the synagogue to commemorate publicly the miracle, and the blessings are recited. They are placed at the south wall and are lit in the interim between the afternoon and evening services. However, the individual's obligation is not fulfilled with the lights in the synagogue; he must light them in his home. . . .

A woman may light them on behalf of her entire household. A child that has reached the age of [religious] training is also obligated.

On the eve of the Sabbath the Hanukkah lamp is lit first and then the Sabbath candles as long as it is later than the middle of the afternoon, and the afternoon service has been recited. There must be sufficient oil to burn for a half hour after the appearance of the stars; otherwise, the blessing will have been invalid. If one kindled the lights near the entrance he should be careful to have something to separate them and the door, to prevent their being extinguished by a wind when the door is opened and closed.

At the conclusion of the Sabbath, Havdalah is recited and then the Hanukkah lights are lit.

Kitzur Shulhan Arukh 139.1–7, 9–11, 14–18

7 HANUKKAH
IN MODERN PROSE

iiiiiii

Eight Golden Hanukkah Lights
A. ALAN STEINBACH

poet, author, and editor of Jewish Book Annual *and of* Jewish Bookland; *recipient of National Jewish Welfare Board Frank L. Weil Award for distinguished contributions to American Jewish culture*

Eight slender Hanukkah lights in our menorah—how tiny, how fragile they appear! And yet, what a trenchant message we read in their quivering light! With rapt fascination we look beyond the flickering flame into the hoary past when aged Mattathias's battle cry reverberated through Mizpah's rocky mountain ridge: "All who are for the Lord, follow me!"

This has become our modern battle cry. Israel's mission is Sha-

95

lom, Peace, and our holy city Jerusalem derives its name from Sha-lom. Therefore, our historic goal has been to promote the ideal of peace as the sine qua non for establishing the universal brotherhood our literary prophets espoused. Unfortunately, in June 1967 the Israelis were compelled to resort to arms in order to insure their survival, and they fought heroically like their Maccabean forebears. But Israel's normal weapon is light, and our goal universal peace.

"All who are for the Lord, follow me!" This moral imperative has been thundered down through the centuries to every generation of Jews, and it is addressed to our contemporary generation. The little Hanukkah lights command us to rise above our opaque human clay and to seek the fountainhead of God's divine light. The pathway to that fountainhead is through the incandescence diffused by the moral tapers in our spiritual menorah: the Torah.

Our objective as Jews must be to harmonize our mundane lives with the divine precepts enjoined in the Torah as God's will. In order to attain this harmony, we must hallow life's tasks upon the altar of love, charity, rectitude, virtue. These must become candles in our inner menorah, the immortal soul God breathed into us. They must become luminous to our fellowman whose light has ceased to shine. Mattathias calls again: "All who are for the Lord, follow me!"[1]

iiiiiiii
=

The Immortality of Israel
LEO JUNG

rabbi and educator; professor of ethics at Yeshiva University; prolific author and editor of many books emphasizing traditional Judaism

"What is Hanukkah?" What is the deepest sense of this festival, its eternal message to the Jew?

"It came to pass," says the Talmud, "that when the Jews overpowered the Greeks and reentered the holy Temple, they found one cruse, one bottle of pure oil, enough for one day. But a miracle happened, and it lasted for eight days."

The light seemed sufficient for but one day, yet it outlasted the expectations of all.

Is not Hanukkah a symbol of Israel, and its light a symbol of his immortality? When nations are victorious they grow ungrateful. But the Maccabees were not ordinary victors. They felt that the spirit which they fought for could sustain them only if it retained its pristine Jewishness. And so, when the Jewish nation finally was driven into Galut, it took along a small lamp with the seal of holiness upon it. "It is for one day only," sneered the enemies. "When the day is over, it will be gone; after some generations this nation will be no more." How could they know the miracle of Israel's history? How could they understand that the light of the rededicated Temple was a promise and a declaration that Hanukkah never ends; that Israel never dies; that the *Ner Tamid*, true Jewishness, burning in the hearts of however few, is brighter than all artificial enthusiasm; that though the tempests may do their worst, they cannot quench this fire.[2]

iiiiiii
—

The Meaning of Hanukkah
THEODOR HERZL GASTER

orientalist and folklorist; author of books on the Jewish festivals; professor of comparative religion at Dropsie University, Philadelphia

First, Hanukkah commemorates and celebrates the first serious attempt in history to proclaim and champion the principle of religio-cultural diversity in the nation. The primary aim of the Maccabees was to preserve their own Jewish identity and to safeguard for Israel the possibility of continuing its traditional mission. Though inspired, however, by the particular situation of their own people, their struggle was instinct with universal implications. For what was really being defended was the principle that in a diversified society the function of the state is to embrace, not subordinate, the various constituent cultures, and that the complexion and character of the state must be determined by a cultural process of fusion on the one hand and selection on the other, and not by the arbitrary imposition of a single pattern on all elements.

Seen from this point of view, therefore, Hanukkah possesses broad human significance and is far more than a mere Jewish national celebration. As a festival of liberty, it celebrates more than the independence of one people—it glorifies the right to freedom of all peoples.

Second, Hanukkah affirms the universal truth that the only effec-

12. Hanukkah lamp. Brass, cast, pierced and engraved. Morocco. Eighteenth century.

tive answer to oppression is the intensified *positive* assertion of the principles and values which that oppression threatens. What inspired the movement of the Maccabees was not simply an abstract and academic dislike of tyranny but a desire to safeguard and evince an identity and way of life which was in danger of extinction. It therefore consisted not only in a fight *against* Antiochus but also in a fight *for* Judaism, the military uprising going hand in hand with an almost fanatical crusade for the internal regeneration of the Jewish people.

The combination was not fortuitous nor was it due solely—as some scholars have asserted—to the pressure of the pietists whom Mattathias and Judah rallied to their cause. On the contrary, it was fundamental. . . . The real issue at stake was not the right of the Jews to be like everyone else, but their right to be different; and victory meant not the attainment of civic equality (which, after all, was what Antiochus was offering!) but the renewal, after its forced suspension, of that particular and distinctive way of life which embodied and exemplified the Jewish mission. The mark of that victory, therefore, was not a triumphal parade but an act of dedication—the cleansing of the defiled Temple. Moreover, when the Jews wished to perpetuate the memory of their achievement, what they chose to turn into an annual festival was not the day of some military success but the week in which the house of God had been cleansed and the fire rekindled on the altar. There is an important meaning in this, one feels, for our own day, and especially in connection with the problem of safeguarding civil rights.[3]

iiiiiii
=

A Single Spark
SAMSON RAPHAEL HIRSCH

rabbi, statesman, philosopher, and leader of Orthodox Jewry in Germany (1808–88); his influence is still evident today

One single spark, loyally treasured in but one single Jewish heart, is sufficient for God to set aflame once more the whole spirit of Judaism. And if all the oil, if all the forces that were to have preserved the light of God in Israel, were to be misused for the light of paganism—even then, one little crucible of oil, one heart which in a forgotten hidden corner, imprinted with the high priest's seal, has faithfully remained untouched and undefiled, this one crucible is sufficient to become the salvation of the entire sanctuary when the right time and hour has come. "And even though all countries were bowed in obedience to Antiochus, if every man forsook the land of his fathers and assented to the king's command, even then, I and my sons and brothers will not forsake the laws of our fathers"—thus spoke the loyal Hasmonean heart of one single hero advanced in years —and Israel's sanctuary was saved. . . .

And if you, yourself, were the only one who still preserved the spirit of the Maccabees in his home, remember that one single Jew, one single Jewish house is ultimately in itself sufficient to serve as foundation for the reerection of the entire Jewish sanctuary.

Translated by Isidor Grunfeld[4]

iiiiiiii
=

The Miracle of Hanukkah
JUDAH L. MAGNES

American Reform rabbi; first president of the Hebrew University in Jerusalem (1877–1948)

The festival of Hanukkah has a rather peculiar history. On the one hand, our ancient literature contains injunctions as to how to observe the festival; on the other, our sages were inclined to obscure its historical background. They were opposed to having the miracle of Hanukkah set down in writing; and, indeed, the books of the Maccabees were relegated by them to the Apocrypha, and the names of the members of the Hasmonean dynasty are not even mentioned in the talmudic tradition.

No wonder, then, that even in ancient times it was asked: what is this festival of Hanukkah? What does it signify?

Its primary purpose is to recall, year after year, the great miracle that was wrought there in the days of Mattathias the Hasmonean, when the iniquitous Hellenist government of the day attempted "to make the Jews forgetful of Thy Law. Then didst Thou in Thy abundant mercy deliver the strong into the hands of weak, the arrogant into the hands of them that occupied themselves with Thy Law." When the Hasmoneans reentered the Temple they found a single cruse of oil, sufficient for only one day, yet they kindled lights from it for eight days.

Whatever be our attitude toward such miracles, it is a miracle that the Jewish people was saved then and that it has survived to this day. Because of such miracles in Jewish history, it is easier for a Jew to believe generally in miracles. Just as the Hanukkah candles are lighted one by one from a single flame, so the tale of the miracle is passed from one man to another, from one house to another, and to the whole House of Israel throughout the generations. The miracle of Hanukkah is thus turned inward, into the soul of each individual. For, at Hanukkah the injunction is that there be a candle for every household, and for greater piety a candle for every member of each household.[5]

iiiiiii
=

The Hebraic and the Hellenic Views of Life
ABRAM LEON SACHAR

founder and first president of Brandeis University; author of A History of the Jews *and other historical works*

The Hebraic and the Hellenic views of life have been often contrasted. The Hebrew stressed reliance upon an omnipotent God and conformity to a divinely sanctioned moral law; he was essentially serious, restrained, willing to recognize his finite limitations. To seek God was the ultimate wisdom, to follow His precepts the ultimate virtue. The Greek accepted no revelation as ultimate; he strove to penetrate to the core of his conceptions, analyzing the very bases of his knowledge. He was blessed with a delicate, subtle reason and with a keen desire to use it, to probe with it, to open the very heart of reality. The Hebrew was inclined to mysticism; he accepted the moral law and would not go beyond it. The Greek bowed to no law but that of complete self-expression. He loved beauty and art, the outdoor life, and every aspect of nature which appealed to his aesthetic sensibilities. Where the Hebrew asked: "What must I do?" the Greek asked: "Why must I do it?" . . . The Hebrew believed in the beauty of holiness, the Greek believed in the holiness of beauty.

The two points of view could not very well be reconciled in an individual. One could not accept a revealed law as ultimate, and yet honestly question the very foundations of life; or submit to a moral law and yet exploit one's capacities without restraint. But was it not possible for both spirits to be present in a whole people, residing in individuals who were splendid examples of each? National life would indeed be ideally rounded out if it developed at once the burning zeal for social righteousness of an Amos or an Isaiah, and the serene wisdom of a Socrates or a Plato, the moral fervor of a Jeremiah and the artistic genius of a Praxiteles.

Unfortunately, the best in the Greek spirit did not meet the best in the Hebrew spirit. The splendid achievements of the philosophers and the artists, their search for truth and beauty, their mellowed humanistic approach, did not come to the East in the wagons of the Greek conquerors. There came instead a degraded imitation of Hellenism, externals with the glowing heart burnt out, a crude paganism, a callousness for the common weal, a cheap sophistry, a cynicism easily undermining old conceptions and older loyalties, but substituting nothing constructive in their place. Too often the gymnasium and the amphitheater meant lewdness and licentiousness; the search for intellectual clarity meant dishonest banter and trickiness; the pursuit of the beautiful meant moral irresponsibility. . . .

In Judah, coming after a long period of priestly sternness and puritanic piety, the Greek ideals wrought havoc. At first only a few more daring souls stepped out of the established conventions. But as their numbers grew, the older generations stood back aghast. The youth of the land were aping names and manners; they were shamelessly displaying their nudeness in the Greek palaestra. More too: they were assimilating the whole Greek Weltanschauung. They were even attacking the laws and the customs in which they were reared. This was no mere passing fad, to be treated indulgently.

The masses were, as usual, not the decisive elements in the conflict. They were fuddled, bewildered, and inarticulate. They traveled in the beaten path, perhaps vaguely wondering where the quarrel lay. But the two extreme factions, Puritans and Hellenists, filled the synagogues and the marketplace with their din as they sought to discredit each other.

Soon Judah was rent by the quarrels of two factions who could not understand each other. Almost every family found itself divided. What was earnest to one group was jest to the other; what was pleasure to one was torment to the other; and neither side gave quarter. Those who loved the Greek ways found Judaism crude and soul-repressing. They looked upon the sacerdotalists as fools if sincere, and as hypocrites if not ready with answers. The stern nationalists, on the other hand, alarmed by the assaults on their mode of life, drew no distinctions in judging the alien culture. Hating lasciviousness, they decried all that was beautiful in Greek art; hating sophistry and irreverence, they decried all that the philosophers taught. There could be no compromise.

Victory, quite naturally, as usual seemed to go at first to the hellenizers. They gathered to them the youth of all classes, the aristocracy, and even some of the priests. Ambitious men discovered that the way to advancement, at least socially, lay in living like Greek gentlemen. By the beginning of the second century the old Judaism was in serious danger of dissolution, threatened with death, not by the mellowed wisdom of ancient Hellas, but by the bastard culture which called itself an offspring. Perhaps Judaism would have been quietly swallowed up as so many other civilizations had been; but at the dramatic moment history worked one of its miracles. Suddenly the hellenizers were thoroughly discredited in a reaction which shifted the whole balance of the Near East, a reaction brought about by the harshness and stupidity of a new Syrian monarch who usurped the throne in 175 B.C.E.[6]

iiiiiiii

Judaism and Hellenism
YEHEZKEL KAUFMANN

late professor of Bible at the Hebrew University in Jerusalem; author of the monumental eight-volume History of the Religion of Israel *(1937–56) and other erudite philosophical publications in Hebrew (1889–1963)*

During the very period in which the edifice of Judaism was being consolidated, the culture of Greece—the glory of polytheistic civilization—was reaching its climax. Both of these cultures have points in common, and yet they are utterly distinct. They were destined to conflict with each other and to influence each other, but they forever remained two worlds. Judaism embodied the idea of divine revelation, of prophecy and the holy spirit. Its faith was in a God who gave man Torah and *mitzvot* to show him the path of life and virtue. It aspired to mold life in accordance with the inspired utterances of its ancient prophets. Greek culture was distinguished by its idea of scientific reason. It aspired to perfect a system of thought, a world view based on rational awareness. It had faith in the redeeming power of the intellect. It created science and philosophy and believed that reason could show man the path of life and virtue.

In the time of Alexander the Great of Macedonia, Greek enlightenment began to be diffused among many nations. It was spread by Greeks and Macedonians who lived in the areas under Hellenistic rule. The upper classes were its primary devotees. In the course of time Hellenism conquered Rome also, and with this conquest attained universal dominion. At the same time Judaism was the heritage of a scattered, exiled, and subject people. The Hasmonean kingdom was a mere episode; Rome put an end to it and vanquished Jewry.

And yet the lesson of history is that the men of that age accepted the Jewish gospel of a redeeming God and rejected the Greek gospel of redeeming reason. The struggle between monotheism and paganism ended with the utter collapse of paganism, and the debris buried Hellenistic enlightenment as well. This is certainly not without significance. It indicates that there was something in Judaism that overbore the great appeal of Hellenism. The heart of man was

13. *Oriental Hanukkah lamp. Brass. Tetouan, Morocco. Nineteenth century.*

captivated by the message of the one supreme God, sovereign and unfettered by blind fate, a God whose sacred moral will governs all, and is the source of man's moral obligation. The spirit of man was elevated by the message of his moral freedom and the injunction "So choose thou life!" The soul of man responded to the tidings of a gracious and merciful God. The moral pathos of prophecy triumphed over the moral philosophy of reason. Men were dismayed and yet heartened by the demand for repentance that Christianity and Islam adopted from Judaism and announced to many peoples. Repentance was the way to the redemption of man. The war upon paganism was at the same time a war upon the idolatrous deification of reason, the faith that rational knowledge could save man. Moral goodness shall redeem, not the power of the intellect! And since man can choose goodness, the keys to redemption are in his hands. The nations knelt before these tidings.

Translated by Moshe Greenberg[7]

iiiiiiii
=

Warriors in a Holy Cause
MORRIS JOSEPH

British theologian (1848–1930); noted for his major work, Judaism as Creed and Life

It is because Hanukkah enshrines memories of the glorious past that it kept its strong grip upon the Jewish heart. In one respect a minor feast, it is in other respects a very great feast indeed. It tells a story of valor which, while it appeals to all who honor courage, is especially calculated to quicken the pulse of the Jew. For it is a story of valor displayed for the Religious Idea, in defense of the solemn trust, in pursuance of the sacred mission, confided to Israel. It is good for Jewish lads to include warriors of their own race in their gallery of heroes, to be able to say: "My people has produced its brave men equally with the Greeks and the Romans and the English." But still better is it for them to feel that these brave men drew their courage from the purest of all sources, from a passionate love of their religion, from a veneration for the good and the true and the morally beautiful. The Maccabees boldly faced overwhelming odds, not for their own selfish ends, but in a spirit of self-sacrificing fidelity to the holiest of all causes. They threw themselves upon the enemy in the temper that takes the martyr to the stake; they did it not for gain or glory, but solely for conscience's sake. They felt that God was calling to them, and they could not hold back. Theirs was an unique effort. Others had, it is true, displayed an equally noble courage on the battlefield; but they had displayed it in defense of their fatherland and their mother tongue, their hearths and homes. The Maccabees fought for these things, but for their religion too, and "to fight for religion was a new thing."

Such heroic constancy may well secure our admiring homage for its own sake. But it claims our reverence also for its results. The victory of the Maccabees was no barren achievement. It rendered solid benefits to the Jewish cause. But for the Maccabees Judaism would probably have perished. It would have gone down before the cruel cunning of the Greeks. And with it would have perished a mighty bulwark against the encroachments of paganism with its gross immorality. The little Maccabean band was like a rock in the midst of a surging sea. Standing almost alone in their day, the heroes beat back the forces that threatened to involve all mankind in a common demoralization. They kept a corner of the world sweet in an impure age. They held aloft the torch of true religion at a time when thick darkness was covering the nations.[8]

iiiiiiii
—

The Martyred Mother
GRACE AGUILAR

British-Jewish author and poet for whom a branch of the New York Public Library was named; many of her extensive writings on Jewish themes in a short-lived career (1816–47) have appeared in several editions and some have been translated into Hebrew and German

During the persecution under Antiochus Epiphanes, the sufferings of the women of Israel must have been as fearful as their constancy and fidelity were powerful proofs of the perfect adaptation of the Law of the Eternal to their temporal and spiritual wants. Never could a religion which made them soulless slaves have become so dear, such a part of their very hearts, that it was easier to endure torture, and slavery, and death, rather than depart from it themselves, or refuse its privileges to their infant sons. Eighty thousand persons, men, women, and children, slain in the forcible entrance of Antiochus into Jerusalem, and forty thousand of both sexes sold into slavery was the horrible preface to the misery which followed. Every observance of the Law, from the keeping of the Sabbath and the covenant of Abraham, to the minutest form, was made a capital offense. Yet, in spite of the scenes of horror so continually recurring, the very relation of which must now make every female heart shrink and quiver—yet were there female martyrs baring their breast to the murderous knife, rather than bow down to the idol or touch forbidden food. Women, young, meek, tender, performed with their own hands the covenant of Abraham upon their sons, because none else would so dare the tyrant's wrath; and with their infants (for whose immortal souls they had thus incurred the rage of man) suspended around their necks, received death by being flung from the battlements of the Temple into the deep vale below; others were hung, and cruelties too awful to relate practiced upon others. Yet no woman's spirit failed; and what must have been their attachment to their holy religion, what their sense of its responsibility, and its immortal reward, what their horror of abandoning it themselves and cutting off their sons from its sainted privileges, to incur martyrdoms like these? It is useless to argue that persecution always creates martyrs, as opposition kindles constancy. The religion degrading or brutalizing woman never yet had martyrs. . . .

Where, in the vast tomes of history, sacred or profane, shall we find a deed more heroic, a fortitude more sublime, than is recorded of Hannah, the Hebrew mother, during the persecution of Antiochus?

Great emergencies will often create great characters; but in the narrative which we have been considering, we read something more in the character of the Hebrew mother than even the heroism which she displayed. By her close connection with her sons, in being brought before the tyrant, and condemned to share their fate, it is clear that though a woman in Israel, her influence must have been supposed of some consequence. That her sons owed their all to her, even to their education, and that her influence on them was very great, we read alike in her own words, and in the appeal of the king to her, to save by her exhortations her youngest. . . . And in the calm courage, the noble words of each of her sons, we learn the education she had given. They had probably been among the valiant, though unsuccessful defenders of their land; among the faithful few who, in the very face of the persecutor, dared to obey the Law of Moses, and refused every effort to turn them from their God. Would this patriotism, this devotedness, have come at the moment needed, had it not been taught, infused from earliest boyhood—by example as well as precept? A mother in Israel could be herself no warrior, but she could raise up warriors—she could be no priest, but she could create priests—she could not face the battle's front, or drive the idolatrous invader from God's holy land—she could not stem the torrent of persecution, and of torture; but she could raise up those who would seek the one, and, by unshrinking death, bear witness to the fruitless efforts of the other; and it was these things this heroic mother did. She had trained up her boys in that faithfulness, the constancy, which could only spring from virtue.[9]

iiiiiiii

=

Theodor Herzl's "The Menorah"
ALEX BEIN

Zionist historian and director of the Central Zionist Archives in Jerusalem

The growth and evolution of Herzl's conception of the Jewish problem since the day when he looked on at the degradation of Dreyfus can be measured almost with laboratory accuracy by a study of the articles which he wrote immediately after the first [Zionist] Congress. He himself was quite aware of the transformation. Two years before, in December 1895, he had been outraged by [Vienna's Chief Rabbi Moritz] Güdemann's declaration that the use of a Christmas tree in Jewish homes—an accepted custom with Herzl's parents—was essentially un-Jewish. Herzl had believed then that it was permissible to interpret the Christmas tree as a "Hanukkah tree"; or it might be looked upon as the celebration of the upward turn of the sun at the winter solstice. Now he wrote an article, entitled "The Menorah," in which he told how he had returned to Judaism, how he regarded the celebration of Hanukkah, and how this festival affected him. The story begins like a fairy tale: "Once upon a time there was a man who had discovered deep in his soul the need to be a Jew." The man was an artist; he had made his peace with the surrounding world; he had long since ceased to concern himself with his Jewish origins and the faith of his fathers. But the ever-rising tide of anti-Jewish sentiment, the incessant attacks on the Jews, tore open something within him "so that his soul became nothing more than an open and bleeding wound." He came by degrees to "a deep inner love" of Judaism, and to the conclusion "that there was only one way out of the Jewish tragedy, and that was a return of the Jews to their homeland." Everyone believed that the man had gone mad. Everyone believed that "the way out" which he had chosen would result in a deepening and intensification of the evil. "But he was sure now that the moral catastrophe in Jewish life was all the sharper because the Jews had lost that inner compensation which had existed so strongly in their ancestors."

Undistracted by the mockery and contempt which were directed at him, the man followed to its logical conclusion the consequences of his conviction. He realized that the first problem was that of the education of the young generation of Jews. He therefore decided to revive the festival of the Maccabees for his children, and to plant in their young souls a feeling of relationship to the past of their people. As he held aloft the nine-branched candlestick he suddenly recalled, in a strange rush of feeling, his own childhood, and the celebration of the festival in his father's house. He looked at the antique symbol, the prototype of which had so obviously been a tree, and asked himself "whether it was possible to bring new life into his petrified menorah form, and to water its roots again as if it were really a tree." And thus the first evening of the Hanukkah festival passed.

"The first candle was lit, and the story of the origin of the festival recited: the miraculous origin of the undying lamp, the saga of the return from Babylon, of the Second Temple and of the Maccabees. Our friend related to his children all that he knew. It was not much, but it was enough for them. When he lit the second candle, it was the children who recited the story to him, and as he heard it from their lips it seemed not only beautiful, but quite new. And from then on he looked forward joyfully to the coming of each evening, always brighter than the evening before. Candle stood by candle in the menorah, and by their light, father and children dreamed their dreams. In the end it all grew into something more than he had sought to tell them, for it had risen beyond their understanding. . . .

"Amid these meditations the week passed. The eighth day came, and now the *shammash*, the servant among the candles, which until

then had been used only for the kindling of the others, burned together with them. A great light streamed out from the menorah. The eyes of the children flashed, but what our good friend saw was the kindling of the light of the nation. First one candle, and dimness all around it, so that the candle was sad and lonely. Then a companion was added to it. Then a third, and a fourth. The darkness is compelled to retreat. The first candles are lit among the young and the poor, and gradually they are joined by all those who love truth and beauty and justice and freedom. When all the candles burn there is admiration and rejoicing for the work that has been done. And there is no office more beneficent and creative than that of a Servant of Light."

Translated by Maurice Samuel[10]

iiiiiiii
=

Hanukkah and the Redemption of the Land
JOSEPH G. KLAUSNER

professor of modern Hebrew literature and of Second Temple history at the Hebrew University in Jerusalem; prolific author of scholarly books and articles; editor in chief of the Encyclopedia Hebraica *(1874–1958)*

The great victory of Judah Maccabeus, whose memory is honored in every Jewish house and every Jewish heart during the eight days of Hanukkah, was the triumph of the Jewish tiller of the soil. It was not the city of Jerusalem, nor the ranks of the wealthy and large landowners, but the obscure village of Modin in Judah, with its peasants whose plot of land was their all, that produced Mattathias the Hasmonean and his sons, who saved Jewish culture and perhaps the whole Jewish race from destruction. We have here a historic fact which speaks more than all the theoretical arguments in the world for the importance of national land and agricultural workers who literally draw their bread from their soil by the labor of their hands, for the sake of the culture, the freedom, the life of the nation.

Zionism knew how to raise the Feast of Hanukkah, that feast of small candles which shed their eternal light from the past into the future, to the height of a new national symbol. Can one ever forget that fine sketch by the founder of Zionism, Theodor Herzl, "The Menorah"? The picture of Herzl standing wrapped in troubled thought, in front of a menorah, is one of the most beautifully symbolic in the life of the leader. But it seems to me that this festival has come to tell the people, through its two-thousand-year-old symbol, of the principle of land redemption, and the creation of a class of workers on the soil that shall serve as a basis for the future existence of the race.[11]

iiiiiii
=

The National Significance of the Maccabean Legacy
SOLOMON RAPPAPORT

rabbi and author; professor of Hebrew at Witwatersrand University, Johannesburg, South Africa

The national significance of the Maccabean legacy for the Jewish people manifests itself in two distinct aspects: the heroic-martial, and the religious-spiritual. The memory of Maccabean faith and valor has created an unbroken tradition of heroic fighting and heroic dying. Throughout Jewish history, from the days of Hannah, who urged her seven sons rather to die than to betray the Law, to the peerless bravery displayed in the revolt of the Warsaw Ghetto and Israel's War of Liberation, the Maccabean spirit of heroism, resistance, and sacrifice was continually in evidence. The sons of Mattathias created a new precious value in Judaism, the value of *Kiddush ha-Shem*, rightly considered as the brightest jewel in the crown of Judaism. They exemplified the Jew of all ages who lived and died for the sanctification of God's Name, the symbol and embodiment of the true Jewish way of life.

The thinkers and poets of the Zionist renaissance aroused the wretched denizens of the Russian Pale to resist their tormentors and reawakened in them the national will to live by holding before their eyes the undying deeds of their Maccabean forebears. Morris

Rosenfeld's "National Songs" evoked in the pogrom-ridden Eastern Jew nostalgic memories of a heroic past, of those ancient days of "blood and glory," when Jews "took to the field and made the foemen yield" ("Hanukkah Candles"). In "City of Slaughter," Bialik chastises his contemporaries for displaying abject cowardice during the pogrom of Kishinev. "Great is the sorrow and scathing" that they "who ran like mice" are "scions of the Maccabees." Tchernichovsky in his rousing poem "A Night in Hanukkah" pours bitter scorn upon the spiritless dwellers of the ghetto who have forgotten to wield the Maccabean sword:

Lo, these are our Maccabees!
 These heaps of bones,
These shriveled hands, these bloodless arteries,
These blighted brains—'tis a miracle they live.
Who live and live not, aged ere their time.

Herzl concludes his vision of the Jewish state with the triumphant hope: "I believe that a wondrous generation of Jews will spring into existence, the Maccabees will rise again." His vision has come true.[12]

iiiiiii
=

Hanukkah and the Rebirth of Israel
YAACOV HERZOG

rabbi and diplomat; Israel ambassador to Canada and director general of the Prime Minister's Office (1921–72)

Hanukkah comprehends Judaism to mean Jewish independence—in the physical and political sense—in that small land on the eastern coast of the Mediterranean where the threefold bond of land, people, and faith was forged for all time. Hanukkah also enshrines the dialogue between Israel and the nations of the world from earliest times. The central theme is of the few against the many, of a people —its soul kindled by immortal dispensation—pursuing its distinctive course through the ages against all odds; a people confident in its faith that no mortal force, whether active or passive, whether of oppression or hatred, whether of discrimination or assimilation, could in the final analysis deny it the fulfillment of its spiritual and national destiny, both for itself and in the broader context of human progress. . . .

The Maccabees of old were not only members of the priestly house and, as such, guardians of Judaism; they were also leaders of their people—generals and statesmen. In summing up political and military prospects, the criteria were the same in ancient times as today. The Maccabees could not have ignored them, and yet they embarked on a revolt against Greek oppression that, in light of what we know today about the balance of forces in those days, must have seemed remote indeed from any chance of success. They acted as they did because failure to act would have meant total physical destruction and spiritual eclipse. But an inner voice told them that if the tragedy of Jewish destiny is a precarious existence on the brink, its triumph is achieved by total commitment to faith through which peril can be challenged and overcome. In our time, over two thousand years later, the sons of the Maccabees faced a situation that, in poignancy and despair, recalled the circumstances in which their forefathers had likewise found themselves. . . .

But the passage of time had not obliterated the spirit of the Maccabees: their resolve, their faith, and the message of their experience bridged the gap of time and guided their heirs in the twentieth century. If archeology one day uncovers the political and military estimates of those who sent Greek forces to crush the Hasmonean revolt, we might assume that their analysis of the Jewish prospects would not be far different from the assessments that were prevalent in 1948. Redemption flashed anew, when every mortal assessment would seem to have denied its validity. The few vindicated their cause against the force of the many. As Hanukkah is celebrated throughout Israel today, its true significance and innermost spirit can be grasped for the first time since the festival was initiated thousands of years ago. . . .

The dialogue of a redeemed people with the world has but begun. The testament of the Maccabees will be vindicated. On Hanukkah let us clasp hands in spiritual fraternity and historical involvement. Let us recall the testament of Mattathias, the father of the Maccabees: privileged indeed are we to live in this generation. May we be worthy of the destiny that summons us forward.[13]

ⅲⅲⅲⅲⅲ
=

The Hanukkah Menorah
DANIEL PERSKY

American Hebraist who wholeheartedly fostered the Hebrew language through teaching and writing; a noted feuilletonist and grammarian (1887–1962)

These candles we kindle. . . . . The "sexton" and the eight candles—the kindler and the eight that are kindled.

The Creator of nature, the Original One, whose origin has no beginning, the Paragon of paragons, the Holy One, Blessed be He —He is the source of light, the quarry rock of illumination. The flame of His holy fire enlightens and warms all of existence in all its infinity, everything in heaven and on earth.

And behold, this exalted "Sexton," the eternal and glorious Kindler, kindled a candle, *the first candle*—His people Israel, the seed of Abraham, Isaac, and Jacob. It is an eternal people; as the days of the heavens and the earth are the length of its duration upon the world. No weapon forged against this nation will succeed, for it draws the sap of eternity from the very altar of God.

In the desert, on the way from Egypt to the land of Canaan, in a period of transition, Israel was given the "Torah of Moses"—the Torah that planted in our hearts the faith in a God of justice and truth, of love and mercy; the Torah crowns us with the splendor of commandments and judgments, traditions and laws. By virtue of the Torah, Jerusalem grew exalted and mighty, was purged in the divine crucible, and purified seven times over. From the Torah we draw the abundance of our vitality, nay, the reason for our existence. Her brightness envelopes our bodies and souls forever and ever. It is *the second candle* and was kindled on Mount Sinai.

Then too, we were presented with Judaism's fundamental of fundamentals, the Sabbath. The delightful of all days, the crown of the week, the day of rest and relaxation, when we may forget our poverty and toil to unite with the Creator of the universe. On the Sabbath we forsake the secular realm and the gloom of reality. We are elevated and joined in holiness with the Source of holiness. We sense the distinction between man and beast, for not by bread and work alone do we live—here are the words of God and the sparks of His spirit. The very exalted "Sexton" Himself lit *the third candle* for us—the Sabbath.

But the Sabbath is not all we have. Throughout the year, from beginning to end, the Lord of creation and the Father of our nation has endowed us with periods of rejoicing and holy festivals: Rosh Hashanah and Yom Kippur, Sukkot and Simhat Torah, Hanukkah and Purim, Pesah and Shavuot. These holidays were appointed to commemorate historic events of old, to serve as milestones in the flow of time, for spiritual self-analysis, for the purification of morals, as a symbol of past freedom, and as a sign of hope and consolation for the future. These festival days introduce joy and beauty into our homes, join us to the national values, strengthen our hands in our fight for survival, and encourage confidence in our ultimate victory. Verily, this is the gift of *the fourth candle*, that the exalted Master kindled.

Let us give thanks to the Rock of Ages for bequeathing to our people *the fifth candle*—the goodly, pleasant, and broad land, that He allowed to our fathers. Eretz Israel is bound to Jeshurun with an unbreakable bond. Deep in that land are anchored the roots of our vitality and culture. Without it our life is not worthy of the name. Though we have been exiled from it, on account of our sins, she has not been exiled from our hearts. When we dwelt on its soil, securely and freely, and when we were far removed from it—at all times she was the head of our joy and pain, the aim of our longings and the chiefmost of our desires. We shall look forward all of our days to the perfect renaissance of the land of Israel, together with that of our people.

Still another candle, *the sixth candle*, the high and mighty Kindler kindled for us—the Hebrew language. The holy tongue, by which the Lord created His world, is also the language of our people. In Hebrew the Torah was given, in Hebrew the prophets prophesied, in Hebrew the early and later sages meditated and wrote, in Hebrew all the generations of our great men struck off the coins of Torah and Judaism, in Hebrew the poets wailed the bitterness of our exile, and in Hebrew they aroused us to hope for redemption and salvation. Our wonderful and eternal tongue, old-new, ancient-young, has always been the vehicle of our meditations and visions. We have never betrayed her; with the reconstruction of Zion and Jerusalem, she too shall be rebuilt.

Our great and variegated literature, the treasury of our spirit and our individuality, from Genesis to this very day, during the course of many periods and lands, through endless sufferings and struggles —is *the seventh candle*, with which the most powerful "Sexton" of all blessed us. Truly, it is a *candle for our feet and a light for our way* in all our physical and spiritual journeyings in foreign climes. It is the guarded treasure of our culture, in which is secreted all that is good and exalted, select and glorious—all that our national genius has created: the treasures of thought and verse, ritual and legend, the sacred and the profane, science and ethics. We have guarded them with love and devotion and we are drawing substance and understanding, wisdom and knowledge from them to this very day, and we shall continue to nourish our soul and heart with them forever.

Yet another candle, *the eighth* and last candle, the Holy One of Israel and its Redeemer presented to us, that we may know that there is an end to our labor and a hope for all who aspire to Him —it is the candle of the Messiah. Even when the Eternal made life very bitter for us, we did not lose hope. Like a pillar of fire in the desert of our wanderings, the vision of the Messiah shone through the woes of the nations among whom we sojourned, in all the splendor and charm of His countenance. This long-held aspiration to be unfettered from the chains of the deep was not symptomatic of a sick heart but of a longing one. As long as our hand holds the torch of the trust in the Messiah, as long as the image of redemption persists in our eye—our knees do not totter nor our feet waver. With head held high and confident tread, with a burning heart we stride with pride to meet the sun rising in the east, the sun that will not cease to shine from Zion, our beloved and the nation of the redeemed.

The Hanukkah menorah's eight candles of Israel shine with power and splendor, they burn and are not consumed. Look at them. There is the "sexton" guarding the candles of his delight lest they be extinguished—those candles that burn bright, unceasing flare, in spite of the whole world.

Translated by Jacob Sloan[14]

iiiiiii
=

Hanukkah Today
HERMAN WOUK

author of best-selling novels, including The Caine Mutiny, The Winds of War, *and* Marjorie Morningstar, *and an exposition of traditional Judaism,* This Is My God

In a thousand years of national existence on the soil of Palestine the Jews over and over drove out oppressors and regained independence, but the Maccabean War, a battle for religious liberty, alone found a place in the rites of our faith. It stood out. It was the Jews' first full-scale encounter with the question that was to haunt them in the next two thousand years, namely, can a small people, dwelling in a triumphant major culture, take part in the general life and yet hold to its identity, or must it be absorbed into the ranks and the ways of the majority? In the two great worlds of current affairs—the Communist empire, which so much resembles an ancient military dictatorship, and the tolerant, skeptical free West—they face the question again.

The Communist position on the Jews is generally, though with less crudity, that of Antiochus. Our religion the Soviets consider a barbarous relic, superseded in wisdom and soundness by Marxism. The training of children in this exploded Semitic superstition goes against good sense and the interests of the state. So the police discourage such teaching, in ways sometimes oblique and sometimes forcible. For Greek religion substitute Marxism, and the Russian Jews are back where their fathers were in 168 B.C.E.—with whatever differences one may find in the relative truth and beauty of the Greek and Communist cultures.

The challenge of the West is different, though just as serious. The proposition is the old one: that the Jews are confronted with a better way of life and should give up their religion for it. Forces that are not coercive, and therefore do not call forth the human impulse to fight them, urge Jews along this path. The position of the government, and indeed the deep conviction of most American leaders, is that the Jewish community has the right to hold fast to the faith of its fathers and ought to do so. What contradicts them is the tidal

force that de Tocqueville long ago marked as the great weakness of a democracy in his unforgettable phrase "the tyranny of the majority." The pressure to emulate neighbors, the urge to conform to popular views and manners, the deep fear of being different—these, in the United States, are the forces of Antiochus. Where the power of the sword long ago failed, the power of suggestion has recently been doing rather better.

It would be pleasant to believe that the stabbing relevance of Hanukkah to Jewish life in America has occasioned the swell of interest in the holiday. But a different and perfectly obvious cause is at work. By a total accident of timing, this minor Hebrew celebration falls close in the calendar year to a great holy day of the Christian faith. This coincidence has all but created a new Hanukkah. . . .

It was entirely natural for a new Jewish generation growing up in the United States to feel each December like children in the dark outside a house where there was a gay party, pressing their noses wistfully against the windows. That Judaism had its own rich and varied occasions of gaiety was beside the point. Most second-generation Jews were but poorly trained in their own faith; and anyway the Christians had a brilliant midwinter feast, and the Jews did not. Some families solved the problem in the simplest way by introducing Christmas trees, Christmas presents, and Christmas carols into their homes. They argued that it was harmful for their children to feel underprivileged, and that the Christmas tree was a mere pleasant ornament of the season without religious content.

Meantime in schools where there were large numbers of Jewish children a dual celebration of Christmas and Hanukkah sprang up, as an official symbol of mutual courtesy and tolerance. This in turn generated a new Jewish interest in Hanukkah. Even those Jews who were celebrating Christmas in their homes—trees, holly, "Born Is the King of Israel," and all—began to find it seemly to add an electric menorah for their windows, and perhaps even to light the candles. This apparently solved the problem by giving the children the best of both worlds. . . .

The aggrandizement of Hanukkah itself is a fortunate accident. The level of knowledge of all Judaism must rise when any part of it happens, for whatever reason, to gain attention. The son of my skeptical friend is not likely to stop after learning about Hanukkah. A lack of clear and satisfying religious identity hurts American Jews most in December. That is why the apparently trifling issue of the

Christmas tree generates such obduracy and such resentment. It rasps an exposed nerve. It is a good thing that Hanukkah is then at hand. If the old custom of Hanukkah money has become the new custom of Hanukkah gifts, that is a minor shift in manners. The tale of the Feast of Lights, with its all-too-sharp comment on our life nowadays, is very colorful. It is of the greatest use in giving the young a quick grasp of the Jewish historic situation. The gifts win their attention. The little candles stimulate their questions. The observance seems tooled to the needs of self-discovery. . . .

Our whole history is a fantastic legend of a single day's supply of oil lasting eight days; of a flaming bush that is not consumed; of a national life that in the logic of events should have flickered and gone out long ago, still burning on. That is the tale we tell our children in the long nights of December when we kindle the little lights, while the great Christian feast blazes around us with its jeweled trees and familiar music.

The two festivals have one real point of contact. Had Antiochus succeeded in obliterating Jewry a century and a half before the birth of Jesus, there would have been no Christmas. The feast of the Nativity rests on the victory of Hanukkah.[15]

iiiiiiii
=

The Menorah or the Tree?
ROLAND B. GITTELSOHN

rabbi of Temple Israel, Boston; author of books on contemporary Jewish problems

One of the most pathetic spectacles in American Jewish life is the Jew who justifies his observance of Christmas on the ground that it is a secular, national holiday, with no religious significance. Though it is in a sense cruel to deprive such a person of his reassuring rationalizations, both honesty and Jewish self-respect require that we face Christmas honestly for what it really is. What, then, is the real significance of those seemingly innocent Christmas customs with which so many of our people delight to adorn their homes?

Like many other ceremonies and symbols of both Judaism and Christianity, the Christmas tree may have originated in pagan life. It was soon given deeply religious significance, however, by Christianity. Its early Christian use was based on a legend that the night Jesus was born all the trees of the forest bloomed and bore fruit despite the snow and ice which covered them. By more thoughtful and theologically-minded Christians, the tree is still meant today to symbolize the resurrection and immortality of Jesus, as well as the wood used for the cross of crucifixion. Grim irony indeed that Jews, so many of whose ancestors were persecuted and perished because of their alleged complicity in the crucifixion of Jesus, should now embrace a symbol of that very event!

One Christian authority summarized the significance of the Christmas tree in these words: "In quieter moments its real significance may be hinted: For it is a symbol of Christ, as the Tree of Life who offers freely to all his gifts of light and life and wisdom."

Of what religious significance are the decorations used on the Christmas tree?

One explanation goes back to Martin Luther, whom the stars in the sky reminded one Christmas Eve of "him who for us men and for our salvation came from heaven."

The tinsel seen on Christmas trees is known as "angel's hair." It is meant to recall the heavenly hosts who are supposed to have attended the miraculous birth of the Christian Savior.

The apples which were once part of the tree's adornment, and the simulated apples more commonly used today, are supposed to remind us of the apple which tempted Adam and Eve in Eden. Christian doctrine teaches that from the seeds of that very apple there grew the tree used for the cross on which Jesus met his death.

Surely the inhibition-removing mistletoe at least is devoid of religious significance? Must we be deprived of this too?

I'm afraid we must. No better description of the place of mistletoe in the Christian scheme of things can be found than in the words of a popular Christmas hymn:

The mistletoe bow at our Christmas board,
Shall hang to the honor of Christ our Lord:
For he is the evergreen Tree of Life.

And the holly wreath? One Christian spokesman tells us that it represents "the crown of thorns which Christ wore on the cross, the little red berries symbolizing the drops of blood."

Not even the gifts so generously distributed at Christmastime can escape our careful scrutiny. They are explained by Christian religious authorities in two ways. One: their purpose is "to supplicate the saints and win forgiveness for sins." Two: they are meant to "emulate the amazing unselfishness of Christ."

Small wonder that the real name of Christmas, which preachers and priests are today doing their proper best to restore, is "Christ's Mass."

A final question remains, the last refuge of the Jew who would cling emotionally to his celebration of Christmas even after he has been assured intellectually that its religious significance is not for him: "But can't we Jews observe Christmas as a secular occasion, without accepting the theology it symbolizes?" Of course we can. That's not the real question. The real question is: *do we have a moral right to?*

What would be our reaction if any significant number of Christians were to begin celebrating Yom Kippur, the holiest day in our religious calendar, as a secular occasion—a day devoid of all sacred significance, a day for unbounded hilarity and exaggerated commercialization? What right have we to expect our devout Christian neighbors to take any more kindly to the dilution of their most sacred day than we would to ours?

This question—and the answer implied by its very asking—are not imaginary on my part. Sensitive Jews, even if not compelled by an inner integrity and self-respect to celebrate Hanukkah rather than Christmas, might well heed the advice of the *Churchman* in its issue of December 15, 1950: "Whatever external elements the festivals of Hanukkah and Christmas . . . may have in common, this fact remains: that Hanukkah is distinctly Jewish and Christmas is as distinctly Christian. . . . This should be remembered to the advantage of both Jew and Christian. . . . If the season of Hanukkah and Christmas is always to be one of peace and goodwill, let both Jew and Christian remember that they have a right to perpetuate and preserve their particular cultural and religious mores and that any attempt at reckless and superficial 'assimilation' are as stupid as they are bound to be futile."[16]

iiiiiii
=
The Challenge of December
EMANUEL RACKMAN

rabbi and educator; past president of the Rabbinical Council of America; professor of Jewish studies at the City University of New York

There was a time when Hanukkah was a festival of secondary importance. It certainly did not rank with the High Holy Days; nor did it even rank with the pilgrimage festivals—Passover, Weeks, and Tabernacles. By no means was its importance comparable to that of the Sabbath. Yet as Jews began to live closely with non-Jews, Hanukkah came into its own.

The economic enterprise of Jews now involves non-Jews in great measure. Our social, political, and even intellectual existence is not isolated from Christianity, and since Christians celebrate one of their most important religious festivals during the month of December, the festival of Hanukkah donned overwhelming importance for Jews.

Jews had to find some way in which they could place the accent upon their own identity. And Hanukkah was catapulted from the status of a minor festival into one of great importance. We too have become involved with Hanukkah gifts, Hanukkah wrappers, Hanukkah parties, Hanukkah savings clubs. . . .

If we would try to accomplish what we should for the preservation of feelings of Jewish identity, we must do more than simply graft a few observances typical of the season on a holiday of our own. We must ponder and continuously discuss the historical background of our festival and all of its ethical, legal, and philosophical significances.

Hanukkah affords us the opportunity to cope with the challenge of our environment in the month of December. However, properly to cope with the challenge requires more mind and heart than we have given it.[17]

8 HANUKKAH IN ART

JOSEPH GUTMANN

Although a minor holiday, Hanukkah is rich in surviving ceremonial objects. Especially in the twentieth century has it assumed major importance and given artists an opportunity for creative play. It is one of the few holidays that has one symbol—the lamp—linked with it, whose artistic development we can trace from ancient times to our own day.

The earliest Hanukkah lamps come from the talmudic period and were probably clay oil lamps with openings for wicks, as we can see in the third–fourth century clay lamp from Palestine, with its three-footed menorah in the center (fig. 1). It was in talmudic times that the Rabbis deliberately set the tone for the holiday by de-emphasizing its militaristic and national aspects, and emphasizing instead the miraculous and religious nature of the holiday: "For when the

Greeks entered the Temple, they defiled all the vials therein, and when the Hasmonean dynasty prevailed against them and defeated them, they made search and found only one cruse of oil, which lay with the seal of the high priest, but which contained sufficient oil for one day's lighting only; yet a miracle was wrought therein and they lit [the lamp] therewith for eight days" (Shabbat 21b).

In the later Middle Ages a metal bench-type oil lamp with a triangular back developed. The earliest surviving examples of this type are said to be from the fourteenth century, because of the Gothic motifs used (fig. 2). This lamp was at first hung on the left doorpost of the house, opposite the mezuzah. It has a ninth servant light placed higher than the other lights.

Along with the use of the bench-type Hanukkah lamp, there arose in the Middle Ages the custom of placing a large standing lamp in the synagogue. This lamp was intended for wayfarers, so that when all were assembled "the miracle might be spread and proclaimed." We can see such a synagogue lamp illustrated in the late north Italian Rothschild manuscript, from the fifteenth century. Next to the Hanukkah prayer, we see mounted on a high pedestal eight tapers in a row (fig. 3).

Apparently from the seventeenth century on, the Hanukkah lamp resembling in shape the Temple menorah appeared. Such a lamp is shown in the *Sefer Minhagim* from Amsterdam (fig. 4), and a large bronze lamp from 1706 has survived from Aschaffenburg, Germany (fig. 5). This large lamp frequently stood toward the south, or to the right of the Torah ark, in Germany, thus commemorating the menorah of the Bible (Exodus 26.35), which also stood toward the south. An unusual feature of this lamp is the hands, emerging from the central shaft and grasping the extended branches on either side.

The bench-type lamp of the Middle Ages developed with infinite variations. A drip pan was added under the oil burners, and sides were added sometimes to the backpiece to allow the lamp to be placed on the windowsill or table. In eighteenth-century Holland simple brass lamps with floral and heart decorations were common. Splendid silver lamps were also produced, such as the Amsterdam specimen of 1719 (fig. 6) or the handsome English lamp made by Jacob Marsh, 1747–48 (fig. 7). Although these lamps carried primarily floral decoration we also possess silver lamps from England with scenes from the prophets, such as the lamp made by John Ruslen in London, in 1709, which has a scene of Elijah being fed by the ravens (fig. 8).

From eighteenth-century Frankfort, Germany, we have a popular type of silver lamp, where two lions flank a cartouche with a nine-branched lampstand (fig. 9). A more elaborate silver lamp with figural and animal decoration, a menorah in the center, and the blessings over the lights on either side of it comes from eighteenth-century Augsburg, Germany. The lamp is crested by the eagle of the Holy Roman Empire (fig. 10). From Germany we also have simple examples of the bench-type lamp made of tin, such as the lamp from 1756 (fig. 11).

The bench-type lamp is at home in oriental countries, as we can note in the eighteenth- and nineteenth-century brass cast pierced specimens from Morocco (figs. 12–13). Bench-type lamps from Iraq of the same period use painted glass and prominently feature magical hands (figs. 14–15).

From sixteenth-century Italy a rare type of the bench variety of Hanukkah lamp has come down to us. Renaissance *putti* and decorations abound, and in the center of the lamps we find a cartouche with the coat of arms of cardinals, such as Cardinal Ippolito Aldobrandini (later Pope Clement VIII) (fig. 16), or the armorial bearings of Avalo de Aragona, who became a cardinal in 1561 (fig. 17). What is the explanation for the cardinal's coat of arms on Hanukkah lamps? Perhaps they were simply tokens of loyalty by Jews who worked as agents for the princes of the church.

From seventeenth or eighteenth century Italy we also have brass bench-type lamps with centaurs, topped by Judith brandishing a sword, since in medieval Jewish folklore she was associated with the Hanukkah holiday (fig. 18).

Bench-type lamps were also made of porcelain, painted and gilded, such as the nineteenth-century one from Gorodnitza, Ukraine. Simple floral decoration and the inscription "to kindle the Hanukkah light" adorn this lamp (fig. 19).

Some rare specimens of the eight-branched Hanukkah lamp have been preserved, such as the silver eighteenth-century one from Frankfort on the Main made by Johann Matthias Sandrart. This lamp rests on four lions rampant; its branches have alternating balls and blossoms. Judith holding the head of Holofernes surmounts the Hanukkah lamp (fig. 20). Another interesting lamp, which comes from eighteenth-century Poland, is in the shape of an oak tree. A peasant motif of a hunter shooting a bear, who is climbing the trunk of the tree to reach the honeypot, adds a bit of whimsey to the seriousness of the occasion (fig. 21). A beautiful lamp made in Frankfort on the Main in the mid-nineteenth century has survived the Holocaust. It was made for Wilhelm Karl von Rothschild and has at its base a rampant lion and unicorn and the coat of arms of the Rothschild family (fig. 22).

Large lamps utilizing architectural forms also begin to appear in the eighteenth century. One unusual Hanukkah lamp of this type comes from Germany and is dated 1814. It is in the form of a classical building with columns and pediment. The inscription on the pediment comes from 1 Samuel 10.1: "Then Samuel took the vial of oil, and poured it." The altar on the pediment is flanked by two stags rampant. On their bodies is the Hebrew word "Samuel," perhaps alluding to the name of the owner. On either side of the altar are three overlapping triangles. The eight oil vials are in the

18. Hanukkah lamp. Brass. Italy. Seventeenth or eighteenth century.

shape of lions. On the steps, connected by chains, are seven silver implements for servicing and fueling the lamp (fig. 23).

Elegant and forceful is the Hanukkah lamp designed by the contemporary artist Ludwig Wolpert (fig. 24). The late Benno Elkan designed a bronze Hanukkah lamp which has Judah Maccabee with hammer in the center, flanked by his brothers. The inscription from Exodus 15.11 reads: "Who is like You, O Lord, among the celestials?" (fig. 25). Another contemporary lamp is by the late Ilya Schor. It has four dreidels on top of the lamp with the inscription "A great miracle happened there." These dreidels can be spun to turn the figures below, which represent great leaders in Judaism— top row, right to left: Moses, Isaiah, Saadia Gaon, Hillel; bottom row: Maimonides, Rashi, Baal Shem, Isaac Mayer Wise (fig. 26).

The joyous aspect of Hanukkah is of course symbolized by the dreidel. Examples from nineteenth-century southern Germany have come down to us (fig. 27). Paul Kirchner in his eighteenth-century print shows the lighting of candles and both children and adults playing games (fig. 28). Similarly, Moritz Oppenheim lets us glimpse into a nineteenth-century German home, where we can witness the kindling of the Hanukkah lights on the windowsill and the children and the adults indulging in games (fig. 29).

The books of Maccabees were not canonized as part of the Hebrew Bible, but were taken over by the church fathers. Whether the panel of the third-century Dura-Europos synagogue shows Mattathias slaying the Jew who is preparing to sacrifice on a heathen altar is not certain (fig. 30). If it is taken from the books of Maccabees, it raises interesting questions on knowledge of these books at an earlier time than previously assumed. No other scenes of the heroic deed of Mattathias are found in medieval Jewish art, but of course it is at home and well known in Christian art. One of the early portrayals of this event is in the eleventh-century Farfa Bible, where at the top we see a Jew about to sacrifice a pig on an altar and Mattathias killing him with a sword (fig. 31).

In a medieval *piyyut*, we also find an adaptation of the story from 4 Maccabees, which describes the martyrdom of the seven brothers. In the fifteenth-century German miniature we see in the uppermost scene two women, who in defiance of the king's decree circumcised their children. They were hung by their breasts in punishment and their children were cast down from a tower. Next we see Eleazar the high priest, whom the king is trying to persuade to offer false sacrifices. The ninety-year-old man refused and is being decapitated in the following scene. The bottom scene depicts the heroic martyrdom of the seven brothers who were burned and mutilated, rather than eat the proffered sacrifices (fig. 32).

In a *Mahzor* from Hammelburg, Germany, dated 1348, we see next to the Hanukkah *piyyut* "I thank you that you were angry," the high priest rekindling the lights of the Temple menorah (fig. 33). The above *piyyut* also has scenes from Judith, an Apocryphal book rejected by the early rabbis, that reappears in medieval Jewish folklore and legend. Judith is shown cutting off the head of Holofernes as he and his army are fast asleep, drunk from a feast. Below Judith and her maid are taking the cut-off head to the gates of the city. The text reads: "This pious and smart woman cut off his head like an ear of corn" (fig. 34).

The fifteenth-century Rothschild manuscript reveals the *piyyut* in bold Renaissance letters. The curtains of the tent are parted and Judith holding the sword in one hand and the head of Holofernes in the other are depicted (fig. 35).

The rich variety of the Hanukkah lamp, the dreidel, and the Apocryphal scenes in medieval Hebrew manuscripts reveal both the joyous, miraculous aspects of Hanukkah as well as its heroic devotion to a sacred cause.

9 A HANUKKAH DRAMA

iiiiiiii
‗

Judah Maccabeus

HENRY WADSWORTH LONGFELLOW

popular American poet and professor of modern languages and belles lettres at Harvard (1807–82); following are sustantial excerpts from his tragedy in five acts on the conflict between Judaism and Hellenism

Act 1. The citadel of Antiochus at Jerusalem

SCENE 1.—*Antiochus; Jason*

Ant.   O Antioch, my Antioch, my city!
Queen of the East! my solace, my delight!

       The dowry of my sister Cleopatra
       When she was wed to Ptolemy, and now
       Won back and made more wonderful by me!
       I love thee, and I long to be once more
       Among the players and the dancing women
       Within thy gates, and bathe in the Orontes,
       Thy river and mine. O Jason, my high priest,
       For I have made thee so, and thou art mine,
       Hast thou seen Antioch the Beautiful?

Jas.   Never, my lord.

Ant.   Then hast thou never seen
       The wonder of the world. This city of David
       Compared with Antioch is but a village,
       And its inhabitants compared with Greeks
       Are mannerless boors.

Jas.   They are barbarians,
       And mannerless.

Ant.   They must be civilized.
       They must be made to have more gods than one;
       And goddesses besides.

Jas.   They shall have more.

Ant.   They must have hippodromes, and games, and baths,
       Stage plays and festivals, and most of all
       The Dionysia.

Jas.   They shall have them all.

Ant.   By Heracles! but I should like to see
       These Hebrews crowned with ivy, and arrayed
       In skins of fawns, with drums and flutes and thyrsi,
       Revel and riot through the solemn streets
       Of their old town. Ha, ha! It makes me merry
       Only to think of it! Thou dost not laugh.

Jas.   Yea, I laugh inwardly.

Ant.   The new Greek leaven
       Works slowly in this Israelitish dough!

       Have I not sacked the Temple, and on the altar
       Set up the statue of Olympian Zeus
       To hellenize it?

Jas.   Thou hast done all this.

Ant. As thou wast Joshua once and now art Jason,
       And from a Hebrew hast become a Greek,
       So shall this Hebrew nation be translated,
       Their very natures and their names be changed,
       And all be hellenized.

Jas.   It shall be done.

Ant. Their manners and their laws and way of living
       Shall all be Greek. They shall unlearn their language,
       And learn the lovely speech of Antioch.
       Where hast thou been today? Thou comest late.

Jas. Playing at discus with the other priests
       In the gymnasium.

Ant.   Thou hast done well.
       There's nothing better for you lazy priests
       Than discus-playing with the common people.
       Now tell me, Jason, what these Hebrews call me
       When they converse together at their games.

Jas. Antiochus Epiphanes, my lord;
       Antiochus the Illustrious.

Ant.   Oh, not that;
       That is the public cry; I mean the name
       They give me when they talk among themselves,
       And think that no one listens; what is that?

Jas. Antiochus Epimanes, my lord!

Ant. Antiochus the Mad! Ay, that is it.
       And who hath said it? Who hath set in motion
       That sorry jest?

Jas.   The seven sons insane
       Of a weird woman, like themselves insane.

Ant.   I like their courage, but it shall not save them.
        They shall be made to eat the flesh of swine
        Or they shall die. Where are they?

Jas.   In the dungeons
        Beneath this tower.

Ant.   There let them stay and starve,
        Till I am ready to make Greeks of them,
        After my fashion. . . .

        SCENE 3. *Antiochus; Jason*

Ant.   My task is easier than I dreamed. These people
        Meet me halfway. Jason, didst thou take note
        How these Samaritans of Sichem said
        They were not Jews? that they were Medes and Persians,
        They were Sidonians, anything but Jews?
        'Tis of good augury. The rest will follow
        Till the whole land is hellenized.

Jas.   My lord,
        These are Samaritans. The tribe of Judah
        Is of a different temper, and the task
        Will be more difficult.

Ant.   Dost thou gainsay me?

Jas.   I know the stubborn nature of the Jew.
        Yesterday, Eleazer, an old man,
        Being fourscore years and ten, chose rather death
        By torture than to eat the flesh of swine.

Ant.   The life is in the blood, and the whole nation
        Shall bleed to death, or it shall change its faith!

Jas.   Hundreds have fled already to the mountains
        Of Ephraim, where Judah Maccabee
        Hath raised the standard of revolt against thee.

Ant.   I will burn down their city, and will make it
        Waste as a wilderness. Its thoroughfares
        Shall be but furrows in a field of ashes.
        It shall be sown with salt as Sodom is! . . .

Act 3. The battlefield of Beth Horon

SCENE 2. *Judah Maccabeus; Jewish Fugitives*

Jud.   Who and what are ye, that with furtive steps
Steal in among our tents?

Fug.   O Maccabeus,
Outcasts are we, and fugitives as thou art,
Jews of Jerusalem, that have escaped
From the polluted city, and from death.

Jud.   None can escape from death. Say that ye come
To die for Israel, and ye are welcome.
What tidings bring ye?

Fug.   Tidings of despair.
The Temple is laid waste; the precious vessels,
Censers of gold, vials and veils and crowns,
And golden ornaments, and hidden treasures,
Have all been taken from it, and the gentiles
With reveling and with riot fill its courts,
And dally with harlots in the holy places.

Jud.   All this I knew before.

Fug.   Upon the altar
Are things profane, things by the law forbidden;
Nor can we keep our Sabbaths or our feasts,
But on the festivals of Dionysus
Must walk in their processions, bearing ivy
To crown a drunken god.

Jud.   This too I know.
But tell me of the Jews. How fare the Jews?

Fug.   The coming of this mischief hath been sore
And grievous to the people. All the land
Is full of lamentation and of mourning.
The princes and the elders weep and wail;
The young men and the maidens are made feeble;
The beauty of the women hath been changed.

19. *Hanukkah lamp. Porcelain, painted and gilded. Gorodnitza, Ukraine. Nineteenth century.*

Jud.   And are there none to die for Israel?
'Tis not enough to mourn. Breastplate and harness
Are better things than sackcloth. Let the women
Lament for Israel; the men should die.

Fug.   Both men and women die; old men and young:
Old Eleazer died: and Máhala
With all her seven sons.

Jud.   Antiochus,
At every step thou takest there is left
A bloody footprint in the street, by which
The avenging wrath of God will track thee out!
It is enough. Go to the sutler's tents:
Those of you who are men, put on such armor
As ye may find; those of you who are women,
Buckle that armor on; and for a watchword
Whisper, or cry aloud, "The Help of God."

Scene 3. *Judah Maccabeus; Nicanor*

Nic. Hail, Judah Maccabeus!

Jud.   Hail! Who art thou
That comest here in this mysterious guise
Into our camp unheralded?

Nic.   A herald
Sent from Nicanor.

Jud.   Heralds come not thus.
Armed with thy shirt of mail from head to heel,
Thou glidest like a serpent silently
Into my presence. Wherefore dost thou turn
Thy face from me? A herald speaks his errand
With forehead unabashed. Thou art a spy
Sent by Nicanor.

Nic.   No disguise avails!
Behold my face; I am Nicanor's self.

Jud. Thou art indeed Nicanor. I salute thee.
What brings thee hither to this hostile camp
Thus unattended?

Nic.   Confidence in thee.
Thou hast the nobler virtues of thy race,
Without the failings that attend those virtues.
Thou canst be strong, and yet not tyrannous,
Canst righteous be and not intolerant.
Let there be peace between us.

Jud.   What is peace?
Is it to bow in silence to our victors?
Is it to see our cities sacked and pillaged,
Our people slain, or sold as slaves, or fleeing
At nighttime by the blaze of burning towns;
Jerusalem laid waste; the holy Temple
Polluted with strange gods? Are these things peace?

Nic. These are the dire necessities that wait
On war, whose loud and bloody enginery

I seek to stay. Let there be peace between
Antiochus and thee.

Jud.   Antiochus?
What is Antiochus, that he should prate
Of peace to me, who am a fugitive?
Today he shall be lifted up; tomorrow
Shall not be found, because he is returned
Unto his dust; his thought has come to nothing.
There is no peace between us, nor can be,
Until this banner floats upon the walls
Of our Jerusalem.

Nic.   Between that city
And thee there lies a waving wall of tents
Held by a host of forty thousand foot,
And horsemen seven thousand. What hast thou
To bring against all these?

Jud.   The power of God,
Whose breath shall scatter your white tents abroad,
As flakes of snow.

Nic.   Your Mighty One in heaven
Will not do battle on the seventh day;
It is His day of rest.

Jud.   Silence, blasphemer.
Go to thy tents.

Nic.   Shall it be war or peace?

Jud. War, war, and only war. Go to thy tents
That shall be scattered, as by you were scattered
The torn and trampled pages of the Law,
Blown through the windy streets.

Nic.   Farewell, brave foe!

Jud. Ho, there, my captains! Have safe conduct given
Unto Nicanor's herald through the camp,
And come yourselves to me. Farewell, Nicanor!

SCENE 4. *Judah Maccabeus; Captains and Soldiers*

Jud.   The hour is come. Gather the host together
For battle. Lo, with trumpets and with songs
The army of Nicanor comes against us.
Go forth to meet them, praying in your hearts,
And fighting with your hands.

Cap.   Look forth and see!
The morning sun is shining on their shields
Of gold and brass; the mountains glisten with them,
And shine like lamps. And we, who are so few
And poorly armed, and ready to faint with fasting,
How shall we fight against this multitude?

Jud.   The victory of a battle standeth not
In multitudes, but in the strength that cometh
From heaven above. The Lord forbid that I
Should do this thing, and flee away from them.
Nay, if our hour be come, then let us die;
Let us not stain our honor.

Cap.   'Tis the Sabbath.
Wilt thou fight on the Sabbath, Maccabeus?

Jud.   Ay; when I fight the battles of the Lord,
I fight them on His day, as on all others.
Have ye forgotten certain fugitives
That fled once to these hills, and hid themselves
In caves? How their pursuers camped against them
Upon the seventh day, and challenged them?
And how they answered not, nor cast a stone,
Nor stopped the places where they lay concealed,
But meekly perished with their wives and children,
Even to the number of a thousand souls?
We who are fighting for our laws and lives
Will not so perish.

Cap.   Lead us to the battle!

Jud.   And let our watchword be, "The Help of God!"
Last night I dreamed a dream; and in my vision
Beheld Onias, our high priest of old,

Who holding up his hands prayed for the Jews.
This done, in the like manner there appeared
An old man, and exceeding glorious,
With hoary hair, and of a wonderful
And excellent majesty. And Onias said:
"This is a lover of the Jews, who prayeth
Much for the people and the Holy City,—
God's prophet Jeremiah." And the prophet
Held forth his right hand and gave unto me
A sword of gold; and giving it he said:
"Take thou this holy sword, a gift from God,
And with it thou shalt wound thine adversaries."

Cap.   The Lord is with us!

Jud.   Hark! I hear the trumpets
Sound from Beth Horon; from the battlefield
Of Joshua, where he smote the Amorites,
Smote the five kings of Eglon and of Jarmuth,
Of Hebron, Lachish, and Jerusalem,
As we today will smite Nicanor's hosts
And leave a memory of great deeds behind us.

Cap. and Sol.   The Help of God! . . .

Act 4. The outer courts of the Temple at Jerusalem

SCENE 1. *Judah Maccabeus; Captains; Jews*

Jud.   Behold, our enemies are discomfited.
Jerusalem is fallen; and our banners
Float from her battlements, and o'er her gates
Nicanor's severed head, a sign of terror,
Blackens in wind and sun.

Cap.   O Maccabeus,
The citadel of Antiochus, wherein
The mother with her seven sons was murdered,
Is still defiant.

Jud.   Wait.

Cap.   Its hateful aspect
Insults us with the bitter memories
Of other days.

Jud.   Wait; it shall disappear
And vanish as a cloud. First let us cleanse
The sanctuary. See, it is become
Waste like a wilderness. Its golden gates
Wrenched from their hinges and consumed by fire;
Shrubs growing in its courts as in a forest;
Upon its altars hideous and strange idols;
And strewn about its pavement at my feet
Its sacred books, half burned and painted o'er
With images of heathen gods.

Jews   Woe! woe!
Our beauty and our glory are laid waste!
The gentiles have profaned our holy places!
          [Lamentation and alarm of trumpets]

Jud.   This sound of trumpets, and this lamentation,
The heart-cry of a people toward the heavens,
Stir me to wrath and vengeance. Go, my captains;
I hold you back no longer. Batter down
The citadel of Antiochus, while here
We sweep away his altars and his gods.

          SCENE 2. Judah Maccabeus; Jason; Jews

Jews   Lurking among the ruins of the Temple,
Deep in its inner courts, we found this man,
Clad as high priest.

Jud.   I ask not who thou art,
I know thy face, writ over with deceit
As are these tattered volumes of the Law
With heathen images. A priest of God
Wast thou in other days, but thou art now
A priest of Satan. Traitor, thou art Jason.

Jas.   I am thy prisoner, Judah Maccabeus,
And it would ill become me to conceal
My name or office.

Jud.   Over yonder gate
There hangs the head of one who was a Greek.
What should prevent me now, thou man of sin,
From hanging at its side the head of one
Who, born a Jew, hath made himself a Greek?

Jas.   Justice prevents thee.

Jud.   Justice? Thou art stained
With every crime 'gainst which the Decalogue
Thunders with all its thunder.

Jas.   If not justice,
Then mercy, her handmaiden.

Jud.   When hast thou
At any time, to any man or woman,
Or even to any little child, shown mercy?

Jas.   I have but done what King Antiochus
Commanded me.

Jud.   True, thou hast been the weapon
With which he struck; but hast been such a weapon,
So flexible, so fitted to his hand,
It tempted him to strike. So thou hast urged him
To double wickedness, thine own and his.
Where is this king? Is he in Antioch
Among his women still, and from his windows
Throwing down gold by handfuls, for the rabble
To scramble for?

Jas.   Nay, he is gone from there,
Gone with an army into the Far East.

Jud.   And wherefore gone?

Jas.   I know not. For the space
Of forty days almost were horsemen seen
Running in air, in cloth of gold, and armed
With lances, like a band of soldiery;
It was a sign of triumph.

Jud.   Or of death.
Wherefore art thou not with him?

Jas.   I was left
For service in the Temple.

Jud.   To pollute it,
And to corrupt the Jews; for there are men
Whose presence is corruption; to be with them
Degrades us and deforms the things we do.

Jas.   I never made a boast, as some men do,
Of my superior virtue, nor denied

20. Hanukkah lamp. Silver. Frankfort, Germany. Beginning of
eighteenth century.

The weakness of my nature, that hath made me
Subservient to the will of other men.

Jud. Upon this day, the five-and-twentieth day
Of the month Caslan, was the Temple here
Profaned by strangers, by Antiochus
And thee, his instrument. Upon this day
Shall it be cleansed. Thou, who didst lend thyself
Unto this profanation, canst not be
A witness of these solemn services.
There can be nothing clean where thou art present.
The people put to death Callisthenes,
Who burned the Temple gates; and if they find thee
Will surely slay thee. I will spare thy life
To punish thee the longer. Thou shalt wander
Among strange nations. Thou, that hast cast out
So many from their native land, shalt perish
In a strange land. Thou, that hast left so many
Unburied, shalt have none to mourn for thee,
Nor any solemn funerals at all,
Nor sepulcher with thy fathers. Get thee hence!
[*Music. Procession of priests and people, with cithems, harps,
and cymbals. Judah Maccabeus puts himself at their
head, and they go into the inner courts*]

SCENE 3. *Jason alone*

Jas. Through the Gate Beautiful I see them come,
With branches and green boughs and leaves of palm,
And pass into the inner courts. Alas!
I should be with them, should be one of them,
But in an evil hour, an hour of weakness,
That cometh unto all, I fell away
From the old faith, and did not clutch the new,
Only an outward semblance of belief; .
For the new faith I cannot make mine own,
Not being born to it. It hath no root
Within me. I am neither Jew nor Greek,
But stand between them both, a renegade
To each in turn; having no longer faith

In gods or men. Then what mysterious charm,
What fascination is it chains my feet,
And keeps me gazing like a curious child
Into the holy places, where the priests
Have raised their altar? Striking stones together,
They take fire out of them, and light the lamps
In the great candlestick. They spread the veils,
And set the loaves of shewbread on the table.
The incense burns; the well-remembered odor
Comes wafted unto me, and takes me back
To other days. I see myself among them
As I was then; and the old superstition
Creeps over me again! A childish fancy!
And hark! they sing with citherns and with cymbals,
And all the people fall upon their faces,
Praying and worshiping! I will away
Into the East, to meet Antiochus
Upon his homeward journey, crowned with triumph.
Alas! today I would give everything
To see a friend's face, or to hear a voice
That had the slightest tone of comfort in it!

Act 4. The Mountains of Ecbatana

SCENE 1. *Antiochus; Philip; Attendants*

Ant.   Here let us rest awhile. Where are we, Philip?
    What place is this?

Phil.   Ecbatana, my lord;
        And yonder mountain range is the Orontes.

Ant.   The Orontes is my river at Antioch.
    Why did I leave it? Why have I been tempted
    By coverings of gold and shields and breastplates
    To plunder Elymais, and be driven
    From out its gates, as by a fiery blast
    Out of a furnace?

Phil.   These are fortune's changes.

Ant. What a defeat it was! The Persian horsemen
Came like a mighty wind, the wind Khamáseen,
And melted us away, and scattered us
As if we were dead leaves, or desert sand.

Phil. Be comforted, my lord; for thou hast lost
But what thou hadst not.

Ant. I, who made the Jews
Skip like the grasshoppers, am made myself
To skip among these stones.

Phil. Be not discouraged.
Thy realm of Syria remains to thee;
That is not lost nor marred.

Ant. Oh, where are now
The splendors of my court, my baths and banquets?
Where are my players and my dancing women?
Where are my sweet musicians with their pipes,
That made me merry in the olden time?
I am a laughingstock to man and brute.
The very camels, with their ugly faces,
Mock me and laugh at me.

Phil. Alas! my lord,
It is not so. If thou wouldst sleep awhile,
All would be well.

Ant. Sleep from mine eyes is gone,
And my heart faileth me for very care.
Dost thou remember, Philip, the old fable
Told us when we were boys, in which the bear
Going for honey overturns the hive,
And is stung blind by bees? I am that beast,
Stung by the Persian swarms of Elymais.

Phil. When thou art come again to Antioch,
These thoughts will be as covered and forgotten
As are the tracks of Pharaoh's chariot wheels
In the Egyptian sands.

Ant. Ah! when I come
Again to Antioch! When will that be?
Alas! alas!

SCENE 2. *Antiochus; Philip; Messenger*

Mess.   May the king live forever!

Ant.   Who art thou, and whence comest thou?

Mess.   My lord,
          I am a messenger from Antioch,
          Sent here by Lysias.

Ant.   A strange foreboding
          Of something evil overshadows me.
          I am no reader of the Jewish Scriptures;
          I know not Hebrew; but my high priest Jason,
          As I remember, told me of a prophet
          Who saw a little cloud rise from the sea
          Like a man's hand, and soon the heaven was black
          With clouds and rain. Here, Philip, read; I cannot;
          I see that cloud. It makes the letters dim
          Before mine eyes. . . .

Phil. [reading] "We pray thee hasten thy return. The realm
          Is falling from thee. Since thou hast gone from us
          The victories of Judah Maccabeus
          Form all our annals. First he overthrew
          Thy forces at Beth Horon, and passed on,
          And took Jerusalem, the Holy City.
          And then Emmaus fell; and then Beth Sura,
          Ephron and all the towns of Galaad,
          And Maccabeus marched to Carnion."

Ant.   Enough, enough! Go call my chariot men;
          We will drive forward, forward, without ceasing,
          Until we come to Antioch. My captains,
          My Lysias, Gorgias, Seron, and Nicanor,
          Are babes in battle, and this dreadful Jew
          Will rob me of my kingdom and my crown.
          My elephants shall trample him to dust;
          I will wipe out his nation, and will make
          Jerusalem a common burying place,
          And every home within its walls a tomb!

        [*Throws up his hands, and sinks into the arms of attendants,*
          who lay him upon a bank]

Phil.   Antiochus! Antiochus! Alas,
      The king is ill! What is it, O my lord?

Ant.   Nothing. A sudden and sharp spasm of pain,
      As if the lightning struck me, or the knife
      Of an assassin smote me to the heart.
      'Tis passed, even as it came. Let us set forward.

Phil.   See that the chariots be in readiness;
      We will depart forthwith.

Ant.   A moment more.
      I cannot stand. I am become at once
      Weak as an infant. Ye will have to lead me.
      Jove, or whatever name
      Thou wouldst be named—it is alike to me—
      If I knew how to pray, I would entreat
      To live a little longer.

Phil.   O my lord,
      Thou shalt not die; we will not let thee die!

Ant.   How canst thou help it, Philip? Oh, the pain!
      Stab after stab. Thou hast no shield against
      This unseen weapon. God of Israel,
      Since all the other gods abandon me,
      Help me. I will release the Holy City,
      Garnish with goodly gifts the holy Temple.
      Thy people, whom I judged to be unworthy
      To be so much as buried, shall be equal
      Unto the citizens of Antioch.
      I will become a Jew, and will declare
      Through all the world that is inhabited
      The power of God!

Phil.   He faints. It is like death.
      Bring here the royal litter. We will bear him
      Into the camp, while yet he lives.

Ant.   O Philip,
      Into what tribulation am I come!

Alas! I now remember all the evil
That I have done the Jews; and for this cause
These troubles are upon me, and behold
I perish through great grief in a strange land.

Phil. Antiochus! my king!

Ant.   Nay, king no longer.
Take thou my royal robes, my signet ring,
My crown and scepter, and deliver them
Unto my son, Antiochus Eupator;
And unto the good Jews, my citizens,
In all my towns, say that their dying monarch
Wisheth them joy, prosperity, and health.
I who, puffed up with pride and arrogance,
Thought all the kingdoms of the earth mine own,
If I would but outstretch my hand and take them,
Meet face to face a greater potentate,
King Death—Epiphanes—the Illustrious!

                                        [*Dies*[1]

10 HANUKKAH IN MANY LANDS

iiiiiii
=
The Graves of the Maccabees
DAVID SHIMONOWITZ

I sit down to rest on a large stone, smooth and white, growing out of a hill which stands stalwart, peering, like a sentinel to the valley below. Looking down, I see boulders and stones, black and white, arrayed as by some hand; delicate blood-red flowers swaying on their tall stems among the burnished stones; beauty arising from a desolation seared by the sun. Where the valley ends there stands an aged carob tree, many-branched and hedged in with rocks. A stag leaps from stone to stone, springs like a flash round the tree and hides again in the shadow. The sun beats down upon me as I walk on the side of the wall of stones which guards the valley.

It is sunrise as I set out for Modin, birthplace of the Maccabees.

151

I jump from one stone to another along the narrow path. What are the tiny forms I see, moving in the valley? I strain my eyes and discern a group of plowmen following their plows. On the other side of the valley a young shepherd wrapped in lambskin leans on his staff and examines me with curiosity. Lambskin on a hot day like this! He has apparently not yet forgotten the cold of the night; or perhaps it is still cool in the shadow of the hill. My limbs crave for the coolness; but the day is short and I wonder whether I can reach Modin before sunset.

I go forward, uncertain of the way. The path? Scores of paths stretch before me. But in the distance I see a polished mirror flashing and my heart rejoices. It is the sea, and now I know that I am near Modin. It is the highest point from which one may see the sea, many hours distant. I climb higher and see the scattered huts hewn out of the rocks. There is still an hour and a half before the sun sinks.

I reach the village.

How wild the country is! Caves and crags, pits and wells partly covered with stone slabs. The little Maccabees must have played hide-and-seek here. Jonathan, Simon, Johanan: "Find me!" And the hills echo: "Find me!" Jonathan, Simon, Johanan leap like stags from stone to stone, scatter over cave and pit; they look for Judah. Judah, "Where are you?" And the hills echo: "Where are you?" Suddenly he appears, climbing out of his hiding place, laughing. The rays of the setting sun tinge the stones. A shepherd bearing a newborn lamb in his arms is going homeward for his flock. The youngest of the Maccabees leaps up, snatches the flute from the shepherd, runs in front of the flock, frolics and makes merry. His mother stands at the door of the tent, shading her eyes. When she learns the cause of the noise she scolds the mischievous children and smiles. Blue shadows creep down from the hills.

But the graves? Near them stand the ruins of a building, hewn out of the rock. The door has been destroyed; there remain only the pillars, thick with weeds. Behind the wall facing the entrance stands an ancient olive tree with a broad and hollow trunk. I sit in the doorway and recapture from the surrounding stillness snatches of song of the past. It was here perhaps that the mother lion sat and sucked her whelps. Judah lay in her lap and could not sleep. He heard the roar of the sea, the cries of the eagles, the echoes of the hills. The crests of the hills are shadowed; mist has covered the

22. Hanukkah lamp. Silver. Frankfort, Germany. Mid-nineteenth century.

valleys; but the eyes of the child are wide open and fixed on the distance. His mother rocks him slowly. She sings softly:

Sleep, my eagle, sleep
All the world is quiet,
Hushed is all the singing

In the gardens round.
Every ship's asleep
On the mighty sea.
Living things are still;
The eagle on his rock,
The wild goat, the lion.

But the child will not sleep. His ears are open to every sound. The mother sings on:

Sleep, oh, sleep, my son,
The chilly night descends;
When cold of night has gone,
Warm morning will be here.
The honey dew,
The rubied sky,
Living things will waken;
The eagle on his rock,
The wild goat, the lion,
And with them you, my son.

Judah stirs, closes his eyes, opens them again. The mother lowers her voice to a whisper:

Everything is asleep,
Songs are stilled.
And you, my cub,
Will grow to strength.
Suck from my breast,
Grow—hunt the prey,
Grow—become a lion.
Now sleep, my son, sleep.

Judah falls asleep, but she remains sitting, afraid to stir. I too fear to move, lest I wake him from his sleep. Suddenly I jump up as if stung; my imagination is playing tricks with me—had clothed me in woman's form so that for a moment I imagined myself a mother, mother to Judah asleep in his cradle.

The last rays of the sun spread over the great stone which covers the cave of the graves, and are caught in the moss that grows in its cracks. It is evident that the heavy stone could not be rolled away from the mouth of the cave but was moved a little from its place. Here is a narrow oblique opening. I push into the cave; and I am swallowed by darkness.

The roof is covered with the handwriting of visitors. Joseph

Rahamin from Acre, Aaron Moshe from Jerusalem, Haim Herman from Elisavetgrad. I erase the scribbling; no stranger shall intrude in this holy place! Weary and spent I stretch out on the floor.

From the moment that I entered the cave I felt a tightness around my breast, a pain of love. I came to visit my heroes in the name of my childhood which was lit up by their glory and glowed in their splendor. My heart is still filled with awe and overflows with love; but before those inanimate blocks of stone my childhood's blessing is stifled and my heart is no lighter than before.

The olive tree outside becomes enveloped with flame—a huge, wonderful Hanukkah light above the graves of the heroes. The Creator Himself has lit it with the fire of His lightning. But now a wild storm bursts out, a cry of distress from a thousand mouths. Myriads of the brave are treading the hillside, coming to bury their leader. The olive tree burns but is not consumed; sparks dance and flare in the darkness. I feel as if I were bewitched by the sparkling tower of flame. My ears detect a muffled murmur, faroff and unceasing—the dirge of the sea in honor of the brave.

The rain pours down, drums on the stones, falls dully into the dust. I gaze up. There is a large undefined blackness between sky and earth, whispering, pleading, despairing, yet humming with hope, like the hum of a brook in spring. Bands of fire pierce its depth, sink immediately and appear again as distant lights. Now they are lit, now dim again. Are they not Hanukkah lights, flickering in the ends of the earth, from the parched deserts of Yemen to the cold snows of the north, in fogbound Whitechapel and in the new ghetto in New York, in an attic in Paris and in a tent in Polesia? For a moment the stones and the thorns that grow among them flare up into fantastic forms, flare up and recede as if fleeing from sudden terror. The darkness is intense. The olive tree has perished, the lightning has ceased for a moment, and I hear broken sounds of lamentation and the tapping of staffs against the stones. Here they hover, these eternal wanderers, fleeing from Yemen and Russia, from the suffocating atmosphere of Whitechapel and New York; they flit like ghosts from rock to rock, feel their way in the blackness with their staffs—weak, dull tapping as of feebleness, decay, despair.

But why do I tremble, why is my body on fire? How the hills resound, like the ring of hammer on anvil! Here they come, tramping, marching on the heights, the multitudes of the brave bearing their leader to his grave. Is the earth crumbling? Are the graves opening? Hush! I hear a plaintive voice. Who is crying? Ah, I recognize the cry, it is Judah. . . . I am here, I am here![1]

ііііііі
=

Hanukkah among Eastern Jews
DEVORA AND MENAHEM HACOHEN

In Persia little notice was taken of Hanukkah, other than the lighting of candles and the recitation of prayers relative to the occasion, as well as a recounting of the Hasmoneans' deeds. On the first night the candle would be lit by the head of the household; the sons would light the others, so as to become familiar with the ritual. The custom of Hanukkah *gelt* was not observed; instead, children of the poor went from door to door for gifts, in each case burning a wisp of grass in order to discourage the "evil eye" from visiting the household. On the last of the eight nights, the father brought forth a large tray of nuts and roasted seeds, which the children grabbed by the fistful, to be eaten in *heder* on the following day. . . .

In Tunisia the Hanukkah candelabrum was suspended on the doorpost opposite the mezuzah and remained there until Purim. The oil and wick were prepared by the mother or grandmother. Beneath the Hanukkah candelabrum was a page bearing the festival blessings. Rosh Hodesh Tevet, which occurs during Hanukkah, was known as "the New Moon of the Daughters," when girls received gifts from their parents and brides were remembered by the grooms. . . .

In Salonika the Hanukkah menorah was in the form of a triangle, with the eight oil-and-wick holes along the base and the *shammash* at the apex. The theme song of the festival was the thirtieth psalm; the traditional "Rock of Ages" (*Moaz Tzur*) was unknown.

Translated by Israel I. Taslitt[2]

iiiiiii
=

Hanukkah Customs among Sephardic Jews
SOLOMON FEFFER

The Jews of Aleppo, who are descendants of the Sephardim who settled in that city after the Expulsion from Spain, practice a unique Hanukkah custom: they kindle an additional light every evening of the eight days of Hanukkah. Their procedure is as follows: on the first evening they kindle one light and two *shammashim*, the second evening two lights and two *shammashim*, until, on the eighth evening, the lamp is aglow with eight lights and two *shammashim*.

According to Tovia Preschel, the Aleppo Jews possess a tradition that their ancestors, who were expelled from Spain on July 30, 1492, wandered for many months before they found a country that was willing to shelter them. When they finally found a haven in Syria, they vowed to kindle an additional light on Hanukkah in thanksgiving to the Almighty.

During the daylight hours of the eight days of Hanukkah, the Jews of Aleppo also kindle the "Lights of the Chieftains" in their synagogue. During the holiday the daily Torah readings consist of various passages from the seventh chapter of Numbers which describe the sacrifices of the chieftains of Israel during the dedication services of the completed Tabernacle in the wilderness. The Aleppo Jews follow the practice of kindling each morning twelve oil lamps in remembrance of the dedication rite of the chieftains of the twelve tribes.

During the joyous celebration of Hanukkah in Aden, children donned blue garments made especially for the festival. The adults also dressed in blue, and the entire family went to the synagogue for the afternoon service, after which they went home, kindled the Hanukkah lamp, and returned to the synagogue for the evening prayers. Thus all the lamps appeared illuminated at the same moment, creating a festive air over the entire city because the burnished copper Hanukkah lamps were all suspended from the doors of the houses. As the people left the synagogue, they were greeted with the noise of explosions and the odor of burning sulfur. These came from the fireworks, "bombs," and matches which were continuously ignited and exploded. The children trembled with joy mingled with trepidation at the strange sounds and beautiful sights.

In Yemen every child was presented with a coin each day of Hanukkah. With this gift he purchased a tiny bag of sugar and a pinch of a red coloring powder. With the sugar and the red powder he prepared a small bottle of sweet red liquid—a sort of "wine"— which was called "Hanukkah drink." The mothers cooked a special Hanukkah delicacy made of peas or lentils. In the evening the little boys and girls of the neighborhood assembled in one of the homes, near the entrance where the Hanukkah lamp was lit, bringing their "wine" and the special Hanukkah dish. The lady of the house spread old rugs on the ground and the children sat down to enjoy their Hanukkah repast. The meal was followed by a verse, sung to the tune of the Simhat Torah hymn "*Mippi El*":

> O Hanukkah, Hanukkah, I look to thee and yearn;
> Do not from me, I pray, thy lovely face upturn.

Every evening a different home was the scene of the neighborhood celebration.

In some Sephardic communities the seventh night of Hanukkah is traditionally dedicated to Jewish women to commemorate their notable bravery during the Maccabean period. Today's Jewish women, and their daughters who are included in the festivity marking this occasion, recall the stories of the martyrdom of Hannah and her seven sons and the heroic act of the beautiful Judith. The women thus feel that they are entitled to special prerogatives. In some communities of North Africa the women and girls filled the synagogue, withdrew the scrolls of the Law from the ark and, each in turn, kissed the scrolls. The rabbi, extending his arm over each of the women and girls, recited the benediction: "He who blessed our matriarchs Sarah, Rebecca, Rachel, and Leah, etc." A special prayer, invoking the Almighty's protection of the ladies, was also intoned. After this ceremony, the evening service was read and the Hanukkah lamp was kindled. Then the women ate cheese dishes and engaged in singing and dancing.

In Salonika girls who were angry with each other would be reconciled as is done on the eve of the Day of Atonement.

Many women refrain from working throughout the eight-day festival, being especially careful to avoid doing needlework, laundry, and other household chores.

In Hebron the Feast of Lights was observed in private and public celebrations which continued all eight days. There were special games to celebrate the occasion. One, called *"Caraça de Sal"* (salt face, i.e., pale bonfire), was played as follows. In a large tub were placed bran, ashes, and a little salt. Then brandy was added and the mixture, after being stirred, was ignited. The lights in the room were extinguished. The faces of the participants, who stood around the tub, now appeared starkly white. Then began the singing, accompanied by gestures and shrieks. In addition, some of the participants barked and others bleated like sheep. There was no limit to the excitement.

Food was collected for public and family dinners, the most important of which was the dinner arranged by the communal society for the children of the schools. The children, too, participated in the gathering of the food, which they commenced on the first day of Hanukkah. Armed with miniature rifles—marking them as Maccabean soldiers—they "shot" and looted and sang, urging the ladies of the households to subscribe liberally to the feast:

Give us heaps of flour;
Your lives will ne'er go sour.
Give us jars of oil;
The Lord your foes will foil.

Other children recited biblical verses containing references to food, translating them into Ladino for those matrons who did not understand Hebrew. If, by chance, the contribution fell short of the expected, the lusty youngsters did not hesitate to remind the reluctant donor of Jacob's gift to Esau: "200 she-goats and 20 he-goats; 200 ewes and 20 rams; 30 milch camels with their colts; 40 cows and 10 bulls; 20 she-asses and 10 he-asses" (Genesis 32.15–16)—the verses cantillated in Hebrew and translated into Ladino. The group did not stir from the house until the desired quota of flour, sugar, oil, or coal was reached. With the "spoils," nightly Hanukkah dinners were enjoyed.

On the seventh day the family celebrations came to a halt and preparations were begun for the great banquet. From the early morning hours the yeshivah students congregated in the streets, carrying burning candles, "shooting" their guns and singing:

Prepare the meals and the great celebration,
When all will share in the Feast of Dedication.

When they reached the home of the president of the community, he lovingly recited the biblical blessing: "The Angel who has redeemed me from all harm—/Bless the lads" (Genesis 48.16) and presented to the *shammash* of the school a sum to be used for the great occasion.

The following day, the final day of Hanukkah, the scene of the celebration shifted to the yeshivah. Every boy came provided with a plate and spoon. The envied one was the possessor of the largest plate. Seated on mats along the walls in opposite rows, each child caught a loaf of bread deftly thrown by the *shammash*. Then the latter's son entered with a large kettle filled with roasted meat and placed a portion on each plate together with sauce. He was followed by his mother, carrying a large tub chock-full of saffron-colored rice perfumed with mouth-watering spices. Immediately there was the sound of rattling plates as they came up empty and descended full to the brim with the delicious mixture. The final touch was a sauce of kidney beans ladled out by the daughter of the *shammash*.

At the conclusion of the dinner the yeshivah supervisor—who throughout the year was the chief examiner of the students—entered, followed by a group of lads carrying pitchers of wine. Each student received a cup, recited the benediction, and, after drinking, joined in the general dancing.

Joyously singing the Grace after Meals in their clear, lusty voices, the pupils stressed particularly the blessing for the land of Israel and ended the Hasmonean festival with a heartfelt: "Next year in a rebuilt Jerusalem!"[3]

iiiiiii
=

Lights in the Frankfort Judengasse
HEINRICH HEINE

As we walked that same evening again through the Judengasse and resumed the conversation about its inhabitants, the well of the Börne spirit was overflowing the more gleefully. For that street, too, which in the daytime presented a gloomy appearance, was then illuminated most cheerfully, and the children of Israel, as my guide informed me, were celebrating their joyous Feast of Lights that evening. It was instituted in the past as an everlasting remembrance of the victory which the Maccabees had won so valiantly in their war against the king of Syria.

"You see," said Börne, "this is October the 18th of the Jews; only that this Maccabean 18th of October is more than two thousand years old and is still being celebrated, whereas the Leipzig 18th of October has not passed the fifteenth year yet and has already been forgotten. The Germans should go to school at Madame Rothschild's in order to learn patriotism. You see, in this little house there lives this woman, Letitia, who gave birth to so many Bonapartes of finance, the great mother of all public loans. But in spite of the world empire of her royal sons, she still will not abandon her little ancestral castle in the Judengasse, and today, because of the great feast of rejoicing, she adorned her windows with white curtains. How happily these little lights sparkle, which she kindled with her own hands, in order to celebrate that day of victory when Judah Maccabee and his brothers liberated their fatherland with the same courage and heroism which Friedrich Wilhelm, Alexander, and Franz II displayed in our own day. When this noble woman looks at these lights, tears come to her old eyes, and she recalls with melancholy delight those younger days when the late Meyer Anschel Rothschild, her beloved husband, would celebrate the Feast of Lights with her, and when her sons were still little fellows and placed little candles on the ground and jumped to and fro about them, as it is a custom in Israel."

Translated by Israel Tabak[4]

iiiiiiii
=

Hanukkah Festival in London's Whitechapel
A. B. LEVY

The Rivoli Cinema is in ruins. One remembers, before the Germans literally brought down the roof, how the children at mammoth Hanukkah parties were invited to do so metaphorically by chairmen who called for cheers for the good lady who presented the prizes.

Twenty-four hundred children would attend, from classes of the Jewish Religious Education Board. Sabbath school choirs would sing. Film comedies were screened and brought shrieks of delight from the little ones. Stepney's mayor, in his chain of office, beamed at them from the platform. A rabbi told them about the valiant Maccabeans who rescued the Temple from the Syrian foe and rekindled the perpetual lamp with a little oil that lasted miraculouly for eight days. And a boy ascended the platform to light the candles in commemoration of that event and, in a sweet soprano, sang the blessings appropriate to this Feast of Lights.

The great audience chanted the popular Hanukkah hymn—and two or three of the youngsters, after singing the first three Hebrew words, may have rhymed them impiously with "The cat's in the cupboard and you can't catch me." But the profanity passed unnoticed in the general singing, and the naughty ones, at the end of the celebration, were given bags of fruit and sweets to take home, just like the rest of the children.[5]

iiiiiiii
=

Hanukkah in a Lithuanian Ghetto
A. S. SACHS

Foggy, rainy, windy autumn is past. Outside it is cold but dry. The frozen snow crunches under foot. The marketplace is filled with sleighs which move about smoothly and quietly without any of the creaking and rattling made by wagons. Business is pretty good. The smooth roads bring many peasants from nearby villages. Goods are being sold, old debts settled, new ones incurred. The marketplace is all abustle. People are free with their money. When pockets jingle, hearts grow lighter; the clouds clear away from the faces; gloom disappears; the stooping, broken figures straighten up.

Long before they had supplied themselves with warm clothing they began wearing lined boots so that the cold was no longer unbearable. On the contrary, all drank in the exhilarating, dry, frosty air. In the houses the double windows had been put up, all holes in the walls had been plastered up and in the cracks of the doors were stuffed strips of old sheepskin which allowed no wind to get through. The stoves had already grown accustomed to the turf and no longer smoked. True, the price of wood had gone down, but then it was not so bad to use the turf for heating. Brozova wood gives out a wholesome, genial warmth which refreshes and penetrates all your limbs, when you come in from the cold into the warm room. It is so pleasant to sit at home, if the lamp does not smoke but gives out a fine bright flame. All payments have been made. The house is warm and light. What more can a Jew wish for?

You sit before an open Gemara, a copy of the *Hatzefirah* or some other work, a pipe in your mouth, telling stories about Antiochus, the tyrant, who oppressed our forefathers and wanted to annihilate them, until the Hasmoneans arose and threw off the yoke of the stranger. You talk about the past and then again you think of the present. . . . "Why does not a Judah Maccabeus arise today?" you wonder, "to free us from the enemy, from the tormentors of Israel?"

Our fathers and our *rebbes* were always so preoccupied around Hanukkah time that they paid no attention to the pranks played on the sliding ponds. The river was frozen and we had a jolly old time on the glassy ice. We performed all sorts of tricks. We skated on our soles and on the edges of our heels which were covered with iron plates. We were experts at fancy skating. We tumbled about and were ashamed to admit that we had been hurt.

In ordinary times we would have been severely punished by the *rebbe* for such goings-on. But on Hanukkah he pretended not to see and winked at all our pranks. "Well, let them know what Hanukkah stands for. Let them know that there once lived a Judah, a Mattathias," the *rebbe* would say good-naturedly when anyone came to him with a complaint that we were turning the river upside down and that a troop of *shekatzim* was about to pounce upon us.

The *rebbe* knew there was no danger; that on Hanukkah we were full of prowess, we, the descendants of the Hasmoneans, in whose veins flowed the blood of Judah the Maccabee. We would beat them. He would therefore not pester us with the usual questions about where we had been and what we had done. Besides, the *rebbe* didn't think it wise to quarrel with us at this time of the year. He knew that we were to bring him Hanukkah money.

On Hanukkah every Jew is filled with pride and energy, with lust for strife and with prowess. The ancient Hasmoneans implanted in us the hope for a good future. Since Antiochus, in his might, had not succeeded in wiping the Jews off the map, no other tyrant would succeed in doing so. The Jewish light, the true, pure, and holy light, can never be extinguished by our oppressors. One vessel of oil is always hidden in the innermost chambers of the Jewish soul. And when all other oils shall grow stale and unholy, then, by a miracle, that small vessel of oil will illumine our dark Galut path. . . .

During the week of Hanukkah all dressed in their good clothes. The stores closed earlier, and if the keeper of the store happened to be your mother, then she would close before *Maariv* so as to see your father light the candles. Then she would stay in the house for the rest of the evening, and neighbors, friends, and relatives would drop in to chat for a while. Your father would become engrossed in a game of chess. The younger people would play cards and the little ones would play other games.

About eight or nine o'clock all would gather about the table to eat the potato pudding which had to come out well in honor of Hanukkah. We sat about the table and chatted good-naturedly. The Jew likes to talk about everything and nothing. But all year round he has no time for talk. The same Abraham Hirsh, the sexton, who even on Purim refused to stay at the house a moment after he had received his Purim money, would on Hanukkah bend back the collar of his greatcoat, blow out the light of his lantern, sit down at the table, and drink and chat: "Hanukkah is long enough—I'll manage," he would answer, when asked whether he had time enough.

There was very little Gemara-studying on Hanukkah. Even the yeshivah students would spend the Hanukkah days in jesting and fooling about. In the evenings the yeshivah students would climb up into the women's synagogue and play cards. The head

23. Hanukkah lamp. Silver. Germany. 1814.

of the yeshivah and the rabbi knew of this, but they said not a word. . . .

The greatest day of Hanukkah was the day when the fifth candle was lit. On that day, everybody had to get Hanukkah money. This was the last day on which this could be done and no one was allowed to put it off. Immediately after morning prayers, we youngsters would put on our warm clothes, the servant would wrap mufflers about our necks and put warm gloves on our hands. Then we would be warned not to go off to the river and begin sliding, lest we fall and hurt ourselves. We went to our relatives for Hanukkah money.

First of all we went to our grandfather, then to our uncle, Yankel Yoshe, then to Aunt Breine and so on, without forgetting a single relative.

At Aunt Breine's we weren't made very happy. Before giving us the money she would shower us with questions: How is mother? What is father doing? Who was at the house last night? What did mother serve? Did Yente send the goose for Friday? Was mother going to bake a potato pudding? Did we give the sexton Hanukkah money? And so forth. And this was not enough. She would take off our mufflers and gloves and treat us to her wonderful pancakes which melt in your mouth! . . .

Finally we were seated at the table and began eating pancakes, impatiently waiting at the same time for the Hanukkah money. As soon as we got the money we shot out of aunt's house, to avoid further questioning. After leaving aunt's house we no longer kept our hands in our gloves, but put them into the pockets of our coats, where the Hanukkah money lay. We didn't walk. We skipped along, getting keen joy out of the jingle of the coins at each step.

For the older generation the day of the fifth candle was a great day. It was the concert of the year. In the evening the cantor and his assistants sang the prayer for the lighting of the candles in the bet ha-midrash, and the town band played all sorts of merry tunes for the rest of the evening. The bet ha-midrash was crowded. The people were all in holiday spirit. All cracked jokes at the expense of Antiochus and his downfall, and talked about the present oppressions and hoped that the oppressors would meet with the same fate as did the ancient one. The cantor said *Maariv,* singing the entire service.

The tune which the cantor sang on lighting the candles was a lively one—a sort of triumphal march, which was later sung at all weddings and other celebrations. When the cantor rested, the band would play songs of triumph and victory. They played the best music they knew. The concert lasted until midnight and then the people, happy, proud, triumphant, would go home filled with joy and hope. During the last three days whenever father lit the candles the children would sing the cantor's tune, just as he had sung it when lighting the fifth candle. The father and children sang. The mother set the table for the members of the family and the guests who were expected. The Hanukkah candles burned brightly and were reflected in the windowpanes.

The Hanukkah candles were small, but they lighted up a great part of our history. They took us back to a time two thousand years ago. And like sun rays falling on dry grass, so did the memories of that tune brighten up and illumine the sad, dark life in the long, dreary Yiddish Galut.

Translated by Harold Berman[6]

iiiiiiii
=

The Festival of the Maccabees in Svislovitz
SHMARYA LEVIN

The first Festival of the Maccabees which I remember fell in the midst of a furious winter, which had "fastened" the rivers in a silent rage, and laid an invisible, bitter hand on the town. The cold burned intensely, the houses dripped icicles throughout the winter months. The chief preparation for the Festival of the Maccabees—at least, as far as the youngsters were concerned—consisted in the making of the tiny leaden tops, four-sided, with a grip protruding at the upper end—the traditional game for this festival. The making of leaden tops was no easy enterprise, and it belonged to the older boys. My brother Meyer was one of the principal manufacturers. The mold was made of four pieces of wood, one for each side, and within the mold had to be cut out—in reverse, of course—the four Hebrew letters which appeared in rotation on the sides of the top: *nun, gimel, he, shin*—*Nes gadol hayah sham*, "A great miracle happened there," an allusion to the drops of oil in the Eternal Light of the Temple, which burned for eight days while the Maccabees were driving the enemy before them. Above and below the mold tapered off into thin lines, to make the grip and the base of the top: then the mold was tied together with cord, and molten lead was poured in from above. It had to be done quickly, because the spoon was of some alloy which melted easily. It had to be done skillfully, too, or else some of the lead would be poured out over the fingers which were holding the mold. And more than one boy would be seen round the festival, carrying a bandaged hand as evidence of his clumsiness. With these tops we played a special game which resembles American put-and-take. As a rule we played for the fun of it; but sometimes we played for money. And this was our introduction to gambling games, later concentrated in cards.

The most moving ceremony of the Feast of the Maccabees is the lighting of the candles. On the first night one candle is lit, on the second two, on the third three—and so on till the end of the eight days which commemorate the period during which the unfed lamp continued burning miraculously in the Temple. The candles were short, grooved, and prettily colored. But the first few nights the ceremony made no impression on me. The fact was that Hanukkah was not then regarded as one of the important festivals in the Jewish calendar. The miracle of the inexhaustible oil in the Eternal Light did not seem to grip the imagination of the Jews, who had become accustomed to miracles on a larger and more imposing scale. And for some reason or other they told us little about the heroic wars of the Maccabees—little or nothing at all. The rabbis were not interested in wars, and pious Jews had the same tastes. It was only years later, with the rise of the forerunner of the Zionist movement—the Hibat Zion, or Love of Zion—that the wheel made a half turn, and Hanukkah became one of the great and important nationalist festivals of the Jewish people. It was then that the lighting of the candles became a significant and moving ceremony.

Translated by Maurice Samuel[7]

iiiiiii
=

Kindling the Lights in Vitebsk, Russia
BELLA CHAGALL

"Children, where are you all? Mendl, Avreml, Bashke, where have you all got lost?" Mother's high voice is heard from the shop. "Where do you run about for whole days? Come, Father is waiting with the Hanukkah lights."

Where would we be? We are standing and warming ourselves at the stove. The day has almost gone. It is now dark. So we are waiting for the shop to be closed.

Mother runs out of the shop like a culprit, apologizes to herself: "Today is a sort of holiday, and I'm still tangled up in the shop. Let us at least gather the children and bless the Hanukkah lights."

All together we go to the big room, where Father is waiting for us.

The room, although large, has only one small window. Father stands with his back to the window, and the scant light from outside is quite shut out. So all of us are standing in darkness, waiting for the little taper to be lighted. . . .

The Hanukkah lamp is small, almost like a toy. But how many things are carved on its tiny silver wall!

In the center are two lions with fiery heads, open mouths; with their legs upraised they hold up the outspread tables of the Law. The tablets are blank, without a single letter on them, but they give forth a light as though they were packed full of sacred wisdom inside.

Around the lions there is a garden. It blooms, a real paradise— it has little vines with grapes, and familiar fruit fallen from the trees. A pair of birds peep out from the branches. And even a big serpent crawls there.

At either side of the paradise there stand on watch two silver pitchers, tiny too, but with fat, stuffed little bellies. They see to it that the paradise does not lack oil. And to gladden one's eyes there is under the lions and birds a little bridge, divided into eight little goblets that are waiting for a flame to go up from them. Father's white hands move among the goblets. From one—Father begins with the first—he pulls out a tiny wick; then he tips a pitcher and pours a drop of oil into the goblet. The wick drinks in the oil, becomes soft and white, almost like a candle.

Father says a benediction and lights the wick. Only one light. Father does not even touch the other goblets. All seven of them stand as though superfluous, empty and cold.

It is not festive at all with only one light burning. My heart tightens, as though—God forbid—a memorial candle were burning.

Its flame is so little that it could be put out with one whiff. No reflection falls from the light onto the dark floor. Even the wall of the paradise is not much illumined. Of the two lions, only one receives a little warmth from below, the other does not even know that something is burning beside him.

My parents and my brothers have gone. I approach the light; I try to pull up its wick, hoping to brighten its flame. But there is nothing that I can grasp with my hand. I singe my fingers. The little flame burns, faints, flickers, trembles all the time. At any moment it will go out; it makes an effort to rise upward at least once, to lick a grape on the silver wall, or to warm one foot of the carved lion.

Suddenly, one after another, drops of thick oil begin to fall from the taper; they clog the little opening of the goblet, and they smother the little flame. The wick begins to smoke and smears the woodwork of the window.

A fresh gray stain is added to the stains that have remained on the window frame since last year's Hanukkah. All the stains shine above the solitary light, almost outshine the light itself. And when the big chandelier is lighted, the large flame of the lamp blows away the last breath of the Hanukkah light.

Why are Mother's Sabbath candles tall and large? And why does big Father bless such a tiny Hanukkah light?

Translated by Norbert Guterman[8]

iiiiiiii
=

Hanukkah in a Nineteenth-Century American Home

ESTHER J. RUSKAY

A broad, roomy kitchen of a sort not found in modern houses. Half of the wall on one side is taken up by a quaint, old-fashioned bake oven; the remaining space is filled by a large-size modern range.

Around the open grate hang long-handled shovels and pokers, and above, on a shelf, rests the coffee roaster, a cylinder of sheet iron, which, turned by the children once a week, sends a delicious fragrance of roasting beans through the house. . . .

Bridget, the servant of fifteen years' standing, has just put away the supper dishes, and, after hanging up the last dish towel, turns and makes a dash for the hearth. "Up wid yez, childern; the Grandmother wants the kitchen tonight to make Hanukkah candles." Before they can demur, she has seized, first one pink-toed youngster, then another, and borne them off in triumph, one under each arm, upstairs, where, after tucking them into bed, she listens to them lisp the "*Shema Yisrael,*" prompting the sleepy voices and demanding repetition when the familiar words do not sound correct to her devout Catholic ear.

Meanwhile the aspect of the kitchen has changed. Grandmother, with three or four old friends, has taken possession. All of them have been well tried in life's furnace, and have issued therefrom dim as to vision, but clear as to soul; a little strict perhaps in their religious demands upon themselves and the younger people, but full of zeal and love for their faith—so full, indeed, that each day is measured only by the number of good deeds it can hold, of service to the needy and destitute, of ministering to the sick and dying.

Upon a side table lie many balls of soft, white twine, which the older boys and girls are twisting into regular lengths, while Grandmother and her cheerful, garrulous friends break the big round cakes of hard yellow wax into small pieces. Later the children help to warm these pieces before the fire, after which, with the length of the kitchen stretching between, they hold the ends of the twine, keeping it taut and stiff while the experienced elders roll the lumps of wax about the twine.

Very gently the aged palms work, and mold the wax that must be free from flaws and impurities, for were not the Maccabees and their victorious hosts careful, before dedicating the Temple, which had been spoiled by the Syrians, that only the purest oil should be used to celebrate their victory? And when the twine is covered evenly and smoothly along its whole polished yellow length, clip, clip, clip, go the scissors next to the yardstick measured against the thin golden line, and clip, clip, again into smaller and still smaller sizes, after which the young people gather them together in even heaps, tying them into neat bundles of forty-four, which bundles are subse-

quently to be presented to friends far and near for the home celebration of Hanukkah. . . .

On the first night of Hanukkah, each child is presented with a
funny little top, called a trendel, which he may twirl round sharply,
and watch as it spins itself out. It is sure to fall with one of its sides
uppermost, and as each side bears a raised Hebrew letter, the
fun of the game hinges upon which letter the player turns up to
view. . . .

Such were some of the preparations for what was to be to young
and old among the descendants of the Maccabee warriors a glad
festival week. After this followed days of cleaning and refurbishing,
of baking and cooking; for most certainly a whole week of games,
of music and song, of gathering together of the various family clans
could not well be lived through without an abundance of the good
things of life. In all these pleasures the children were allowed their
full share.

Nor were the poor forgotten. Fortunate winners in any of the
games of chance (which, by the way, because fully permitted and
enjoyed during this one week of Hanukkah, never suggested themselves as an indulgence during the rest of the year) were compelled
to put half of their winnings into the boxes fastened upon the inside
of the closet door, the one marked PALESTINE, the contents of which
were taken out twice a year and sent to Zion, the other for the home
poor.

Each evening, after the lighting of the candles, the children's
tuneful voices mingled with the deeper ones of the elders in the
grand old harmony of the Hanukkah hymn, and before the tiny wax
tapers had begun to burn down in their sockets, and even while the
shammash was still sending up his sputtering appreciation of his
position in front, the children, helped and abetted by the older
folks, entered upon an evening of such unrestricted enjoyment and
pleasant family intercourse as is rarely witnessed in these too-busy
and too-enlightened days.[9]

24. *Hanukkah lamp. Brass. Designed and executed by Ludwig Y. Wolpert.
New York. Contemporary.*

iiiiiiii
=

With American Soldiers in World War II
ZELDA POPKIN

The Marines had come back from the capture of Tarawa. They were
encamped on an island in the central Pacific, on a ridge three thousand feet above sea level, tough, seasoned fighters who had lived
with death and yet had not forgotten how to cherish the gentle
things that belong to home.

Chaplain Jacob Philip Rudin had traveled the tortuous, corkscrew "little Burma Road" to their mountain encampment, to celebrate with them the festival that honors another group of valiant warriors against tyranny—the Maccabees. The chapel was a tent, sides rolled up, open to the whistling mountain winds. The pulpit was a home-made table, covered with a blanket. There were no chairs. The men stood around in a semicircle. There were no electric lights. It was necessary to hold Hanukkah services early, to be finished before the sun went down.

Chaplain Rudin filled the menorah with the little orange candles, so that the barren pulpit would look less bleak. He lighted the *shammash* and the single candle for the first night of Hanukkah. The men recited the blessings, sang "Rock of Ages." The Jewish Welfare Board's Hanukkah gifts were distributed.

The service and the daylight came to an end together. The *shammash* and the single candle burned bravely against the encroaching night. "Then," Chaplain Rudin wrote, "a lovely and unexpected thing happened. As we stood there in the semigloom and as I was finishing my talk, the wind blew through the tent and it set the flame flickering from side to side in the closely set rank of candles. And while we watched, the entire menorah was ablaze. I let it burn. It was as though we were sharing together all the eight days of the festival in one sudden, miraculous moment.

"It was night now but atop that distant mountain and in the midst of war, all the lights of Hanukkah gleamed through the darkness and made it bright with their golden message of courage and faith and hope."

On Hanukkah, the Jew is fully prepared to believe in miracles. He retells the story of the tiny vessel of oil which burned eight days and assures himself that when a man has faith anything can happen—even Hanukkah latkes in the jungle. When Chaplain Seligson visited with the soldiers at isolated outposts in Assam, he found their memories of the traditional observance were poignant. His box of JWB religious supplies contained the candles and menorah, but holiday latkes were only a fond dream. The makings were nonexistent. Who had ever seen fresh eggs in the jungle?

Suddenly, the miracle began to happen. A new unit moved into the area, bringing a Jewish mess sergeant who had in civilian life made knishes and latkes. He furnished willingness and a recipe. The chaplain went out to find the ingredients.

Investigation revealed that in the village of the Naga hillmen, chickens had been seen. These naked headhunters had been known from time to time to bring eggs into the native bazaars. Chaplain Seligson changed his paper rupees into silver and haggled with the headhunters. Volunteers, for once pleased to do KP, began to peel endless sacks of potatoes. Mess Sergeant Levine brought his aides, McAllister and McCoy, and mass production of GI latkes commenced. . . .

Officers and soldiers stationed near London decided to reverse the familiar procedure of accepting the holiday hospitality of the local community and to act as hosts themselves. As their guests for a Hanukkah party they chose 120 Jewish orphans who had lost their parents in the blitz of London's East End, and held their party at the orphanage. Chaplain Judah Nadich told the story of the festival and led the singing of Hanukkah songs. Mickey Mouse films were shown and gifts distributed. Most welcome were gifts donated by the servicemen themselves—candy, cookies, chewing gum—rare and almost priceless delicacies, saved by the men from their rations and packages from home, and presented as Hanukkah *gelt*.

In the evening, impressive services were held at the Bevis Marks Synagogue, in London, the oldest synagogue in the English-speaking world. Jewish soldiers of the American forces joined with their allies from Britain, Canada, France, Czechoslovakia, Poland, and Holland, heard chaplains of the United Nations conduct the festival service with the choir of the Great Synagogue.

To this stirring religious military service, there is vivid contrast in the celebration which Chaplain Edward T. Sandrow reported from Alaska. The Arctic weather is bitter, the Arctic night long and inky black. Across the ice, the heavy boots of scores of soldiers crunched —men in parkas, mukluks, fur hats, manborne fortresses against snow and sleet. They crowded the warm, lighted mess hall whose windows were blacked out by the thick rime of heat within and frost outside. Tables were set. Volunteer army cooks (a medical corps lieutenant and several enlisted men) dished up latkes and gefilte fish.

"All activity is temporarily halted as we light the Hanukkah lights," the chaplain wrote. "A mood of seriousness, of historical reflection pervades the atmosphere. For a moment we forget our war. We are transplanted in time and space to Judea. We praise God for a military and spiritual victory which in its time brought surcease to Jewish pain. We sing "*Maoz Tzur*" and "Rock of Ages." There is hope in the air. There are dreams of victories to come, of a return to home and loved ones, of happiness in all its potential richness.

"Then a babel of sounds bursts forth, shrieks, laughter. The gefilte fish and GI latkes are on the table. They are rapidly consumed. More songs follow. Then instrumental music by a captain and a corporal. The Hanukkah lights themselves seem to dance. We play dreidel for small stakes. The dreidels themselves are works of art. The candles sweat and droop and play along with us. Reluctantly, the evening comes to a close. Self-appointed KP's begin the job of cleaning the mess hall. We sing "America" and "*Hatikvah*." The men start filing out. They are well fortified against cold and darkness. In the midst of war, they have celebrated Hanukkah 5704/1943, linked to a deathless, vibrant way of life."[10]

iiiiiiii
=

Miracles for a Broken Planet
CHAIM POTOK

Hanukkah is the Festival of Lights. It commemorates an ancient Jewish rebellion against oppression, during which the Temple in Jerusalem was miraculously recaptured from pagan hellenizers and rededicated to the worship of God. The candles of Hanukkah celebrate that rededication. They also help brighten the long winter nights.

But I remember a Hanukkah when darkness almost overpowered the light.

It was the first week of November 1938. The final years of the Depression lay like a polluting mist across the streets of New York. On afternoons when it did not rain I would play on the sidewalk in front of the plate-glass window of the candy store near our apartment house. The bubble of darkness on the other side of the world bumped only vaguely against my consciousness. I was very young then, interested more in Flash Gordon and Buck Rogers than Adolf Hitler.

One afternoon I was near the candy store, in the cardboard box that was my rocket ship, when an elderly couple walked slowly by; I caught some of their frightened words. Before supper that evening I saw my mother standing over the kitchen sink, her head bowed, and heard her whispering agitatedly to herself. Later, my father came home from work, drenched in weariness; he turned on the radio and became wearier still.

That night I lay awake in my bed and saw the pieces of the day come together and form a portrait of terror.

A Jewish boy had shot a German, the old people had said. We will pay dearly for it, very dearly.

The boy had been sent by his parents to live with his uncle in Paris, my father had murmured. Then his parents were deported to Poland.

The boy went out of his mind, my mother had said in a voice full of fear. He did not know what he was doing.

He wanted to kill the German ambassador, my father had said. He wanted the world to know about the suffering of Germany's Jews. Inside the embassy he made a mistake and shot and wounded a subordinate instead.

He was out of his head with grief, my mother had said. He could not have known what he was doing.

I lay very still in my bed, thinking of the boy who had shot the German and wondering what the Germans would do to the Jews. Two days later the subordinate died.

In the weeks that followed I dreamed about the synagogues that were burning all over Germany, about the Jews who were being sent to concentration camps, about the looted stores and smashed shop-windows, One day I stood in front of our apartment house and imagined our street littered with glass, shattered glass everywhere, the plate-glass window of the candy store splattered across the sidewalk, the store itself burned and gutted. I imagined the entire block, the neighborhood, the city heaped with broken glass and thick with the stench of fire. The days of that November and December began to go dark, until it seemed all the world would soon be of shades of darkness: dark sun and dark moon, dark sky and dark earth, dark night and dark day. I was a child then, but I still remember that darkness as a malevolence I could touch and smell, an evil growth draining my world of its light.

My world seemed thick with that darkness when Hanukkah came that year on the twenty-fifth of December.

I remember my father chanting the blessings over the first candle on the first night of the festival. He was short and balding, and he chanted in a thin, intense voice. I stood between him and my mother, gazing at the flame of the first night's candle. The flame seemed pitiful against the malignant darkness outside our window. I went to bed and was cold with dread over the horror of the world.

The next night two candles were lighted. Again my father chanted the blessings before the lighting and the prayer that follows when the candles are burning: "We kindle these lights on account of the miracles, the deliverances, and the wonders which Thou didst work for our fathers. . . . During all eight days of Hanukkah these lights are sacred. . . . We are only to look at them, in order that we may give thanks unto Thy Name for Thy miracles, Thy deliverances and Thy wonders."

I wanted a miracle. But there were no miracles during that Hanukkah. Where was God? I kept dreaming of burning synagogues.

On the eighth and final night of the festival I stood with my parents in front of the burning candles. The darkness mocked their light. I could see my parents glancing at me. My mother sighed. Then my father murmured my name.

"You want another miracle?" he asked wearily.

I did not respond.

"Yes," he said. "You want another miracle." He was silent a moment. Then he said, in a gentle, urging voice, "I also want another miracle. But if it does not come, we will make a human miracle. We will give the world the special gifts of our Jewishness. We will not let the world burn out our souls."

The candles glowed feebly against the dark window.

"Sometimes I think man is a greater miracle-maker than God," my father said tiredly, looking at the candles. "God does not have to live day after day on this broken planet. Perhaps you will learn to make your own miracles. I will try to teach you how to make human miracles."

I lay awake a long time that night and did not believe my father could ever teach me that. But now, decades later, I think he taught me well. And I am trying hard to teach it to my own children.[11]

iiiiiiii
=

Hanukkah in a Monastery
ISAAC NEUMAN

In the hard winter of 1940 I was seventeen years old. In my hometown in Poland, there was no coal for us Jews of the ghetto. Day after
day, I would rise early in the morning to queue up at one of the coal
dealers, waiting patiently for my turn. However, since the supply of
coal was limited, and the Germans and the Poles were given theirs
first, by the time I reached the gate there was never anything left.

One day as I was returning from hours of waiting in the coal line,
I took a different route home. The temperature was far below zero,
and a biting wind blew in my face. As I was passing a little monastery, I decided to enter and thaw my half-frozen limbs. A kindly
monk asked me whether I wanted food. When I nodded, he mo-
tioned to me to follow him. He led me through a long, dark corridor
and into a pig shed. He asked me to wait there, and promised to
return soon with some hot soup. . . .

The monk returned with a steaming pot of potato soup. I squatted
on the floor, and my nostrils were filled with a mixture of hot
potatoes and onions, as well as odors of the pigsty. When I finished
my soup, the monk handed me a small piece of bread. I broke it into
little pieces and used it to wipe out every last bit of the potatoes.
When this was done, I licked the spoon until it was completely dry.
My hunger was only half quelled, for I had not had a good meal in
days. I thanked my newly found friend and asked him if there was
any work for me on the premises. He hesitated. Finally he said that
if I didn't mind sleeping with the pigs, I could stay awhile, doing odd
jobs around the place. But on one condition, that I never go beyond
the monastery gate.

I agreed.

I immediately started on my job, which consisted, among other
things, of tending the ovens, cleaning the kitchen, and catering to
the needs of the pigs. . . .

From time to time I would be called away from my routine work
and asked to substitute for one of the altar boys inside the chapel
of Saint Martin. I enjoyed this new status but it made me feel ill at
ease. I felt somewhat hypocritical, as a Jewish boy, carrying a big

portrait of the Madonna and standing on the altar together with the faithful. At times my lips would mumble a Hebrew prayer while the brethren carried on the mass.

As December approached, I became more restless than ever. Memories of home and the festival of Hanukkah at Grandmother's house flooded my heart, I could not help remembering Grandfather shining the brass menorah, and all the grandchildren preparing the wicks. I remembered the sweet smell of Grandmother's pancakes and of the Palestinian olive oil used for frying them as well as in the menorah.

My restlessness became unbearable as the melodies of the Hanukkah holiday kept returning to my mind. The hum of them was without interruption. It was as if my phonograph of memories had gone mad and I did not know how to turn it off.

If I could only do something to chase these melodies away! I was sure that, if I could only light one candle and recite the blessing over it, the melodies and memories would disappear.

25. Hanukkah lamp. Bronze, cast. By Benno Elkan. Germany. Early twentieth century.

In the little monastery chapel hundreds of candles were lit every day, and here I was, with not even one candle to light on the first night of Hanukkah.

From time to time, as I passed through the semidarkened nave of the chapel and noticed a candle which had been snuffed out, I wanted to take it, hide it in my pocket, but how could I? These candles were designated for Saint Martin, Saint Barbara, Saint Joseph, and the Madonna. Certainly their donors had not brought them to be used for a Jewish festival.

One evening as I was turning off the lights and snuffing out the last few burning candles, I noticed a mass of wax that had been dripping down on the floor from one of the small side altars. Aware that this would never be used again, I carefully scratched it off the floor and hid it in my pocket. I returned to my abode, lay down, and tried to sleep. Exhausted as I was from a full day's work, sleep would not come.

Sure you have the wax, you could even make your own candle, but where, where would you light it?

It was past midnight when I fell asleep. I dreamt about Grandfather shining the old brass menorah. When he finished he called on me. I was very small, and he pinched me on my cheek and said: "Tonight you light the first candle." Then I awoke and found myself still in the pigsty. At first I wanted to cry, but then I decided I was too old for that. Instead I started to search for a place where I could light my candle.

One of the smaller buildings used as dormitories for the monks had a trapdoor into a small attic. It was a hole used by the chimney sweep. After a lot of perilous climbing on lintels and woodwork, I made my way up through that opening. I felt my way in the darkness of the tiny attic and found nothing but dust and gravel. In the darkness my fingers felt the outline of a chimney. I felt it from top to bottom. Where the chimney narrowed, there was on each side a little ledge, half a brick in width, and I took out my wax and began to knead it. I tore off one of the fringes of my prayer shawl and placed it in the center of the wax. When I finished rolling it, I lit the candle and placed it on the ledge.

My heart was bursting with joy as, in a barely audible voice, I chanted the "*Maoz Tzur*." For a moment I thought I felt my grandfather's pinch on my cheek. Happy memories filled my heart. The walls of the cloister disappeared. The cold, hunger, and misery of daily life vanished. Once again I was part of a link in the long chain of the tradition of Judaism. Not even a squeak at the trapdoor turned me aside from the burning taper.

Not until I felt a bony hand on my shoulder did I realize where I was.

It was the hand of Peter, a lay brother in the monastery. I had never liked Peter. I never trusted him. From the way he had eyed me, I had constantly feared he would turn me over to the Nazis.

Come on, why don't you say it?

Yes, I am a Jew, I have been hiding here, serving as an altar boy, eating your food and enjoying your hospitality. Go ahead, why don't you call the Gestapo? I don't care anymore.

Peter's eyes moistened. Silently he stood there. After endless agonizing seconds he said: "Let us sing together '*Maoz Tzur.*' "

He actually knew the Hebrew words and melody. We continued together.

The two shadows on the wall merged into one.[12]

iiiiiiii
=

Hanukkah Celebration in the Warsaw Ghetto
CHAIM A. KAPLAN

December 26, 1940

Hanukkah in the ghetto. Never before in Jewish Warsaw were there as many Hanukkah celebrations as in this year of the wall. But because of the sword that hovers over our heads, they are not conducted among festive crowds, publicly displaying their joy. Polish Jews are stubborn: the enemy makes laws but they don't obey them. That is the secret of our survival. We behaved in this manner even in the days when we were not imprisoned within the ghetto walls, when the cursed Nazis filled our streets and watched our every move. Since the ghetto was created we have had some respite from overt and covert spies, and so Hanukkah parties were held in nearly every courtyard, even in rooms which face the street; the blinds were drawn, and that was sufficient.

How much joy, how much of a feeling of national kinship there

was in these Hanukkah parties! After sixteen months of Nazi occupation, we came to life again.

This time we even deceived the *Judenrat* itself. It tried to ban the
holding of Hanukkah parties without a permit from a special office
set up for this purpose. But this too took effect only on paper; the
Judenrat was fooled. Hundreds of celebrations were arranged and
the stupid *Judenrat* did not get a single penny.

Today is the second day of Hanukkah, and I have already taken
part in two celebrations. One was a celebration organized by the
courtyard committee for both festivity and revenue—more pre-
cisely, a celebration arranged by myself and my co-workers, since I
am the president of the committee and since I instigated this party,
which was completely successful. We enjoyed ourselves and we will
give joy to the poor people of the courtyard.

Just now I returned from a celebration at the Zionist soup kitchen.
On every holiday the guests here arrange themselves at small tables,
sip tea, and nibble on some sort of baked goods. But that is not
important. That is only on the outside, for the sake of appearances
before strange eyes. The important thing is the presidium, which is
headed by Kirszenbaum and Kaminar, to the right and left of whom
sit all the leaders of Warsaw's Zionists, who speak and debate with
words that go straight to your heart.

This year's Hanukkah celebration was very well attended. We
almost forgot that we are only allowed to go as far as the corner of
Nalewki and Swietojerska streets. Dr. Lajfuner gave a speech full of
jokes and we all laughed heartily. There was one truth in his speech
which should be stressed: "In all the countries where they want to
bury us alive, we pull the gravediggers in with us." Witness czarist
Russia, Poland, and Romania. Nazi Germany will have the same fate
—and in our own time.

There were also historical and scientific speeches, sermons, and
all kinds of talks, Kaminar, Dr. Lajfuner, Kirszenbaum, Dr. Weis-
man from Suwalki, Bloch, Dr. Schiper, and I all spoke. Everyone
used Yiddish except me; I "ruined" the evening by speaking in
Hebrew.

Translated by Abraham I. Katsh[13]

iiiiiiii
=

Hanukkah 1942 in the Vilna Ghetto
HERMAN KRUK

The ghetto adheres strongly to tradition. All holidays are celebrated with great enthusiasm. On Thursday a Hanukkah program was presented in the theater auditorium by the police. Following addresses by the officers, awards were presented to those policemen who have been on the force since its inception. The second part of the program consisted of a revue in which jokes were made at the expense of one another. A second Hanukkah program is being arranged by the religious circles.

The kindling of Hanukkah lights was permitted in the ghetto, but it was limited to one candle a night. The reason—scarcity and expense of candles.

The employees of the *Judenrat* received an extra Hanukkah ration —two kilograms of bread, two boxes of matches, and one egg.

Translated by Shlomo Noble[14]

iiiiiiii
=

Hanukkah in Nazi-Occupied Belgium
MOSHE FLINKER

excerpts from a diary written by a devout Jewish boy when he was sixteen years old; two years later he died in Auschwitz

December 4, 1942

Now I end today's notes. I hear a heavy sigh coming from my mother.

I had thought that in honor of Hanukkah, salvation, or at least a part of it, might have come; instead, we get new troubles.

December 7, 1942

During the last few days nothing important has occurred, either to me or around me. We lit the fifth candle tonight, and Hanukkah, the Feast of Lights, is drawing to a close. I cannot hope any longer for miracles on this Hanukkah. Every day more and more Jews are being deported—now from one place, now from another. They say that the Germans have special personnel who go around town trying to find out where Jews are living, and they show the Germans these locations, and the Germans come and take our brothers away.

December 12, 1942

Thursday was the last night of Hanukkah. My father, young brother, and I lit the candles which we had obtained, though not without difficulty. While I was singing the last stanza of the Hanukkah hymn "*Maoz Tzur*," I was deeply struck by the topicality of the words:

> Reveal Thy sacred mighty arm
> And draw redemption near,
> Take Thy revenge upon that
> Wicked people that has shed the blood
> Of those who worship Thee.
> Our deliverance has been long overdue,
> Evil days are endless.
> Banish the foe, destroy the shadow of his image.
> Provide us with a guiding light.

All our troubles, from the first to this most terrible one, are multiple and endless, and from all of them rises one gigantic scream. From wherever it emanates, the cry that rises is identical to the cries in other places or at other times. When I sang "*Maoz Tzur*" for the last time on Hanukkah, I sang with emphasis—especially the last verse. But later when I sat on my own I asked myself: "What was the point of that emphasis? What good are all the prayers I offer up with so much sincerity? I am sure that more righteous sages than I have prayed in their hour of anguish for deliverance and salvation. What merit have I that I should pray for our much-needed redemption?"[15]

iiiiiiii
‗

Lights Are Kindled in Bergen-Belsen
PHILIP R. ALSTAT

A challenging test of loving obedience to the divine commandments presented itself in a Nazi concentration camp with the advent of the Hanukkah festival. The pious Jewish inmates there were determined to kindle Hanukkah lights and chant the appropriate Hebrew blessings. Be it remembered that they were not freemen but abject slaves temporarily permitted to live and toil until their strength gave out. Death lurked on all sides and at all times. Moreover, even if they could manage to avoid detection by their sadistic taskmasters, they lacked the essential materials—Hanukkah candles and a menorah. Where, when, and how did such a seemingly impossible thing come about?

Yet it did happen on the first night of Hanukkah, 1943, in the Nazi concentration camp of Bergen-Belsen. The Jewish inmates there were more than ordinarily depressed then, for the day before they had witnessed how two Nazi officers ordered the Jews holding foreign passports to come out of their barracks and shot them down in cold blood. . . .

Of the 1,126 holders of Peruvian passports only 11 were spared for some mysterious reason. One of these fortunate 11 survivors, Rabbi Israel Shapiro, better known among his Hasidim as the Blazhever Rebbe, now residing in Brooklyn, N.Y., was the central figure of that macabre Hanukkah celebration we are about to describe. . . .

Living in the shadow of death and not knowing when their own turn would come, the Jewish inmates were nevertheless determined to celebrate Hanukkah in the traditional manner and draw whatever spiritual strength they could from the heroic story of their Maccabean ancestors.

But where did they get the candle essential for a Hanukkah ceremony? From their meager food portions, the men saved up some bits of fat. The women, on their part, pulled out threads from their tattered garments and twisted them into a makeshift wick. For want of a real menorah, a candle-holder was fashioned out of half a raw potato. Even Hanukkah dreidels for the dozen children in the camp were carved out of the wooden shoes that inmates wore.

At great risk to their lives, many of the inmates made their way unnoticed to Barrack 10, where the Blazhever Rebbe was to conduct the Hanukkah ceremony. He inserted the improvised candle into the improvised menorah and in a soft voice began to chant the three traditional blessings. On the third blessing, in which God is thanked that "He has kept us in life, and preserved us and enabled us to reach this time," the *rebbe*'s voice broke into sobs, for he had already lost his wife, his only daughter, his son-in-law, and his only grandchild.

The assembled inmates joined him in a chorus of weeping, for all of them had also lost their own families. In low voices, choked by irrepressible sobs, they struggled to chant the traditional hymn "*Maoz Tzur*," which proclaims steadfast faith in God, the Rock of their strength.

On regaining some composure, the *rebbe* tried to comfort them and instill new courage and hope. Referring to the words of the second blessing, that "He wrought miracles for our fathers in days of old," the *rebbe* asked: Is it not anomalous to thank God for miracles He had wrought for our ancestors long ago, while He seemingly performs none for us in our tragic plight? In answer to his own question he said: By kindling this Hanukkah candle, we are symbolically identifying ourselves with the Jewish people everywhere. Our long history records many bloody horrors our people have endured and survived. We may be certain that, no matter what may befall us as individuals, the Jews as a people will with the help of God outlive their cruel foes and emerge triumphant in the end.[16]

iiiiiiii
=

A Hanukkah Candle in Auschwitz
MOSHE PRAGER

It is said that everything depends on luck. Even for those who were taken to the gas chambers in the death camp of Auschwitz, everything depended on luck.

There were times when the executioner was in a great hurry and had no time to prolong the torture of the condemned. At such time the road from the "death cars" to the ovens was short. But on other occasions the road was unbearably long and wearisome. When the trainloads kept coming at a steady flow and the ovens could not accommodate them, the emissaries of the devil would take their time, endlessly tormenting the wretched Jews. Those emissaries were far worse than their master. Satan had invented a method of quick and efficient mass murder, while his underlings kept murdering the same people over and over again.

On that snowy night the "death train" was unloaded as usual, and its new transports were led to the main entrance of Auschwitz, where the inscription could be seen above the gate, ARBEIT MACHT FREI (Work Is Freedom). The chief *Kapo* was in no rush. He did not prod the faltering marchers. He did not use his crop on their bowed heads. Nor did he use the familiar lie, "Move on, dirty Jews, move on to the big bathhouse. Move on!" That night the secret order from the camp commander was to direct the new arrivals to the cabins of the "labor squads" and arrange a "game" in honor of the Jewish festival, the Feast of the Maccabees.

The brutish face of the chief *Kapo* took on an air of anticipation, and he spoke in mock sympathy: "No rush, Jews, no rush! It's your holiday today. A good meal is waiting for you. Your bones are too dry and brittle. Can't use them to make a decent fire. In your honor we have kindled all four furnaces today, and all their chimneys will be letting out billows of smoke and tongues of fire. It is your festival of lights, Hanukkah, as you call it!"

"Hanukkah!". . . That word, spit out at the crowd by the villain, hovered in the air over the heads of the oppressed and desolate multitude, suspended like the spark that is suddenly released with a clap of thunder. Could that spark touch that extinguished clod of humanity and stir it up?

Fortunate spark!

For the greater part of the multitude the spark went unnoticed. "What is Hanukkah?" But here and there someone *was* touched by it. "Hanukkah? Was such a thing possible? Satan is ruling the world; there is no miracle of salvation." The spark reached them, but it died out. Only in one spot did the spark take hold and turn into a flame. "Hanukkah! Hanukkah in spite of it all! A single glimmer of light from the divine Source can ultimately vanquish all darkness and evil!"

The sacred spot where the flame was kindled was in the heart of one Rabbi Efraim, the elder of the clan, the head of the court of one of the Jewish communities.

The throng moved on toward death and extinction. And in the terrible darkness the spark lit up the will to rebel. Satan was preparing for his show, intending to degrade those led to slaughter, but in the hearts of the doomed a note of dogged defiance was struck.

When the multitude was crowded into a narrow cabin too small for anyone to sit down, the old rabbi began to speak.

"My fellow Jews, it's Hanukkah today! Satan himself told us so! Granted, this is an unholy place, but we mustn't neglect to kindle the Hanukkah lights. We will kindle the holy Hanukkah candles right here in this cabin!"

"You couldn't be serious!" someone yelled out in an anguished voice.

"Go ahead, go ahead! Light your candles. Pure olive oil and ritually acceptable wicks," another person said, laughing derisively.

"Look over there," a third person cried out. "Those fires out there, they are ours, they are for us," and he pointed at the burning ovens outside the window.

"Nevertheless, today is Hanukkah, my fellow Jews!" The old rabbi spoke again, raising his voice. "Who needs oil and wicks? Every Jew is a candle, even as it is written, 'The soul of man is the light of the Lord.' In the soul of every Jew there is a cruse of oil sealed with the divine Word and reserved for a time of need. When the time comes the cruse opens, shaken by the holy command, and the treasured light is kindled in every Jewish soul, and the flame, the divine flame, begins to rise!"

The rabbi's face glowed, and sparks flew from his eyes. In his soul the cruse of oil was preserved in all its purity, and was now burning with a holy flame. It was obvious that in his great fervor the old rabbi had much more to say. But Satan in the guise of the chief *Kapo* tore into the cabin.

"Filthy Jews, I promised you a good meal for your festival, and I am going to keep my promise! I will give you regular hotel and restaurant service—to fatten you up. But first I will teach you a lesson in the good manners we observe in this camp. Rule one: We have prepared boiling soup for you, and we will pour it into the palms of your hands. Rule two: A twenty-gram slice of bread was allotted to each one of you. Every ten men will get a whole loaf and will divide it among themselves without using a knife. Rule three: Two grams of margarine will be given each one of you tonight. You will lick it off your fingers, at my order!"

The starved and degraded crowd seized the promise of food like a drowning man grabbing for a straw. The chief *Kapo* and his assistants began to distribute the dabs of margarine.

"Each ration of margarine is seven hundred calories, enough for doing one week of work. Each pat is a day of life," the *Kapo* explained in a methodical German tone. He was determined to squelch the last spark of humanity in the hearts of the starved inmates, and to instigate fights among them. "Every able-bodied Jew will get a double portion," he added as an afterthought.

It was the turn of the old rabbi to get his portion.

"You, grandpa, I'll give you a double portion," the *Kapo* laughed loudly, and in his mirth he dropped bits of margarine on the floor and ordered the old man to pick them up.

"A miracle, a miracle!" the old rabbi whispered. He quickly went down on his knees, carefully picked up the crumbs of fat from the floor, and put them inside the flap of his long coat.

"Ha ha ha, you old glutton," the *Kapo* railed at the degradation of the old rabbi. The crowd of humiliated Jews stood there, failing to understand the rabbi's intention.

"The bread and the boiling soup you will get in exactly one hour. In the meantime you can lick the fat which is melting on your fingers."

The *Kapo* left the cabin. He went to get his friends and let them share his enjoyment of watching the Jews being degraded.

"My dear friends, this is truly a miracle!" the voice of the old rabbi was heard. "I picked up the crumbs for a holy purpose. We can now light Hanukkah candles! For the sake of the Hanukkah candles we should be willing to give up all our margarine. I will light my portion! A miracle from heaven!"

"A Hanukkah candle! A Hanukkah candle!" The words aroused shouts of joy.

"To fulfill the commandment!" the old man responded, and as he spoke he pulled some threads out of his lapel from which to make wicks and held up the flap of his coat with the bits of fat inside.

"Where will we put the fat so we can light it up?" the old man mumbled to himself, thinking out loud.

"I have a small silver spoon which I had been hiding," someone called out from the crowd.

"I will give you the cover from my pocket watch," another person said.

26. *Hanukkah lamp. Silver. By Ilya Schor. New York. 1957.*

"Perhaps you can use the buttons from my coat," an elegant woman said as she pulled the buttons off her coat.

"Excellent idea! A true *mitzvah!*" The rabbi smiled and took a few buttons. They were made of tin, and after the cloth lining was removed from them they became adequate containers for the melted fat.

All preparations for lighting the Hanukkah candles were completed.

The old rabbi's face shone.

"The whole purpose of lighting the Hanukkah candles is to publicize the miracle, for in the end the forces of holiness will overcome and triumph over the forces of evil and ungodliness! So, let us light the Hanukkah candles on the windowsill, so that the villainous enemy will know that his end is near. . . ."

The old rabbi stood before the window through which he could see the smoke of the ovens rising up to heaven, and intoned the blessing over the miracle of the oil, kindling the holy flame in everyone's heart.

"These candles are holy—"

The old rabbi sang the Hanukkah hymn, and many joined him in the singing.

"Rock of ages, let our song—"

"*Kreuzdonnerwetter!*" The *Kapo* came running in, shouting at the top of his lungs. The light in the window had caused a general alarm.

"These are Hanukkah candles. You yourself reminded us about Hanukkah," the old rabbi spoke confidently, like one who had attained his goal and had nothing to fear.

"Hell and damnation! You will pay dearly for this, all of you. And you, impudent old man, you first!" the *Kapo* screamed, his voice bristling with disappointment, seeing that his plan had been foiled.

That night the residents of the camp tasted of the miracle of Hanukkah. In their hearts, as well as in the heart of their tormentor who had vowed to take revenge, a feeling remained, a feeling that the small flickering lights on the windowsill had scored a victory over the chimneys of the giant crematoria and even over death itself.

Translated by Mordecai Schreiber[17]

iiiiiii
=
Hanukkah in the Soviet Union
JOSHUA ROTHENBERG

Because it is a minor holiday, a holiday little distinguished from weekdays, and perhaps also because Hanukkah does not lend itself very well to antireligious propaganda, as its theme is the struggle against foreign invaders and oppressors, it has rarely been discussed or attacked in the Soviet press and literature.

Among Soviet Jews Hanukkah is hardly noticeable. The lighting of the candles is observed by only a small number of Orthodox Jews. In addition to the fact that lighting candles in one's home is a conspicuous act of religious adherence, it is difficult to secure the small Hanukkah candles. Although the Soviet government allows non-Jewish cults to manufacture candles for the needs of their rites, and to sell them at a profit to the adherents of their faith, no such rights are granted to Jewish religious associations. Hanukkah candles are not produced legally in the Soviet Union, either by religious associations or by private persons.

Old Jews occasionally engage in producing and selling the holiday candles. The Soviet press will "expose" from time to time the "manufacturers of candles" and accuse them of "profiteering." Thus, for example, *Znamia Kommunizma* [January 24, 1964] of Odessa charged "the former employee of the Odessa synagogue, Auerbach, with manufacturing candles at home" and "selling them on Hanukkah to believers at speculative prices."[18]

iiiiiiii
=

A Hanukkah Party in Riga
ALLA RUSINEK

What a marvelous idea! We are going to Riga in December. Natasha, Basja, Olja, Bettie, and three boys. We decided to go at one of the last parties—just decided and that was that. None of us has any idea of how we will make it, but we all know we'll manage somehow. . . .

We are going for four days—December 4, 5, 6, and 7. The fifth of December is the holiday of the Soviet constitution, so there will be no work. And the sixth and seventh are the weekend. But the most important thing is that these days are the Jewish holiday of Hanukkah. That is what really made us think about going to Riga. In Moscow almost nobody really knows how to celebrate Jewish holidays. And if they do celebrate, then they do it very symbolically in a Zionist way. But in Latvia all the rituals are carefully observed, and young people of our age know them as well as their parents. The whole of Jewish Riga will celebrate Hanukkah in families or in groups, but certainly according to all religious rules. And we want very much to see and to join in this celebration. . . .

We arrived in Riga just in time for the lighting of the first Hanukkah candle. (Now I know something about it.) We went to beautiful Ruth's apartment, where the party was going to take place. Ruth has changed a lot since 1967, but she is still the same hospitable and easygoing girl. We are both a little reticent. It is so difficult to get rid of the unpleasant aftertaste of what separated us two years ago and was one of the reasons for my retiring. But we shall try our best, shall we not, Ruth? Isn't the idea that unites people more important than all the trifles that occasionally separate them? And I shall never forget that you were the first to tell me about Israel and what it meant to be Jewish. You brought me salvation in your beautiful hands saying: "Look . . . Listen . . . Read!" I remember your hands holding picture postcards with a blue sky and orange trees or thumbing a volume of Dubnov's *History of the Jews* or showing me a record of Yaffa Yarkoni. You gave me part of your great love for Israel and for this I shall always be grateful. . . .

The evening had not yet begun. We discussed the new songs we had learned. For us songs were a main source of inspiration.

"Let's have a contest—one song from Riga, then one from Moscow. Then we'll see who knows more."

"OK." Riga began with a Hasidic song: "The Lord will rejoice over you [O Israel] as a groom rejoices over his bride." A wonderful song! But I winked at Natasha; we answered with one of our best: "Nation shall not lift up sword against nation, neither shall they learn war anymore." They were delighted. The contest continued. Riga won: many more songs, nearly all of them in Hebrew or in Yiddish, while most of ours were in Russian. But "Nation shall not lift up sword against nation" was recognized as the best song of the evening. And we knew something else that nobody, I was sure, knew in the Soviet Union—three Israeli folk dances. We had learned them from American tourists on the night of Simhat Torah. We danced and Riga admitted defeat.

Then someone spoke. A middle-aged man told us the story of Hanukkah. He was excited, looking at something far away. He was there then, fighting together with Judah Maccabee, cleansing the holy Temple, lighting the oil in the small jug. He had quite forgotten that he was in the twentieth century, thousands of miles away from his Holy Land, among young people born in Galut, and that he was telling the story of their ancestors—a story some of them had never heard before.

A thoughtful silence fell in the room full of standing people. And then one of Ruth's family began to recite the benedictions and lit the first candle. I could not follow his biblical Hebrew, so I looked around. I looked at the Jewish faces in the light of the candles. Their eyes reflected the glimmering flame, or perhaps it was their inner flame, aroused by the story of Hanukkah. Every time I see Jewish faces around me, I feel happy and safe. I touched Natasha's hand. "Look, aren't they wonderful, these people? They look like Israelis." But how could I know, never having been there? They were beautiful and that was why they looked like Israelis.

And Jewish eyes—eyes that can tell you everything, eyes that reveal, eyes that beg, demand, but seldom laugh. Eyes that live their own lives separate from their faces. Eyes that make me strong and sad, proud and frightened.

The boy, Leib Khnokh, could be described in two words—eyes and beard. Huge, black, sad eyes and a curly black beard. I wondered if Mary, his pretty girl friend, was not afraid of his eyes. There was one boy who was always laughing and couldn't stand still for a moment. He was full of energy, joy, and youth. His name was Izja Zalmanson. He was very young, good-looking, strong. Why shouldn't he be happy and gay? Why should we always carry the burden of our victory? We might be the first generation of happy Jews. (*Leib Khnokh, aged twenty-six, an electrician, was arrested on June 15, 1970. Sentenced to ten years of imprisonment in a hard-labor camp. Mary Khnokh (née Mendelevitch), twenty, student, arrested on June 15, 1970, pregnant. Released at the end of 1971. Arrived in Israel with her newly born son. Izja (Israel) Zalmanson, age twenty-two, student. Arrested on June 15, 1970. Sentenced to eight years in a hard-labor camp.*)

I looked at the Jewish faces. My dear people, I love you, I love my distant motherland. I wish that all of you will soon be in Israel and we will celebrate Jewish holidays at home. All of you are struggling for emigration to Israel, but I don't want you to become heroes because heroes appear when the people are in trouble. Pharaoh, let my people go without making them heroes!

The benedictions were over and I finished my prayer. Wine, cookies, jokes, conversation. The Riga boys helped us to learn the words of a new song. They wrote them down easily in Hebrew. Unbelievable![19]

iiiiiiii
=

An Israeli Boy in Moscow
ARIE L. ELIAV

A Jewish boy lived in Moscow at the time when his father, a friend of mine, was there as a diplomat from Israel. When Hanukkah drew near—the last that my friend's family was to spend in Russia—the eleven-year-old boy asked permission to pronounce the blessing over the Hanukkah candles in the synagogue. It was three years since the child had had any contact with Israel, its scenery, customs, and holidays, and he was eager to get home. It was no wonder that at every religious or national holiday he was consumed with a hunger for the atmosphere of Israel.

The custom to have a boy recite the blessings over the Hanukkah candles is practiced in Israel and in many other Jewish communities. When I mentioned this to the synagogue elders in Moscow, they were eager to let the boy bless the candles after the rabbi's blessing.

Unlike the great holidays in the fall, Hanukkah is not known to many Jews in the Soviet Union. The elderly and aged do not attach great importance to the festival, which symbolizes heroism in war, the overthrow of foreign rule by rebels and fighters, and the glorious feats of Jewish guerrillas more than two thousand years ago. Most of the young people are not at all familiar with this festival and its significance in Jewish history. In the past forty years the symbols of Hanukkah have slowly been lost. Even the bravest of Jews in the Soviet Union would not dare to light the Hanukkah candelabrum at home to commemorate a national rebellion. The familiar spinning tops, pancakes, and other holiday customs have almost entirely disappeared.

Nevertheless, despite the bitter cold of the Russian winter, many hundreds of Jews converge on the synagogue in Moscow to witness the lighting of the first candle of Hanukkah. Most of them are old, swathed and wrapped up in their heavy black overcoats and dark woolen scarves, which they do not take off even during the service. But here and there, particularly along the sides of the building, one sees beneath the fur caps the bright eyes of boys and girls luminous with curiosity.

That year, after the rabbi of Moscow had recited the blessing over the candles in the large ancient silver candelabrum set on the pulpit, the boy went up and blessed the little colored candles in the small bronze candelabrum he had brought from Israel. His hands shook and his voice trembled with emotion. He almost choked over the first words of the blessing, but recovered in the second verse. His voice rang out clearly.

Years passed. Then one day I visited my friend at his home in Israel. He told me that one of the teachers in the school which his son attends had asked the pupils to write a paper on the theme "Memories of My Childhood." My friend said that his son did not like to talk to his friends or even to his family about his impressions of Moscow. But for some reason he had decided to choose "Hanukkah in Moscow" as the topic of his paper. And this is what he wrote:

"In the fifteen years of my life I have traveled and seen much more than the average boy. I have visited twelve countries, including the Soviet Union. Not everyone is allowed to visit Russia. Luckily, my father was sent there on a mission for the state of Israel. That is how I came to live abroad where I absorbed impressions I shall never forget.

"The thing that impressed me most was the condition of the Jews in the Soviet Union. This is not clear or understandable to anyone who lives here and merely reads about it in the papers. Only by actually experiencing the atmosphere on the spot can one feel what happens to the Jews in that country. The Israeli delegates do not have much to do there, but a cheerful word can at times bring a ray of light into the hearts of the Jews. . . .

"During our last Hanukkah in Moscow I was given permission to light my small candelabrum in the synagogue. My heart beat rapidly as I entered the synagogue. I could hardly see what was going on around me. I almost forgot all the blessings I had learned. After the traditional evening service, the rabbi lit the synagogue candelabrum, reciting the blessings in a dry voice. Then my turn came, I was frightened by the large crowd that had gathered there. I walked to the pulpit with trembling knees and lit the candles. Then the little flames gave me courage. I knew I had to say the blessings and to sing well while hundreds of eyes were focused on me. As I pronounced the blessings, I saw the eyes of the Jews lighting up and I began to sing "*Hanerot Hallalu.*" In the middle of the chant a mysterious conductor seemed to have given a signal—and the worshipers joined me in a tremendous chorus.

"When I left the synagogue, I was filled with the feeling of having helped, of having been a messenger of comfort who brought light and hope to his people."

Sometime later I was present at a Hanukkah party in Bet Hillel, a Jewish student club in one of the large universities in the United States. The building was new and roomy. A charming student chanted the blessings over the candles in a perfect Hebrew that was tinged with an American accent. Lovely girls handed out the traditional pancakes, and the entire group of about 120 boys and girls sang festive songs in English and Hebrew. Between these songs I told them stories about Israel, including the one about the Israeli boy who lit the Hanukkah candles in the Great Synagogue of Moscow. When I finished my story, I noticed that the eyes of the students had become serious and sad; they were like the eyes of the young Russian Jews I had seen, the eyes I had come to know so well as a result of my experiences in the Soviet Union.[20]

27. Dreidel. Wood, carved. Southern Germany.
Beginning of nineteenth century.

ііііііі
=

With Sephardic Children and Teachers in Jerusalem

JOSEPH J. RIVLIN

In past years Jerusalem would witness countless parades of the pupils of Sephardic schools during the Hanukkah holiday period. Led by their teachers and singing lustily, the children carried little bags in which they collected contributions of food and drink for the Hanukkah meals. Hanukkah, as a rule, occurs in the week in which is read the scriptural portion *Mikketz*, which includes the verse "Go again and procure some food for us" (Genesis 43.2). These words were repeated melodiously by the children thousands of times during the parades.

The teachers of the Sephardic schools made their own circuits. They visited the homes of the Jewish quarter to invite contributions for a great Hanukkah feast. In front of each home they sang an ancient Ladino melody, invoking God's blessings upon the donors. In return, they were given gifts of beans, oil, garlic, onions, rice, flour, coal—and money.

These articles of food, together with meat purchased with the money gifts, were saved up until the eighth day of Hanukkah. On that day a magnificent feast was prepared after much baking and cooking and roasting. Huge kettles were brought to the Talmud Torah in the Old City near the Johanan ben Zakkai synagogue. First appeared the children, their parents, and the teachers. Then came the dignified arrival of the "Chief Rabbi, the Diadem upon Our Heads, the Foremost in Zion," who took his stand on the *bimah*. All the pupils then recited in a loud voice the verse "Go again and procure some food for us," repeating it 321 times! This number represented the numerical value of *Shaddai* (Almighty) and *B.H.* (Blessed be the Lord!). The rabbi kept track of the correct count with the aid of a heap of beans. Then a selected group circled the *bimah* seven times, carrying the kettles of food on their heads while they recited benedictions in honor of the rabbis, teachers, and children.

Now the real festivities began. One of the teachers called out: "Would you like bread?" The lusty reply was: "Yes!" "Beans too?"

"Yes!" "And rice?" "Yes!" "What about meat pie?" "Yes!" "And lashes?" "No, no, no!"

The food was served in large, flat bowls, some filled with rice and the others with beans. There were also many varieties of meat pies. These were placed near the door of the synagogue. The poor, the widowed and the orphaned brought their plates and were helped to heaping portions. Hundreds of loaves of bread were also distributed.

With the departure of the poor, each pupil received a loaf of bread, a meat pie, and a bowl of rice and beans. To amuse the children, some of the pies were filled with cotton instead of meat. When one of these cotton-filled pies was opened a roar of delight erupted. Each pupil was also given a gift of five coins before going home.

The teachers, now left alone, partook of a special meal which was prepared with greater elegance and ended the day with appropriate songs and hymns.

The Hanukkah celebration was called in Ladino "*Miranda de Hanukkah*" or, in Hebrew, "*Shulhan Arukh shel Hanukkah*."

Translated and adapted by Solomon Feffer[21]

iiiiiii
=

Jerusalem Candles
MENASHE

I remember the first time they lit the lights in Jerusalem. Down at the corner of the road there was a streetlamp. The little bowl of light hung up there in the darkness like a bright moon, a pool of light shed gracefully at its feet. Here again, a kind of signal, little beacons of light throughout Jerusalem, repeating the message as you pass, "Here we are again, it's been a long time." All over Jerusalem there are lights. In Geulah and Kerem Avraham, in Meah Shearim and Mahneh Yehudah, in Jaffa Road and Ben Yehudah Street, in Rehavia, by the King David and the Jaffa Gate, by the synagogue of the Tiferet Yisrael and at the Western Wall.

But tonight it is not only the streetlamps that are illuminating the city. For as you pace the quiet byways in the evening, at every window between the drawn curtains the little candles flicker, like elfish winking stars, curtseying and tipping their hats to you as you go by saying: "Good evening; a Happy Festival, a Happy Hanukkah."

At first there are only two, but as each day passes and each evening you retrace your steps through these streets, the lights grow and grow, as though the rumor of your passing had spread to all the other little elfish flames, till on the last day there they are, all crowding at the windows, bobbing and shining, bright and slender, lighting your path as you walk, turning the open street into a star-roofed synagogue.[22]

iiiiiiii
=

Hanukkah in Israel
JACOB KABAKOFF

During the modern period, the Zionist movement accentuated the national aspects of the Hanukkah festival and utilized to the fullest its heroic symbolism. Hanukkah became a special occasion for Zionist celebrations and meetings in behalf of the movement for rebuilding Palestine.

In the homeland itself, Hanukkah took on a public character which only a people rooted in its own soil could impart to it. If the kindling of the lights is elsewhere the hallmark of the festival celebration, it is only in Israel that the lights are all-pervasive. Large electric menorahs are lit atop public buildings, institutions, and synagogues, and they adorn the water towers of the settlements. In Jerusalem, for example, the Knesset building has its menorah, and in Tel Aviv the Great Synagogue is traditionally the site of candle-lighting. The menorah casts its light above ancient Masada, and the army camps, too, are decorated by menorahs during the festival.

Annually students and hikers visit Modin, the cradle of the Hasmonean revolution, on the eve of Hag ha-Makkabim, the Feast of the Maccabees. On the first day of the festival, thousands of members of the Maccabi sport movement gather at the ancient site of the

Maccabees to enact an impressive ceremony. An honor guard stands at attention while the Israeli flag is raised; then a bonfire is lit and torches are kindled.

The ceremony marks the beginning of the torch relay which transports the flame of Modin to various cities and settlements in Israel. The torchbearers proceed along a designated route and light the torches of runners who await them at specified positions. In Jerusalem, the president of the state of Israel receives the first torch and an appropriate public ceremony is conducted during which the festival lights are kindled.

From the president's home the torch is taken to Mount Zion, where menorahs are lit in memory of the victims of the Holocaust. Lights are also kindled at a public ceremony held at the Western Wall. In other cities and towns, the torches are awaited at municipal centers or at public squares, where they are greeted with fanfare and paraded through the streets.

A torch lit at Modin is also dispatched to America as a symbolic link with the American Jewish community. In 1974 it was brought by soccer star Mordecai Spiegler, who was accompanied by two children whose fathers were killed in the Yom Kippur War. The torch was extinguished during its flight on El Al to New York, where it was relit. Runners then carried the symbolic torch through the city streets.

Schools, youth organizations, and national institutions have done much to enhance the spirit of the festival. The fact that the entire eight days of Hanukkah are traditionally a school holiday adds greatly to the festive atmosphere. It is preceded by intensive educational preparation in the classroom and is highlighted by ceremonies, dramatic presentations, and musical offerings. A special activity of nursery and kindergarten children is the making of their own menorahs. Schoolchildren also take home to their parents gifts they prepare in the classroom.

Special open-air celebrations for teenagers are marked by torch relay races and processions. The Gadna (Youth Cadet Corps) sponsors a torch relay from the Jordan Valley to Haifa, where the torch is presented to the mayor of the city.

Hanukkah serves as an occasion to dispense charity and practice community welfare. Various institutions, including hospitals and old-age homes, utilize the festival to sponsor festive meals at which gifts are distributed. The absorption centers for new immigrants and the army installations also serve as places of special activity. At Kfar Habad, Hasidic women bake thousands of potato pancakes as part of their "Operation Hanukkah" for wounded soldiers, widows, orphans, and frontier settlers, and distribute them together with food and wine.

The Histadrut or Labor Federation, founded during Hanukkah on the twenty-eighth of Kislev, 1920, holds various celebrations in observance of this anniversary. The WIZO and other women's organizations schedule their annual bazaars for the week of the festival. In Haifa an annual Mother's Day is marked at this time of the year. Hanukkah is also traditionally a time for the dedication of new buildings and the founding of new settlements. The Tel Aviv Museum, for example, was dedicated during the festival, as were various strategic new settlements established by Nahal groups.

The eight days of Hanukkah are also widely used by Israelis for touring the land and for meetings and conferences. Hanukkah events and dances abound in hotels and other public places. In Israeli homes, as everywhere in the Jewish world, the festival serves as an occasion for family gatherings and parties.

The kibbutzim, even the nonreligious ones, serve as the proving grounds for the development of new patterns of holiday celebration. Because of their tightly knit structure, they afford a unique opportunity to plan organized programs for the entire eight days of the festival, during which various aspects are stressed. In the member units of the Ihud ha-Kevutzot ve-ha-Kibbutzim (Union of Collective Settlements), for example, each day of Hanukkah has a special character.

The ceremony marking the first night is the most impressive. At a designated time, ushered in either by siren blasts or by holiday melodies played over the public-address system, the lights go out throughout the entire kibbutz. At a given signal, parents and children proceed together in a parade of torches or gaily colored lanterns to a central point where a public candlelighting ceremony takes place. In some kibbutzim a torch relay contest is held prior to the candlelighting. This is followed by a festive meal and gathering in the settlement dining hall, which is decorated with placards, maps, and exhibits in the spirit of Hanukkah. Menorahs adorn the tables and are lit by individual family groups. In various settlements representatives of different age groups are called upon to light the candles on successive nights.

The Hanukkah evenings have their moments of both seriousness and fun. One evening may be devoted to a discussion of the Hasmonean period, while another may be given over to the theme of Jewish heroism. In some kibbutzim the heroism of the Jewish woman through the ages is highlighted. A literary evening may be arranged, concluding with the distribution of gift books to the members. Hanukkah folklore and the anniversary of the founding of the Histadrut may serve as the themes on other evenings.

The arts are employed to augment the holiday spirit. Pageants, plays, readings, lectures, quizzes, films, slides, and musical offerings add to the celebrations. In some kibbutzim the children's band plays Handel's *Judah Maccabeus* and other appropriate numbers. A special evening may be devoted to the various kinds of kibbutz endeavor, such as agriculture, fruit-growing, beekeeping, and the like. The members will vie with each other to create original menorahs representing their specific branch of work.

In the kibbutz Hanukkah is also a time for contests—for decorating, baking, making menorahs, and above all for frying *levivot*, or potato pancakes. No kibbutz celebration is complete without an evening devoted to this activity, and members at the various tables compete in preparing this delicacy on individual kerosene stoves. In the spirit of Hanukkah, also game nights are arranged and special gifts are distributed to the children.

The Hanukkah festivities in the kibbutzim are the product of careful planning on the part of cultural committees striving to incorporate not only the symbolic and folkloristic values of the festival but also its warm social and familial aspects.

II HANUKKAH IN POETRY

iiiiiii
=

Table Hymn for the Sabbath of Hanukkah
ABRAHAM

*the author is identified from an acrostic formed by the first letter of each stanza
in the Hebrew version; although there were rabbinical objections to the singing
of this frolicsome hymn, it was included in a prayer book published in Salonika
in 1557 and later reprinted in other liturgy collections*

Eat dainty foods and fine,
  And bread baked well and white,
With pigeons, and red wine,
  On this Sabbath Hanukkah night.

Refrain
Your chattels and your lands
    Go and pledge, go and sell!
Put money in your hands,
    To feast Hanukkah well.

Capons of finest breed
    From off the well-turned spit
The roasts that next succeed
    Each palate will surely fit.

Joints tender, poultry young,
    Rich cakes baked brown in pan;
"A-greed" is on every tongue,
    "Set-to" laughs every man.

No water here they carry,
    Their steps fade fast away;
Over wine we all will tarry,
    Two nights in every day.

Our ears no more shall tingle
    At sound of the water's fall;
But, red wine in cups come mingle,
    And shout in chorus all,

Our fields and our lands
    We will pledge, we will sell,
To put money in our hands
    To feast Hanukkah well.

Translated by Israel Abrahams[1]

ïïïïïïï
—

Shabbat and Hanukkah Dispute before Me
SOLOMON BEN ELIJAH
''GOLDEN SCEPTER''

astronomer, poet, and grammarian who lived in Salonika (c. 1422–1502);
this poem, depicting a disputation between the Sabbath and Hanukkah on the
day they coincide, was published in an early sixteenth-century Mahzor.

Quoth Shabbat to Hanukkah:
   I lay claim to priority!
   For who are you and your upstart brood?
   On me the great and awesome God forbore
   From all creation's work that He had done (Genesis 2.2).

Quoth Hanukkah to Shabbat:
   Why do you assail and harry me?
   On my eight days the whole Hallel is said
   But on your single day not even once.
   And why do you declaim: "Watchman, what of the night?
      Watchman, what of the night?" (Isaiah 21.11)

Quoth Shabbat to Hanukkah:
   My additional prayer for the early rain is superior,

28. Hanukkah celebration. From Jüdisches Ceremoniel, *by Paul C. Kirchner, Nuremburg, 1726.*

Even better "A burnt offering for every Sabbath in addition to
the regular burnt offering" (Numbers 28.10).
Why do you glorify yourself with Hallelujah,
You who are bare, denuded of offerings?

Quoth Hanukkah to Shabbat:
My lustrous lights are kindled first and yours come after (on
Sabbath eve).
I'm mentioned first in "Blessing the land," and later you in
the prayer "Have mercy" (in Grace after Meals).
All your allusions and all your words, are they not
"These shall march *last*, according to their standards"?
(Numbers 2.31)

Quoth Shabbat to Hanukkah:
I am constant like the virtuous bride of one's youth
Summoned every seven days as a king's honored daughter,
But you, like a mistress affrighted in the night,
Are summoned once annually at the appointed season.

Quoth Hanukkah to Shabbat:
Your light may be eyed and made use of,
But for mine "it is permitted only to look at them."
Your anthem (Psalm 92) may be sung by all, but mine (Psalm
30)
Only by those born into priesthood,
When the Temple rebuilt becomes the holy of holies.

My decision:
Desist from your disputation.
Now you are linked together in love
Beware, lest a sin be committed
Desist and I'll vindicate both of you.

I avouch that no dispute need be between you
Why should you stir up and contest your love?
YOU, SHABBAT, most eminent of festivals, remit your claims,
Most beauteous for mankind, grace is distilled from your lips.
YOU, HANUKKAH, you are a redeemer, none but you can bring
redemption.

                              Translated by A. Alan Steinbach

ÏÏÏÏÏÏÏ
=

The Banner of the Jew
EMMA LAZARUS

an American Jewess who received wide recognition for her poetic abilities; her poem "The New Colossus" is on the Statue of Liberty (1849–87)

Wake, Israel, wake! Recall today
   The glorious Maccabean rage,
The sire heroic, hoary-gray,
   His fivefold lion-lineage:
The Wise, the Elect, the Help-of-God,
The Burst-of-Spring, the Avenging Rod.

From Mizpeh's mountain ridge they saw
   Jerusalem's empty streets, her shrine
Laid waste where Greeks profaned the Law,
   With idol and with pagan sign.
Mourners in tattered black were there,
With ashes sprinkled on their hair.

Then from the stony peak there rang
   A blast to ope the graves: down poured
The Maccabean clan, who sang
   Their battle anthem to the Lord.
Five heroes lead, and following, see,
Ten thousand rush to victory!

Oh, for Jerusalem's trumpet now
   To blow a blast of shattering power,
To wake the sleepers high and low,
   And rouse them to the urgent hour!
No hand for vengeance—but to save,
A million naked swords should wave.

Oh, deem not dead that martial fire,
   Say not the mystic flame is spent!
With Moses' law and David's lyre,
   Your ancient strength remains unbent.
Let but an Ezra rise anew,
To lift the *Banner of the Jew*!

A rag, a mock at first—erelong,
  When men have bled and women wept,
To guard its precious folds from wrong,
  Even they who shrunk, even they who slept,
Shall leap to bless it, and to save.
Strike! for the brave revere the brave![2]

iiiiiii
=

The Feast of Lights
EMMA LAZARUS

Kindle the taper like the steadfast star
  Ablaze on evening's forehead o'er the earth,
And add each night a luster till afar
  An eightfold splendor shine above thy hearth.
Clash, Israel, the cymbals, touch the lyre,
  Blow the brass trumpet and the harsh-tongued horn;
Chant psalms of victory till the heart takes fire,
  The Maccabean spirit leap newborn.

Remember how from wintry dawn till night,
  Such songs were sung in Zion, when again
On the high altar flamed the sacred light,
  And, purified from every Syrian stain,
The foam-white walls with golden shields were hung,
  With crowns and silken spoils, and at the shrine,
Stood, midst their conqueror-tribe, five chieftains sprung
  From one heroic stock, one seed divine.

Five branches grown from Mattathias's stem,
  The Blessed Johanan, the Keen-eyed Jonathan,
Simon the fair, the Burst-of-Spring, the Gem,
  Eleazar, Help-of-God; o'er all his clan
Judah the Lion-Prince, the Avenging Rod,
  Towered in warrior-beauty, uncrowned king,
Armed with the breastplate and the sword of God,
  Whose praise is: "He received the perishing."

They who had camped within the mountain pass,
　Couched on the rock, and tented 'neath the sky,
Who saw from Mizpeh's heights the tangled grass
　Choke the wide Temple courts, the altar lie
Disfigured and polluted—who had flung
　Their faces on the stones, and mourned aloud
And rent their garments, wailing with one tongue,
　Crushed as a windswept bed of reeds is bowed,

Even they by one voice fired, one heart of flame,
　Though broken reeds, had risen, and were men,
They rushed upon the spoiler and o'ercame,
　Each arm for freedom had the strength of ten.
Now is their mourning into dancing turned,
　Their sackcloth doffed for garments of delight,
Week-long the festive torches shall be burned,
　Music and revelry wed day with night.

Still ours the dance, the feast, the glorious psalm,
　The mystic lights of emblem, and the Word.
Where is our Judah? Where our five-branched palm?
　Where are the lion-warriors of the Lord?
Clash, Israel, the cymbals, touch the lyre,
　Sound the brass trumpet and the harsh-tongued horn,
Chant hymns of victory till the heart take fire,
　The Maccabean spirit leap newborn![3]

ïïïïïïï
=

An Interpretation of Hanukkah
RUTH F. BRIN

short-story writer, poet, and interpreter of Jewish liturgy

The light of freedom burns bright and hot
at the crossroads of decision.

In the marketplace at Modin
Mattathias stood in the heat and the light
for only an instant.

He heard the offer of the tyrant:
silver and gold, honor and the king's friendship,
but he, in his freedom, chose another way.

Without hesitation, he chose the Law of God
for himself and his family,
though it meant warfare and death.

When we sing the holiday blessings
let us ponder the solemn choices of those men
who fathered our freedom,

When we light the Hanukkah candles
let us remember the grave choices
freedom illuminates for us.[4]

In Darkness Candles
MICHAEL I. HECHT

author of The Fire Waits, *a collection of prayers and poems; rabbi in Cleveland Heights, Ohio*

Lord, You create day and night,
Rolling away light before darkness,
Darkness before light.
    Thank You for the darkness.
    Without it we could not appreciate the light.
    By the darkness we can measure blessing—
Health by sickness,
Laughter by tears,
Riches by poverty,
Freedom by oppression.

In the darkness of the night
The Maccabees lit a flame
Which still illuminates our lives.
Thank You for the challenge that they met.
In centuries of night
Men rose at midnight and lit flames.
And by those slender lights,
From torn and tear-soaked prayer books,
They pleaded for Your mercy
And asked an end to exile's night.
Thank You for the answer to their prayers.
Thank You for restoring Israel's light.
But still night reigns
In all the world.
Thank You for unfinished tasks.
In the darkness
Teach us to light candles.
Teach us to light candles,
Even as we did tonight
In memory of ancient light after darkness.
A candle is small.
Not far from where it brightly flames
The darkness closes in.
But candles light other candles,
And light draws strength from light.
Each night of life let us add candles:
The candle of hope.
The candle of faith.
The candle of brave deeds.
The candle of freedom . . .
Thank You for the darkness
Thank You for the light.[5]

iiiiiii
=

The Festival of Hanukkah
RUBY FOGEL LEVKOFF

one of three American poets honored at the 1967 Stroud International Festival of the Arts in England

The candles burn against the brink of years,
flashing their shadows through the centuries
back to an old beginning—the fiery, fierce
devotion that once stirred the Maccabees

to triumph over a tyrant. *The Temple stood;*
the Temple was destroyed . . . its altar dark—
except for one small flame—that somehow would
burn like the Faith lit from an ageless spark.

Now flashing through the dark of histories
of people harried by hatred's troubled night,
stand the tall shadows of the Maccabees—
as if God willed each year, "*Let there be light!*"[6]

iiiiiii
=

The Eternal Light
MOSHE DAVIS AND VICTOR RATNER

Dr. Davis: historian and educator, head of the Institute of Contemporary Jewry of the Hebrew University; Mr. Ratner: public-relations consultant and free-lance writer

A candle is a small thing.

But one candle can light another.

And see how its own light increases,
as a candle gives its flame to the other.

You are such a light.

Light is the power to dispel darkness.

You have this power to move back
the darkness in yourself and in others—
to do so with the birth of light
created when one mind illuminates another,
when one heart kindles another,
when one man strengthens another.

And its flame enlarges within you
as you pass it on.

Throughout history,
children of darkness have tried
to smother this passage of light
from man to man.

Throughout history, dictators large and small
have tried to darken, diminish
and separate men by force.

But always in the end they fail.

For always, somewhere in the world,
the light remains;
ready to burn its brightest
where it is dark;
a light that began
when God created the world:

". . . *Who coverest Thyself with light as with a garment.*"

And every free people has remained free
by resisting those who would
extinguish in men the light
of freedom,
of love,
of truth.

To do our daily part to increase this light,
we must remember that a candle alone is a small thing,
a man alone is a small thing,
a nation alone is a small thing.

Remembering this,
we must recognize something much more
than our indispensability to others.

We must also remember their indispensability to us.

We cannot hope—
either as individuals or nations—
to reach our highest capabilities
until we help those around us reach theirs.

29. "A Hanukkah Evening." By Moritz Oppenheim (1800–82).

To be strong
the strong must serve.

"*These lights we now kindle. . . .*"

These words accompany the lighting
of Hanukkah candles in the home,
and in the heart,
to commemorate the eternal bridge of light
which reaches from creation itself
to the radiant spirit of freemen.

In this spirit is celebrated
the Festival of Hanukkah—
the Festival of Light—
wherein the candle that gives its light
to the others is called
"the servant candle."

You too are strongest . . .
when you serve.[7]

iiiiiiii
=

Meditation on Hanukkah
CHARLES REZNIKOFF

a native New Yorker who wrote fiction, drama, and verse, and served as editor of the Jewish Frontier *and as a contributing editor of* The Menorah Journal *(1894–1976)*

The swollen dead fish float on the water;
the dead birds lie in the dust trampled to feathers;
the lights have been out a long time and the quick gentle
    hands that lit them—
rosy in the yellow tapers' glow—
have long ago become merely nails and little bones,
and of the mouths that said the blessing
    and the minds that thought it

only teeth are left and skulls, shards of skulls.
By all means, then, let us have psalms
and days of dedication anew to the old causes.

Penniless, penniless, I have come with less and still less
to this place of my need and the lack of this hour.
That was a comforting word the prophet spoke:
Not by might nor by power but by My spirit,
　　said the Lord;
comforting, indeed, for those who have neither
　　might nor power—
for a blade of grass, for a reed.

The miracle, of course, was not that the oil
　　for the sacred light—
in a little cruse—lasted as long as they say;
but that the courage of the Maccabees lasted to this day:
let that nourish my flickering spirit.

Go swiftly in your chariot, my fellow Jew,
you who are blessed with horses;
and I will follow as best I can afoot,
bringing with me perhaps a word or two.
Speak your learned and witty discourses
and I will utter my word or two—
not by might nor by power
but by Your spirit, Lord.[8]

iiiiiiii

A Night in Hanukkah
SAUL TCHERNICHOVSKY

Hebrew poet of distinction ranked next to H. N. Bialik; composer of idylls and sonnets, author of stories and philological studies, and translator of many classical works (1875–1943)

Shadows and shades of death hold sway this night,
Heaven and earth are darkened like the grave,

The winds in the forest dance about the trees,
An instant calm, then thundering from all sides,
And moaning softly to awake the dead,
Crying pitifully, heaving sighs;
But in the dark night and its howling storm,
The city, wrapped in snow, prepares for sleep.

Over the housetops on the wings of the wind
Hover dark hosts—the shadows of the night,
Lifeless and still, that were a mighty band,
Staring with sockets that were anguished eyes:
"Lo! These are our Maccabees! These heaps of bones,
These shriveled hands, these bloodless arteries,
These blighted brains—'tis a miracle they live,
Who live and live not, aged ere their time—
Sans strength or power, but with craven cowardice
Bent double like a willow o'er the brook;
They have not seen God's light, their life's a coin,
Their hapless soul knows not what beauty is;
In chains of the king's law, dogma and its bonds.
This errant folk plod on and sin for bread.

·"We breathed our last in the hot and fiery waste,
In a land of drought where leopards prowl the hills;
From thirst, from famine, pricked by the sword of death,
Rent by the lion's jaws and beasts of prey,
On crosses by the wayside crucified,
Sword in hand we fell on the battlefront,—
We died, but thought that they who came after us,
Sword in hand, they would avenge our blood,
That day the horn would sound in Lebanon,
The strong arise, banners unfurled to Zion!
Was it for *these* we hoped? A race unschooled
To freedom, feeling not its iron bonds,
Unruffled when the wonted stones are thrown;
A nation of slaves who spurn their heritage
Surely will be cut off; their sword of pride
Rust has worn away."

Ere the last lamp of the Feast of Lights is out,
While the crickets chirp, the townsfolk turn to bed;

Then their desires awake, take human form,
Their ardor, hatred, anger and their strife
For honor, gods or a tiny loaf of bread.
The tempest groans—dread cries of the jungle depths,
The forest trees moan—dying men that sigh—
And bend their crown and shake their leafless boughs,
And rear their naked trunks toward the clouds.

Translated by L. V. Snowman[9]

iiiiiii
=

To Soviet Jewry: A Hanukkah Invocation
CHAIM LEWIS

poet, essayist, and editor in Johannesburg whose writings have appeared in leading journals in both England and America

Each year this season
these fingered flames
hallow the dark.
I embrace God, my Redeemer,
in a molten ritual
of candlelight:
my people's history
kindled to a pious
candle's girth, filching
noonday light
to break the plotting dark.

The lights gather
the dry fagots
of martyred days
to burn with zealot
fire. I hang on the promise
rooted in the flames—

Will tomorrow's dawn
break through prison walls?

Will the joy of running
waters loosen the bound
despair of stone?

The lights on my window ledge
peer into the void
to show a tarrying
Messiah the way.[10]

iiiiiii
=
Mattathias
ABRAHAM M. KLEIN

Canadian Jewish poet whose four books of verse and only novel, The Second
Scroll, *won him acclaim throughout the English-speaking world (1909–72)*

Of scabrous heart and of deportment sleek,
And reeking like an incense superfine,
The Hebrew renegade laid hold the swine
And raised it as a flattery to the Greek . . .
His dagger flashed, truly a lightning streak;
The blood gushed from the swine-heart which, in fine,
Did the Lord's altar all incarnadine . . .
In truth, there is sore vengeance now to wreak!
And Mattathias, man of Modin, cool
With old age grew all warm with wrath; he threw
Discretion to the winds like a false jewel,
And on the instant, zeal-possessed, he slew
The knave. Behold within a single pool
A swine's blood and the blood of traitor Jew![11]

ііііііі
=

Candle Lights
ABRAHAM M. KLEIN

Dead heroes ride the chariots of the wind;
Jew phantoms light the candles of the sky.
Old war cries echo in my memory;
The ghosts of five brave brothers stalk my mind.
And this because my father and his kind
Are lighting heirloom'd candelabra, aye,
Are singing praises to the One on high,
This night in which past battles are enshrined!
As sweet as were the sweet songs of degrees
That David sang rejoicing, is this rite
My sire rejoicing sings; and as the sight
Of almond blooms that burst on springtime trees
In sight of this menorah, and of these
Eight blossoms breaking on a winter night![12]

12 HANUKKAH IN THE SHORT STORY

iiiiiii
=

The Battle Of Modin
HOWARD FAST

historical novelist and short-story writer; author of the prize-winning novel about the Maccabean revolt, My Glorious Brothers, *from which the following episode is excerpted*

And in the month of Tishri, when the sweet breath of the new year was all over the land, Apelles returned. So things have a beginning and an end—even Modin.

Judah laid his plans well. He was tireless; day and night he worked, planned, schemed, and day by day, the store of long, slender spears mounted. A village condemned was Modin. We dug our bows out of the ground. We made new arrows. We turned our plows

223

into spears. We put a razor edge upon our knives. And already, even now, it was to Judah that people brought their woes. "And six children, Judah ben Mattathias—" "We will make provision for the children." "And what will a man do with his goats?" "Our stock goes with us." It was Lebel, the teacher, who pleaded his case. "I am a man of peace, of peace." He came to the Adon, his bloodshot blue eyes wet with tears. "Where is the place of a man of peace in Israel today?" And the Adon called for Judah, who listened and nodded.

"Will our children grow up like savages in the wilderness?"

"No," Lebel said.

"Or Jews who cannot read or write?"

Lebel shook his head.

"Then make peace in your heart, Lebel!"

Then Judah told the Adon that the few slaves in Modin must be freed. "Why?" "Because only freemen can fight like freemen," Judah said. The Adon said: "Then ask the people. ... ." And thus was our first assembly in the open valley. From the nearby villages of Goumad and Dema, people came to listen, and the synagogue would not hold them all, so Judah stood on the fragment of ancient stone wall to speak, and he said to the people:

"I want no man who is faint of heart to follow me! I want no man who cares more for his wife and children than he cares for freedom! I want no man who counts the measure when he pours it out! I know a road that leads in only one direction, and who travels it must travel light. I want no slaves or bondsmen—turn them away or put weapons in their hands!"

"Who are you, to talk like that?" some of them cried.

"A Jew out of Modin," Judah said. There could be an incredible simplicity about him—yet a cunning measure of the people he spoke to. "And if a Jew should not speak, then I'll be silent"—and he began to climb down. But they shouted at him:

"Speak! Speak!"

"I don't come with gifts," he said simply. "I come with blood on my hands—and there will be blood on yours when you listen to me."

"Speak!" they told him. And afterwards, when twenty men from Goumad came armed, to seek him out, they asked in the village:

"Where will we find the Maccabee?"

And the people of Modin directed them to the house of Mattathias. Thus it was in the days before Apelles came back. . . .

And then Apelles returned.

In the morning, Nathan ben Borach, thirteen years old and fast as a deer, came leaping down from the hillside, calling: "Simon! Simon!" But all the people heard, and when I reached him, I had to push through the press of the people. "From where?" I asked him. "From the west." "And how far?" "Two or three miles—I don't know how far. I saw the gleam you told me to watch for, and then I saw the men and I came."

"We have time," Judah decided, quieting them. "Go to your houses and bolt the doors and close the shutters—and wait." He had a little silver whistle that Ruben had made for him. "When I call you, come—those who have spears with spears and the rest with bows. Watch your shafts when you drop them and shoot well."

"And the men from Goumad?"

"It's too late," Judah said, "and this will be for Modin."

"We could go to the hills now," someone said.

"And we could bend our knees to Apelles. Go to your houses, and those of you who have no heart, stay there, stay there."

They did as he said, and doors closed and the village became silent. The Adon and Rabbi Ragesh and Judah and Eleazar and I stood in the square and waited. I had my knife in my belt, and under his cloak Judah wore the long two-edged sword of Pericles. Then Jonathan ran from the house and joined us. I would have sent him back, but Judah looked at me and nodded—and I held my peace. A moment later, Johanan joined us, and with him was Ruben ben Tubel, cloaked and clenching his hammer under his cloak. Close together, the eight of us waited, until presently we heard the beat of a drum and the metallic clash of armor—and then the mercenaries came, first a rank of twenty, then Apelles in his litter, then sixty more in three ranks of twenty, no horsemen now, for which I breathed a sigh of relief, but walking among the mercenaries a Jew, a white-robed Levite whom I recognized as one of the Temple attendants from Jerusalem.

The slaves set down the litter, and Apelles hopped out, grotesquely magnificent in a golden mantle and a little red skirt. How well I remember him as he stood there in the cool Judean morning, the apostle of civilization, his hair carefully set and curled, his cupid bow lips delicately rouged, his pink cheeks carefully shaven, his jowls underlined with a golden necklace, his capon bosom swelling the golden mantle, his fat thighs setting off his flounced skirt, his

30. *Mattathias slaying a traitor. Fresco. Dura-Europos synagogue. Syria. Third century.*

little feet encased in high silver sandals that wound up his dimpled calves.

"The Adon Mattathias," he greeted us, "the noble lord of a noble people." My father nodded, but said nothing. "And is this a welcome?" he lisped. "Are eight men a fitting delegation for your warden?"

"The people are in their houses."

"Their pigpens," Apelles smiled.

"We will call them if you wish," the Adon said, gently and respectfully.

"Presently, presently," Apelles agreed. "You suit my mood. There is a civilized way of doing everything. Jason!" he cried, waving at the Levite.

Hesitantly, the Jew joined him. The man was afraid. His face was as white as his cap, and his tiny beard and his two tiny mustaches trembled visibly.

"Now welcome, Joseph ben Samuel," my father said gently, "to the poor hospitality of Modin."

"Shalom," the Levite whispered.

"An ancient greeting, a warm greeting," the Adon said. "And peace unto you, Joseph ben Samuel. Our house is enriched with an elder of the tribe of Levi."

"He comes to the sacrifice," Apelles lisped smilingly. "The great king to his poor wardens saith thus, 'My heart is heavy with this dark folk and their dark worship. An unseen God makes a secretive and vile people.' So saith the king to me, his poor warden, and what else should I do but obey his orders? Yet I brought the good Jason here, a Levite, so that you might sacrifice in your own way." He clapped his pudgy hands, and two mercenaries fetched a bronze altar they had been carrying and set it down before us. It was a slim thing, about four feet high, and crowned with the figure of Athena.

"Pallas Athena," Apelles said, mincing around the altar. "She was my own choice—Wisdom. Knowledge comes first and then civilization. Is that not so? Later Zeus and the swift Hermes. A complete man is a full man, is that not so? Make a flame, Jason, and burn the incense—and then we will have the people forth to see the Adon do honor to this noble lady."

"Yes, make a flame, Joseph ben Samuel," my father said. "Pallas Athena—later Zeus and his swift Hermes. Make a flame, Joseph ben Samuel."

Looking at the Adon, never taking his eyes off the Adon, the Levite approached the altar. Then, with one quick step, my father reached out a long arm, seized the Jew, and, in a motion so quick I could scarcely follow, drew his knife and plunged it into his heart.

"There is your sacrifice, Apelles!" he cried, hurling the dead Levite against the altar. "For the goddess of wisdom!"

The shrill sound of Judah's whistle broke the morning air. The two mercenaries who had brought the altar leveled their spears and came at us, but Eleazar raised the altar and flung it at them, bowling both over. Apelles turned to run, but Judah was on him, his first grasp short and stripping off the golden mantle. Half naked, Apelles tripped and fell, rolled over, and then squealed wildly as he saw Judah above him. With his bare hands, Judah killed him, lifting him by the neck and snapping it suddenly, as you do with a chicken, so that the wild squeals stopped and the head lolled.

Then, for the first time, I saw Judah fight. The mercenaries were driving down on us, their brazen shields lapping, their shovellike spears leveled. Judah drew his sword; I picked up the spear of one of the groaning mercenaries Eleazar had struck, and Eleazar had gotten from somewhere a wine mallet, an eight-foot pole with twenty pounds of wood at the end of it, used for mashing grapes in a deep cistern. The blacksmith joined us with his hammer, but it was Eleazar who broke the first rank of spears, charging in and using the long heavy pole as a flail. Judah was beside him, sword in one hand, knife in the other, never pausing, never still, quicker than I had ever dreamed a man could be, a stroke here, a cut there, always in motion, always making a circle of steel around him with the sword.

It was not a long battle, and my own part was small. The spear of a battle-maddened mercenary tore my cloak, and I closed with him and broke my spear on his shield. We rolled on the ground, he trying to draw his sword, I cursing the neck plates that impeded my fingers. He half drew his sword, and I stopped trying to throttle him, but beat his face in with my clenched fist and continued to beat at the bloody face even after he was dead. I took his sword, and all of this seemed like hours but could only have been a minute or two at most, yet the people of Modin had already poured out of the houses, some with spears and some with bows, and the world was full of that wild screaming that goes on in a battle—and the mercenaries were no longer in orderly ranks with lapped shields, but in clumps and clusters, and a good many of them on the ground and others running.

But around Judah and Eleazar and Ruben they made a knot, as if these three must be torn down and offered to whatever gods mercenaries worshiped, or the world would end surely; and there I went, where my brothers fought, and there too the Adon came, knife in hand, cloak torn and bloodstained. I killed another man— I remember yet the blasphemous ease of slaughter—running through the small of the back, severing his spine just beneath his armor; and I saw the Adon drag down another, an old wolf, truly, and terrible in the strength of his wiry arms—and then it was done, and Judah and Eleazar and Ruben and my father and I stood panting and gasping for breath with twelve dead and dying men at our feet, and what remained of the mercenaries fled.

They fled through the streets and the Jews followed them with arrows and slew them. They fled into the houses where they were hunted down and fought like wolves until they were slain. They fled up the hillside, pricked all over with arrows, and yet they were dragged down. We took no prisoners; these were mercenaries we fought. The last one was dragged out of a cistern where he crouched, soaked in olive oil, and a spear was driven through his heart.

And then the battle of Modin was done. Only eight Jews were dead, although at least fifty, including my father, bore wounds of the fight; but every mercenary had died. Apelles was dead, as was the Levite. Of the *nokhri*, only the slaves who bore the litter remained.

So I tell it here, I Simon, the least of all my glorious brothers, and as I tell it, the fighting in Modin was finished. . . .

So the village moved out of Modin and northward, and now we were armed. We carried spears and swords and bows, and we were a grim band as we wended our way through the terraces, higher and higher. In Goumad, where we paused to rest and where the people brought us milk and fruit and wine, we told the story of the fight, and when we left Goumad, twelve families of that village were with us. We did not recruit; we did not harangue. When they asked: "For how long?" we answered: "Until we are free." Until the land is cleansed over, three times, as it is written.

With nightfall, we camped on a lonely mountainside, and as the sun set, we prayed and remembered the dead. Now, after the weariness and strangeness of the day's journey, some of the children began to weep, and their mothers comforted them, singing to them: "Sleep, my lamb, my woolly lamb; slumber, little waif of God. Never fear the darkness; your pure heart fills it with light . . ." that song which was old already when Moses heard it from his mother's lips.

I sat by a fire, and Judah plucked my arm. I followed him, and we climbed up the face of the cliff, higher and higher, until we saw the Mediterranean, all bathed over with the final, rosy hue of sunset. Then Judah pointed down through the valleys to Modin, and I saw a glow that was not of the sunset. The village was burning. For over an hour, we stayed there, watching it, never speaking, but watching it burn, and at last, Judah said:

"They will pay—for every lick of flame, for every drop of blood, for every hurt."

"It will not bring Modin back."

"We will bring Modin back."[1]

ꞮꞮꞮꞮꞮꞮꞮ
=

His Pride Was Too Much
HOWARD FAST

There came to me a man and wife out of the town of Carmel in the far South, and the man, Adam ben Lazar, tall and dark and hawklike and unbending, as so many of those who live close to the bedouins are, said to me: "And thou art the Maccabee?"

"Not the Maccabee, who is my brother Judah. Are you new in Marah that you don't know Simon ben Mattathias?"

"I am new, and I come to be judged by a child." But his wife, who was round and lovely, yet worn and terrible with grief, said nothing.

"And yet I judge," I said. "If you want other judgment, go to the Greeks and find it."

"You are bitter the way the Adon your father was bitter, Simon ben Mattathias."

"What I am I am."

"Like him," his wife cried suddenly, pointing to her husband. "The men in Israel were emptied and hatred was poured in. I want no more, so separate us and make us strangers to each other."

"Why?" I asked the woman.

"Shall I tell you, when every word is wiped in blood?"

"Tell me or don't tell me," I said, "for I make no marriages and break none. Go to the rabbis or the *kohanim* for that, to the old ones, not to me."

"Will the old ones understand?" the man demanded coldly. "Listen, Simon, and then send me where you will, to hell or to the arms of your brother, the Maccabee."

"We are married twelve years," the woman said, "and we had a daughter and three sons," and she said it in almost those singsong tones of the teller in the marketplace. "Bright they were, and round and beautiful and a blessing in my heart and my house and in the eyes of God. Then the warden, whose name was Lampos, set up his Greek altar in the marketplace and told the people to come and bend their knees and burn incense. But he"—whirling on her husband and pointing an accusing finger at him—"he would not bend his knee, and the Greek smiled with pleasure . . ."

"With pleasure," Adam ben Lazar nodded, wooden-faced. "He

was the right man for the South. For if there are hard men in Judea, you will find harder if you travel south."

"So he slew my little girl," she said, "and he hung her body on the rafters over our door, so that the blood dripped on our doorstep, and all day and all night, the mercenaries sat there, drinking and eating and watching, so that we should not cut down her body and give her burial—"

Without tears she told this. I judged in the open, sitting on a rock, and sometimes the people listened. Now they listened, and more and more came, and as she told her tale, the people were packed around, shoulder to shoulder.

"This for seven days, and when the Sabbath came, with his own hands this Lampos cut the throat of my little boy and hung the body up beside the girl, the girl who was already foul with corruption and smell. Yet we must live there. All around the house stood the mercenaries, day and night, with their spears linked, so that a mouse could not crawl through. Then, on the third Sabbath, Apollonius came to consult with his warden, and it was great sport—" Her voice dried up; she did not cry or appear to be moved, but her voice dried up.

"It was great sport and the Greeks love sport," her husband said, nodding. "With his own hands, Apollonius cut the throat of the third child, for he pointed out to us that a people who could not bend a knee, to God or man, were an abomination on the face of the earth. It was merciful to kill the young, he said, so that mankind could look forward to a time when it would be rid of Jews forever, and then all the world would be sweet with laughter."

"And the next week, they slew our firstborn and hung the body beside the others," the woman added in her terrible singsong tones. "And all in a row, the four bodies hanged, and the birds came to feed upon them; but we could not cut them down, we could not cut them down, and the flesh that came out of my womb rotted away. So I hate him, my husband, even as I hate the *nokhri*, for his pride was too much and it destroyed everything I loved."

She did not weep, but an anguished sigh came from the people listening.

"His pride was too much," she said, "his pride was too much."

There was silence then for what seemed to be a long while, a silence broken only by the weeping of those among the people who did not hate too much to weep. Yet I could not judge and I said so, motioning to Ragesh, who stood there, listening. "Come and judge," I asked him. "You are a man of years and a rabbi." But Ragesh shook his head, and like two lost and eternally tormented souls, the man and his wife stood in the circle of the people—until Judah pushed through them and stood before her, such sorrow and love on his young and beautiful face as I have not seen before or since on the countenance of any human being. All she said of death and the making of death seemed to wither away in the face of this man who was the very embodiment of life, and he took her two hands in his and pressed his lips to them.

"Weep," he said softly, "weep, my mother, weep."

She shook her head.

"Weep, for I love you."

And still she shook her head hopelessly and damned.

"Weep, because you lost four children and gained a hundred. Am I not your child and your lover—then weep for me, weep for me or the pain of your children will lie on my heart and destroy me. Weep for me and the blood on my hands. I am proud too, and I wear my pride like a rock around my neck."

Slowly, it came, a crinkling of her long dark eyes, a bit of moisture there, and then tears—and then long, screaming moans as she fell to the ground and lay there. Her husband picked her up in his arms, weeping even as she did, and Judah turned from them and passed through the people, who made way for him. He walked through them, his head bowed, his hands hanging by his sides.[2]

iiiiiii
=

The Last Hour
DAVID FRISHMAN

author of numerous stories and feuilletons, both in Hebrew and Yiddish, and translator into Hebrew of many works of the great European writers (1861–1922)

Outside the wind wails and shrieks. The rain sweeps upon the roofs and beats upon the windowpanes. But within, the house is full of light and joy, radiating in every corner, glowing in every heart.

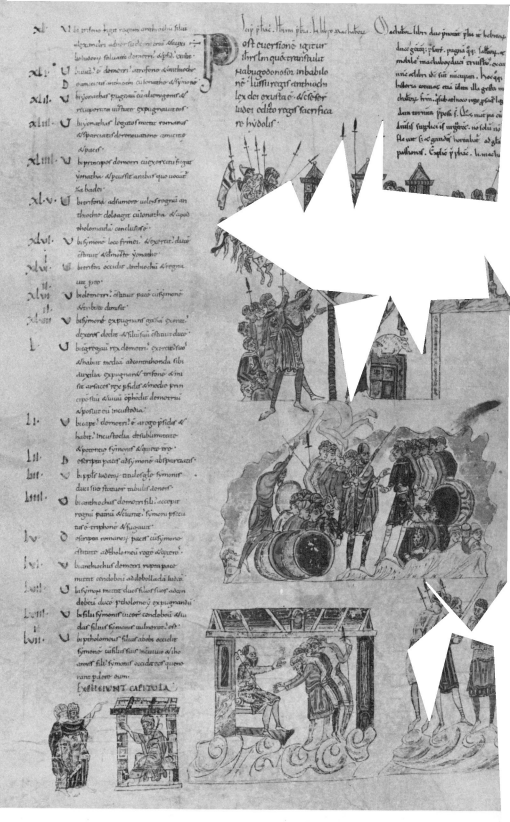

31. Mattathias slaying a traitor who is sacrificing on an altar. Farfa Bible. Catalonia, Spain. Eleventh century.

Upon the silver Hanukkah menorah there shines the eighth candle tonight, and opposite it the waxen *shammash* stands bent and molten, its fire flickering and dying.

In the tapestried armchair Grandmother sits, attired in her comeliest garments, garments worn on Sabbaths and on holidays. Her eyes are bright with happiness. The folds of her silken shawl fall from her head; her jeweled earrings sparkle and send little lightnings from beneath her ears. All of us gathered about her and I on her footstool, my head resting on her knees, entranced; she sits, in profound thought, her lips shut, only her eyes gleaming with inspired light. Truly the secrets of God are hidden in those eyes, full of wisdom and eternally bright! Her forehead is infinitely wrinkled; her back is bent, almost humped, her hands quiver, her very voice quivers—but her eyes, they are young, they are eternally bright!

Silence! From her cloud of dreams she raises her heavy weary head. "My children, I am old and gray, am I not? My days outnumber the sands on the shore of the sea and my nights defy computation, but the words which I am about to tell you this evening are even older than I am myself, older than myself by thousands of years, and I, my dear children, must tell you these words which fill my heart even to overflowing."

Outside the wind still wails and shrieks in an eerie voice. But the voice of Grandmother rises above the cry of the wind. She speaks:

"My children, you are expecting, no doubt, that I will tell you of the miracle of Hanukkah. That is your error. The story of Hanukkah and the deeds of Antiochus you have heard long ago. I have it in mind, however, to tell you of that which took place in Jerusalem in the reign of Antiochus five or six years before the miracle of Hanukkah. It is the tale of a little Hebrew lad who came to *heder* one day and began bitterly to cry, not because he was being beaten there, forsooth, but because there was an aching in his heart and in his soul an anguish. Truly these words are full of sorrow and great bitterness."

And Grandmother is suddenly silent. Her eyelids slowly droop as in a dream. And I, all anticipation, sit at her footstool, my head resting on her knees.

The streets of Jerusalem. Rays of sweetness and light pour from heaven upon the goodly dwellings of Israel. From horizon to horizon the sky extends, a perfect blue, save for bits of clouds slowly wandering above like travelers spent with journeying. A clear warm breeze gently rustles the leaves. This summer is verily a warm one —this summer of the year 3590 of the divine creation.

In the street the children romp and play. They are happy; they laugh; they sing. Beneath their feet the golden sand is scattered; above their heads there burns a golden sun. Their hearts swell with happiness. Of a sudden, they hear the shout of the crier: " 'Tis time, my children, to go to your studies. Hurry then, hurry to the *heder*." As suddenly the children stop and look hither and thither. A tall old man stands before them. His beard is white and falls upon his chest, and his eyes gleam as he looks upon them with a despairing bitterness. Who does not know this ancient graybeard? Who does not recognize Rabbi Jose, the son of Joezer, of the city of Tzeradoh?

As he stands there and stares at them a kindly contentment shines from his face; on his eyelashes there cling large tears. "These are the remnants of Judah," he mutters to himself, "and this is the staff upon which our nation is to lean. The young ones are still ours." As one entranced he stands there, stands and dreams in the drowsiness of summer.

What had befallen his people in these latter days? True it was that they were living in the land of Israel, yet the land was not Israel's. This country was now subject to the whims of the Greek Antiochus Epiphanes, who at this time was carrying on his military expeditions in Egypt, while the wicked Andronicus was sent to Palestine to fill his place as governor. This tyrant was now reigning with a mighty hand, seeking to root out the last spirit of Judaism which still lingered in abandoned corners, and to plant in its stead a spirit of Hellenism. By converting Jewish customs into Greek and by setting up Greek gods he was slowly but surely spreading that spirit over the land. The streets of Jerusalem ceased to be called by their Hebrew names; Greek ones were assigned instead. Hebrew coins went out of circulation; Greek currency took its place. Hebrew names disappeared; Jews were known by Greek cognomens. Hebrew flags waved no more from the public buildings; Greek ones fluttered vauntingly upon their poles. Even from the courthouse of the Sanhedrin they took the Hebrew standard and hung a Greek one in its stead. The high priest, who still strove for the ideals of his nation, was replaced; and his office given to Menelaus, a man of heathen inclinations.

"Still are the young ones left to us, still are the sucklings of the kindergarten ours," he says, and again his face is filled with bitterness and again he cries: "To the *heder*, children, to the *heder*."

In compliance, the young boys hasten in all directions, and little Joezer, the youngest son of Rabbi Jose, follows them eagerly. With such a sun shining in all its splendor it is no light thing to leave the open air beneath the blue sky to shut oneself up in a *heder*. With merry hearts the young lads cross the bridge of Kedron. They stop near a Greek toyshop. Little Joezer gazes into its show window, transfixed, as if his feet were nailed to the spot. Suddenly there appears upon the threshold of the shop a Greek slave. He yells at the boy in a shrill, angry voice. Young Joezer runs with all his might, and stops to look neither to right nor to left. He passes the farm of Jehoshaphat, the bridge of Antiochus, and the fields of the washers, till he comes to the market of Andronicus. Here he stops for a while and wistfully regards the souvenirs sold by the Greeks, toys and talismans brought from Athens and from Sparta and from Byzantium. Here are golden sandals, chains of pearls, silver stars, and here images of horses and of dogs and of man, wrought in wood and stone, works of an artist. And all these things glitter and gleam in the sun and are pleasing to the eye. All at once he recalls that he is in a hurry and that he must go to the *heder*. When he comes to ‚the open land which lies behind the Temple he halts. Here in the northwestern portion a gymnasium had been erected, where the Greeks taught the Hebrews all forms of acrobatics and the art of fighting. The boy stood enraptured at the sight of young Hebrews exercising themselves in the open air. How good it must be to be thus always under the warmth of the sun and in the coolness of the breeze, he thought. Two Hebrew boys enter the ring, and quick of hand and fleet of foot, they engage in a spirited struggle, each attempting to vanquish the other, and after some time, both falling to the ground, the surrounding crowd lustily cheering the Hebrew champions. There next enters the ring a Hebrew lad, naked to the waist, who begins to dance with all the charm and perfection of the art, while the lyre and the drum emphasize his motion. Happiness and joy is everywhere. Only upon the heart of Joezer, of little Joezer, does there come a pang of sorrow, for he has remembered that he must hurry to *heder*. But his feet are as glued to the place; he stands there transfixed, his eyes do not leave the ring. This is new youth, he thinks, these are new games, new sports, new joys. His evil spirit, however, does not allow him to leave this spot. Already four hours have passed, and still the lad is watching the sports in the gymnasium. The sun has already climbed to its central height in the heavens. And a great terror possesses little Joezer. Half a day is already gone, and he has not yet been to *heder*. What will be the words, the sharp, bitter words which his teacher will fling at him? What will be his warm reception? And already he imagines the severe words of the rabbi and already he sees his angry face, and already he hears his harsh voice. He rouses himself from his trance, and runs, runs.

And as he runs there follow him visions that he had beheld in the gymnasium—boys and girls, half naked, seem to pursue him. The dances and the combats, the exercises and the acrobatics, the music of the lyre and the beat of the drum are again with him. And from all these remembered sounds there rises louder and sterner the voice of his rabbi, scolding and wrathful. He hurries faster and faster, his feet do not seem to touch the ground; he is already in the street of the *heder*. His heart pounds violently, he stops for a moment before the door of the *heder* to rest and wipe the perspiration from his brow. So silent it is that he hears the beating of his heart. A second passes—and his hand is on the doorknob. Another—and he is already within the classroom. A great terror and darkness fall upon him, and his legs are weighty as with lead. What is this? A silence as of death reigns today in the classroom. A spirit of mourning, of speechless mourning, pervades the whole room. The boys sit silent and motionless. No one says a word, no one even winks an eyelash. Truly the *heder* is different today from what it was yesterday. Even the rabbi stands leaning upon the desk—his brow wrinkled and resting upon the palm of his hand, his eyes shut. Suddenly he raises his head, and his eyes catch sight of little Joezer. "My son, you are late this morning, very late, but you did good in coming, even if late."

Could it be? His voice was soft and kind, softer than poured oil, and his words full of compassion and regret, words that fall deeply into the heart of little Joezer. When did his rabbi last speak to him in this fashion? Whence came this voice, so full of bitterness and sorrow and yet so full of warmth and pity? At this very moment the conscience of the little boy hurt him for having wasted the whole morning, for having come late. "My son," continues the rabbi, his voice quivering, "my son, take your book and study your lesson, for ere you will know it this hour will be the last . . . tomorrow we cease to learn Hebrew." His voice is choked with tears . . . all the boys in the *heder* shudder and commiserate with their rabbi, an old man weeping like a child. "Our last fire they have quenched, our language they have taken from us"—he can hardly refrain from tears —"and what will we now teach our children. How will they now be able to know the spirit and the splendor and the greatness of their people?"

He passes his hand over his eyes; he weeps; the children weep. And in this silence and sorrow little Joezer finds himself bewildered: his heart beats loudly, and in that moment a new spirit had come into him, a new soul had entered into him.

"So this, my children, is our last hour. Tomorrow we cease to study our language." The voice of the rabbi is heard a third time, but it is a voice no longer filled with bitterness and sorrow, but with softness and pure compassion—a voice which seems to say: "Tomorrow all existence will fade from off the face of the earth and only wilderness will reign instead."

The young boys take their books and hasten home. And as young Joezer takes his books, his hands quiver and his eyes are washed with tears. Never up to this day did he understand his lesson so well, never up to this day did the words of the rabbi sink so deeply in his heart. On this day one of the world's languages will be borne to the grave; on this day a nation will be lost among the nations; on this day a land will perish from among the lands. And the young lad, in his heart, knows and understands these things. And as his rabbi speaks to him these words of kindness and warmth, his voice sweet and pleasant, his explanations clear and memorable, they are like secrets of God emanating from the square letters, whose like he had never heard nor seen before. Then did the lad make an inward vow never to step within the Grecian gymnasium.

The sun has set. Within the *heder* the darkness has cast its shadows into every corner and nothing is heard save the voice of the rabbi trembling as he studies the Law of God this last, last hour.

Outside before the door of the *heder* is heard the voice of the passing men, loudly speaking Greek, and the whole street seems full of joy and happiness. . . .

The light in the Hanukkah menorah has long since flickered out. In the armchair Grandmother sits; her hands cover her eyes; she is silent. She has ended her story—outside the wind has long since ceased its wailing and its shrieking, but in the house there are shadows and silence and sorrow.

Translated by Abraham M. Klein[3]

ïïïïïïï
=

The Living Menorah
AVIGDOR HAMEIRI

Israeli editor of literary magazines, playwright, novelist, and expressionist poet who wrote several volumes of verse; recipient of the Bialik Prize

This incident was reported in the newspapers at the time. But the newspapers distorted and misrepresented it. Let me tell it as it really happened.

We were in the frontline trenches. It was winter, the second year of the war.

At that time the beast in man had already begun to assert itself, the urge to kill and torture, not as a necessity of war, but for its own sake, for the sadistic joy of killing.

For some months the front had been quiet. Deep snow covered the landscape. There was no talk of action.

First Lieutenant Erich S. sought some diversion to break the monotony. And what could be more diverting than to witness the agony of a fellowman squirming in pain?

Some say this is a Slavic trait, others that it is also a Magyar streak. And Lieutenant S. was of mixed Slavic-Magyar descent. But I suspect that it is a generally human characteristic.

Lieutenant General Von Greulchen's latest order directed against deserters read: "Anyone apprehending a traitor in the act of deserting may punish him in any manner he desires without resort to a court-martial, short of inflicting the death penalty, which must be approved by a regularly constituted court-martial."

This order pleased Lieutenant S. "In any manner he desires. . . ." How many "manners" had been invented by Satan? "Anyone apprehending a traitor. . . ." What's easier than that? If one wishes one can catch such deserters any day of the week.

Lieutenant S., anxious to find a traitor, found one—Pfc. Hayyim Yosef David.

Hayyim Yosef David . . . that's a beautiful name. It had potentialities.

Especially when the bearer of the name was such a strange creature, a *yeshivah bachur*, a man set apart by strange mannerisms, who donned phylacteries for his daily prayers, read Hebrew books, and always went about with an expression of benignity on his face and the joy of Hasidic communion in his eyes.

This joyousness irritated Lieutenant S. It acted upon him like an acid.

One day he could bear it no longer and addressed himself to the Pfc.: "Pfc. Hayyim Yosef David, why are you always so happy? Do you really think this war was arranged as a diversion for us? What's the expression of joy on your stupid mug?"

Hayyim Yosef David answered him simply: "Sir, why shouldn't I be happy when this war purifies humanity?"

"How do you mean 'purifies'?" the officer asked, his face suffused with bewilderment.

"Suffering purifies, sir, suffering purifies."

Lieutenant S. remained unenlightened. Then a thought seemed to strike him. He pondered the matter for a moment, then muttered: "I'll purify you pretty soon." His Turanian-Slavic blood coursed more rapidly in his veins in pleasant anticipation. His hands trembled with a strange delight. He visualized what was coming.

He not only visualized it but later actually witnessed it. And we too, all of us, saw it. We saw it and felt faint, that's all; we did not go mad, we did not bite our own flesh, we did not kill each other. We did none of these things. It happened in this way.

It was Hanukkah.

Hayyim Yosef David lit the candles, blessed them, and sang devoutly as though his very soul were rising to higher spheres.

We sat in the dugout and watched him. We listened to his singing as he poured out his heart in love and compassion, his voice modest, intimate.

Suddenly Lieutenant S. entered. All of us rose as he entered. Hayyim Yosef David did not notice him and continued singing. Then we saw the lieutenant's eyes turn pink with anger, his face became suffused with blood, his hands began to tremble.

32. Scenes of the Maccabees. Miscellany. Germany. Fifteenth century.

He muttered a few words which we did not understand. Then he walked out with a determined air. It was obvious—he had decided to act.

And we all had the feeling that Hayyim Yosef David's fate was sealed.

Toward evening of the following day, Hayyim Yosef David was

included in the guard detachment. That same night he was brought
back in chains. The lieutenant himself brought him in.

Then followed the terrible rumor: "Lieutenant S. personally
caught Pfc. Hayyim Yosef David as the latter began crawling toward
the enemy lines."

Now what?

Now the punishment, without trial, according to the order from
headquarters.

Not capital punishment, naturally. Just punishment. We turned
pale trying to imagine what this could be. Our hearts began pounding strangely, like the ticking of mechanically faulty clocks.

The lieutenant issued a strict order: "Quiet. There must be no
noise. All must be calm and silent. It is to our shame that there are
among us creatures willing to sell themselves to the enemy. This
shame must remain secret, among ourselves, and among ourselves
we will punish the criminal."

"Among ourselves" Lieutenant S. brought in the offender, put
him up against the wall, then addressed us.

We did not hear what he said. Our ears were shut against the voice
of the human refuse that lectured to us on justice, fairness, courage,
and the homeland. We tried not to listen, but some of the words
forced themselves on our attention: "If suffering purifies man, as
you, Hayyim Yosef David, so joyfully tell me, you will now have a
chance to become purified. I will give you a special Jewish opportunity to become purified, one that you will like. You will at the same
time obey a command. And now, Hayyim Yosef David, do you admit
your guilt?"

Hayyim Yosef David, bound like a thief, looked at the ground and
answered, as if in song: "Before the King of kings, yes, but before
you, sir, before man, I am not guilty."

"What," the lieutenant shouted laughing savagely, "what? Not
before me? Very well! In that case, Hayyim Yosef David, you will
purify yourself before your God. Now you will be purified. I will not
kill you. I have no order nor right to do so. I don't want to, either.
But I do want to purify you. You, Hayyim Yosef David, will light
your candles!"

"Yes," he answered.

"And you will bless them loudly!"

"Yes."

"And you will be purified of your sins!"

He issued an order and a soldier came in carrying a bucket filled with a black viscous liquid. It was hot steaming tar. The bucket was placed near Hayyim Yosef David, his bonds were loosened, and the lieutenant commanded:

"Dip your hands into it, your fingers!"

Hayyim Yosef David evidently was not aware of the bucket's contents. He did not know that it was hot. He was oblivious to everything.

He dipped the fingers of both hands into the liquid and a quiet groan escaped him, penetrating our hearts.

"Quiet, you dog! Shut your mouth, traitor! Did you think this was honey?"

Hayyim Yosef David stood there, his hands dripping hot tar. They trembled and squirmed in great agony. His face was contorted with pain.

"Sir," he said like a stupid child, "sir, it hurts, it hurts terribly."

"Raise your hands up," the lieutenant shouted, "up to your head. Wrists straight against the wall, palms out. Now stand against the wall, with your back to it. Rifleman Kalman, tie his hands to the wall so they can't slip."

Rifleman Kalman drove four big nails into the wall, two about each hand, and bound the hands to the nails with wire.

Hayyim Yosef David stood thus like a two-branched menorah, the fingers covered with tar constituting ten black candles.

We sensed what would follow. We wanted to leave, one by one. The lieutenant shouted at us: "No one will stir from his place! For whose benefit do you think I am punishing this traitor, if not for yours? So that you should see and learn! And now," he turned to Hayyim Yosef David, "now pronounce the blessing!"

At this moment Hayyim Yosef David paid no attention to the lieutenant. He did not exist for him at this moment. He turned to us and chanted in a low sad voice, in Hebrew: "This is coming to me because I had forgotten that it was Hanukkah. Even I forgot. Yesterday was the seventh day already and I thought it was only the first day. For a whole week I had forgotten. For the first time in my life I had forgotten. You pity me? Don't pity me! Oh, oh . . ."

The lieutenant struck a match and lit the fingers of Hayyim Yosef David. But he continued talking: "I am suffering, suffering. The pain is passing from the fingers to the brain. My brain hurts . . . because I had forgotten . . . one must never forget . . . especially Hanukkah. One must never forget . . . Hanukkah is the celebration of *our* war, the celebration of the war of God. In the present war we

have forgotten the war of the living God, we have forgotten Mattathias, the high priest. I have seen him, here on the ice on the
window. Look, there he stands . . . waiting for my benediction. I will
pronounce the benediction and you answer, Amen!"

He sang the benediction in a voice full of sacred sorrow and
suffering, his face suffused with a transparent glow, tears rolling
down his cheeks.

His fingers were aflame; his face was like a flaming torch. The
blood rushed to our heads as we stood by. For a moment it seemed
that we would fall to the ground. Nausea overcame us. We closed
our eyes.

When we opened them, Hayyim Yosef David was no longer in our
midst. He had been taken somewhere, perhaps to the hospital,
perhaps to be buried. We never saw him again. Suddenly one of us
cried out, and with a face alternately flushing and turning pale,
dragged us to the frozen window. The panes were covered with icy
designs and flowers of frost. But etched in frost, on one side of the
pane was the image of an old Jew.

We stood rooted to the ground and stared at each other.

"He must have drawn it himself," one of us remarked skeptically.

"Fool," retorted another, "does this look like a design made by
human hands?"

We had forgotten for a moment that Hayyim Yosef David's hands
were no longer hands, that they had become a sacred menorah.

Translated by Shlomo Katz[4]

iiiiiiii

Hanukkah Money
SHOLOM ALEICHEM

*pseudonym of Shalom Rabinovitz, the renowned humorist of Yiddish literature;
born in 1859 in Russia and died in 1916 in New York; a prolific writer
known as the "Jewish Mark Twain," his masterful stories were extremely popular among the Jewish masses and have been translated into many languages*

Can you guess, children, which is the best of all holidays? Hanukkah
of course.

You don't go to *heder* for eight days in a row, you eat pancakes every day, spin your dreidel to your heart's content, and from all sides Hanukkah money comes pouring in. What holiday could be better than that?

Winter. Outside it's cold, a bitter frost. The windows are frozen over, decorated with beautiful designs, the sills piled high with snow. Inside the house it's warm and cheerful. The silver Hanukkah lamp stands ready on the table, and my father is walking back and forth, his hands behind his back, saying the evening prayers. When he is almost through, but while still praying, he takes out of the chest a waxen candle (the *shammash*, to light the others with) and starting *Alenu*, the last prayer in the regular services, signals to us:

" '*Shehu noteh shamayim . . .*' Nu! Nu-o!"

My brother and I don't know what he means. We ask: "What do you want? A match?"

My father points with his hand toward the kitchen door. " '*Al ken nekaveh lekha . . .*' E-o-nu!"

"What then? A bread knife? Scissors? The mortar and pestle?"

My father shakes his head. He makes a face at us, comes to the end of the prayer, and then, able to speak again, says: "Your mother! Call your mother! I'm ready to light the candle!"

The two of us, my brother and I, leap for the kitchen, almost falling over each other in our haste.

"Mother! Quick! The Hanukkah candles!"

"Oh, my goodness! Here I am! Hanukkah lights!" cries my mother, leaving her work in the kitchen (rendering goose fat, mixing batter for pancakes) and hurries into the parlor with us. And after her comes Braina the cook, a swarthy woman with a round plump face and mustache, her hands always smeared with grease. My mother stands at one side of the room with a pious look on her face, and Braina the cook remains at the door, wipes her hand on her dirty apron, draws her greasy hand over her nose, and leaves a black smear across her face.

My father goes up to the lamp with his lighted candle, bends down and sings in the familiar tune: "Blessed art Thou, O Lord . . ." and ends ". . . to kindle the light of Hanukkah."

My mother, in her most pious voice, chimes in: "Blessed be He and blessed be His Name." And later: "Amen." Braina nods her approval and makes such queer faces that Motel and I are afraid to look at each other.

"These lights we kindle," my father continues, marching up and down the room with an eye on the Hanukkah lamp. He keeps up this chant till we grow impatient and wish that he would reach his hand into his pocket and take out his purse. We wink at each other, nudge and push each other.

"Motel," I say, "go ask him for Hanukkah money."

"Why should I ask?"

"Because you're younger, that's why."

"That's why I shouldn't. You go. You're older."

My father is well aware of what we are talking about, but he pretends not to hear. Quietly, without haste, he walks over to the cupboard and begins to count out some money. A cold shiver runs down our backs, our hands shake, our hearts pound. We look up at the ceiling, scratch our earlocks, try to act as if this meant nothing at all to us.

My father coughs.

"H'm. . . . Children, come here."

"Huh? What is it?"

"Here is Hanukkah money for you."

The money in our pockets, we move off, Motel and I, at first slowly, stiffly, like toy soldiers, then faster and faster with a skip and a hop. And before we have reached our room we lose all restraint and turn three somersaults one after the other. Then hopping on one foot we sing:

Einga beinga
Stupa tzeinga
Artze bartze
Gola shwartze
Eimelu reimelu
Beigeli feigeli
Hop!

And in our great joy and exuberance we slap our own cheeks twice, so hard that they tingle.

The door opens and in walks Uncle Benny.

"Come here, you rascals. I owe you some Hanukkah money."

Uncle Benny puts his hand into his vest pocket, takes out two silver gulden, and gives one to each of us.

Nobody in the world would ever guess that our father and Uncle Benny are brothers. My father is tall and thin; my uncle is short and fat. My father is dark, my uncle is fair. My father is gloomy and silent, my uncle jolly and talkative, as different as day and night, summer and winter. And yet they are blood brothers.

My father takes a large sheet of paper ruled off into squares, black and white, and asks us to bring him a handful of dry beans from the kitchen, dark ones and white ones. They are going to play checkers.

Mother is in the kitchen rendering goose fat and frying pancakes. My brother and I are spinning our dreidel. My father and Uncle Benny sit down and play checkers. . . .

At this point my mother comes in from the kitchen, her face flaming from the heat.

Behind her comes Braina with a large platter of steaming pancakes. We all move toward the table. My brother Motel and I, who only a moment ago had been fighting like cat and dog, make up quickly, become friends again, and go after the pancakes with the greatest gusto.

In bed that night I lie awake and think: how much would I be worth if all my uncles and aunts and other relatives gave me Hanukkah money? First of all there is Uncle Moishe-Aaron, my mother's brother, stingy but rich. Then Uncle Itzy and Aunt Dveira, with whom my father and mother have not been on speaking terms for years and years. Then Uncle Beinish and Aunt Yenta. And how about our sister Ida and her husband Sholom-Zeidel? And all the other relatives?

"Motel, are you asleep?"

"Yes. What do you want?"

"How much Hanukkah money do you think Uncle Moishe-Aaron will give us?"

"How should I know? I'm not a prophet."

A minute later: "Motel, are you sleeping?"

"Yes. What now?"

"Do you think anyone else in the whole world has as many uncles and aunts as we have?"

"Maybe yes . . . and maybe no."

Two minutes later: "Motel, are you asleep?"

"Of course."

"If you're asleep, how can you talk to me?"

"You keep bothering me so I have to answer."

Three minutes later: "Motel, are you awake?"

This time he answers with a snore. I sit up in bed, take out my father's present, smooth it out, examine it. A whole ruble.

"Think of it," I say to myself. "A piece of paper, and what can't you buy with it! Toys, knives, canes, purses, nuts and candy, raisins, figs. Everything."

I hide the ruble under my pillow and say my prayers. A little later Braina comes in from the kitchen with a platter full of rubles. . . . She isn't walking, she's floating in the air, chanting: "These lights we kindle. . . ." And Motel begins to swallow rubles as if they were pancakes.

"Motel?" I scream with all my might. "God help you, Motel! What are you doing? Eating money?"

I sit up with a start . . . spit three times. It was a dream. And I fall asleep again.

The next morning after we have said our prayers and eaten breakfast, our mother puts on our fur-lined jackets and bundles us up in warm shawls and we start off for our Hanukkah money. First of all, naturally, we stop off at Uncle Moishe-Aaron's.

Our Uncle Moishe-Aaron is a sickly man. He has trouble with his bowels. Whenever we come we find him at the washbowl after having come in from the back yard, washing and drying his hands with the appropriate prayer.

"Good morning, Uncle Moishe-Aaron!" we cry out together, my brother and I. Our Aunt Pessil, a tiny woman with one black eyebrow and one white one, comes forward to meet us. She takes off our coats, unwinds our shawls, and proceeds to blow our noses into her apron.

"Blow!" says Aunt Pessil. "Blow hard. Don't be afraid. Again! Again! That's the way!"

And Uncle Moishe-Aaron, a little man with a moth-eaten mustache and ears stuffed with cotton, dressed in his old ragged fur-lined jacket and with his quilted skullcap on his head, stands at the water bowl, wiping his hands, wrinkling his face, blinking at us with his eyes, while he groans out his prayer.

My brother and I sit down uneasily. We are always miserable and frightened in this house. Aunt Pessil sits opposite us, her arms folded across her chest, and puts us through her usual examination.

"How is father?"

"All right."

"And your mother?"

"All right."

"Have they killed any geese yet?"

"Oh, yes."

"Did they have much fat?"

"Quite a lot."

"Did your mother make pancakes yet?"

"Yes."

"Has Uncle Benny come yet?"

"Yes."

"Did they play checkers?"

"Yes."

And so on and so on. . . .

Aunt Pessil blows our noses again and turns to Uncle Moishe-Aaron.

"Moishe-Aaron, we ought to give the children some Hanukkah money."

Uncle Moishe-Aaron doesn't hear. He keeps on drying his hands and comes to the end of his prayer with a drawn-out groan.

Aunt Pessil repeats: "Moishe-Aaron! The children! Hanukkah money."

"Huh? What?" says Uncle Moishe-Aaron, and shifts the cotton from one ear to the other.

"The children. Hanukkah money!" Aunt Pessil shouts right into his ear.

"Oh, my bowels, my bowels," groans Uncle Moishe-Aaron (that's the way he always talks), holding his belly with both hands. "Did you say Hanukkah money? What do children need money for? What will you do with it, huh? Spend it? Squander it? How much did your father give you? Huh?"

"He gave me a ruble," I say, "and him a half."

"A ruble! Hm. . . . Some people spoil their children, ruin them. What will you do with the ruble, huh? Change it? Huh? No! Don't change it. Do you hear what I say? Don't change it. Or do you want to change it? Huh?"

"What does it matter to you whether they change it or don't change it?" breaks in Aunt Pessil. "Give them what they have coming and let them go on their way."

Uncle Moishe-Aaron shuffles off to his room and begins to search through all the chests and drawers, finds a coin here, a coin there, and mutters to himself:

"Hm. . . . How they spoil their children. Ruin them. Simply ruin them."

And coming back, he pushes a few hard coins into our hands. Once more (for the last time) Aunt Pessil blows our noses, puts on our coats, wraps the shawls around us, and we go on our way. We run over the white frozen crunchy snow, counting the money that

33. The high priest kindling the Temple menorah.
Hanukkah piyyut, Mahzor. Hammelburg, Germany. 1348.

כִּי אֱמֶת וֶטוֹב   אָז וְנֵך הֵטִיבָה שׁוּעִי לְקָשׁוּב
אִי רֵטֵס מֵקֵשׁ מֵעַל עוֹלָה לְפַשׁ אָבְנָה וְאִזְבְּרֵה יְמֵי קֵדֶם
אֲשֶׁר קְרָאֹנִי בְּנֵּטֵם אָדָם   בְּרֵיהֶם אַזְרִירֵה וְלֹא אֵרְוָב
אֲפִירֵה צֵרָחָה וּמִקְמֵה אַטְוֹזֵבֵל אֲרָמָה הֵסֵרְיר וּמָשִׁיעֵי נֵּבַס

Uncle Moishe-Aaron has given us. Our hands are frozen, red and stiff. The coins are copper, large and heavy, very old six-kopek pieces, strange, old-fashioned three-kopek pieces rubbed smooth and thin, groschens that we've never seen before, thick and green with age. It's hard for us, in fact impossible, to figure out how much Hanukkah money Uncle Moishe-Aaron has given us.

Our second stop for Hanukkah money is at Uncle Itzy's and Aunt Dveira's, with whom my parents have not been on speaking terms for many years. Why they don't speak to each other I don't know, but I do know that they never speak, although they go to the same synagogue and sit next to each other on the same bench. And at the holidays when it comes to auctioning off the various honors, they always try to outbid each other. A fierce battle takes place each time. The whole congregation takes sides, helps them to bid, eggs them on.

The *shammash*, who acts as auctioneer, stands on the platform, working hard. His skullcap is off to one side, his prayershawl keeps slipping off his shoulders.

"Eighteen gulden for *Shishi*!

"Twenty gulden for *Shishi*!"

The bidding gets hotter and hotter. My father and Uncle Itzy are bent over their Bibles, from all appearances unaware of what is going on. But every time one of them bids the other one raises it.

The congregation enjoys the spectacle and helps along. "Thirty . . . thirty-five . . . thirty-seven and a half. . . ." But the battle is between my father and Uncle Itzy, and they continue the bidding until one or the other has to give up.

And yet whenever there is a celebration in the family, a birth, a circumcision, a bar mitzvah, an engagement party, a wedding or a divorce, the feud is forgotten. We all attend, exchange gifts, make merry, drink together and dance together like the best of friends.

"Good morning, Uncle Itzy! Good morning, Aunt Dveira!" we cry out together, my brother Motel and I, and they receive us like honored guests.

"Did you come all this way just to see us, or was there something else on your mind?" Uncle Itzy asks and pinches our cheeks. He opens his purse and gives us our Hanukkah money, a new silver twenty-kopek piece to me and another one to my brother. And from there we go straight to Uncle Beinish's. . . .

The next place we go to for Hanukkah money is our sister Ida's. Since she was a child Ida has always been a lugubrious creature. No matter what silly little thing happened, she could always be counted on to burst out crying. She was always shedding tears over her own or other people's troubles. But when she became engaged to Sholom-Zeidel, that was when she really cried! Perhaps you think it was because the young man didn't please her. God forbid! She had never even seen the man! No, she wept because a bride is supposed to weep before her wedding. When the tailors brought her trousseau she wept all night long. Later, when her girl friends came for their last party together she ran off to her room every few minutes to weep into her pillows. But she was really at her best on her wedding day! That day she didn't stop crying for a minute. . . .

When we come into the house, Sholom-Zeidel greets us heartily.

"Well, well! Look who's here! I'm glad you came. I've been waiting. I have some Hanukkah money for you!"

And Sholom-Zeidel takes out his purse and hands each one of us several shiny silver coins. And before we can even count how many he has given us, his hand flies out, *pinch, fillip* go his fingers, and our ears and noses feel the sharp sting.

"Leave them alone! Haven't you tortured them enough?" our sister Ida begs him with tears in her eyes, and calling us aside, fills our pockets with cake, nuts, and figs, and gives us Hanukkah money besides.

We make our escape as quickly as we can and hurry home.

"Well, Motel," I say, "Let's get down to business. Let's figure out how much money we've collected. But I'll tell you what. You wait. First let me count mine and then you'll count yours."

And I begin to count. A ruble and three twenty-kopek pieces, four gulden, five grivnye, six piatekas . . . how much is that altogether? It must be a ruble and three twenties and four gulden and five grivnye and six piatekas. . . .

My brother Motel won't wait until I am through, and he gets busy with his own finances. He moves each coin from one hand to the other and counts.

"A twenty and a twenty are two twenties, and one more is three. And two gulden is three twenties and two gulden and a grivnye and another grivnye and one more—that makes two twenties and three gulden, I mean three gulden and two twenties. . . . What am I talking about? I'll have to start all over again from the beginning."

And he starts all over from the beginning. We count and we count and we can't get the total. We figure and we figure and we can't get it straight. When we get to Uncle Moishe-Aaron's old piatekas, huge sixes, smoothly rubbed threes, and swollen groschens we get so mixed up that we don't know where in the world we are. We try to exchange these coins with our mother, our father, with Braina the cook, but it doesn't work. Nobody wants to have anything to do with them.

"What sort of piatekas are those? Who palmed them off on you?"

We are ashamed to tell, and we keep quiet.

"Do you know what," says my brother Motel, "let's throw them into the oven, or outside in the snow, when no one is looking."

"What a smart boy you are!" I tell him. "It would be better to give them to a beggar."

But just to spite us no one comes to our door. We wait and we wait and not a single one appears. We can't get rid of Uncle Moishe-Aaron's present.

Translated by Julius and Frances Butwin[5]

iiiiiiii
=

The Little Hanukkah Lamp
ISAAC LOEB PERETZ

prolific author of Hasidic stories and folk tales, Peretz (1852–1915), together with Mendele Mocher Seforim and Sholom Aleichem, is considered one of the three modern Yiddish literary classicists

After all, it's Hanukkah! Therefore, I'm going to tell you how a Jew by the name of Shloime-Zalmen, who had once been rich and lost everything (may you not meet with a like fate!), pulled himself up again with the aid of a little Hanukkah lamp.

And don't make the mistake of thinking that this little Hanukkah lamp was made of gold! Not even of silver! It was actually made of brass, and it was quite broken at that. It was just an old hand-me-down from generation to generation . . . twisted out of shape too, and one of its eight candle-holders was broken.

Suddenly Shloime-Zalmen became prosperous again.

How so? This has nothing to do with the subject. Nevertheless, since you insist I'm going to tell you.

They say that once, when he came across a soldier on the street carrying some iron bars, he bought them from him cheap. On coming home, when he tried to file the iron, what do you think he found? Gold! Stolen from the bank, you know.

However, when a Jew suddenly gets rich he turns everything upside-down. First of all, our Jew changed his clothes. He became a "Deitsch" and his wife a regular "Frenchie." She promptly threw away her *sheitel*. Two sons they had, so they took them out of the Jewish *heder* and placed them in the *goyisher* gymnasium. Then they began to change the appearance of their home. There was, for instance, the bookcase full of sacred works. Who needs sacred works? So they sent them to the house of study as a gift. The case itself, an old one, they chopped up into kindling for the oven. In its place his wife placed a full-length mirror: all of a sudden she felt like seeing herself from top to bottom! So they called in the junkman and they sold him the old furniture for next to nothing. In place of it they bought Louis XIV antiques, small, charming, gilded, and upholstered, but with twisted little legs on wheels. A pleasure! People were afraid to sit down on them.

Then they had some old silver: little *etrog* boxes and spice holders, which they sold for a fraction of their value or gave away as wedding gifts to their relatives. Then they bought fine glassware and crystal, fancy flowerpots and vases, in keeping with the fashion of the world, "modern" so to speak.

And since the world is a revolving planet, before long everything began going upside-down for Shloime-Zalmen—with the buttered side down. He could no longer send any money to his sons abroad, was barely able to postpone payment on his notes to his creditors, and nowhere was there the possibility of getting a loan.

Matters got worse and worse. He rummaged about; there wasn't even anything left to pawn. Louis XIV had fallen apart, the fine glassware and crystal was shattered, a few broken pots remained, held together with plaster.

So they lived in dire need.

And when you live in dire need you begin to think a bit about your Jewishness.

Shloime-Zalmen's wife borrowed a *Teitsch-Chumesh* from a neighbor and she'd read it. Now Pan Solomon, the erstwhile Shloime-Zalmen, reverted back again to plain Shloime-Zalmen. Once in a while he'd put on his *tallit* and *tefillin* and recite his prayers.

Once, when Hanukkah came around, he had a strong desire to kindle the Hanukkah lights and to pronounce the benedictions over

34. *Scenes from Judith. Miscellany. Germany. Fifteenth century.*

them. Little candles they managed to get. They then went into the kitchen for a slab of wood on which to fix the candles, but they found none, not even a splinter of kindling.

Suddenly, Shloime-Zalmen recalled that long, long ago, he had found once an old Hanukkah lamp and had thrown it up on top of the oven.

"Shloime-Zalmen," begged his wife, "do climb up and take it down."

So, risking life and limb, they placed a chair on the table which they shoved alongside the oven. Shloime-Zalmen climbed on top of the heap. The chair wobbled and squeaked, indeed Louis XIV was groaning. But at last the Hanukkah lamp was brought down safely.

It was so thickly covered with dust that they managed to wipe it off only after much effort. Then Shloime-Zalmen began to recite the blessings over the lights.

And this he did every day until the eighth day, However, that last night they'd have to go to bed without supper. That wasn't so jolly! And Shloime-Zalmen sat on one side of the table and his wife sat on the other, and they both fell into deep painful thought. It looked very much as if they'd have to die of hunger.

Suddenly there was a ring at the door. So they opened it. In came a young man, an acquaintance of theirs who was an agent for all sorts of things.

"What is it you want?" they asked him.

The agent could barely keep back his laughter. He told them that a crazy Englishman had just come to Warsaw. He was clean-shaven, or perhaps it was just a woman in disguise . . . bought up all kinds of broken things . . . in fact, at the very moment he was waiting in the vestibule.

"Let him come in!" said Shloime-Zalmen. "We'll surely find something. After all, I've been a householder for such a long time."

Shloime-Zalmen and his wife exchanged looks. What sort of old things did they have, they wondered? In the meantime, the Englishman had come in, couldn't wait long enough to be asked in, and then, too, the door stood invitingly open. He took off his fur coat, and when he caught sight of the little Hanukkah lamp he grabbed it up like a hot pancake. He held it in his trembling hands. His eyes sparkled peculiarly.

"Didn't I tell you *meshuggeh*!" whispered the agent.

"*Wie viel, wie viel!*" chanted the Englishman in German.

In short, they sold the Hanukkah lamp, relying entirely on the crazy Englishman's sense of fairness. They took whatever he offered.

After the Englishman and the agent left and the couple were alone, Shloime-Zalmen exclaimed:

"Really *meshuggeh*!"

"And maybe perhaps it was Elijah the prophet?" added his wife. "He might, you know, have paid us a visit on account of the merit we earned with our lighting of the Hanukkah lamp."

Nonetheless, they had enough for supper that night, and for breakfast the next morning, and also something to go to market with.

The money they got proved really lucky. The wheel of fortune began to turn backwards and up again.

And once more Shloime-Zalmen started calling himself Pan Solomon.

When things go well, everything goes well. Shloime-Zalmen and his wife received from their children abroad letters full of *naches*. The son in London had become an engineer, had risen in the world, had got married. He invited his father and mother to come to London and get acquainted with their daughter-in-law.

So they went.

After rejoicing with their son and his wife at home they set out to view the sights of London, first public buildings and factories, then theaters, concert halls, and exhibitions.

One day, they were taken to an art museum. Just try to imagine how stunned the old couple were when in one of the exhibition halls in a glass case they came face to face with their little old Hanukkah lamp! They recognized the laughing lions, the little trees with the birds on them, one of the crooked legs, and one of the half-broken candle-holders.

"So he wasn't at all *meshuggeh*!" concluded *Mr.* (now in England) Solomon.

"And it wasn't Elijah the prophet, either," added *Mrs.* (now in England) Solomon.

To talk loudly, in fact to ask questions, in the presence of their young English daughter-in-law didn't seem quite proper.

So they began to think about it. . . .

Nu, maybe you, too, would like to think about it? . . .

Translated by Nathan Ausubel[6]

iiiiiii

The Extra Flame
CURT LEVIANT

professor of Hebraic studies at Rutgers University; author of short stories and essays and translator of Hebrew and Yiddish classics

Harry Samson took the Hanukkah lamp out of the cabinet and stood resolutely in the middle of the living room. "Tonight I'm going to light the candles by the front window," he announced to his wife.

He watched his wife's eyes move away from her book and up to his face. "You've always lit them in the kitchen," she said.

"Not always. You remember in New York—"

"These past four years have not been New York."

Harry paced the living room floor. "For once I don't want to hide it. So this is a hick town in the South. So what! The lights are supposed to be seen for many reasons. For the passing of a stranger as a reminder. For everyone to see how the Jewish spirit manifested itself over tyranny."

His wife, Vera, understood, but . . . "This isn't a Jewish community where you might wake someone from his lethargy and make him aware of his Jewish heritage. Here? It's not enough that we're the only Jews here, do you want them talking too?"

Harry curled his fingers around the lamp. "No more hiding. This is a holiday of lights. A light in the darkness is no light at all."

They looked at each other in silence, suddenly understanding the meaning of the words, feeling the loneliness of four years of isolation. In the small community even the people's names were so Anglo-Saxon that you couldn't even have the pleasure of conjecture —maybe . . . maybe he's a Jew. Scattered in the nearby towns were a few Jewish families, but not nearly enough to make a *shul* or a community center.

So the Samson home became synagogue and house of study combined. But a house of meeting it could never be. On the horizon stood the day when Harry and Vera would be able to leave town, when Harry would have a teaching job in the city. There they wouldn't be island-dwellers. There they would participate once more in communal life. But as a substitute for communal prayer,

פִּי אֲגַבָה וַ

וַהֲשׁוֹב אֶ

הֵטִיָה סֹוּ

לִקְטֹוב ' אֵ

אֹורֹבָּֽהִי בַּק

בְּעָלַעִלָב ' יַ

לַנְשֹׁוֹב ; אָב

וְאֹוֹבְרָה יְמֹ

קֹדֶם ' אֲשֶׁד

קֹרַאֹוּגֹֽצֵי כַּ

פְּנִבְּתָם אֹוֹדִ

אֹוֹדַהֲתֶם אָ

אֲנִדָה וְלֹא אֲרַדֶם ; אֲשִׁיחָה צָרֹֽוֹה וּנְקָמֹֽית אֲנַטְיֹוֹפֶּבַּס ' אֲבַּח חֹסֹרַדִי וּבִּי
וּמְשִׁיחִי נָבַּס ' אֲוֹרִי עֲמִי פֹּהַקֹרַיֹצֹוּבִּי לַהֲרַבֵּס " יְבַּ/"
יַעֲשֹׁ וַיַעֲשֹׂ סוּגֹסֵי פַּלַדֹּרֹוֹת ' בְּמֹֽוֹ רֹוֹכְבַּס שְׁנֹוּסֵי לַפִּירֹוֹת ' מֹוֹצֶה לַהַ/
הָרֹאֹוֹת בַּהֹֽוֹרַ עִיר נִכְבָּרֹֽוֹת ' קָדֹוֹשֹׁ "

35. *Judith and Holofernes.* Mahzor *in Miscellany.* Ferrara [?], Italy. *Circa 1470.*

Harry discovered that the dignity and gifts of the spirit were anywhere and everywhere. Wherever the willing man roamed, desert or
oasis, there they were.

Their neighbors were silent, distant people. Like Fire Chief
Brown across the street, estranged not only from the Samsons, but
from his other neighbors as well. A silent, brooding man looking as
if a guilt rode perpetually on his shoulders. He was never close with
anyone. He just did his job. Possibly it was his public job that

prevented intimacy, but then again maybe not. No one bothered to analyze it. Harry's other neighbors, too, were polite but distant friends. At times, in his loneliness, he thought that the vague shadow of white-hooded knights still hovered about the town. Their sporadic activity in the area troubled him, and an inner fear took hold of him when he thought he saw an unfriendly look in the townspeople's eyes.

And so the Samsons' companionship was centered around the "family" of his school, where the teachers were always the antibiotics of intelligence against the disease of ignorance. And from these they sustained their social nourishment.

It was the first night of Hanukkah. As on each holiday, their aloneness was accentuated by the starkness of no one's sharing their joy. Harry carried the candle-holder and placed it on the sill facing the street. He put the first candle into position and lit it with the *shammash* candle. He sang the blessings sweetly, looking at his wife. Her eyes were focused on the flame, as if seeking out its mystery.

Harry's hand shook as he passed the flame to the candle. The fire grew in his mind and transformed itself momentarily into a quick nightmare of hooded men and burning crosses. He waited anxiously for the next day.

Business on the street as usual. He taught his classes the rudiments of chemical construction; his wife shopped in the local stores; the world remained a tiny norm. That evening he lit the second candle. Still the quiver of the flame reflected in his mind. Soon someone would inquire. He was impatient for someone to ask— "Why?"

The next day a question was asked.

Fire Chief Brown stopped him on the street, saying: "Excuse me, Mr. Sampson, but, uh . . . can you tell me where you buy those little candles? The ones . . . you were burning in your window last night."

"Why?" he expected him to ask, "why?" But Harry was ready with an answer.

"You can't get them here." Harry forced a laugh. "You get them ten miles out in the supermarket. You know. A few Jewish families are scattered around there." Harry watched Brown's face. His lips didn't form the word *Why.* Then Harry would ask him: "Why did you want to know, Mr. Brown?"

"Thought I would test them for . . . fire hazard, quick-burning quality, and . . . we can't be too careful, you know."

They both laughed, Harry again exploding the artificial smile into a laugh. "Yes, you can get them at the supermarket," he repeated foolishly.

When he told his wife the story, she laughed and said: "Maybe he's Jewish." Harry joined in with the joke. "Maybe I'm a fire chief." But underneath his tongue the words were forming: what will he really do with them?

Two days later he saw some men talking on the street. They were huddled together strangely. He couldn't hear what they were saying and his sensitive mood imagined the worst. "He packs a powerful wallop," said one man, raising his fist. But then he heard: "That Mantle sure is a ballplayer."

He walked by the firehouse, purposely, wanting to meet Mr. Brown, wanting to bring the situation to its inevitable conclusion. He saw him standing there, an intense look on his round face, the lips puffed out, the eyes half closed. He was about to say something. Harry signaled for his attention by lifting his head upward in a half nod.

He'll tell me about the fire hazard. And I'll have to remove the candles from the window. But Mr. Brown was silent. He just looked at Harry, made another motion, as if to walk toward him, but then walked slowly back into the shaded firehouse, his hands in his pocket.

The continued silence of the town hung heavily like a curtain in Harry's mind. By the fourth night he was ready to remove the candles from the window. All he needed was an official excuse. His zeal had done nothing but set him on edge. His wife noticed it. And maybe she was right. All this would have been fine in a Jewish community. But here? Here it was just stubbornness. His wife's thoughts were now, somehow and mysteriously, his own. With each lit candle the insides of his head buzzed with vague fears. Something had to come. It was slowly building up. He knew it. He breathed it in the air of the streets. He saw it in the looks of the people's eyes. He heard it in the rumblings of daily life.

As soon as he finished lighting the fourth night's candles he resolved: "This is the last night." As if confirming his decision, the phone rang. There it is, he thought. He stood watching the candles as his wife answered the phone. The little flames leaped higher and higher and disappeared into the air. Yet more flames always sprang up from the wick. Thus our people against the tyrants, he thought. He let his eyes relax, filling them with light, filling his whole being with the warmth of the light.

"It's for you, Harry." His heart bounced with the leaping flames.

"This is Fire Chief Brown," he heard the voice say. Get those candles off the window, he thought. But instead, a soft voice said: "Do those candles have to burn in the window?"

Very subtle, thought Harry. "How do you mean?" Harry's voice was not his own. The cords in his throat tightened as he spoke. The sound was in a higher, odder pitch. He swallowed.

Mr. Brown continued. "Is it part of the religious ceremony to do that?"

Come out with it, Harry thought, and tell. Don't suspend me, then stab me. Tell me now. "Let me explain the significance of the candles, Mr. Brown—"

Harry was cut short. "Don't bother explaining. Just tell me, is it better if they burn in view?"

"Yes," Harry's thoughts exploded. "It is better if they are seen, if they communicate their message to the others—"

"Good. That's all I wanted to know. The message was communicated. Thank you." And click—the phone was dead. Harry looked at the mouthpiece for a while and set it back.

"What's the matter, Harry?" his wife asked. She stretched her hand out to him. He took her warm hand into his and felt his fingers trembling against hers. The nervousness leaped with the touch into her. "What is it? What did he say?" The edge of her lips quivered. "You're all upset."

"I don't understand. He said, 'The message was communicated.' "

"Harry," she said softly, but there was a tone of firmness in her voice. "Since you started this candlelighting in the window you haven't been the same. You worry about every word, every sound, every flame. Either go back to the privacy of the kitchen, or accept your own move."

Harry knew his wife was right, but still he felt that his wife was deserting him, by asking about it in the open, by verbalizing what had previously been unsaid. Gloomily he looked at the candles and at the street below, scanning the houses across the street mechanically. His mind was playing tricks again. Two of his four candles had gone out already. In the window opposite his, symbolically enough in Mr. Brown's window, the reflection of his Hanukkah lights were shining. He looked at their reflection. Suddenly he called his wife.

"Come quickly. I'm having a vision."

Vera came running, afraid something was wrong with him.

"Look. Look across the street. In Mr. Brown's window."

She held her breath. They couldn't believe it. A living reflection.

Strangely, a third candle appeared to be shining in Mr. Brown's window, while only two remained in Harry's window.

"He's burning Hanukkah lights," Harry shouted, patting his wife on the arm. "Vera, do you know what that means? Hanukkah lights by Mr. Brown."

Across the street, the lit candle illumined Mr. Brown's shadowy, brooding features, and the flickering flames cast a glow on his face as he lit the fourth candle.

"A light from the darkness," Vera whispered, "another miracle."[7]

13 HANUKKAH ODDITIES

SIDNEY B. HOENIG

Because the Feast of Lights was not confined to the synagogue but found its fullest observance and celebration in the home, in an atmosphere of relaxation and freedom from any restraint, not limited to ritual food (e.g., matzah) or locale (e.g., sukkah), it attained great popularity for entertainment. Its joy goes beyond formal religious practice. Hence it includes gambling, mystic numerology, talmudic riddles; acrostics, Hasidic explanations, and cryptic allusions. The participant found pleasure in juggling the name and meaning of Hanukkah, in finding biblical references which "proclaimed" and "foresaw" the holiday, and in giving an added mysterious *hiddush* (novel interpretation) to the concept of freedom and to the historic event.

There was leisure while the Hanukkah lights burned—no one

engaged in manual labor or even studied. Many would take to card-playing, usually forbidden during the rest of the year. On Hanukkah it was regarded not as gambling but as a sport of wits; even Rabbi Levi Isaac of Berditchev did not frown upon it. Chess, *kvitlach,* and dominoes were other pastimes. Intellectuals would seek to demon-strate their mental acumen in even a lighter and imaginative vein, but always relative to the festival's import. Scholars would thus vie with each other in interpreting *ketowes*, or riddles.

iiiiiii
=
The Dreidel

Most popular of all Hanukkah sport was and is today the game of dreidel. As the name from the German *dreihen*, "to spin," implies, this is a spinning top (in Hebrew *sevivon*). This top was popular in medieval Germany; its letters in Latin characters: *N—nisht* (noth-ing); *G—gantz* (all); *H—halb* (half) and *S—shtel* (put), were trans-ferred to popular Jewish script and usage. Symbolically the top recalls the "turnover" of events when Judah the Maccabee's few forces vanquished and toppled the many in Antiochus' army. The natural sequence of events was overturned: the strong were spun into the hands of the weak, as enunciated in the *Al ha-Nissim* prayer of Hanukkah.

To justify the gambling, many interpreted the game as a disguised form of studying. When the Jews were not allowed to engage in the study of the Law, they would assemble to play the game and at the same time discuss the Law orally.

The Hebrew letters *nun, gimel, he, shin* on the dreidel are usually explained as the initial letters of the phrase that epitomized the great event—*Nes gadol hayah sham*, "A great miracle happened there." However, these letters became directions for a put-and-take game, indicating *nun*—take nothing; *gimel*—take all; *he*—take half, and *shin*—put in the pot. In Israel the letters are changed to *nun, gimel, he, pe*; the *pe*, meaning *po* (here), refers to the Temple area; but this was not universally accepted.

Though the playing of the teetotum (dreidel) originated in

medieval days and was very popular in mid-nineteenth century London under its name, derived from the letter T on one side, meaning *totum* ("take all"), it was given a Jewish characterization by the rabbis' "discovery" that the letters were "prophesied" in the Bible. Confirmation was found in the biblical portion read in the Hanukkah period, i.e., in the story of Judah's coming to Goshen. The Bible relates that when Jacob planned to visit Joseph in Egypt and to settle there temporarily, he sent Judah to precede him, "to point the way . . . to Goshen" (Genesis 46.28). The Hebrew letters of *Goshna*, "to Goshen," are similar to those on the dreidel, emphasizing that Jacob's son Judah as well as Judah the Maccabee preceded to show the way for all Israel. Since the letters on the dreidel are equal in number to the letters in *Mashiah*, Messiah (both are equivalent to 358), many believed that the Messiah of the House of Judah would be the appointed one, to show the way for further miracles for Israel. The struggle of the Hasmoneans was seen as a symbolic reversal of the bondage of Goshen.

In the East European schools of the pre-Hitler period the children during the early part of the month of Kislev would be busy carving dreidels from wood or casting them in lead. An allusion to the wood product was found in the prophetic reading (*haftarah*) of the week: "And thou, son of man, take thee one stick, and write upon it: For Judah, and for the children of Israel, his companions" (Ezekiel 37.16). Thus the dreidel of wood spelled "unity" for Israel.

The letters were also mystically interpreted as alluding to the components of man's being as indicated in the Hebrew: *nefesh*—soul, *guf*—body, *sekhel*—mind; this is *hakol*—all that characterizes man.

It was also observed that the four letters (358 in gematria) are equivalent numerically to *nahash*, the serpent or evil spirit. The dreidel is spun to topple evil and to bring forth the messianic era establishing God's kingdom. The Hebrew phrase "God is king, God rules and shall rule" is also the equivalent of 358.

In sum, it was stressed that the world is like a dreidel. Everything is set forth in cycles; things change and spin but all emanate from one Root. The dreidel reflects the game of chance in life as an on-going event. Its letters are also the initials of the phrase "You redeemed Your very own tribe; Mount Zion" (Psalms 74.2).

ⅲⅲⅲⅲⅲ
=

The Dreidel and the Grogger

The student who sought mystic interpretation even in the common-place mode of play on Hanukkah and on Purim asked why we make noise with the grogger on Purim but spin the dreidel on Hanukkah. He found his answer in the manner both instruments are held. The grogger is held below, and the noise is produced by the holder's

*36. "Kindling the Hanukkah Candles."
Woodcut. By Jakob Steinhardt.*

action, symbolizing that intervention on Purim came from below—
by Esther's plea to the king and Mordecai's cry before the royal
gates. But the Hanukkah miracle came from above—through divine
intervention. Hence the spin is made holding the dreidel on its top,
designating that it is the Almighty who spins all worldly events.
There is also an interpretation in reverse. The motion of the spinning dreidel on the table indicates the mundane earth's rotation;
Hanukkah eventuated from physical battles. Purim, however,
emerged through prayer and fasting; its spiritual aspect is illustrated
by holding the grogger upward.

iiiiiii
=

Hanukkah Gelt

The custom of giving Hanukkah *gelt* (money) to the poor, to teachers, and to other communal functionaries is of comparatively recent
origin, probably from the seventeenth century. It may be a carry-
over from the admonition in the Book of Esther of "sending portions to one another and gifts to the poor." In some circles, teachers
in the *hedarim* received monetary bonuses from the schoolchildren's
parents throughout the week of Hanukkah, emphasizing the dignity
of Torah learning and its reward.

Giving Hanukkah *gelt* undoubtedly became popular also because
it provided children with money for their dreidel playing and students for their card games. Even the traditional Hanukkah song
"*Maoz Tzur Yeshuati*" (Mighty Rock of My Salvation) served to ac-
cumulate pennies. By changing the opening word *maoz* (mighty) to
maot (money), the first line was made to read "Mighty money is my
salvation." This amusing semantic byplay was always in the spirit of
holiday gaiety. The serious vein of the chant was never compro-
mised.

ïïïïïïï
=
Cardplaying

The dispensation to play cards on Hanukkah stemmed from its generally falling in the latter part of December, when the night of the Nativity was observed by the Christian world. The Jews called it *Nital Nacht* (from *natoli dominus*) and interpreted it as *Nicht toren lehrnen*—not permitted to learn. Therefore the time was spent in cardplaying, which was called *klein shas* (small Talmud), or *kvitlach spielen*—paper playing. The dispensation for general cardplaying was attributed to the days being those on which *Tahanun* (the propitiatory prayers) are not recited.

The *kvitlach* was a special game consisting of thirty-one numbered cards, artistically colored. These represented the thirty-one kings against whom the Israelites fought on their entrance to Canaan, a biblical prelude to the Maccabean victory.

ïïïïïïï
=
Biblical Allusions

Despite the great zeal displayed in many a Jewish home for the festival of Hanukkah, its official place in the list of holidays is only minor. This status derives from its origin in postbiblical days and its ordination by the *bet din* of Hasmoneans, in contradistinction to the major festivals and the Awesome Days which have their traditional foundation in the Bible. The books of the Maccabees saw the light of day long after the canon of the Pentateuch and the Prophets had been closed. Prophetic vision had already ceased when Judah the Maccabee triumphed. Consequently the Hasmonean books were automatically excluded from the canon by the measuring criterion of the Bible. Purim, also in the minor category, fared better. The popular Scroll of Esther was sufficiently acknowledged to be included among the Twenty-four Books.

Since Hanukkah is only of rabbinic origin, many have questioned the use of the liturgic phrase: "Blessed are Thou . . . who hast sanctified us by Thy commandments and commanded us to kindle the light of Hanukkah." A prayer invoking God's name is recited ordinarily for the fulfillment of a *mitzvah* specifically stated in the Bible. For Hanukkah such commandment is nonexistent. A rabbinic law needed special authorization to be included in the liturgic category. Such was found in the application of the general biblical exhortation: "You shall act in accordance with the instructions given you and the ruling handed down to you; you must not deviate from the verdict that they announce to you either to the right or to the left" (Deuteronomy 17.11). This, the sages said, meant that adherence to rabbinical laws was originally imposed upon every Jew by the Torah itself. Hanukkah was elevated to the status of other rabbinic ordinances like kindling the Sabbath lamp and reading the Megillah. Since every Jew is obliged to follow the decisions of the Rabbis, the observances must be fulfilled as if they were laws of Moses. Only thus did Hanukkah, though of rabbinic origin, receive Mosaic sanction.

Nonetheless, rabbinic authors were not satisfied with the general declaration that the observance of the Hanukkah festival was added to and became part of the 613 commandments. Such blanket support gave meager luster or strength to the holiday. More definitive sources, more distinct and specified notations in the Pentateuch were sought. Any allusion, farfetched as it might be, was better than a wholesale clause. The adage "Search the Scriptures well" served as sufficient inspiration and sanction to motivate an effort to find the Feast of Lights ordained in the Bible.

The first reference to the festival was presumed in the creation story. "Let there be light" (Genesis 1.3) was the divine command, and since the numerical value of the word *yehi* ("let there be") is twenty-five, declared the Rabbis, it is thereby recorded that on the twenty-fifth day of Kislev the light of the menorah shall burn in every home.

The portions of Genesis read during the festival month abound in allusions. Hanukkah is "hinted at" in the wrestling of Jacob with his adversary. Triumphantly Jacob exclaimed when he prevailed: "I have seen a divine being face to face, yet my life has been preserved" (Genesis 32.31). Whereupon, "the sun rose upon him" (*va-yizrah lo ha-shemesh*) (ibid. 32). This latter phrase was ingeniously interpreted to apply to the Hanukkah celebration. Instead of *shemesh*, "sun," by a change of vowels, the word was read *shammash*, "sexton light." Since the total of Hanukkah lights is thirty-six, this was found to be the numerical value of the word *lo*, "upon him," in the biblical verse. Thus even the Pentatuch declared that "the *sexton light* was to *kindle* the other *thirty-six*."

The particular portion read on Hanukkah week, Genesis 41–44.17, served as a rich source for many observations regarding the festival. The *soferim*, or scribes, who counted the letters of the weekly portion to guard against scribal errors found that this portion contained 2,025 letters, the same number that encompasses the entire story of the holiday. The *ner*, or light, of Hanukkah, has the gematria or numerical value of 250; for *nun* equals 50 and *resh* is 200. This sum, when multiplied by 8, the days of the festival, totals 2,000. Because Hanukkah begins on the twenty-fifth day of the month, 25 is added, raising the final total to 2,025. Thus, later generations, reading the 2,025 letters in the portion, would remember all about the feast.

The prayer for Hanukkah, *Al ha-Nissim*, "For the Miracles," also was linked with the same weekly portion. Reading the story of Joseph's meeting with his brethren, it was recalled that Joseph gave each one gifts. "But Benjamin's portion was five times that of anyone else" (Genesis 43.34). These "five times" are literally in the Hebrew "five hands," and in *Al ha-Nissim*, the term "hand" is also repeated five times: "Thou hast delivered the strong into the *hand* of the weak, the many into the *hand* of the few, the impure into the *hand* of the pure, the wicked into the *hand* of the righteous, and the arrogant into the *hand* of those who occupy themselves with the study of the Law."

We have already seen that reference to the dreidel was found in Genesis 46.28 when Jacob sent Judah to Egypt. The struggle of the Hasmoneans was indeed a heritage from Goshen, since the Hasmoneans were the "tribute-bearers [*hashmanim*] . . . come from Egypt" (Psalms 68.32).

In Leviticus 23, all major biblical holidays and their manner of observance are enumerated. Then chapter 24 opens with the passage: "Command the Israelite people to bring you clear oil of beaten olives for lighting," a direct reference to the cruse of pure oil stamped with the seal of the high priest which the Hasmoneans found among the ruins of the Temple. This allusion to Hanukkah after the listing of all the major holidays bears special import. While it is only in the minor class, its significance is enhanced in that it is accorded the place of honor in the opening phrase of the new chapter.

The enumeration of the various utensils used in the First Temple by Solomon, as recorded in a second prophetic reading of Sabbath Hanukkah (1 Kings 7), must have inspired the Maccabees to cleanse the Second Temple and to rekindle the menorah light to shed luster upon coming generations.

iiiiiii
=

Acrostics

The name Maccabee, is, according to mystical or pilpulistic students, simply the initial Hebrew letters of the biblical phrase "Who is like You, O Lord, among the celestials" (Exodus 15.11). These words emblazoned on the battle standards fired Judah's army with invincible faith and religious zeal to enter the field of combat against the Syrian infidels.

The rubric "Maccabee" also is formed by the name of Judah's father: *M*attityahu *K*ohen *B*en *Y*ohanan. His children perpetuated their stalwart father's name when they used the first letters for their own surname.

Searching into the sources of genealogy, others recognized Maccabee as a combination not of initial letters but of the last letters of the names of the patriarchs, Avraha*m*, *Y*itzha*k*, Yaako*b*. Maccabee (MKBI) was the progenitor of the Hasmonean priestly dynasty, even as the first letters in the name indicate *mamlekhet kohanim Bet Yisrael*, "kingdom of priests of the House of Israel."

Scholars have also advanced various explanations of Hasmonean, the name applied to all the sons of Mattathias. The Hasidic student would find concealed in the name "Hasmonean" those elements of the Jewish religion which the Syrians had aimed to abolish, and he would interpret the letters in the following manner:

חדש	New Moon celebration
שבת	Sabbath
מילה	circumcision rite
נדה	laws of menstrual purity
ארוסה	sanctity of the betrothal
יחוד השם	belief in the unity of God

Attempts were made to ascribe new meaning to the name Hanukkah. With great ingenuity, therefore, they read Hanukkah as two words, *hanu* and *kah*, "they [the Maccabees] rested [from their fighting] on the twenty-fifth [day]." Thus the Hasmonean struggle and ultimate victory on the twenty-fifth day of Kislev was chronicled in the name.

The talmudic controversy between the schools of Shammai and Hillel concerning the laws of kindling the lights was also used to interpret the word Hanukkah. According to the Shammaites the lights were to be kindled in a descending order: eight on the first day, seven on the second, and so forth. On the eighth day only one candle was lit. The school of Hillel proposed an ascending order: one on the first day and finally eight on the last day. The final decision is recorded in the name itself as follows:

ח	eight
נרות	candles
והלכה	and the law is
כבית	according to the school of
הלל	Hillel

To demonstrate how these letters reflected the detailed controversy would be a novel scholastic achievement. Some students attempted it and succeeded, thus:

Shammai's view:
ח נרות ופוחת כל השבוע
(Eight candles diminishing nightly during the week.)

Hillel's view:
חד נר ומוסיף כל השבוע
(One candle to be added nightly.)

The accepted opinion:
חכמים נמנו וגמרו כבית הלל
(The rabbis decided in favor of the school of Hillel.)

In sum, Hanukkah adds up to eighty-nine, as does the word *guf*, "body," manifesting the physical prowess of Judah "the hammer" or "the general" (*matzbi*).

ⅲⅲⅲⅲⅲ
=

Riddles

During the long nights of the eight-day festival the rigorous study of the Talmud is inhibited. Yet, the yeshivah student continued to nurture his mental acumen with pilpul, gematrias, and *notarikon*— casuistry, arithmetical puzzles, and word abbreviations. These riddles, known as *ketowes*, whose spelling and meaning are in themselves enigmatic, have been regarded as an outgrowth of the *kvitlach*, the "card and paper" games mentioned above, which provided pleasant indoor sport during the holiday season. It has been suggested that the word *ketowes* derived from the root *katav*, "to write," since the answers to riddles required writing the figures or letters. Others have suggested that *ketowes* is borrowed from a Slavonic root *katowcz*, meaning "fun" or "tricks." Another view is that the word is derived from the French *chatoullier*, "to play." Its usual meaning was "solution," hence the Yiddish maxim *Zekhus avos ken ketowes* (Merit of the fathers is not a solution).

In general, these are in the form of arithmetic puzzles, to which the number forty-four is always the final answer. This total represents the sum of all the candles used on Hanukkah week, adding the eight *shammashim* serving the menorah to the thirty-six original candles. These thirty-six lights, symbolic of the tractates in the Talmud possessing the Gemara commentary, served also as an inspiration to rekindle the belief in the thirty-six "righteous individuals" who, according to tradition, are found in every generation. These sustain the light of Israel because of their invincible faith.

Interesting examples of the *ketowes* are found in dialogues, especially in the student-teacher question-and-answer method. "Can you calculate the number of candles from the lesson?" The group had just completed the tractate Gittin and was now celebrating the *siyyum* with unbounded Hanukkah joy. The pupils were dumbfounded. "Can there be any possible relationship between Hanukkah and Gittin?" Only the genius of the class knew, and he quoted the rule from Gittin 5b: "He who brings a divorce bill (*get*) from beyond the sea (*ha-yam*) must add another witness before the tribunal to validate the proceedings." The pupil continued: "The equivalent of *get* is 12, and the numerical value of *ha-yam* (the province of the sea from whence the divorce bill is brought) is 55. By subtracting this *get* from its source (55 minus 12), we obtain a remainder of 43. By adding one more task, the appearance before the *bet din*, our final total will be 44, corresponding to the number of candles of the week."

A further illustration of such Hanukkah numerical gymnastics is contained in a story about the renowned scholar Israel Israelin. Seated at his table and enjoying the latkes, he suddenly asked his pupil, Yozel, to prove the number of candles by removing his coat. "What has *my coat* to do with Hanukkah?" asked the scholar. Only when the teacher told him to use gematria, did he find the answer. "The numerical value of my name Yozel is 53, and my coat *begged*, has the gematria 9. When my coat is removed from me (53 minus 9), I remain with 44, corresponding to the total of Hanukkah lights."

Such exercises in numerical juggling served as a pretext for giving the students a deserved Hanukkah holiday. After the talmudic lecture, a rabbi once remarked: "What appropriate phrase from the Song of Ascents shows the exact total of lights? Then you will be excused." The answer, recalling the tense and perilous Hanukkah struggle, was found in Psalms 124.8, "Our help is in the name of the Lord," and the preceding passage in the psalm revealed all: "The trap [*pah*] broke and we escaped." The student gave the deduction: "The gematria of *pah* is 88; this is broken in half, leaving 44 (the total of candles) and now we may escape."

Our concluding word relates to the popular psalm of Hanukkah, "A song for the dedication of the Temple" (Psalms 30.1), with its finale:

> You turned my lament into dancing,
> You undid my sackcloth and girded me with joy (ibid. 12).[1]

14 HANUKKAH SIDELIGHTS

||||||||

The Festival Names

Hanukkah literally means dedication, inauguration, consecration. The term "dedication offering for the altar" (*hanukkat ha-mizbeah*) is used in the Pentateuch (Numbers 7.10). However, the word *hanukkah* is found only once in the Bible, when Ezra and Nehemiah dedicated the walls of Jerusalem: "They sought the Levites out of all their places, to bring them to Jerusalem, to keep the dedication [*hanukkah*] with gladness" (Nehemiah 12.27). As a festival the name first appears in *Megillat Taanit* 9 and refers to the dedication of the Temple and the altar.

In 1 Maccabees, Hanukkah is referred to as "the dedication of the altar": "Judah and his brothers and the entire congregation of Israel decreed that the days of the dedication of the altar should be kept with gladness and joy at their due season, year after year, for eight days from the twenty-fifth of the month of Kislev" (4.59). In 2 Maccabees the festival is called "the purification festival": "We are about to observe 'the purification festival'; and we are writing to you to ask if you will also observe these days of the festival. . . . For it was He who delivered us from grave dangers and purified the Temple" (2.16–18).

The historian Josephus called Hanukkah the Festival of Lights: "We observe this festival, which we call the Festival of Lights, giving this name to it, I think, from the fact that the right to worship appeared to us at a time when we hardly dared hope for it."[1] It appears that Josephus did not know why Hanukkah is thus designated.

Both names—Hanukkah and Festival of Lights—complement each other in expressing the meaning of the holiday. Hanukkah, like other festivals, has dual significance—religious and national. Hanukkah refers specifically to the dedication of the Temple and its worship. Festival of Lights alludes to the tapers and torches lit to mark the military victory over the Syrians and the reestablishment of Jewish hegemony. Professor Solomon Zeitlin wrote: "The name Hanukkah bears the religious connotation in the commemoration of the dedication of the altar, while the name Festival of Lights is in commemoration of national liberty which the Jews won from the Syrians. However, after the destruction of the Second Temple, when the Jews lost their national state and were segregated as a religious community, the name Festival of Lights disappeared and only the religious name Hanukkah remained."[2] In modern Israel, Feast of the Lights (Hag ha-Urim) is frequently employed.

Hanukkah is also known in Jewish literature as Feast of the Maccabees and Festival of the Hasmoneans.[3]

iiiiiiii
=

Judah's Surname

Judah was the first to be called Maccabee; subsequently, the surname was applied to his kinsmen and his followers. The origin of this surname is shrouded in uncertainty. The Hebrew original source has been lost; the earliest extant record is the Greek Makkabaios, which has been transliterated into Hebrew. Maccabee may be derived from the Hebrew word meaning "hammer," equating Judah with its great strength. Dr. Zeitlin maintains that the Hebrew *makkaba*, literally "hammerhead," was applied to Judah because of the shape of his skull, claiming that it was a common practice in the Hellenistic world to name men according to physical characteristics.[4]

It has been claimed that the family name of the Maccabean dynasty is Hasmonean. According to Josephus, Mattathias's great-grandfather was named Hashmon, meaning rich, prince, or noble.[5] Perhaps it derives from a geographical locale (Joshua 15.27).[6] Others maintain that Hasmonean was applied to Mattathias because he was a priest or a "prince," as were his descendants.[7]

iiiiiiii
=

A Glaring Omission

While the author of 1 Maccabees reveals a deep devotion to Jewish laws and ideals, the words "God" and "Lord" are conspicuously missing, although the divine Presence pervades the volume. This avoidance appears to have been deliberate on the part of the author.[8]

iiiiiiii
=

The Eight-Day Miracle
ELIYAHU KITOV

Why do we observe Hanukkah for eight days, since the miracle of the oil occurred only for seven days, there having originally been sufficient oil for one day? Many of the great scholars have offered a variety of answers. The following are some of their explanations:

1. The first day of the festival commemorates the miracle of the military victory. "On the twenty-fifth of Kislev the Jews rested from battle with their enemies." They therefore celebrated the day, just as Purim celebrates the day when the Jews "rested from their enemies." The remaining seven days commemorate the miracle of the oil.

2. The very discovery of the one remaining jar of pure oil that was marked with the high priest's seal was itself a miracle.

3. The discovered oil was divided into eight portions to last the eight days required for the production of new oil. Till then the menorah was to be lit for at least a brief hour every evening. Miraculously, the minute measure of oil poured into the menorah each evening burned the entire day.

4. After the menorah was filled with all the available oil, the jar remained full as before.

5. All the oil was emptied into the menorah, but after the lamps had burned all night, they were found next morning still filled with oil.

6. The Greeks prohibited circumcision; this decree was the harshest of all the decrees they issued, its aim being to annul the covenant between God and Israel. When the Hasmoneans prevailed against their enemies, they rejoiced over the renewal of the covenant of circumcision, which is set for the eighth day in a child's life.

7. The first night they made thin wicks, which could only draw a minute measure of oil; they also apportioned the oil itself, of which they poured only a little into the menorah. Miraculously, the lamps burned in full light all night, and the same occurred every remaining night.

8. The jar itself absorbed some of the oil so that there did not remain even sufficient oil for one day.

9. The Greeks wanted to uproot faith in divine Providence from the Jewish heart. They wanted to implant the belief that the events of nature occur only in accord with mechanical laws. Many Jews inclined to their views. Events, however, convinced them that all existence reflected divine Providence; that even when the world functioned in accord with natural law, it still remained totally depen-

dent on the hand of God and His providence. From the miracle they understood that the natural function of oil is also a miracle.

10. The very fact that they did not despair from lighting the lamps even the first day, despite the knowledge that they would be unable on the morrow to fulfill the Torah's command to light "a perpetual lamp," was in itself a great miracle; a miracle which enables the people of Israel to endure through all generations and every exile. Had they always tried to surmise what the future held in store for them, they would long since have lost the capacity to survive. The people of Israel have, however, placed their trust in God, and they have rejoiced whenever they were given the opportunity to abide by His word.

Translated by Nathan Bulman[9]

iiiiiii

Candlelighting in Daylight

In Jerusalem it is customary to kindle the Hanukkah lamp in the synagogue not only in the evenings but also in the mornings when the recital of the blessings is omitted. Two rationales are advanced for this practice: first, lighting the lamp in the morning when lights are not needed adds emphasis to the commemoration of the miracle; second, it aids those who were unable to kindle the lamp on the previous evening to know the number of lights required on the following evening.[10]

Among the laws of Hanukkah prepared for soldiers by Israel's Chief Rabbi Shlomoh Goren when he was chief chaplain of the Israel Defense Force, we find the following. Soldiers in fortified positions and in the front lines, fearing that the enemy will espy them if they kindle the Hanukkah lights at night, should light them a half hour before sunset and extinguish them immediately after sunset. If this is not possible, they should feel as though they are fulfilling the commandment through the candles being lit at their military base.[11]

37. *Hanukkah commemorative coins minted in Israel.*

ⅲⅲⅲⅲ
=

Electric Substitutes for Hanukkah Lights
J. DAVID BLEICH

The suitability of electric lights for use in place of the usual Sabbath candles and as a substitute for the traditional Hanukkah menorah has been a recurrent theme in halakhic literature since the invention of the incandescent bulb. Numerous responsa expressing conflicting viewpoints have been written on this topic.

The halakhic principle governing the lighting of the Hanukkah lamp is the dictum "Kindling constitutes performance of the *mitzvah*." For this reason the lights, once properly kindled, need not be relit should they become extinguished. But on the other hand if the lamp, at the time of kindling, contains an insufficient quantity of fuel, additional fuel should not be added; rather, the lamp must be extinguished and relit. On the basis of this principle Rabbi Zevi Pesach Frank, late chief rabbi of Jerusalem, peremptorily dismisses consideration of the halakhic feasibility of an electric Hanukkah menorah. Electric current is not stored for future use but is consumed as it is generated. Thus the requisite amount of "fuel" is not immediately available at the moment the lamp is turned on. The lamp is dependent upon continous generation of power to remain lit. Hence the act of kindling in itself is insufficient to cause the lamp to burn for the prescribed period of time. An identical line of argument is advanced by R. Shlomo Zalman Auerbach in the third chapter of his *Meorei Esh*, a classic monograph on the halakhic ramifications of electricity. . . .

Rabbi Frank raises yet another objection. He questions whether the turning on of an electric switch constitutes an act of kindling. He expresses doubt as to whether this is to be deemed a "direct action" or an "indirect action" and enters into a further discussion of whether a "direct action" is indeed required or whether an "indirect action" is sufficient with regard to the fulfillment of *mitzvot*. . . .

R. Yitzhak Schmelkes maintained that since electricity is in common use throughout the year, use of electric lights on Hanukkah does not constitute "publicizing the miracle." Rabbi Eliyahu Kletzkin and Rabbi Y. E. Henkin both assert that the Hanukkah menorah, since it is modeled upon the candelabrum used in the Temple, must contain fuel and a wick. Electric bulbs do not incorporate these features and, hence, in their opinion, cannot be used as Hanukkah lights. Both Rabbi Eliezer Waldenberg and Rabbi Mordecai L. Katzenellenbogen disagree and present evidence supporting their contention that neither wick nor fuel is essential for fulfillment of this obligation. Rabbi Waldenberg nevertheless expresses doubt with regard to the utilization of electric bulbs for this purpose. . . . While there is some disagreement with regard to the specific grounds for its disqualification, none of the above authorities approve the use of an electric Hanukkah menorah for fulfillment of the *mitzvah*.[12]

iiiiiiii
=

The Most Popular Ritual

In the late 1950s a study of Jews in a midwestern suburb known as Lakeville revealed that kindling the Hanukkah candles was the most frequently observed ritual, exceeding even the Passover seder—the only two rituals practiced by a majority of the respondents. In fact, the Hanukkah candlelighting ceremony was more prevalent in the homes of this Jewish community than in their parents' homes.[13]

iiiiiiii
=

Hanukkah Greetings in the Venice Ghetto

During the Middle Ages, Jewish residents of the Venice Ghetto observed a unique rite during the Festival of Lights. Embarking on gondolas, they rowed through the canal streets, and when they passed a home where the Hanukkah lights were burning in the windows or outside the doors, they greeted the dwellers with a blessing and a gay Hanukkah song.[14]

iiiiiiii
=

Hanukkah among Reform Jews

Isaac M. Wise, who introduced Reform Judaism in the United States
and founded its major institutions, suggested in 1865 the elimination of the Hanukkah lights.[15] Six years later the Augsburg Synod,
with delegates mostly from German Reform congregations, introduced a resolution urging the appropriate commemoration of
Hanukkah, which had been neglected in many Reform Jewish congregations and schools. The rationale for this resolution was to
counteract the celebration of Christmas by many Jewish families "in
direct opposition to Jewish consciousness."[16]

iiiiiiii
=

Marranism and Hanukkah

El Macabeo: Poemo Heroico, an epic poem by Dr. Miguel de Silveyra,
was first published in 1638 in Naples, where the author had fled
from Spain after appearing as a witness for a defendant on trial
before the Holy Office of the Inquisition. Silveyra was a New Christian, that is, of Jewish descent, and there is a probability that he may
have been a Marrano. Hailed as a masterpiece, his poem was reprinted in Madrid in 1731 and published in an Italian translation in
1810. Concerning Silveyra's choice of the Maccabean revolt as the
theme for his epic, Dr. Yosef Hayim Yerushalmi has written: "He
could not have been blind to the fact that, while the so-called Maccabean saints were venerated by the church, in essence the story of
the Maccabees was one of a great moment in Jewish history. Again,
while among medieval Jewry the Maccabean revolt had been generally quite underrated (except by the author of the *Yosippon*), among
the Marranos themselves, perhaps because of their reliance on the
Apocrypha, the Maccabean tradition seems to have played a certain
role."[17] Dr. Yerushalmi cites a few examples of this tradition: "A
Marrano woman of Trancoso in the 17th century . . . was considered
a 'saint' and was held to be a descendant of the Maccabees. A similar

instance is recorded in Brazil in 1591, of a mother and two daughters known as 'Machabeas.'. . . . Among the Judaizing rites charged against Antonio Homem and his circle in Coimbra was a vestigial observance of Hanukkah, called there 'a Paschoa das Candelilhas.' "[18]

iiiiiiii
=

The Maccabees in Christianity

Hanukkah is mentioned in the Gospel of John: "It was the Feast of Dedication of the Temple at Jerusalem; and it was winter" (10.22). There is evidence that the early Christians were intrigued by the Hanukkah festival and its heroes.

The Jewish Scriptures do not include the books of the Maccabees, but relegated them to the Apocrypha. However, 1 and 2 Maccabees have been accepted as canonical by the Catholic Church. This was confirmed by the councils of Florence (1441), Trent (1546), and Vatican I (1870), which reiterated that these works were inspired by God.[19]

Indeed, the Roman Catholic Church considers the Maccabees among her saints. Abbot Aelfric (c. 955–1020), known as Grammaticus, who was considered "the most distinguished English-writing theologian in his time," included the history of Judah Maccabee in his *Lives of the Saints* (996–97) so that the Maccabean struggle might serve as a motivation "to inspire the struggle for English nationhood."[20]

According to sources gathered by Yom-Tov Lewinski, about a thousand years before Michelangelo (1475–1564), whose masterpiece "Moses" is in the Roman church San Pietro in Vincoli, a marble coffin with seven compartments was taken to this Catholic house of worship. In these compartments are allegedly the bones of the seven sons of Hannah slain by King Antiochus. According to a legend the king, consternated by the uncompromising heroism of these Maccabean brothers who chose death rather than bow to an idol, ordered their bodies to be placed in a beautiful marble casket. The casket was interred in the city of Antioch and a church was built on its site. The anniversary of their death, or, according to some sources, the spiritual "Birthday of the Maccabees," was fixed on the first day of August and was denominated by the early Christians as *Commemoratio Sanctorum Macchabaeorum Martyrum*, Commemoration of the Sainted Maccabean Martyrs. In church usage the "birthday" of a saint meant commemoration. While the August 1 date is listed in the oldest ecclesiastical calendar (702–6), the commemoration is no longer observed.

In the sixth century, when Antioch was destroyed by an earth-quake, the marble casket was removed and eventually was taken to Rome and, on orders of the pope, lodged in San Pietro in Vincoli. With the passing of many generations, the Maccabean coffin was forgotten. In 1876, during excavations under the steps of the church's entrance, the casket was uncovered and identified by Cardinal Rampolla and others as that of Hannah's seven sons. The cardinal later wrote a book on this subject, published in 1899 in a French translation, entitled *Martyre et sépulture des Macchabées*.

According to Jewish tradition, Hannah and her sons are buried near Safed at a place called Kerem.[21]

Zot Hanukkah

The eighth and last day of Hanukkah is called *Zot Hanukkah* (This Is the Dedication). It alludes to this day's scriptural portion dealing with the dedication of the Tabernacle, which states: "This was the dedication offering for the altar" (Numbers 7.84). Great rejoicing was customary on this day, as on Simhat Torah, the last day of Sukkot. Eating elaborate meals, narrating legends of Jewish heroes, and playing games were included in the day's gaiety. In some communities the eighth day was dedicated to Judith; the women would read in Old Yiddish the story of this heroine in *Zos Hanukkah Bikhel* by Elhanan ben Issachar (Frankfort on the Main, 1712).[22]

iiiiiiii

Hanukkah and Sukkot

The author of 2 Maccabees underscores the similarity between Hanukkah and Sukkot. It might even be interpreted as equating Hanukkah with Sukkot. Following the account of the cleansing of the Temple by the Maccabees, we read: "They celebrated it for eight days with rejoicing in the manner of the Feast of Tabernacles, mindful of how but a little while before at the festival of Tabernacles they had been wandering about like wild beasts in the mountains and caves. That is why, bearing thyrsi and graceful branches and also palm leaves, they offered up hymns to Him who had given them success in purifying His own place of worship" (2 Maccabees 10.6–7). These verses seem to intimate that the Maccabees, embattled against their enemies, were unable to observe Sukkot in the traditional manner. When Jerusalem was liberated their first thought was to observe the festival of Sukkot to compensate for their failure to do so at the appointed season. Eager to have other Jews join in the celebration, they dispatched letters to Egypt to advise the Jews of their decision: "Now [we write] urging you to keep the days of the feast like the Feast of Tabernacles in the month of Kislev. . . . We are now about to celebrate the purification of the Temple, on the twenty-fifth day of Kislev. We thought it only right to tell you, so that you too may celebrate [these days] like the Feast of Tabernacles" (2 Maccabees 1.9, 18).[23]

38. Israeli stamps with Hanukkah lamps.

The talmudic dispute concerning the order of kindling the Hanukkah lights was likewise linked to Sukkot (Shabbat 21b). The school of Hillel maintained that on the first day one light is lit and thereafter they are progressively increased. The school of Shammai held that on the first day eight lights are lit and thereafter they are gradually reduced; their reason was that the order should correspond to the sacrifices on Sukkot, when thirteen bullocks were sacrificed on the first day and one less on each succeeding day (Numbers 29.12–32).

To this day marked similarities exist between Hanukkah and Sukkot. Both are celebrated for eight days. On both festivals, even though only one is biblical, the complete Hallel (Psalms 113–118) is recited. Rejoicing is the motif in both: Sukkot is called the "Season of Our Rejoicing"; the Maccabees decreed that "the days of the dedication of the altar should be kept with gladness and joy at their due season" (1 Maccabees 4.59) and "as a time of feasting and rejoicing" (*Megillat Antiochus* 71).

iiiiiiii
=

General Allenby's Entry into Jerusalem

On December 11, 1917, during the festival of Hanukkah, General Edmund Allenby, commander in chief of the Egyptian Expeditionary Force of Great Britain during World War I, having received the flag of surrender from Jerusalem dignitaries, triumphantly entered the Holy City on foot at the head of his entourage, thus terminating Turkish rule. It was about five weeks after the British government's issuance of the Balfour Declaration, which promised "the establishment in Palestine of a national home for the Jewish people."

In festive mood, the Jewish populace turned out on Jaffa Road to greet Allenby and his staff, who had released them from the truculent yoke of the Turks. The Jewish Jerusalemites viewed the liberation as another miracle which—appropriately on Hanukkah—brought renewed hope to them.[24] A contemporary editorial in *The Maccabean*, the official American Zionist organ, waxed enthusiastic: "Faithful Jews were celebrating the Festival of Lights, the Maccabean victories of centuries long past, while in Palestine the British army took the citadel for which the Maccabees fought and in defense of which thousands of Jews in different periods of history gave up their lives. Jerusalem has fallen many times, but only of this time in the modern period may it be said that it has been delivered. . . . The British [Balfour] Declaration came first, and as if to give assurance of the sincerity of its pledge, Jerusalem was taken, and a reaffirmation of the pledge was given in the rare courtesy and magnanimity which attended the entrance of General Allenby into the city."[25]

iiiiiii
=
Handel's Oratorio "Judah Maccabeus"

The Maccabean triumph is the theme of the majestic oratorio "Judah Maccabeus," composed by George Frederick Handel (1685–1759). It was commissioned by Frederic, Prince of Wales, to commemorate the return of the Duke of Cumberland from Scotland after the decisive victory of the battle of Culloden on April 16, 1746. A Greek scholar, Reverend Thomas Morell, wrote the libretto based on 1 Maccabees and on Josephus' *Jewish Antiquities*. In his dedication, Dr. Morell compared the duke to Judah Maccabee: "To His Royal Highness Prince William, Duke of Cumberland, this faint portraiture of a truly wise, valiant, and virtuous commander as the possessor of the like noble qualities. . . ."

The oratorio was first performed at Covent Garden on April 1, 1747. Handel personally conducted it at thirty-eight performances. The Jews of England were so enthralled by Handel's glorification of a Jew as hero that they evidently attended the performances in large numbers and are credited with its great popularity.[26] Among the oratorio's solos and choruses still popular in the musical world are Judah's call, "Sound the Alarm"; the triumphal chorus, "See the Conqu'ring Hero Comes"; the duet, "A Lovely Peace"; and the final chorus, "Hallelujah."[27]

15 THE HANUKKAH CUISINE

The Feast of Lights recalls the dedication of the Temple in Jerusalem following the victory of the Hasmoneans over the Syrians. To emphasize the miracle of the cruse of oil found in the Temple, which was sufficient for only one day but burned for eight days, foods fried in oil are served on Hanukkah. Further evidence of the appropriateness of using oil derives from the fact that the Hebrew words for Hasmoneans (*Hashmonaim*) and for eight (*shemoneh*), the number of days of the festival, contain the Hebrew letters for oil (*shemen*). Latkes—pancakes fried in oil—have been the distinctive Hanukkah delicacy for centuries. Kalonymus ben Kalonymus, who lived in Italy in the fourteenth century, composed a Hanukkah poem extolling latkes. A folk proverb states: "Hanukkah's latkes teach us that one cannot live by miracles alone." While the variety of latkes is legion, the most popular are those made with grated potatoes. Some are made with cheese, fruits, and yeast. In oriental countries sugar and sesame seeds are added to the pancakes.

According to the *Code of Jewish Law*, dairy dishes are featured on Hanukkah to commemorate the heroism of Judith, reputed to be a member of the Hasmonean family. Various legends associate the Apocryphal story of lovely Judith with the Maccabean revolt. She gained an audience with the enemy general Holofernes, who invited her to a banquet at which she partook only of dairy foods. She fed the general milk and cheese until he was parched and then offered him liberal portions of wine to quench his thirst. When he fell into a drunken stupor, she killed him. Learning that their general was dead, the soldiers fled and the Jews were saved. Thus the dairy foods serve as a reminder of Judith's valor and the Maccabean triumph. This custom was instituted as early as the fourteenth century.[1]

On the last day of Hanukkah schoolchildren in the Old City of Jerusalem, accompanied by their teachers, would go from house to house of the affluent Jews singing songs and chanting repeatedly, "Buy us a little food" (Genesis 43.2). The householders responded by giving the children fruit, vegetables, fowl, oil, flour, onions, and other foods and sometimes coins with which to purchase food. With whatever they collected they would prepare three meals: one for the poor, one for their teachers, and the third for themselves. Small pieces of dough baked with a meat filling were one of the tidbits served. To enhance the merriment of the occasion, several pieces of dough were usually stuffed with absorbent cotton.

Similar traditions prevailed in other oriental countries. In the marketplace Yemenite children sold hot potatoes and a drink made with peaches to earn money for their Hanukkah festival meal.

In Hebron the women held their own celebration on the last night of the holiday, at which they made macaroni together and then ate it with salted cheese while engaging in light conversation.

In Turkey the elders of the community, carrying platters of pancakes, visited the affluent Jews to collect Hanukkah *gelt* for the poor. In exchange for their contributions each was given three latkes. Bukharan Jews baked cakes with coins inside and distributed them to teachers and indigent relatives.

East European Jews gave special consideration to the Sabbath of Hanukkah. On that day they would eat two different kugels—one in honor of the Sabbath and the other for the glory of Hanukkah. Another highlight of the Sabbath of Hanukkah was a roast goose or duck from which the schmaltz (fat) was reserved for Passover. *Gri-*

benes (scraps), stuffed neck roasted and fried with onions, and giblets were also among the popular Hanukkah delicacies of East European Jews.

Hanukkah being a home festival, many families set a festive table every evening of the holiday. The enjoyment of the meals is heightened by singing hymns and songs, posing riddles, playing dreidel games, and telling humorous stories.[2]

iiiiiiii

Recipes for Hanukkah
HANNA GOODMAN

GEBRATENE GANS (ROAST GOOSE)

10–12 pound goose	onion powder
6 apples, quartered	garlic powder
salt and pepper to taste	1 ½ cups orange juice
paprika	

Remove all the fat from the goose. Stuff the goose with the apples. Salt and pepper it, and sprinkle with the paprika and onion and garlic powders. Put on a rack and roast in a 425° oven for 30 minutes. Remove as much of the fat in the roaster as possible. Baste with a third of the orange juice. Lower the heat to 325° and continue roasting, basting the goose with the balance of the orange juice every 30 minutes. Again remove all the fat accumulated in the roaster. Roast the goose until you are sure it is tender (the time required for roasting depends on the age of the goose). If possible, roast the goose in advance. Cool and carve in serving pieces, reserving the apples. If necessary, roast again until tender. Serve with the apples. 8 servings.[3]

39. A runner in the annual Hanukkah torch relay from Modin to Jerusalem. 1951.

DUCK À L'ORANGE

	4–5 pound duck	1	tablespoon vinegar
	salt and pepper to taste		juice of ½ lemon
½	cup white wine	1	cup water
2	oranges	1	bouillon cube
1	tablespoon sugar	1	orange, sliced for garnish

Roast the duck for 20 minutes in 450° oven. Pour off the fat. Lower the oven heat to 350°. Sprinkle the duck with salt and pepper and baste with the wine. Roast until the duck is tender.

While the duck is roasting, prepare the sauce. Grate the rind of the oranges. Combine the sugar and vinegar, and bring to a boil. Add the juice of the oranges, lemon juice, the water with the bouillon cube, and the grated orange rind. Simmer for 5 minutes.

Disjoint the duck and arrange on a platter. Remove all the fat from the roaster in which the duck was roasted and add all the brown juice left in the roaster to the orange sauce. Pour the sauce over the duck.

Garnish with orange slices. 4 servings.[4]

MASHED POTATO KUGEL

4	cups potatoes, mashed	4	tablespoons margarine, melted
	salt and pepper to taste	1	teaspoon onion powder
4	eggs, beaten		ground meat (optional)
2	tablespoons farina or semolina		

To the mashed potatoes, add salt and pepper, eggs, farina or semolina, margarine, and onion powder. Mix well.

Grease well a round baking dish, and put in the potato mixture. Bake in a 375° oven for 45 minutes or until brown. 8 servings.

This potato mixture can be made into individual croquettes. Stuff the mixture with ground meat, and form into long shapes. Fry in oil until golden brown, or bake in a well-greased baking pan in a 375° oven for 20 minutes, depending on the size of the croquettes.[5]

PLAIN NOODLE KUGEL

½ pound medium noodles, cooked	salt and pepper to taste
5 eggs, beaten	6 tablespoons margarine, melted

Mix the noodles with the eggs, salt and pepper, and 3 tablespoons of melted margarine.

Grease a baking dish with the rest of the margarine. Heat it in the oven. When the margarine is hot, pour in the noodle mixture.

Bake in a 375° oven for 1 hour. 6 servings.[6]

FRUIT LATKES

2 cups flour	1 can pie-sliced apples or
½ teaspoon salt	1 can pineapple chunks
3 teaspoons baking powder	oil for frying
1 egg, beaten	confectioners' sugar
2/3 cup orange juice	

Sift together the dry ingredients. Add the egg and the orange juice. Beat well. Batter will be heavy. Add the well-drained fruit of your choice. Drop by spoonfuls into deep oil at 375°. Fry until brown. Drain on paper toweling. Sprinkle with confectioners' sugar. Serve hot. 6 servings.[7]

SUFGANIOT (ISRAELI LATKES)

½ package dried yeast	1 teaspoon salt
1 cup warm water (105°–115°)	1 egg, well beaten
2 cups flour, sifted	oil for frying
2 teaspoons sugar	

Sprinkle the yeast over the warm water. Let it stand until dissolved. Sift the flour with sugar and salt, and add the egg. Add the yeast, and beat well until the mixture is thoroughly blended. Cover and put in a warm place (85°) to rise until it doubles in bulk.

Place oil in a frying pan to half the height of the pan and heat. When the oil is hot, drop the batter by spoonfuls into the oil. Fry on both sides until latkes are a golden color. Drain well on paper toweling. Sprinkle with granulated sugar. Serve hot. 6 servings.[8]

COTTAGE CHEESE PANCAKES

1	cup cottage cheese	½	teaspoon sugar
2	eggs, separated	¼	teaspoon salt
1½	tablespoons cornstarch		

Blend the cottage cheese, egg yolks, cornstarch, sugar, and salt. Beat the egg whites until stiff and fold into the cottage cheese mixture. Drop by tablespoons on a hot, greased griddle. Lower heat and cook on one side until puffed and dry. Then turn with a spatula and brown lightly on the other side. Serve with fruit, berries, sour cream, or jelly. 2 servings.[9]

POTATO PANCAKES

4	large potatoes, grated	¼	teaspoon pepper
3	tablespoons matzah meal	1	teaspoon onion powder
3	eggs, beaten		oil for frying
1	teaspoon salt		

Care should be taken to have all the ingredients ready for immediate use before grating the potatoes. (Grated potatoes that are left standing turn brown.) It is desirable to use 2 pans at the same time to expedite frying the pancakes.

Grate the potatoes, and squeeze out as much water as possible. Mix the grated potatoes, matzah meal, eggs, salt, pepper, and onion powder. Heat oil in a frying pan. When the oil is hot, drop the potato mixture by tablespoons into the oil. Fry on both sides until brown. Remove from the oil, and drain on paper toweling.

The pancakes can be fried in advance and frozen. Before serving, lay the pancakes in one layer on a foil-lined cookie sheet and reheat in a 375° oven for about 20 minutes. Serve with applesauce. 6 servings.[10]

MENORAH SALAD

	lettuce leaves		lemon juice
8	pineapple rings	8	maraschino cherries
8	small bananas		

Arrange the lettuce on flat plates for individual salads, or on one large platter. Place the pineapple rings in a line to form the base of a menorah. Cut off the bottom of the bananas so that one end is flat, and scoop out the other end so that it will hold a cherry. Dip the bananas in lemon juice, and stand the flat ends in the pineapple rings. Set the cherries on the banana tops. Serve with cottage cheese and, if desired, sour cream. 8 servings.[11]

16 CHILDREN'S STORIES FOR HANUKKAH

iiiiiiii

The Dolls' Hanukkah
SADIE ROSE WEILERSTEIN

author of twelve books for children in a successful writing career; twice the recipient of the Jewish Book Council's juvenile award

(age level four to eight)

Everybody at Ruth's and Debby's house loved Hanukkah. Even the dolls did. There were five of them: Anna, Joan and Rebekah, Didie —he was their baby doll—and dear old Judah Maccabee.

Judah Maccabee was a rag doll, but a very handsome one. Aunt Ann had sent him to Ruth and Debby when they were only three years old. It was on Hanukkah, so of course they named him Judah

Maccabee. Daddy made him a helmet and a spear and shield, but he didn't wear them every day. It's hard to hug a doll with a helmet and shield on, and Ruth and Debby were always hugging Judah Maccabee. But every year, when Hanukkah came around, they took the shield and helmet out of its box and dressed Judah Maccabee most splendidly in his armor. How brave and handsome he looked as he stood guard over the menorah! It was no wonder the dolls loved Hanukkah. Wouldn't you if you had Judah Maccabee in your own family?

> Judah Maccabee,
>   Brave and tall;
> Judah who helped
>   To save us all.

But there was another reason why the dolls were glad when Hanukkah came. It was on account of the Hanukkah pancakes, the latkes. Ruth's and Debby's dolls always had pancakes on Hanukkah. It began in this way. Mother was out in the kitchen frying pancakes. It was the first night of Hanukkah. Ruth and Debby were helping. Sizzle, sizzle! went the butter in the pan. Mother poured in the batter, when suddenly—

> A little bit of batter
> Went spatter, spatter, spatter!

The spatters were brown in a minute.

"Look at them, Mother," said Ruthie. "They're like teensy little doll pancakes."

"We could feed them to our dolls," said Debby. "Let's!"

And they did. They set the doll table with their blue-and-white doll dishes, and seated their dollies around it. There was a pancake apiece for Anna, Joan, Rebekah and two for Judah Maccabee.

They didn't give any to Didie.

"He's only a baby," Ruthie explained. "Pancakes might not be good for him."

It was while the dolls were at supper that a thought came to Debby. "If the dolls eat pancakes, they ought to light lights. It isn't right to have the pancakes without the lights."

"But where could we get a menorah little enough for the dolls?" asked Ruthie.

"We could make one," said Debby, "out of clay."

And that's what they did. Ruthie fetched a ball of clay, and Debby rolled it and patted it until it looked like a fat little sausage.

Pat, pat, pat!
Make it smooth and flat.

She sang.

Then Ruth took a pencil and poked eight little holes in the clay. She made another one for the *shammash* candle, and the doll's menorah was ready. Mother found a box of yellow birthday candles for Hanukkah lights.

After that, Judah Maccabee lighted Hanukkah candles every night: one on the first night, two on the second night, three on the third, then four, five, six, seven, eight. Ruth and Debby helped him. They sang the blessing for him, too. First Daddy would light the candles in the big menorah. Then Judah Maccabee would light the candles in the little menorah. The dolls sat in a circle and listened most respectfully. They didn't as much as stir—until

Up flared the tiny lights,
  And then
Every doll smiled, Amen.

"The dolls are so sweet," said Ruth and Debby, "we ought to give them Hanukkah presents."

So, on the fifth night, when all the relatives came to dinner and everyone got Hanukkah presents, there were gifts for the dollies, too.

Rebekah was given a gay, knitted cap; Didie a cunning bonnet with blue ribbon rosettes; Joan a pair of doll skates; Anna a wee apron with real pockets. But the best present of all was Judah Maccabee's. Cousin Danny brought it to him. You'd never guess what it was! A blouse, a pair of shorts, a hoe, a spade, and a pickax.

"There," said Danny, as he laid the pickax over Judah Maccabee's shoulder. "He's a *halutz* now, a real Israeli farmer!

He'll dig and he'll sow;
He'll make the green fields grow!
He fought with sword long years ago;
Today he'll fight with pick and hoe;
He'll plow and he'll sow!
To Israel he'll go!"

How proud Ruth and Debby were of their dear Judah Maccabee now that he was a *halutz*! Daddy stood Judah next to the blue-and-white box.

"We had better give him Hanukkah coins," he said. "He'll need a lot of them to buy land. Let us fill up his box."

He put his hand into his pocket and drew out four quarters. Clank! Clank! they dropped into the box. Grandpa put Hanukkah coins in, too. So did Mother and Grandma and Aunt Frieda and Danny and Judith. Then it was Ruth's and Debby's turn. First each of them dropped a nickel in the box for herself. Then—Debby put a penny in dolly Anna's wee hand. Clinkety, clink, the penny was in the box. She put a penny in Didie's hand. Clinkety, clink, Didie's penny dropped into the box. Ruth did the same with Rebekah and Joan.

As for Judah Maccabee, he stood straight and proud with the pickax over his shoulder, and guarded the box with its precious pennies. It was the happiest Hanukkah he had had in all his life.[1]

40. A runner and escorts in the annual Hanukkah torch relay arriving in Jerusalem from Modin.

iiiiiiii
=

Hanukkah in Old Venice
LILLIAN S. ABRAMSON

author of Jewish juvenile books; actively engaged in Jewish and general education

(age level five to nine)

Ruth and David lived in the lovely city-state of Venice about seven hundred years ago, during the Middle Ages. Venice had winding canals instead of streets and arched stone bridges that crossed over the canals.

Hanukkah was such fun in Venice! Every evening, after the candlelighting ceremony, Ruth and David put the menorah in the window or, if it had a hook, they hung it *outside* on the wall of the house. They watched the bright candles cast their light upon the waters of the canals.

On the last night of Hanukkah, when the menorah was full, Father called to Ruth.

"Put on your cape," he said, "we are going into our gondola."

Ruth was overjoyed for she knew what that meant. They would row up and down the canals until they saw a shining menorah. Then they would burst into song, greeting each Jewish home with cheerful melodies.

Suddenly she looked down and saw David, who was standing there sadly.

"Can't I come just this once?" pleaded David. "I can sing in a good loud voice. And I'll spot every shining menorah."

"He can sit next to me and I'll watch him," added Ruth.

Mother and Father looked at each other and smiled at the same time.

"Well, David is growing up!" they said. "Come along, too."

They stepped down carefully into the flat-bottomed gondola and took their seats.

"How dark and quiet it is," whispered David. "But it's not too dark for me. I'll spot every Jewish home with a shining menorah."

Just then they were joined by a neighboring family. Father and his friend took turns rowing through the Grand Canal, which wound its way through the city.

"Aren't there any Jewish families here?" wondered David.

Then they turned into one of the smaller canals.

"Here we are!" announced Father, for suddenly they saw the lights. House after house had a bright menorah either on its windowsill or hanging outside. Cheerful, bright lights!

They stopped the slender boat in front of each house and sang and sang and sang. First they sang "*Maoz Tzur*," then they sang "*Hanerot Hallalu*." They sang "*Al ha-Nissim*" and they even sang portions of the Hallel.

After a while Father called out: "Time to start back. We've greeted every Jewish home by now."

They deftly turned the gondola about and started the smooth ride back. They were just passing a small side canal when David shouted:

"Look, another Jewish home!"

He pointed to a small glow in the water. Alongside was a small home with a menorah that was almost dark, for only one candle was still glowing.

They all burst into song at the top of their voices. The people in the house rushed to the window and waved gleefully, joining in the songs.

Everybody in the boat looked at David gratefully.

"Just to think," said Mother, "that one Jewish home would have been ungreeted on Hanukkah if not for the youngest rider here."

David leaned on Ruth's shoulder and fell asleep. He dreamed of happy faces smiling to him through the windows and lively hands waving to him, and bright Hanukkah lights shining across the dark waters of the Venice canals.[2]

iiiiiiii
=
The Old Dreidel
MORRIS EPSTEIN

late editor of World Over, *a magazine for Jewish children, and professor and chairman of the Department of English at Stern College for Women, Yeshivah University; in addition to scholarly works, he has written extensively for children (1921–73)*

(age level five to nine)

Everything in the house was topsy-turvy.

Gita and Jerry were getting ready for the Hanukkah play. The play would be presented that evening in the Hebrew school. And there were so many things still to be done!

Mother was sitting at the sewing machine. Quick as a flash, in-and-out, out-and-in, went the needle. And then, snip-snip, went the scissors. Mother was putting the finishing touches on the costume Gita was going to wear in the play.

Father had a carton of cotton before him on the table, and he was pulling off great gobs of the white, woolly stuff. He was making a beard for Jerry. Now he tried it on Jerry's face.

"Glub-glub!" said Jerry. "You covered-glub-my mouth!"

"That's all right," giggled Gita. "You don't have to *say* anything in your part anyway!"

"But I have two parts, smarty!" replied Jerry. "You've only got one!"

It was true. Jerry was going to be one of Mattathias's soldiers and then, later, he would pull off his beard and pretend to be the little boy who discovered the tiny flask of oil in the Temple.

Gita's part was much more important. But, after all, she was older. Gita was to be the Narrator. She would tell the story of Hanukkah before the play began.

"Would you like to rehearse your part?" asked Father. "Last chance before dinner. After that, you know, off to school we go."

"All right," said Gita. She drew herself up to her full height, looked at her audience of three, and cleared her throat. "Ahem," she said.

"Our play tonight," she began, "tells the Hanukkah story. Many centuries ago, an evil man named Antiochus became king of Syria and conqueror of Jerusalem. Antiochus thought he could destroy our religion. 'I am god,' he roared. 'The Jews shall not keep the Sabbath! They must bow down and worship our Greek idols!'

"He sent twenty-two thousand of his best soldiers to carry out his command. Soon they had looted the Temple in Jerusalem of its holy objects. They drove grunting pigs into the Temple. They sold many women and children into slavery.

"One day, Antiochus' soldiers came to the little village of Modin. There an old priest named Mattathias surprised everyone by rebelling against the king. When he saw a pagan sacrifice being performed in the marketplace, he became very angry. He killed the king's officer.

"Now Mattathias had to flee. Gathering his five stalwart sons and a band of hardy men, he fled to the hills. Antiochus sent four armies against him. The evil men went down like bowling pins before the hacking blows of the Maccabees. At last, in 165 B.C.E., Judah Maccabee, the son of Mattathias, and his men recaptured Jerusalem. On the twenty-fifth day of Kislev, the Jews poured into the Temple. They cleaned it and scrubbed it.

"They could find no oil to relight the menorah in the Temple. And then, a little boy found a small cruse of oil. They lit the lights and the oil burned for eight full days. Since that time, we have celebrated Hanukkah—which means dedication—for eight days. On the first night of Hanukkah, we light one candle. On every night thereafter we light an additional one until our menorah has eight candles in a row.

"In this way, we commemorate the Festival of Lights and the Triumph of Freedom. And because Hanukkah is such a joyous holiday, we give presents to our friends and relatives. And now—on with the play!"

Gita paused and curtsied very prettily.

Mother and Father clapped their hands and congratulated Gita. Only Jerry remained silent.

"Don't you think Gita did a swell job?" asked Father.

"Sure," Jerry said. "Only . . . only she left out one thing. She didn't say that we play dreidel on Hanukkah!"

"Oh, silly!" cried Gita. "That's a *new* game. The Maccabees didn't play dreidel!"

"Now, hold on a minute, Gita," Father said. "I wouldn't be so sure of *that*. In fact there's an old story which says that the Hanukkah top *was* invented during the time of the Maccabees."

"Tell us!" Gita and Jerry exclaimed.

"Well, it's a very short legend, really. When Antiochus ruled Palestine, he did not permit the Jews to study the Torah. *You* told us that, Gita.

"To escape the king's spies, our ancestors would meet in hidden places. While one person acted as a lookout, the rest would study our Torah by heart. If soldiers were heard approaching, the lookout would cry out a warning. The group would quickly separate and hurry away through back doors and buried passages.

"One day, someone thought of a dreidel game to fool the king's men. They kept a top on the table. If a soldier managed to slip by the lookout, all he would see was a group of Jews gathered together to play a game. In that way, the little Hanukkah dreidel saved many lives.

"Later on, the letters *nun*, *gimel*, *he*, and *shin* were placed on the dreidel. Do you know what they stand for, Gita?"

"Yes," said Gita. "*Nes gadol hayah sham*—A great miracle happened there."

Suddenly Mother poked her head out of the kitchen. "Did I hear someone say something about saving lives?" she asked with a smile.

"That's right," said Father.

"Well, I'd like to save four right now. I've just whipped up a stackful of potato latkes. Anybody care for some?"

There was a mad scramble for the kitchen, where a plate piled high with crusty, delicious latkes stood temptingly on the table.

"Mom," said Jerry, "you just made the fastest miracle I ever heard of!"[3]

iiiiiii
=

Bee-utiful Candles
LEONARD JAFFE

this whimsical story of tiny people is from the author's first publication, The Pitzel Holiday Book

(age level five to nine)

The Pitzel-sailors had forgotten to get Hanukkah candles the last time they sailed over the Star of David Lake, and now, with Hanukkah only one day away, there wasn't a single Hanukkah candle anywhere in Pitzel-land! Oh, there were plenty of dreidels and there would be stacks and stacks of potato latkes, but who ever heard of Hanukkah without Hanukkah candles?

All the Pitzels were sad, of course, but saddest of all were the children. They could hardly eat breakfast that morning, and when they left their snug little houses under the strawberry bushes, they couldn't think of playing. In fact, all David and his sister Sarah and their friends could think of doing was to sit in the shade of some violets and poke the ground with their feet!

A hummingbird was watching them. He didn't know why they were sad, but he didn't care. "Pitzel children should always be laughing," he said to himself, "and in a minute they will be!" Then he darted over and began flying around their heads—backwards! Debbie, Sol, and Harvey did laugh at this trick, and some of the others smiled. But when the hummingbird stopped and hung perfectly still, right there in midair, the Pitzels all laughed out loud. All except one, because David wasn't laughing. He wasn't even smiling. He was listening.

Suddenly David jumped up—the hummingbird's hum had reminded him of something!

"Bees!" he shouted. "And bees make wax, don't they, hummingbird?"

"All the time," answered the hummingbird.

"Then we're saved!" David cried. "We can get wax from the bees and make our own Hanukkah candles!"

"Not so fast!" said the hummingbird. "If you want wax from the bees, you'll have to ask their queen for it, and from what I've heard about *her*, you'll never get it!"

"Anyway, we've got to try—it's our only chance!" said David. "What's the queen's name, hummingbird? I'll ask her myself. I'm not afraid!"

"Let's see, I knew her name once . . . Mel—lifica; yes, that's it—Queen Mellifica!"

"All right, Queen Mellifica—here I come!" David announced, bravely throwing out his chest.

But Sarah could tell David didn't feel at all brave. "Wait for me!" she called after him as he started off. And hand in hand, brother and sister walked down the path to the hollow tree where the bees lived.

Now, Queen Mellifica really wasn't a bad queen, no matter what the hummingbird had heard. But she did have her "bad days," and, unluckily for David and Sarah, this was one of them. And so when the Lord of the Queenbee Chamber came to tell her that two Pitzels were outside the hive waiting to see her, she almost flew off her couch, crying out:

"Impossible, impossible! You know very well, Lord Apis, that

41. A Bukharan family celebrates Hanukkah. Florentine Quarter, Tel Aviv.

today is one of my bad days! I'm in no condition to see anyone, and certainly not Pitzels, whoever *they* are. Send them away!''

"Forgive me, Your Majesty," Lord Apis quietly answered, "but I

42. An Israeli family kindles the lights. Tel Aviv. 1959.

think you should see them. You need a little cheering up, and the Pitzels are—well, they're so funny! You never leave the hive, of course, and so you cannot know what funny creatures there are in this world!"

"Funny? In what way are the Pitzels funny?"

"Well, first of all," Lord Apis went on, "they have no wings—they have to walk all the time! As if that weren't enough, the poor things have only *four* legs, instead of six! But the funniest part of all is, they walk on only *two* of their legs, while the other two just hang—JUST HANG!"

"Enough!" laughed the queen. "If what you say is true, have them brought to me immediately!"

Lord Apis hurried to the entrance of the hive to tell David and Sarah that the queen had graciously consented to see them. Then he ordered one of the drone bees to fly them up to the throne room.

David and Sarah mounted on the drone's back and up they went, breathing in the soft, sweet smell of the honey and passing row after row of bee cells, each waxen row glowing with a different color. At last they reached the highest point of the hive, the throne room itself, shining in a blaze of gold!

Standing now in the presence of the queen, David made a real bow, while Sarah curtsied to the floor. They stayed that way, waiting for the queen to speak. But it took some time for the queen to speak. The Pitzels seemed even funnier to her than Lord Apis had described them.

Finally, she controlled herself and said:

"Why have you come? Tell me quickly, for I must get my rest. Yesterday, you see, I laid 4,281 eggs! You might tell that to your queen, by the way—4,281 eggs in one day!"

"We Pitzels have no queen," Sarah said in a whisper.

"What, no queen, NO QUEEN! Now I understand why you go around like that, on only two of your legs! Anything can happen without a queen! . . . Oh well, come to the point—what is it you want?"

David cleared his throat. "Wax, Your Majesty. We Pitzels need wax."

"Wax?! Whatever for? I can see you don't live in a hive, so why would you need wax?"

"For candles," David replied.

"And what are candles?" the queen asked. "What do you do with them?"

"Burn them, Your Majesty."

"Burn them? Then what is left of the wax?"

"Why . . . nothing!" David said.

"NOTHING?" Queen Mellifica could hardly believe what she was hearing. "You mean you'll take my good wax and make it into things called candles only in order to burn them up until there's nothing left? In other words, you want my wax—for nothing! . . . Well, this must be some kind of Pitzel joke, and I suppose it all comes again from not having a queen to guide you, but I assure you, we are not amused! I bid you good day!"

"Oh please, Your Majesty," David cried out. "We do want your wax for something, something very important. You don't understand about candles. You see, when the sun goes down tomorrow we Pitzels start celebrating our holiday of Hanukkah. Hanukkah is a wonderful, a beautiful holiday—but only if there are candles. Hanukkah is even called the Feast of Lights! It lasts for eight days, and each day we light one more candle until, on the last day, the special candlestick is full. And while the candles burn and their flames dance in the air, they make us think of the time when our freedom and our Temple were won back for us by the good, the brave, the magnificent Maccabees—"

"*Macca*-bees, *macca*-bees?" interrupted the queen. "I've never heard of *those* bees before, though I dare say they're distant relatives of ours—*we* are honeybees, you know. . . . Well now, that's a completely different story! If those candles of yours make you think of bees—macca or any other kind—they *are* important for you to have! In that case, you're welcome to the wax!"

David and Sarah began shouting: "Thank you, thank you!" but the queen quieted them. "Please, please, I have a head-buzz as it is! Now then, my workers will spend the rest of the day filling up on honey and they'll be ready with your wax tomorrow morning. Where shall I send them?"

"To the Star of David Lake, Your Majesty," David said. "Uncle Ben has his workshop there. He's a sculptor; he'll know how to make your wax into candles."

Queen Mellifica nodded. Then slowly, with great dignity, she rose up from her throne and began flying out of the room. Just before she left, however, she said to herself—loud enough for David and Sarah to hear:

"The macca-bees may well have been as brave as those Pitzels say. But I wonder if *their* queen ever laid 4,281 eggs in a single day!"

David and Sarah giggled as they flew back down out of the hive.

Outside, their friends were waiting, and when David and Sarah told them what had happened, they all raced home to spread the wonderful news.

Soon Pitzel-land looked like a carnival. Mother and father Pitzels, grandmother and grandfather Pitzels, and aunt and uncle Pitzels sang and danced with the children in the streets. And up in the air they tossed their heroes, David and Sarah, again and again and again!

The celebration didn't last very long, though, because Uncle Ben climbed up on a mushroom and, using a morning glory as a loud-speaker, called out:

"Fellow Pitzels—your attention, please! If we want to be ready for the bees tomorrow morning, we must start making the candle molds right away!"

The Pitzels realized Uncle Ben was right; without another word they followed him to the lake. There, they began rolling up bits of clay and covering them with the plaster Uncle Ben was mixing in the meantime. They worked and worked, and it was night before they were finished.

What a sight all those plaster casts made in the moonlight—it looked as though the shore were covered with a forest of tiny white trees!

"You can go home now," Uncle Ben told them. "When the plaster is dry, the clay will have to be taken out, and that's a job only I can do with my special tools. But I could use one person to help me."

"Let me!" David cried, and before his mother had time to say no, all the other Pitzels shouted: "Yes, David! Let David!"

So David stayed up that whole night helping Uncle Ben remove the clay from the middle of the molds.

The sun was just stretching over the edge of the sky when the Pitzels gathered on the shore again. No one spoke. Everyone was thinking the same thing—the candle molds are ready, yes, but would Queen Mellifica keep her promise?

Then a strange thing happened. Although by now the sun had fully risen, it suddenly got very dark. The Pitzels looked up—it was the bees coming toward them, covering the sky in a huge swarm! The Pitzels cheered.

With Lord Apis in front, the bees landed in a most orderly fashion.

"Do you think each of your workers could fill a hole like this with his wax?" Uncle Ben asked, holding up a mold in front of Lord Apis.

Lord Apis smiled. "Any one of my workers could fill *ten* of those holes!" Then he buzzed out a command.

The bees quickly scattered, each of them settling on top of a mold and letting his wax drip down into the hole. As soon as a bee was finished, a Pitzel ran up and pushed a piece of thread through the center of the wax. The thread was for the candlewick, of course.

"We must be off now," said Lord Apis when all the holes had been filled with wax and all the candlewicks were in place. "We were glad to help you, but it is rather a shame you couldn't have done such a simple thing yourselves. However, we can't all be bees!"

"That's right," smiled Uncle Ben, and the Pitzels waved until the bees were out of sight.

"My friends," said Uncle Ben, "when you're quite sure the wax is hard, you may break open the plaster shells and take out your Hanukkah candles! As for me, I'm going to get some sleep now, and David should do the same!"

"He certainly should!" said David's mother. "But look, he's asleep already!"

And so he was, right there on the shore, with his arms tight around one of the candle molds. He was still hugging the mold when his father carried him home and put him to bed.

David slept until the smell of potato latkes woke him up. Rubbing his eyes, he walked into the dining room. "Happy Hanukkah!" cried his mother and father, grandmother and grandfather, and Sarah and Uncle Ben.

In the middle of the holiday table was the menorah with one candle in it, a gay orange-colored one.

"David, you will light the menorah tonight," his father said, "and for a *shammash* you can use the candle in that mold you're holding."

David looked down at his hand—he hadn't even realized he *was* holding a mold. He quickly broke it open. Inside was a candle as golden as Queen Mellifica's throne room itself!

David lit the *shammash,* and with it, the other candle. And, at the same time, the very same thing was happening in every other house in Pitzel-land![4]

iiiiiiii
=

The Magic Top
JUDAH STEINBERG

a Hebrew teacher in Bessarabia, he achieved fame as a creator of children's literature in Hebrew including textbooks, stories, fables, and Hasidic tales (1863–1908); two collections of his stories were translated into English

(age level six to ten)

Now, once upon a time, there lived a widow whose name was Dinah. She had two sons: Nadab, who was twelve years old, and Amaziah, who was two years younger. Dinah was so poor that she often had not money enough to buy a loaf of bread. Many were the days when the meal could not satisfy three, and not a crumb passed her lips.

Hanukkah drew near, and Dinah had no pennies for tops.

Nadab made the best of his lot, and did not worry his mother. "Surely, better days are coming," he comforted himself, "and then my mother will buy me a pretty Hanukkah top—a *galgelon*—with wings—a real flyer! Perhaps even next year!"

But the naughty Amaziah plagued his mother by whining all day long. His mother could not withstand his tears, so she took her last pennies that she had saved for supper, and bought a Hanukkah top —one for the two boys.

Nadab didn't have the heart to touch the top, for he knew how it had been bought, with his mother's bread. She had gone hungry all day, feeding her portion to her sons; and now it was night, and she had nothing wherewith to break her fast.

Amaziah, however, made merry over the top. He took it between his fingers and spun it on the table. The top danced from edge to edge of the table and dropped on the floor, where it whirled merrily on. Amaziah, gleeful, hopped in front of it and let it have its way, to go where it would. The top spun to the door and lingered spinning on the threshold. Amaziah rushed to open the door to see if the top would fall outside. Then the top fled out of doors. From street to street and from place to place it whirled, with the two boys after it. It forsook the town. By that time the children were at the end of their strength and could only follow it with their eyes. They watched it climb hills and descend into valleys, until at length it vanished.

Nadab wept bitterly, for he thought of his hungry mother and the pennies she had intended for a loaf of black bread. Amaziah wept, too, but his cry was: "Where is my top? I want my top!" . . .

It was now dusk, and the children thought to go home, but they had lost the road. They sat down on a grassy bank and cried and cried: Amaziah from cold and hunger, and Nadab at the thought of his mother.

"Is it not enough that she is hungry, that she must also have to fret because we are not home?"

At the sight of the setting sun the children were afraid. Never were they allowed out-of-doors after nightfall. Then Nadab prayed: "O God, have pity on my mother. Take us back to her."

No sooner had Nadab made this short prayer than he spied a dove fluttering her wings. He ran to her, and sobbed out his woe. The dove said: "I will take pity upon you for I pity your mother. I, too, am a forsaken mother. My fledglings left my nest and never flew back. I feel sure that you are not more than a few yards distant from your village. As for your top, it is close by." And the dove pointed to a forest which had suddenly sprung up. "Go to this wood. In its depths is a cave, at whose mouth lies a serpent. Enter the cave and go far into it. There is your top. But be warned. A wizard lies in wait for you. If you utter a word or even wink your eye, you will be caught in his snare."

The boys did as they were bid. In the forest they found an old man, blind in one eye, seated on a heap of bones. He winked at the boys; but they did not wink back. In his hand was a pretty top, which he displayed before their gaze, twirling it in his fingers. Nadab looked at it hard; it seemed to be perfect in all its parts. But in a moment he noticed that the Hebrew letters were missing. In their stead were images and idols. Then Nadab knew that this was the wizard. He kept his lips closed tight. Amaziah was about to cry: "There is my top!" But Nadab was too quick for him and clapped a hand over his mouth so that he could not speak. Then they hurried on.

Once in the forest, they counted several trees, turned to the right, and took seven steps, and there was the cave, and at its mouth lay a large serpent. The boys were terrified; but a voice called to them: "Count the *tzitzit* of your four-cornered garment; if you find eight threads in each corner, do not fear, but enter the cave."

Amaziah looked at his fringes, and lo, on the one side were only six threads, and on the other the seventh was torn; Nadab's set was perfect, so he went into the cave, while his brother waited outside.

At the mouth of the cave Nadab found himself in thick darkness, and he trembled. He went back and forth many times, groping along the walls like a blind man hunting for a door. At last, from the right, there shone a great light. Nadab realized that this must be a doorway, so he felt along, unlatched the bolt, and found himself in a huge court. Its floor was of inlaid marble, its walls were mirrors, and its roof was as the sky of a starry night. In the middle of the court there stood a golden menorah on a high pedestal. It had eight branches, but the branches were not like those on our lamps. Upon every branch was a dove with outstretched wings, holding in her bill a precious stone. The place was bathed in light as of the moon. Each stone was engraved with a Hebrew letter. Read together the letters spelled *Nerot Hanukkah*: "Lights of Dedication." The mirrors in the walls multiplied the lights into thousands, reflected back and forth, till the whole place was ablaze.

In the court was also a golden table with ivory thrones round about it. On the highest throne sat an old man, above whose head, on the back of the throne, was carved MATTATHIAS THE PRIEST. On the other thrones, with their names above them, were his five sons, Johanan, Simon, Judah, Eleazar, and Jonathan.

When Mattathias saw the child, his eyes softened. He arose, and taking from the table a loaf of bread, handed it to Nadab, saying: "Here, good little boy, here is your top. From a loaf of bread it came, and into a loaf of bread has it returned forever. Take it to your mother. When you are hungry, eat of it, and you will taste whatever your desire. The loaf will last forever."

Then Mattathias gave Nadab a golden top with wings. Judah Maccabeus arose and girt a sword of pure gold on the thigh of Nadab, saying: "This is a Hanukkah present from the sons of Mattathias."

Then Jonathan led Nadab outside, where he joined his brother. Jonathan bade them: "Close your eyes." They obeyed.

Then a voice commanded: "Open your eyes." They did so, to find themselves standing just outside the gate of their village.

Quickly they ran home. Their mother was overjoyed to see them, for it was dark and she had begun to worry. Her joy grew when she heard the story of Nadab.

The loaf of bread was as Mattathias had promised. When she wished for meat or fish or milk or wine, she had but to taste the loaf, which never failed.

Such fun as Nadab had with his top and sword! The sword was not sharp or keen, but it gave its owner charmed power over the boys who played at battle with him.

Amaziah was sullen. Whenever he ate of the loaf his conscience smote him.

Every boy who heard the story of the brothers set forth in search of the forest and the cave. But not a trace could be found.

Translated by Emily Solis-Cohen, Jr.[5]

iiiiiiii
=

The Story of Hanukkah
DEBORAH PESSIN

author of Jewish children's books and recipient of the juvenile award of the Jewish Book Council of the National Jewish Welfare Board

(age level seven to eleven)

For many, many years the Jews lived happily in Palestine. The farmers raised fine crops of grain and fruit and vegetables. The shepherds in the hills grazed their flocks of sheep and goats. Carpenters, tailors, and shoemakers worked in their shops. Children played and studied happily. In the beautiful Temple at Jerusalem, Jews from all parts of the country came to pray and sing songs of thanksgiving to God.

Then a cruel Syrian king became ruler of Palestine. His name was Antiochus. Syria, the country north of Palestine, was larger and stronger than Palestine, and so its king made himself the ruler of the Jews in Palestine.

Antiochus was a cruel and foolish king. He wanted every one to obey his every command. And because Antiochus followed the Greek gods he ordered all the people to pray to these gods, to observe the Greek holidays, and to call themselves by Greek names.

The Jews would not obey the king's orders. They refused to pray to the Greek idols, to give their children Greek names, and to eat forbidden food. They continued to observe the Jewish festivals, to study the Torah, and to speak Hebrew. They did not want to have a cruel stranger rule over them. Many of them were ready to die rather than give up their religion. These Jews were known as Hasidim because they were pious and God-fearing. There were some Jews who obeyed the king, but they were few in number,

Antiochus sent many of his soldiers into Palestine to make the Jews obey him. The soldiers entered the beautiful Temple in Jerusalem and set up idols there. They carried off the golden menorah and the holy vessels made of gold and silver. They set up idols in all the towns and cities and ordered the Jews to pray to them. Anyone found observing the Sabbath or the holidays was punished and even killed. The Syrian soldiers robbed the people, too.

Year after year it went on. The fields lay barren. Knowing they would be robbed of their harvests, the farmers did not till the soil. People no longer walked freely through the streets of Jerusalem. Men hid in caves to study the Torah. No one went to the Temple. The *Ner Tamid*, the Everlasting Light that had never been permitted to go out, no longer burned. Nor did the music of the Levites fill the streets of the Holy City. There were Greek idols in the Temple, and the sound of drunken soldiers singing through the night.

Year after year the people lived and died under the hated rule of Antiochus. And year after year they became stronger in their worship of God. . . .

At last something happened in Modin, a town near Jerusalem. One day, a Jewish priest called Mattathias was walking through the marketplace. There he saw a large idol, and near it, many Syrian soldiers. The marketplace was crowded with merchants and farmers who had come to buy and sell.

Suddenly Mattathias noticed that one man, a Jew, approached the idol and kneeled before it. Mattathias grew hot with anger. He pulled out his sword, and quick as a flash, he killed the traitor. Mattathias's five sons were with him. When they saw what their father had done, they ran to his side to protect him from the soldiers.

Then Mattathias raised his sword high and cried: "Whoever is with the Lord, follow me." The men in the marketplace could hardly believe their eyes. An old man, his sword raised high, was calling

בימים ההם בזמן הזה

43. The Hanukkah lamp atop the Knesset (Parliament)
building in Jerusalem. 1948.

upon them to fight Antiochus, the powerful king. And there stood
the Syrian soldiers, frozen with fear.

"We are with you!" cried the men of Modin. And they ran to join
Mattathias and his five sons.

Mattathias and his followers went off to hide in the hills of Judea.
Every day more people came to join them.

Judah, the strongest and boldest of Mattathias's sons, became the
general. He trained the men to be soldiers. And his army grew
slowly, day by day. It was never as large and strong as the Syrian
army, for the Jews were a small nation. But it was made up of brave
men who were not afraid to die.

At last the army of Judah began to fight the Syrians. They camped
in the hills, and at night they would come down and attack small
companies of Syrian soldiers. Then, like shadows, they faded into
the hills again.

The men called their leader Judah Maccabee. For Maccabee

means "hammer," and Judah was like a hammer pounding at the enemy.

Antiochus sent more and more soldiers into Palestine, but the Maccabees defeated every Syrian army. Judah and his men drove them from city to city, and at last, out of Jerusalem. Then Judah and his followers marched into the Holy City.

The people of Jerusalem opened wide the gates to the brave Maccabees. They threw flowers before the soldiers who had won back their freedom. And the Maccabees strode happily through the streets of the Temple, while the people sang and danced around them.

But there were no *kohanim*, or priests, at the gates of the Temple to greet the Maccabees. There were no Levites to meet them with songs of praise and thanksgiving. The Maccabees threw open the gates of the Temple themselves. They stepped through the gates into the courtyards. Then they stopped short, and some of them covered their faces and wept. The strong, brave soldiers who had fought against the powerful Syrians wept because the courtyard of the Temple was overgrown with thick, tangled weeds and shrubs.

But Judah quickly entered the Temple, and the men followed him. There, in the Temple, they saw the idols that Antiochus had set up. On the altar there was a sacrifice to the Greek god Zeus. The Maccabees looked at Judah, their leader.

"We must clean the Temple," Judah said. "We must make it ready for use again."

They set to work at once. They took out the altar and built a new one in its place. They threw the idols out of the Temple and scrubbed the places where they had stood. They pulled out the weeds and tangled shrubs from the courtyards. And they brought a new menorah and new holy vessels into the Temple, vessels of silver and gold.

At last, on the twenty-fifth day of the Hebrew month of Kislev, their work was finished. They opened the gates of the Temple, and the people of Jerusalem streamed into the courtyards. The children came dancing, flowers woven in their hair. The men brought sacrifices. They danced and sang in the courtyards, while the priests prayed and the Levites played on their harps and flutes and cymbals. And there was great joy throughout the land.

And there is a story which tells that the Maccabees could not find holy oil to pour into the menorah. There was but one small flask, and they said it could burn for only one day. But they poured it into the menorah and watched it burn, while the priests prepared fresh oil. And behold, there was a miracle. The oil lasted not one day, but eight.

For eight days the people streamed in and out of the Temple, bringing gifts and singing psalms of thanksgiving to God. They called the holiday Hanukkah, which means "dedication."[6]

iiiiiiii
=
The Great Hanukkah Strike
BAMI

(age level seven to eleven)

Everything was topsy-turvy and the whole community was seething with excitement. The news was sensational, and no one talked about anything else. There was no doubt about it. It wasn't just a rumor.

The Hanukkah candles were going on strike.

That was their unanimous decision. Well—almost unanimous. Because one voice refused to join ranks with the others: the *shammash* candle. The oil and the wicks and the tallow; the orange-tinted candles and the multicolored ones—all were firm. They would not burn this Hanukkah!

Here and there a few people were stunned into sadness. They knew they couldn't have a Hanukkah without lights. They even thought of declaring a three-day fast to mourn the terrible situation. Another handful of people, those who never bothered about Hanukkah at all, were, sad to say, quite pleased. "So the candles are on strike?" they snickered. "Fine. We don't care. We'll be on strike with them."

But most of the people were just plain confused. It was a frightening thing to plan a fast for three whole days. But then, on the other hand, to join the candles in a strike? What would happen to the holiness and fun of Hanukkah? Cancel out Hanukkah? It would be the first time such a thing had happened in hundreds, no, thousands of years!

"It's an emergency!" cried some hotheads. "Let's make electric menorahs!"

"Never!" thundered the others. "It must be candles or oil or no Hanukkah at all!"

The children were especially mixed up. They always had thought that Hanukkah was their holiday. It meant listening to the story of Judah Maccabee and eating potato pancakes and playing Hanukkah dreidel—and everything. Hopping up and down, the children kept asking the grownups: "Why? Why? Why? WHY? are the candles going to strike? There must be a reason. Please, tell us!"

Reason! As if those silly candles needed a reason. They seemed to have lost their heads. Thought of themselves as glorious suns, not simple little candles. Once they used to act their parts in a friendly glowing way. When it was time, they would flicker without a fuss. Now their anger had flared forth and they flaunted their pride before the whole community. They had even written an editorial and placed it on the front pages of all the newspapers. What nerve! Anyway, here's what the editorial said:

"Kislev the 17th
"Little Hanukkah candles of the world, unite! In solemn assembly we decree a strike. We hereby inform everyone, big and small, fat and tall, that they will have to do without us this year.

"We admit that we feel sorry for all children everywhere. But it's the only way for us. What's the good of burning with all our might if hardly anyone cares? We try our best to remind you of the heroic struggle of our ancestors, the glorious Maccabees. But does everyone pay attention? Ha! Some don't sing "*Maoz Tzur*," some think it's just a silly old custom, and some don't even know it's Hanukkah!

"Some light us only as an ornament, never seeing our inner flame, never realizing that we stand for victory over tyranny. We're not just tallow and wick. We have a soul. We stand for Jewish history!

"Well and therefore! The strike which we have proclaimed and decided upon unanimously—except for the *shammash*—will go on until we have satisfaction.
"(signed) *The Hanukkah Candles*"

The days rolled by and matters got worse. People had never given so much thought to plain everyday things like candles until this had come up. Hanukkah was fast approaching, and still no solution. The candles had become silent and refused to say a word. They all refused to do their duty, except the *shammash*. The lowliest candle of them all, the one who didn't even have the right to stay on the same level with the other candles in the menorah—he was the only one who wasn't going to strike. But what good would that do?

"Wait a minute!" someone cried. "Let's talk to him. Let's go to the *shammash* candle. We'll plead, we'll request, we'll do anything!"

So a small delegation, with serious faces, came to the *shammash*. He received them courteously, nodding his wick in welcome.

"Listen to our plea," said the committee. "We are not worthy, perhaps. But think of our children. How will it be for them to grow up in a world without Hanukkah?"

And the *shammash* promised. He would talk to his fellow candles. He couldn't promise anything, but he would try. The people were hopeful again, but nervous. It was just one day to Hanukkah.

The *shammash* worked hard, and at last two-thirds of the striking candles relented. They would burn. But the rest of the candles were firm. The answer was no. They would not shed a drop of tallow for the cause.

Finally the *shammash*, weary with pleading, straightened up and said:

"I am the most humble among you. Each of you uses me to be lit up. True, I am your servant, but you can't get along without me. I am the only one who can go from one candle to another to light you. None of you may change places. You can't lower yourselves to light one another. I am lit on each of the eight days. I stay in my place and do my duty without question. Now then, I accuse you of trying to destroy the holy festival of Hanukkah. And, on my oath as a *shammash*, I swear not to serve you this Hanukkah—or ever again. Unless you break up your strike, right now!"

The strike was over. Next day was a happy day in the world. Never had Hanukkah been celebrated with so much joy. In the fight for keeping alive Hanukkah, the *shammash* had fought like a true Maccabee and had won new glory. Tradition kept him from being placed on the same level as the other candles. True enough. But who said he couldn't be higher than all of the rest?

That's where the people placed him. And today, the *shammash* in many a menorah is placed a little higher than the others. From his position of honor he gladly descends to do his duty.

Then he climbs back up, and reminds the world that Hanukkah is a thrilling festival whose meaning we must never forget.[7]

iiiiiiii
=

One Hanukkah in Helm
YAACOV LURIA

educator and lecturer in creative writing and modern literature; free-lance writer

(age level nine to thirteen)

A beggar, a stranger, came to Helm, and the people shut their doors on him.

It was the week of Hanukkah, a cold time. And yet the people of Helm, who were known everywhere for their kindness, peered through their frosted windowpanes at the ragged little man but kept their doors closed to his knocking.

How did such a thing happen? Helm, you see, was a very special place. An ordinary town had one or two or, at most, a half dozen beggars. Helm was so poor that half the town had become beggars. This was a fine arrangement since no decent householder in Helm ever refused anyone asking for charity. One half of the townspeople gave alms, the other half took alms. A rich man never worried that giving charity might make him poor. He could always turn beggar and get back the wealth he had given away.

To be sure, some people seem to have been born to worry. One such worrier was Yoneh Shmeryl, the president of the Beggars' Benevolent Brotherhood of Helm. Yoneh Shmeryl's head, let me tell you, was like a clock: a hundred little wheels were turning inside it all the time.

Now, one day, as Yoneh Shmeryl was mending the thatch on the roof of his house, he fell to asking himself questions. All kinds of foolish questions came jumping at him like rabbits, but he had wise answers for all of them. Yet one question chilled him to his very bones: *What would happen if, God forbid, there should be more beggars in Helm than there were charity-givers?*

It took much stroking of his beard before he brought forth the answer: Some unfortunate chap would be without a patron. . . . Without a patron there would be no charity. . . . Without charity the poor man would starve—*oy gevalt!* A dreadful danger hung over the town! At once he called a meeting of the Beggars' Brotherhood in the synagogue. His fiery words of warning brought cold shudders to his fellow beggars. With one voice they cried out: *No strange beggars must henceforth be allowed in Helm. All doors must stay shut when they come knocking, not a penny should be given them.* Otherwise the beggars pledged that they would leave in a body and take their business elsewhere.

What choice did the rest of the Helmites have? Without beggars Helm would be ruined! Everyone had to agree: let whatever the beggars demanded be done.

And so it was that the little man, a beggar from who knew where, came to Helm and found himself shunned. From the synagogue, of course, he couldn't be shut out. He sat warming himself by the stove, stuffing scraps of felt into the holes in his boots and thinking aloud to Gimpel the *shammash*.

"If only I had a crust of bread . . . ," mused the beggar. "With a bread crust I could make latkes in honor of Hanukkah."

Gimpel straightened up so suddenly that his yarmulkeh almost fell off his head. "Latkes for Hanukkah from a crust of bread!" he cried. "Unbelievable!"

The stranger's sharp black eyes twinkled pleasantly. "Hanukkah is a holiday of miracles. I can do what I say."

All at once Gimpel felt the bravery of a Bar Kochba within him. "I don't care what Yoneh Shmeryl will do," he told the stranger. "I will get you your bread." And he pulled his cloak tightly around him and rushed out into the cold.

"Don't forget a grater and a skillet. And maybe a mixing bowl!" the stranger called after him.

In less time than it takes to say the Eighteen Blessings, the *Shemoneh Esreh*, Gimpel had run to the baker and gotten a stale hallah. From this one and that one he borrowed a skillet, a mixing bowl, a wooden ladle, and a grater. Whipped on by Gimpel, the secret came galloping through the town. "Hanukkah latkes from a crust of bread—imagine!" Everyone dropped what he was doing and followed Gimpel. At the head of the crowd marched Yoneh Shmeryl waving his rolled-up umbrella like a sword.

When they reached the synagogue, the stranger gave one and all a hearty *shalom aleikhem*, hitched up the sleeves of his robe, and began to grate the bread into the mixing bowl. When there was just a tiny heel of hallah left, he stopped. "If I only had a few pinches of salt and pepper . . . ," he murmured.

In an instant someone brought forth salt and pepper shakers.

Then the beggar sighed gently: "A drop of fat would be good too." Immediately a jug of goose fat appeared. Slowly, a very little at a time, he dusted the pepper and salt over the bread and poured the fat into the skillet.

Furiously Yoneh Shmeryl cried out: "Brother Jews, you are being fooled. From bread, salt, pepper, and goose fat you cannot make latkes!"

Said the stranger: "You may give me forty lashes if I lie." Yet his forehead furrowed in a frown, as if he were not quite satisfied.

Timidly, Gimpel reached into his pocket and produced an onion. The stranger's eyes lit up. "What harm can an onion do?" he asked.

Beyleh the watercarrier's widow now spoke up. "I happen to have a few eggs in my shawl. Perhaps . . ."

44. A Hanukkah lamp atop a watertower. Tel Aviv. 1937.

"Eggs? Why not eggs?" the stranger agreed, and into the bowl they went. And now he rubbed his hands together. "Ah, will you taste latkes now! Truthfully, there are some who insist that a touch of potatoes brings out the flavor just right. I like a simple batter."

At this point Shprintze the midwife, a woman big as an elephant, held out two tremendous handfuls of potatoes. "Let it be a first-class miracle. Something to tell our great-grandchildren!" she trumpeted.

"With potatoes I can make latkes too," sneered Yoneh Shmeryl.

"You are right," agreed the stranger. "I don't need them."

"What—you refuse my gift?" cried Shprintze in such a terrible voice that the lamps in the synagogue flickered.

"No charity to strange beggars—you agreed!" bleated Yoneh Shmeryl. "Otherwise we leave Helm!"

"So leave! Go with my blessing!" bellowed Shprintze. She towered over the little stranger while he grated the potatoes and stirred them into the batter.

And suddenly a delicious aroma—warm and peppery and fatty good—came billowing through the synagogue—and there were latkes turning golden brown! The bellies of the Helmites rumbled. Hungrily they watched the little stranger scoop a pancake from the skillet, make a quick blessing, and begin crunching away.

Yoneh Shmeryl demanded: "I must taste for myself!" He had devoured two pancakes and was biting into a third before he announced: "Helmites, these are the best pancakes I have ever eaten!"

"A miracle! A Hanukkah miracle!" cried the Helmites, and they came surging forward to taste the wonderful latkes.

And magically more of everything sprang up—more skillets, more goose fat, more onions, more potatoes. As fast as the latkes were done, the Helmites gobbled them up. Bottles were opened, *le-hayyims* were drunk—and all at once they were singing and dancing. When everyone had danced and sung himself out, Yoneh Shmeryl himself carried the stranger off to spend the night on a warm feather bed.

Nu, it was almost Passover before the Helmites let the little miracle-maker go. They went back to their old ways, welcoming wayfarers with warm hearts and open hands. And their Hanukkahs after that were specially joyous, for they were remembering more than one miracle.

Now Helmites, as you may have heard, were not the most clever people in the world. Yet sometimes a wise child did arise among them. "Ah, what a head he has!" they would marvel. "Someday he will make latkes from bread crumbs yet!"[8]

ⁱⁱⁱⁱⁱⁱⁱⁱ
=

The Pan of Oil
CHAVER PAVER

pen name of Gershon Einbinder; writer of popular children's stories in Yiddish and author of plays and novels (1901–64)

(age level nine to thirteen)

The little hills were already covered with snow, and the day itself was snow-laden. A wind swept out of the woods and tore at the roofs of the houses and the village.

The house that stood at the edge of the village was quiet like the others, the people in it were also asleep. It was dark in all the rooms, but the house was not completely dark. In the window that faced the broad winding road stood a pan of oil; there was a wick in the pan and it burned through the night. It shed a light far off toward the roads that fanned out from the village.

It was a thing of continual wonder to the village folk that with the coming of winter's snow and frost, the owner of that house placed the pan of oil in the window, lit the wick, and let it burn all through the night until daybreak. And it had been noted, too, that as soon as the winter was gone, when the snows melted and the hills turned green again, the light no longer burned in the window, and the house slumbered in darkness like all the rest.

The man who owned the house was named Abraham, and he had four children, two boys and two girls. He was the only Jew in the village, a man who loved work, who worked from sunup to sundown. He raised thousands of chickens, and he also had eight cows and a big dog. His children, when they were quite young, climbed over all the hills in the summer. In winter they stayed indoors and played with their dog. At first they paid no attention to the fact that their father lit the pan of oil every night during the winter, but when they grew a little older they wondered about it, but said nothing.

They said nothing, that is, until one night when they gathered to celebrate Hanukkah. Their father, Abraham, told them the story of the holiday and lit the menorah. It was then that the oldest of the children, consumed by curiosity, took advantage of the occasion to ask about the pan of oil.

"Father," he said, "I understand from all you have told us about the holiday that we light candles for each night of Hanukkah, for eight days, that is. But why do you burn a light in the window every night of the winter, even when it is not Hanukkah?"

The question made Abraham thoughtful. He closed his eyes and was silent for a while. When he opened them there was a smile on his face, and he began to tell them the story.

"It all started twenty years ago," he said. "I was a young man then, nineteen years old. Both my parents died suddenly that year, in the same week, and I was left alone, without friends, without money and without a trade to work at. I was very worried, and after much thought I decided to leave my hometown and go out into the world and seek my fortune.

"It was wintertime. Snow lay over the fields, and it was so cold that my nose and ears froze as I walked. But I was lighthearted. I shrugged away all my cares and walked on for a whole day until night began to fall. I was then in the midst of a long stretch of woods and a snowstorm began to rage. By this time I was quite tired and began to worry that I would be swallowed up by the snow in the strange region. So I gathered up my strength and began to run, in the hope that I would soon come to an inhabited area.

"I ran for a long time until I could go no farther. My strength had given out and I fell in a heap of snow. Not a human was to be seen or heard anywhere. White fields enveloped me all around and the storm raged on. I stretched out on the snow. I was so tired and overheated from running that the snow seemed soft, like a pleasant bed.

"Suddenly I saw, as in a dream, a light shining from somewhere in the distance. I opened my eyes with difficulty and looked, but there was no light. I told myself that I had imagined it, so I closed my eyes again. But again the light appeared. I started into the distance; yes, there was really a light. The gleam seemed to be coming from a house; its glow seemed to be beckoning me to a warm, pleasant home.

"When the owner opened the door for me, I fell into a dead faint, and for two weeks I lay in bed with a high fever, practically unconscious. When I was finally able to understand what was going on around me, I saw an elderly Jewish couple and their young daughter, all of them deeply worried about my health.

"In time I became completely well. The old Jew told me that the night I arrived was the first night of Hanukkah. He had lit the first candle and he placed it on the windowsill. That was the light that had gleamed for me when I was lost among the white fields. It was the light that brought me to this house, my children, in which you now live.

"I told the owner all about myself. He listened to me and then said that if I liked I could stay with him and help out on the farm. I decided to stay with him. That was twenty years ago. The old man and his wife passed away a long time ago. I married their daughter. You probably guessed it—she is your mother.

"Since that time, as soon as winter descends and the snow and frost arrive, I light the pan of oil. I put it in the window every night so it will shine far over the road, to give heart to those who might be out late in the night, so they will not get lost and perhaps be overcome in the snow."

That night, after the story, the children lay down on their beds but they could not fall asleep for a long time. When they finally dozed off they dreamed of snowy fields, of night, of a snowstorm roaring in the darkness and of a man all covered with snow, floundering about and crying. Then the gleam of a flame in a pan of oil appeared and the snow-encrusted man, overjoyed, ran with all his might toward the glow.

Translated by Benjamin Efron[9]

iiiiiiii
=

Reuben Lights a Torch
SOL KLEIN

(age level nine to thirteen)

He stood so still that at first he seemed only a deeper part of the darkness.

"Reuben?" she whispered softly.

He turned, and they made their way to each other across the flat roof of the house. A cloud moved over the moon, and a chill wind crept down from the hills of Judea.

"Reuben," she said, "you haven't been thinking of it again?"

"Yes, Mother."

"Reuben, I can't let you go. They'll kill you, as they killed your father."

"They won't catch me," he said. "They are heavy men, and I am light of foot.

"They are many and we are few," she said without hearing him.

Gently, he took her hand and stood beside her. "Look, Mother," he said, "what do you see?"

"Only darkness."

"Only darkness," he repeated, "in our bright city of Jerusalem. Before they came, lights danced on our streets and highways."

"You are only a child," she said dully.

"Mother," he said, "listen. What do you hear?"

"Only the wind, my son."

"Listen," he said again.

"From the houses where the enemy dwells," she said, "I hear the sound of laughter."

"From the Syrians," he picked up her words, "the sound of drunken laughter. Who but the enemy laughs in the city of Jerusalem, while we cringe like mice on our dark roofs at night? I must go, Mother. I am only a child in your eyes, but my place is with Judah."

The cloud slipped from the face of the moon. Under the yellow light Jerusalem lay silent, like a dead city.

"Go," she said at last, "you are a man. Your place is with Judah."

For a moment they clung to each other, then he seemed to melt from her side. She heard the sound of his feet as he made his way from the roof of the house. She saw him glide like a shadow through the slumbering streets. Then he was gone, and she felt a quiet joy she had never known before. He was only a boy, but she had given a soldier to Judah Maccabee.

Reuben picked his way through the twisting streets, for he knew the city well. He knew where there were heavy trees to give him shelter, and he knew the narrow alleys where he could melt into the shadows. He knew where the Syrians slept, and where they came at night to drink and shout.

At last he reached the outskirts of the city. He sprinted across an open field and beyond it to the highway.

On and on he ran through the night, the wind singing through his hair. Dawn was rising when he cleared a bend in the road. With a startled cry he froze in his tracks. He was face to face with a company of enemy troops. Before he could move, rough hands reached out and seized him. Questions were rained upon him from every side.

"Why did you cry out, young one?"

"Surprised were you, like a deer coming upon a hunter?"

"Or it might be, like a spy for your Judah, son of Mattathias."

"Speak! What are you doing at this hour along an empty road?"

"Silence!" a stern voice suddenly broke into the babble of voices.

Reuben found himself looking up at the captain of the company, a heavy-faced man with gray eyes embedded in puffs of flesh.

"We are no fools," the captain told the boy. "We know you Judeans are ready to die rather than utter a word. You are on your way to Judah Maccabee. Speak, am I wrong?"

"You are not wrong," Reuben said quietly. "I would die rather than utter a word to comfort my people's tormentors."

"A brave lad," the captain said with a short laugh. "But you shall not die. We have need of lads like you to see that our helmets shine and our tents are in order. There are many ways of serving Antiochus."

Once more rude hands seized the boy, and the company marched on down the road. After an hour they turned into a lane that led to a forest. Among the trees stood rows of enemy tents. Men were moving about, rubbing the sleep from their eyes and preparing their morning meal.

The captain called Reuben into his tent. The restless gray eyes looked the boy up and down.

"You seem a healthy boy," he said at last. "That is well, for there

45. *Hanukkah lamp of torches burn on the eighth day of Hanukkah by the side of the Western Wall, Jerusalem.*

is much work to be done. While the men eat, you shall clean their tents. If you shirk your tasks, we have ways of punishing which will make even a brave son of Judea cry out.''

Reuben turned to go, when again the Syrian spoke.

''It will please you to hear,'' he said slowly, ''that your Maccabees plan a raid upon us this night. Our spies have not been idle. When your friends attack, we shall be prepared to receive them.'' And with a wave of the hand, he dismissed the boy and sprawled out to rest on a mat in a corner of the tent.

Silently Reuben made his way among the men, who followed him with hard, curious eyes and taunting shouts. But Reuben felt nothing but the boring eyes of the captain. And in his ears his words echoed like drumbeats: "We shall be prepared to receive them."

Reuben moved from tent to tent, straightening mats and piles of clothes. As he worked his mind raced feverishly. How to warn them! They would descend upon a camp which they thought asleep, and armed men would leap from trees, their weapons raised to strike. On the silent rooftop, his mother had said he was a man. But he was only a boy who had walked into the hands of the enemy.

When the tents were tidy Reuben was given piles of helmets to shine. Soldiers came and went, preparing for the night raid. One of them brushed against the boy as he sat before a tent and stumbled, dropping an unlit torch he was carrying.

"Out of the way!" he said angrily, and recovering his balance, he walked on, muttering under his breath. Reuben stared at the torch, his heart beating out a sudden hope. Quickly he glanced about him. No one was looking his way. He crawled forward slowly, picked up the torch, and tucked it into the loose folds of his tunic. The next instant he was back among the helmets.

The day wore slowly on. When evening came, the captain called his men together and gave them their last instructions. In the shadows Reuben stood, trying to still the beating of his heart. He had hidden the torch in the small tent where he was to sleep alone. If they discovered it they would kill him. But he had told his mother he was a soldier. A curt command from the captain, and the men dispersed to take their positions.

Reuben went to his tent and lay waiting in the dark. The moments crept by, and the hours. Utter silence around him. Sleep tugged at his eyes. With the palms of his hands he beat his temples to keep himself awake.

Then it came, footfalls like distant whispers. The Syrians stirred in the trees, setting the leaves whimpering. Nearer they came, the feet of the Maccabees, muffled thuds creeping down from the hills.

Reuben strained his ears till the blood throbbed in his head. Nearer came the stealthy march of feet. The march of freedom from the hilltops, from the deep caverns, from the secret places of the land.

The camp stirred softly, like a beast awaking from sleep. Reuben crept to the door of his tent. Vague shadows loomed beyond the camp. The shadows grew larger, drew closer and closer.

Reuben grasped his torch.

"Mother!" his lips quivered. "Mother!"

And then his hands grew firm. Another instant, and the torch flared, a jet of flame in the dark.

"Brothers!" he shouted. "The enemy is prepared."

Shouts of fear and anger rang through the trees. Men leaped to seize him, but the boy darted like a hare between their hands. A spear whirred past his ear, and Reuben threw the torch to the ground and stamped out its flame. Again the darkness shielded him as he fled to the edge of the encampment, into the arms of the Maccabees.

The battle raged till dawn. When the sun rose, a weary band of Maccabees made its way triumphantly back to the hills. At their head walked Judah Maccabee, and beside him was the young lad from Jerusalem, his face turned to the sun.[10]

||||||||
=

Seven Sacrifices

JOSEPH GAER

folklorist, editor, and author of numerous popular books on Judaism and other religions

(age level eleven to fourteen)

Of wicked rulers there have been many in the world. Yet it would be hard to find one worse than Antiochus the Madman who conquered Jerusalem 175 B.C.E.

He treacherously entered the Temple of Jerusalem, plundered its holy vessels, and emptied its treasury. Still this mad tyrant was not content.

At his command idols were set up in the Temple. Altars were built before the gilded idols. Pigs were killed upon these altars. Opposite the idols, and within sight of the slaughtered swine, a throne was erected for Antiochus to sit on, and a platform near the throne for the judges whom the king had appointed. Then the Madman ordered all the Jews of Jerusalem to be brought before him in a long procession.

"I now give you a new religion," said the king to the Jews. "You must all become Greeks, like me."

They who readily bowed before the Greek idols, ate of the swine's flesh, and promised to give up their old religion forever were set free and rewarded with presents.

But they who refused were whipped with heated rods and tortured in many cruel ways.

The weakhearted in Israel obeyed the king's command. But the brave and pious remained faithful to their holy Law.

As the number of those who refused to obey the Madman grew, the more insane became the king's cruelty. And the crueler the king's tortures were, the more determined grew the pious and the faithful in Israel.

One day the king's soldiers brought before Antiochus and his judges a woman with seven boys clinging about her.

"Are they all your children?" the king asked.

"These seven are my seven blessings from the God of Israel," the woman replied.

The king beckoned to the oldest boy to draw near, and asked him: "What is your name?"

"My name, Your Majesty," answered the boy, who was fifteen years old, "my name is Abraham, after the first of our forefathers who broke the idols in his father's house."

The king sneered, and with his bony finger he pointed across the hall toward the row of gilded idols.

"Bow before those gods!"

"It is written in the holy Law," the boy said, "it is written: 'I am the Lord thy God! Thou shalt have no other gods before Me!' "

The king's eyes narrowed in anger.

"If you refuse to do my bidding, I shall have your tongue cut out for the words you have just spoken. Obey, then, and bow down before my gods!"

Abraham folded his arms in defiance.

"Shame and woe upon me the moment I'm frightened by the words of a tyrant, and forget to fear Him who created heaven and earth!"

The king's face turned pale, and the king's face turned red, and he shouted:

"Take this boy and torture him until he is dead!"

Abraham was led away to his martyrdom.

His mother raised her eyes to heaven and whispered:

"The Lord hath given, and the Lord hath taken away. Blessed be the Name of the Lord!"

And the children responded:

"Amen!"

"And what is your name?" the Madman asked of the second boy.

"My name, Your Majesty," the boy replied as he came forward, "my name is Isaac, after the second of our great forefathers. Isaac was thirteen years old when he was brought to the altar of God, and I am thirteen years old this day, and just as ready to die if it is God's will."

The king lifted a dish of swine's meat.

"Eat this, and save yourself from the fate that befell your stubborn brother!"

Isaac shook his head with resolution.

"That which is forbidden I cannot do," he said.

"Take him!" Antiochus shouted hoarsely. "Take him and do to him as you did to his brother!"

When Isaac was taken away, the mother whispered:

"Thy ways, O Lord, are beyond the understanding of mortals!"

The king called the third boy forward, and asked:

"What is your name?"

"My name is Jacob," the boy replied. "I am eleven years old, and my uncle who is my teacher says I'm a very bright boy."

The king and the judges laughed at the boy's frankness.

"Now, Jacob," said the king in a good humor, "be a good boy and listen to me. Bend your knee and bow your head to my gods there. That cannot possibly hurt you, can it?"

"Those?" Jacob asked, and pointed to the idols.

"Yes, those," the king said hopefully.

"Oh no!" Jacob shook his head.

"But why not, foolish boy?"

"It is written: 'Thou shalt have no strange gods before me.' That's why."

"If you refuse to do my bidding," the king threatened, "I shall order the whipping rods to be made red hot and with these you'll be punished."

"The cruelty of the tyrant," said Jacob coolly, "is only of the hour. But the world stands forever."

"Take him away!" Antiochus foamed at the mouth and gritted his teeth. "Take him away!"

When Jacob was killed, his mother sobbed:

"Strengthen, O Lord, my weakening heart!"

As she said this, she felt the hand of her youngest squeezing her hand to assure her that he was near.

"And what is your name?" the king shouted to the next boy, who was hardly nine years old.

"My name, Your Majesty, is Joseph," the boy replied.

"Why do you call me 'Your Majesty'?" The king thought of a new approach to the child.

"Because it is written that honor and respect are due to the rulers of the earth."

"Will you honor my commands then?" the king asked.

"Those commands that are within your right to give I shall obey," the boy solemnly promised.

"Then I command you to bow before these!" And the Madman pointed to the row of wooden images.

"It is written: 'Hear, O Israel, the Lord our God, the Lord is One!' But of these there are many. Surely they cannot be gods."

"Take him!" the king shouted to his men.

And Joseph, too, was taken away.

"O Lord!" the mother sobbed. "Ten thousand leagues is the depth of the sea, but deeper still is my grief!"

"And what is your name?" the king asked of the fifth boy, who was six years old.

"My name is Moses, after Moses the Lawgiver," the boy replied proudly.

"I have heard of him," the king said sourly. "Now, tell me, will you bow before my gods or won't you?"

"I will," said Moses.

"You will?" the king gasped.

"You will, child?" the mother gasped.

"I will bow to them, if that idol over there in the center asks me to do so," Moses quickly added.

"Foolish boy, how can a thing of wood talk?" the king said.

"Shame on you, foolish king!" Moses turned on him. "Like unto the Pharaohs of Egypt you are a worshiper of useless things. Look at your gods!" Moses pointed his little finger at the images. "Look at them! They have feet, but can they walk? They have hands, but can they move them? They have ears, but can they hear? They have eyes, but can they see? They have mouths, yet they cannot even ask one to bow to them!"

"Take him away!" the Madman shouted to his executioners.

The king then called the sixth child before him, a little black-eyed boy of four, who came forward with his tongue stuck out.

"Why do you stick your tongue out?" the king asked.

"Cut it out," said the little boy. "Isn't that what you're going to do?"

"Oh no!" the king assured him and drew the child to his knees. "I won't hurt you if you'll be a good boy. Now, what is your name?"

"My name is David. I am named after the king from whose children there shall come the Messiah."

"Who taught you that little speech? Your mother?"

"Yes, sir!" said David very politely.

"Now, David, you have seen how your brothers were killed. You don't want to die like that, do you?"

"No, sir!" said David emphatically.

"Then listen to me and bow down before those gods over there."

David turned to his mother, and he saw her shaking her head.

"No, sir! I won't!" David said, and his young voice began to tremble.

"You are so young, child," the king pleaded. "Your brothers were older and have lived some time. But you haven't even begun to enjoy life. Better listen to me and do as I tell you."

David looked at his mother again, then broke out in tears.

"No, no! I won't do it!"

"Take him away!" the Madman shouted.

"O Lord!" the mother sobbed as David was led away. "Your trial is beyond my strength!"

Then the king called forward the last of the children, a little boy not yet three years old.

"What a beautiful child!" the judges exclaimed.

"What a beautiful child!" the king too, exclaimed. And taking the child upon his knee, he asked: "What is your name?"

"Solomon," the child replied, and looked up frightened at the cruel face of the ruler.

"That's a nice name," said Antiochus. "Be then as wise as Solomon after whom you are named, and do what I tell you to do. Then I'll give you whatever you will ask for."

"No," the child answered.

"I will adopt you as my son and bring you up as a prince," the king promised.

"No." The child was firm in his reply.

"You do not need to bow to those idols," the king whispered in little Solomon's ear. "I'll drop one of my rings and you'll bow down to pick it up for me. That's all you have to do."

"Woe unto you, mighty Antiochus!" the mother spoke up. "You are a ruler of a great empire, but you urge a little boy to deceive your own judges by bowing down for the ring that they may think he is bowing down to your idols."

"How cruel of you to let your children be killed like this!" the Madman reproached the mother.

"Before you talk of cruelty to others," the mother answered, "look at your own hands that are wet with the blood of innocent children."

The mad king recoiled upon his throne and looked at his bony hands with great horror, then wiped the imaginary blood off on his cloak.

"If your mother will not spare you," the king growled, "then I shall not, either!"

And he commanded his executioners to kill the child.

"Let me embrace him before you take him away from me," the mother pleaded.

When the child was given her, and she gathered him in her arms, her heart weakened.

"Please, let me die before him!" she pleaded.

"It is written in your Torah that a mother and her child should not be killed on the same day," the king taunted her.

"Have you obeyed all the commandments in our Torah that you also wish to obey this one?" the mother demanded.

But the king would not listen to her, and the child was taken away.

Then the mother, who had come in surrounded with sons like a proud fortress, left the hall alone, like a defenseless city. She walked out on the roof of the Temple, and cried:

"Abraham, Father Abraham! Behold, you have built one altar for your son; but I have built this day seven altars. You were only tried,

46. The Western Wall, Jerusalem, during Hanukkah. 1968.

and your son was spared; but I was tried and my seven sons were sacrificed. O Lord! Into your hands I now trust my soul also!"

She walked out to the edge of the high roof and threw herself down to her death.[11]

iiiiiii
=

A Syrian Diary
JOSEPH HALPERN

British Jewish educator; author of textbooks and other writings

(age level eleven to fourteen)

It was while on a visit to a village in the West Country that I became acquainted with the local "lord of the manor." He lived in a ruined castle off the main road, and he invited me to look at some old papers he had found in an attic. He was very patriotic and was going to give them all to his local council for their wastepaper collection. "Don't do that," I said, "there may be some valuable documents among these papers. It would be a tragedy to destroy them."

"We must all do our bit to help to win the war," he answered. "But," he added with a smile, "you're welcome to look through them and keep whatever you want."

It was fortunate that I had half an hour to spare before my bus was due to take me to the next center I had to visit. For among these old papers was a priceless document. It was written in Greek and filled about ten quarto sheets, but I had only to read a few lines to realize its importance. It was the diary of one of the personal attendants of the Syrian king Antiochus IV! This heathen had been at the court of the mad king who had tried to crush the Jewish religion at the very time that Judah the Maccabee had raised his standard of revolt. This heathen had been present at all the important interviews and conferences between Antiochus and his generals, and had made a note of them in his diary. As I read my excitement grew, and I did not notice how quickly the time was passing.

"You'll miss your bus," my host said quietly, but I was too absorbed in my reading to hear him. Three hours passed before I lifted my eyes from the document, but my face was filled with triumph.

"I am sorry I have no accommodation to put you up for the night," the lord of the manor began. "Don't worry about me," I broke in, "I shan't be able to sleep in any case. I've made one of the finds of the century. The whole world will want to read this story of Hanukkah as told by this heathen courtier of Antiochus. It completes the picture we have from the Jewish side in the books of the Maccabees and in the Talmud. Tell me, how did such a document happen to come into your possession?"

"I've no idea. Oh, of course. A grandfather of mine visited the Middle East about eighty years ago. I remember now the bundle of papers he brought back with him. Some Arabs had sold them to him. He thought they were part of the Apocrypha, but when he showed a sheet to the authorities they wouldn't look at it. Apparently they had been badly deceived by some previous forgeries a year or two earlier. In disgust my grandfather threw them into the attic in which you found them."

Here are the first extracts. Naturally, I am translating the dates and many of the expressions into a form that you will understand. It is a private diary and it was a good thing for the author that it never came into the hands of Antiochus.

"April 13, 167 B.C.E.
"My name is Callo, and my great-grandfather was a Greek officer in the army of Alexander the Great, may his memory be blessed. It is a pity that we have so few Greek soldiers at court now. Our king, Antiochus IV, has surrounded himself with a gang of barbarians, cowardly men from over the sea, who flatter him shamelessly. In their eyes he can do nothing wrong, and they worship him as a god. And he, like a fool, believes them. About six months ago he actually issued a decree that all his subjects should be one people and that everyone should leave his own laws. Most of the subject nations readily obeyed him. It didn't matter to them what gods they worshiped, and he was vain enough to believe them when they started calling him Antiochus Epiphanes, Antiochus the man-god. But there was one people who had the pluck to refuse to obey his decree. You should have seen what happened in the throne room this morning when the reports from the provinces were read.

"Antiochus (in my circle we call him Epimanes, the Madman), beamed from ear to ear when Nicanor related how the whole of

Syria from Antioch to the gates of Egypt trembled at his word. At the mention of the name Egypt, Antiochus' face went black. He remembered how he had been forced to turn back in his campaign against the Egyptians last year.

"But his face turned purple when Nicanor went on to say that the Jews had refused to obey his command. Apparently one of our officers had come to one of their villages and had set up an altar to Zeus. He had then called on the leading citizen to offer up sacrifice. He happened to be a Jewish priest. Not only had he refused to do this, but when another Jew came forward to offer the sacrifice he had struck him down and killed our officer (I hope he was a mercenary). Our men had tried to hush up the incident. But this troublesome Jew had rushed to the mountains with his five sons and had started a revolt against Syria. Hundreds, some say thousands, of Jews were joining them and stern action appeared necessary.

"Antiochus was almost speechless.

" 'Those Jews,' he spluttered, 'how I hate them. I have pulled down the altar to their God and set up an altar to Zeus in their Temple at Jerusalem. I have burnt their holy books and destroyed their finest buildings by fire. I shall not be beaten by a handful of rebels. Their religion shall perish from the earth. My will shall be done.'

" 'Hear, hear,' sang the gang of mercenaries in chorus. But we still have a few of the Greek nobility at court, and Trypho, a strapping young fellow who will make a name for himself one day, had the courage to speak up.

" 'Sire,' he cried, 'may I remind you of the way in which your illustrious ancestor Alexander treated the Jews.' (A flattering beginning in order to get Antiochus to listen to his words. Antiochus has as much right to be called a descendant of Alexander as I have—and that's none at all.)

" 'Speak on,' said the king, regaining his composure a little.

" 'Your majesty will recall . . .' "

This was the end of the first scroll of the manuscript. The next sheet did not give the actual speech, but seemed to run on well. This is what it said:

"Trypho reminded Antiochus of the scene outside Jerusalem when Alexander's army was marching to capture it. My great-grandfather had been present, and I had often heard the story from my grandfather's lips.

"The advance guard were already rubbing their hands with glee at the prospect of looting Jerusalem, for they had heard that it was a very rich city and contained huge stores of gold and silver. Suddenly the order was given to halt. From the city a procession was approaching, more than a mile long, and all the citizens were dressed in white. At their head appeared a band of uniformed men (we learned later that they were priests) led by a young man clothed in purple garments and wearing a golden miter on his head. (Simon the Just, the high priest, they called him.)

"At the sight of him our Alexander stepped forward and bowed his head to the ground in worship. Our guards were speechless and thought he must have gone out of his mind. Parmenio, however, had the courage to go up to Alexander and ask why he was doing this strange thing.

"A bellow as though from a bull interrupted Trypho's story.

" 'We do not want to listen,' shouted Antiochus, 'to your old wives' tales of centuries ago. I know you are going to say that Alexander had seen this man in a dream before his conquest of Asia and that he therefore allowed the Jews to worship God in their own way. But it is all lies, lies. . . .'

"By this time Antiochus was foaming at the mouth in his frenzied fury, and Clito the chamberlain wisely told us that the royal audience was over. Only Grazi the butcher remained, and as I left I heard him dictating, in the king's name, the measures by which to put down the Jewish rebellion. I caught the words Eleazar and Hannah. Poor souls, I can imagine the torture Grazi has made ready for them. Not for nothing has he earned the title "the Butcher." But then he is one of the mercenary gang.

"December 7, 167 B.C.E.
"The Jewish revolt has lasted a year already. But it will soon be over. Mattathias, their leader, has just died. His five sons will probably quarrel among themselves as to who should succeed him. And that is where our chance will come. I am sorry that it may all soon lead to nothing.

"December 1, 165 B.C.E.
"Those Jews! Lysias, the viceroy, came back to Antioch today a beaten man. His was the fourth army that Antiochus had sent against them. Apparently the death of Mattathias had not weakened them. In fact, they grew stronger and more troublesome. Their

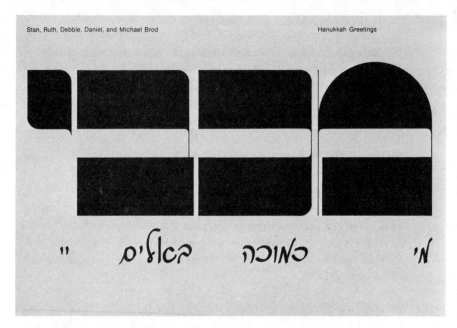

47. *Hanukkah greeting card. By Stan Brod. Cincinnatti. 1972.*

48. *Hanukkah greeting card. Shanghai, China. 1945.*

leader, Judah, must be a remarkable man. He cannot have a large army, and it is only poorly equipped. We have the resources of the world at our disposal. We have even made use of our famous corps of elephants. Yet we cannot defeat them in battle. Now that Lysias has lost Beth Sura, the road to Jerusalem is open. Will they take it? It would be funny if they recaptured their Temple on December 25, because that was the day on which Antiochus defiled it and built an altar to Zeus there three years ago. I should like to see Antiochus' face if that happens. He might think there is something in this Jewish God after all. I am beginning to think so myself.

"March 12, 164 B.C.E. "Antiochus IV is dead. He died in Persia, and reports say that on his deathbed he confessed that all the miseries that had come upon him in the last few years were due to the fact that he had plundered the Temple of the Jews at Jerusalem and had tried to dishonor their God. I can quite believe it. The story of the miracle of oil is still being told in the bazaars at Antioch. Judah did enter the Temple on December 25 last year. The priests purified the Temple and found there a small bottle of oil with the seal still on it which showed that it had not been touched by any gentile hands. That oil would normally be enough for only one day. But it takes eight days to make a new supply and the Jews have a law that the perpetual lamp, once lit, must never be allowed to go out. They were worried about what to do. And then the miracle happened. That little bottle of oil burned for eight days until the new supply was ready."

I brought the manuscript to the light to see some small words at the bottom of the page, when it caught fire. The only light I had was a candle, since I was in some out-of-the-way village where electricity and gas are still considered luxuries. The parchment was so brittle and dry that in a moment nothing was left of it. What a good thing that I had translated as much as I have.[12]

iiiiiiii

A Dreidel for Tuvi
MORRIS EPSTEIN

(age level eleven to fourteen)

The little village of Yud in the province of Kaf nestled in a valley surrounded by majestic mountains. It was a quiet community, with low houses, a marketplace, cobbled lanes, and a gabled synagogue older than any inhabitant could remember.

Most everyone in the village retired quite early in the winter. One by one, the lights blinked out in the homes of Yud. Soon the whole village was fast asleep, and all the windows were dark, except two. One of them belonged to the shop of Berel the blacksmith. The other was in the modest home of the widow Surah, almost at the very outskirts of the village.

Berel the blacksmith was very busy at this time of year. During the day, there were horses to be shod and wagon wheels that needed hammering. And at night, with Hanukkah so close at hand, Berel performed his duties as the only dreidel-maker in the entire province of Kaf.

In the cluttered quarters of the smithy, a pot of lead hanging over the fire began to bubble. Berel reached up to a high shelf and took down the last dusty dreidel form. It was stubby and made of a hard wood, with little openings along the top and a hinge and clasp that kept its two sides together.

Aiming carefully, he poured the molten metal into the little holes in the wooden form. When the lead had cooled off, he opened the clasp and folded back one side of the form. A row of gleaming Hanukkah dreidels faced him. One by one he took them out and spun them.

"This one's good," he said, "and this one, and this . . ." He stopped. One dreidel refused to spin. Berel grasped it firmly between thumb and forefinger and twirled it. This time it spun beautifully, longer than any other dreidel. Berel smiled, pleased with his handiwork.

He yawned and put away his apron and his tools. He was struggling into his greatcoat when he heard a noise, a *clickety-click-click*. The last little dreidel, the stubborn one, had rolled off the edge of the bench. Berel stooped, picked it up, and placed it back. He pulled on his heavy fur cap. *Clickety-click-click*; the dreidel was on the floor again. Absentmindedly, Berel picked up the dreidel and stuffed it into the pocket of his coat. He drew on his mittens, put out the lamp, locked the smithy, and trudged down the deserted cobblestoned street.

Berel was almost home when his eye was caught by a ribbon of light across his path. Looking up, Berel found himself before the window of the widow Surah's home. Surah was sewing a patch on a boy's shirt. Nearby sat little Tuvi, reading from a book, his crutches lying on the floor beside the chair.

Tuvi looked up. "How brave were the Maccabees, Mama," he

said. "They fought the soldiers of cruel Antiochus and drove them out of the Holy Land."

"Yes, Tuvi, Hanukkah reminds us of wonderful days, when God performed miracles for us," replied Surah, a catch in her voice.

"You mean the miracle of oil, Mama? The little bottle of oil that burned in the menorah in the Temple for eight days? I wish I were a Maccabee, Mama. I'd fight for you. I wish I could earn a good living, so that you might have a fine house and never worry about anything!"

"Ah, Tuvi," sighed his mother, "those are fine wishes, but I would trade them all for one wish of my own. If only you could walk again, Tuvi . . . But what use is it to wish for Hanukkah miracles, when I have not even been able to buy a dreidel for you, my child."

Berel retreated into the shadows. Everyone in the village knew Tuvi. The boy had been struck years ago by a runaway horse. The doctor said that the wounds had healed well enough. The boy *should* walk, and perhaps one day would. If, somehow, something could *force* Tuvi to walk, just once. . . . On the other hand, perhaps nothing could help . . .

Berel sensed a moistness in his eyes. Reaching into his pocket for his handkerchief to blow his nose, he felt something hard and cold leap into his hand. He drew out the dreidel that had fallen to the ,smithy floor. He stared at it, then walked to the door and knocked loudly. When the widow Surah opened it, he said gruffly:

"I was going home and saw your light. Tuvi is probably asleep. Will you give this to him in the morning?" He thrust the dreidel into the hand of the astonished Surah and vanished into the night.

The next morning Tuvi sat outside his mother's house, a blanket across his knees. The widow Surah's house was at the top of a hill and Tuvi could see the whole village from where he sat. He had his dreidel, and a large book lay on his lap. Again and again he twirled the dreidel on the cover of the book. It was no use: the dreidel went *clickety-click*, or at most, *clickety-click-click*, and then fell sadly on its side.

"Please, dreidel, *please!*" begged Tuvi. "If you won't try, how will you learn to spin by Hanukkah?" Tuvi looked hard at the dreidel. He read the words on the four wings: *Nes gadol hayah sham*—A great miracle happened there—and they seemed to twinkle at him. "*Nes gadol*," breathed Tuvi, and he spun the dreidel. *Clickety-click-click* went the dreidel, rolling to the edge of the book. "*Nes gadol hayah sham*," whispered Tuvi, and he twirled the dreidel with all his strength.

"*Clickety-click*-ZOOM!"—and the dreidel began to spin. It tapped the book twice, bounded past Tuvi's nose, and bounced on the ground. *Click!* and it was on the edge of the long sloping hill. CLICKETY! Now it was going down, spinning on a cobblestone, bouncing to a rock, hopping from slippery stone to mossy rain gutter, spinning down, down the hill, gleaming when its wings caught the sun, beckoning to Tuvi as if to say: "Come, Tuvi. If you really want me, come and get me!"

Tears started in Tuvi's eyes. He gripped the arms of his chair till his knuckles were white. "I can't!" he cried. Then his eyes brightened with firm determination. "My dreidel!" he said. "I won't lose my dreidel! I WON'T!"

Startled passersby stopped in the street. They saw a thin boy rise quivering from his chair. The blanket dropped to the ground. Tuvi, his arms stretched out like balancing poles, took a step forward, and another, and a third. He stumbled, fell, and rose. He tried again, and this time took six steps before he fell. Now he was on his feet again, tottering, running crazily, flying down the hill, following the spinning Hanukkah top, crying at the top of his voice: "Dreidel, wait for me! I'm coming!"

At the foot of the hill the dreidel struck a sharp stone and came to a sudden stop. In a flash, Tuvi was upon it. He scooped up the dreidel; followed by the gawking crowd, he walked slowly home.

Several days later, on the first night of Hanukkah, the villagers of Yud were squeezed into the widow Surah's home. The house was stuffed with the gifts they had brought: crisp latkes, fragrant tea, a roast goose, dumplings, new clothes for Tuvi and his mother. There was talking and singing and laughter and eating.

A hush fell over the room. The crowd parted to let Tuvi through. He walked proudly to the window and placed two orange candles in the menorah that stood on the sill. The widow Surah lit the *shammash* candle and with it the candle on the right.

"We thank Thee, Lord, for Thy miracles, in days gone by and in our own," sang the widow Surah.

And the village of Yud in the province of Kaf rejoiced until the whole valley rang with happiness and the purple mountains round-about reflected a beauty unsurpassed in all the wide, wide world.[13]

iiiiiiii
=

Five
AUTHOR UNKNOWN

(age level eleven to fourteen)

The jeep left a trail of dusty clouds as it sped along the desert road. The sun, setting in the west, cast a purple hue on the gray puffs of dust. To the east, the faintest trace of darkness appeared. The rest of the sky was blue, bright blue, fading into pink and finally fiery red above the western hills. Evening was coming but it was still day. It takes a long time for night to fall in the Negev.

Moshe drove a little faster. The jeep bounced roughly on the rocky road. Road! Back in America they would call it a path. This road wasn't paved with cement or asphalt—just sand and dirt and rocks! The only way you could tell the "road" from the surrounding countryside was by its wheel ruts and tire marks. But this was the Negev. We've just begun, Moshe thought to himself. We've just begun. Just wait a few more years . . . wait and work . . .

Moshe stepped on the accelerator. *Whoops!* "Who put that rock there?" Moshe asked out loud, as the jeep shot into the air. When they reached earth again, Moshe and the jeep, they hit hard. The steel shaft in the back settled with a loud clang! Hope it doesn't break, worried Moshe . . . this whole trip for nothing!

After a little rise in the road, Moshe could see the kibbutz. What a pretty sight! Not very elaborate or comfortable—but it was home. A real home, in your own land, thought Moshe.

He drove straight to the machine shop. A clanking sound came from within but no one could be seen.

"Hayyim! Hayyim!" Moshe shouted. "Where are you?"

"Here I am!" came an answering voice. "You blind or something?"

"Where?"

"OK, OK, I'll come out."

From underneath a tractor came two feet, then the rest of a man in greasy overalls. This was Hayyim.

"Did you get the shaft?" asked Hayyim.

"Yes, it's in the jeep. Lucky the boys at the other kibbutz had an extra one. As soon as our order from the factory comes in, we'll have to rush it down there. This was their last spare."

"Well, don't just stand there!" yelled Hayyim in mock anger. "I want to get this tractor in shape tonight so's the boys can go out early in the morning. Here, I'll give you a hand."

Carefully, they lifted the shaft from the jeep and took it into the shop.

"There," said Hayyim. He clapped his hands as if trying to brush the dirt off, but only succeeded in smearing the grease some more. Moshe leaned against the door.

"Hayyim," he began slowly. "About tonight . . . I mean, fixing the tractor tonight. I think we'll have to stand guard tonight. They're out again!"

"Who's out again? The stars? Stop being romantic!" And Hayyim broke out a few short bursts of laughter.

"And you stop being so funny," said Moshe. "I'm serious. The Arab raiders are out again. The boys down at the other kibbutz warned me. They were there last night. Burned five chicken coops and broke one of the lathes before the boys managed to drive them away."

Hayyim looked at Moshe, seriously this time.

"So, they're at it again! Haven't had enough!" He muttered some other things to himself, but Moshe couldn't hear.

"OK," said Hayyim finally, "no tractor tonight. Tonight we fight Arabs! Come, let's tell the others."

At the assembly hall, Moshe told all the men what he had heard at the neighboring kibbutz. There was no panic, but everyone was grim—and disappointed.

"Smack in the middle of Hanukkah!" said one of the men. "I thought we'd have a little holiday this week. Looks like we've got to relive Hanukkah every year! Oh, well."

"What about the menorah on the water tower?" asked another man. "Should we light it tonight?"

"I don't think so," called out another. "Best not to attract too much attention tonight."

Then Hayyim stood up.

"It's getting late. Everyone go home, put up blackout curtains, and light your Hanukkah menorahs. Then come back to the dining hall."

They lit the menorah in the assembly hall. Five candles—it was the fifth night.

After supper, guards were chosen and assigned to their positions. It was a cool night, black and starry. Hayyim and Moshe took up

49. Hanukkah greeting card. Vienna, Austria. Circa 1935.

their position near a little hillock to the south. They sat quietly, each busy with his own thoughts.

"You know, Hayyim," said Moshe, breaking the silence, "it just doesn't seem right. About the menorah on the water tower, I mean. I think it should be lit."

"But we agreed," said Hayyim, "we agreed it would be better this way. No good to attract attention."

"It still doesn't seem right. Especially on Hanukkah. You know what I mean?"

"No, what do you mean, 'especially'?"

"Well, on Hanukkah we celebrate the victory of the Maccabees over their enemies. Right? And what was their biggest weapon? Faith! They believed with perfect faith that the Almighty would help them to victory. They were fewer than the enemy, they had less arms than the enemy—but faith made them strong! And *we* don't want to light the menorah. It's almost as if we didn't have faith in God!"

Hayyim didn't feel right either, but he said: "You know it's not that, Moshe, it's—"

"I'm going!" Moshe started to get up.

"Where are you going?"

Moshe didn't answer.

"Hey!" yelled Hayyim. But it was no use. Moshe disappeared into the night. Hayyim wanted to run after him—but he couldn't leave the post unguarded. He checked his gun and settled down to wait.

Only four hundred feet away, in a dried-up creek bed, sat five Arabs. They spoke in whispers.

"Do you have enough fire bombs?" the leader asked one of his men.

"Fifteen, sir."

"Good. They're very quiet tonight. Must've gone to sleep early. Ten more minutes and we attack!"

Silence. Seconds ticked into minutes. A slight breeze made the only noise. Suddenly—

"Look!" said one of the Arabs. "A light—up there!"

"Sh-h-h!" whispered the leader. "There's another! Three! Four! *Five*!" Silence. "That's all—*five* lights! They know we're here. They even know how many we are and they're signaling for help! We'll be surrounded! Let's get out of here—*fast*!"

In hurried excitement, the Arabs fled. In their fright they even forgot to be quiet.

Hayyim, at his post, heard the commotion. He cocked his gun. Just then Moshe came running back to his friend.

"Moshe!" whispered Hayyim, "they're here! Flash on the searchlight, quick!"

The light went on—and all they could see were five Arab figures disappearing into the darkness.

"They've run away," gasped Moshe, still out of breath. "Five of them! I wonder why they ran. You didn't shoot, did you?"

"No," said Hayyim in amazement. "I didn't do a thing. I didn't even know they were here till they ran. They just ran. Guess we're safe now."

They rounded up the other guards and went back to the kibbutz.

"I still can't figure it out," said Hayyim. "Must be a miracle—a Hanukkah miracle!"

"Yes," said Moshe, "must be."[14]

iiiiiiii
=

A Menorah in Tel Aviv
YA'AKOV

(age level eleven to fourteen)

"Hey, DAVID! What are you dreaming about?"

David blinked and saw his two friends sitting almost in front of him on the curb. Tel Aviv has some very busy streets, and he hadn't noticed his friends coming.

Joseph was still waiting for an answer. At last, David said: "About a menorah for Hanukkah."

What he did not tell the boys was that he was trying to think of a way to ask his father about a menorah. They had thrown out their old metal one when mother had been housecleaning before the summer. It had been bent and rusty, and the wax drippings from last year's colored candles were still stuck on it. He remembered father saying: "By next Hanukkah I'll surely have a job and then we will buy a beautiful new menorah."

But only last night, when David was about to remind his father, the dog-eared record book with the family budget was open on the table. David saw his father chewing the end of his pencil. He knew what that meant. There wasn't much work in the building trade these days. David swallowed his words and left the house.

Reuben broke in on his thoughts. "We were just talking about Hanukkah lamps, too," he said.

"Not just about any old menorah," Joseph corrected him. "Think of it, David, they are going to build a giant steel tower right here in the center of Tel Aviv. Maybe like the Eiffel Tower in Paris! And on top will be a mighty Hanukkah lamp. Each light will be a million candlepower! The papers said so today. All of Tel Aviv will be lit!"

David's face lit up with sudden joy. "Really?" he cried. "If . . . if that's so, we won't have to light a menorah in our homes!"

Joseph roared: "You believe everything, don't you! Didn't you realize that I was just joking?"

"And even if they build a giant-size Hanukkah lamp I would still want to light candles of my own," said Reuben. "You ought to see how beautiful our menorah is—it's all hammered silver, decorated with lions and birds, and the candle-holders are small and graceful."

"Our Hanukkah lamp uses oil," said Joseph. "You pour a little oil into each holder and light it. And then I ask my father to place the lamp on the windowsill that faces the street, and I go down to the street and look up at our window."

David closed his eyes and said: "I think it would be wonderful to build a giant menorah. When I grow up and become an engineer I will build a huge tower in the center of Tel Aviv. I'll put a great menorah on top of it and each candle will shine with the power of a million candles, and nobody will have to light his own menorah at home. On Hanukkah everyone will be amazed, because the night will be as bright as day."

"Say, I've got an idea," Reuben broke in. "Suppose we all go out on the first day of Hanukkah and look at the windows of all the homes to see who has the most beautiful menorah."

"Swell!" cried Joseph.

"Nothing could be more beautiful than a real giant menorah," David said, with a break in his voice.

Finally, he gave in. He could not tell his friends his troubles. Maybe there wouldn't even be a Hanukkah lamp at all in his house this year. And even if there would be one—it surely would not be made of hammered silver or burn pure olive oil.

Until the very day before Hanukkah, David had no chance to

speak to his father about a menorah. His father had still not found any work. David nibbled his bread and cheese and wondered how to start the conversation. At last, after a small pile of green olive pits had accumulated on his father's plate, he suddenly said: "Dad, what do you think? Would it be possible to build a giant menorah at the top of a tower in the center of Tel Aviv, with a million candlepower for each light?"

"What for?" his father asked. "Where did you get such an idea?"

"If there were only a menorah like that, everyone would be able to go outside and enjoy it. We wouldn't need our own menorah. Then those who could not afford a beautiful menorah of hammered silver would not be"—he finished bravely—"ashamed of their tin menorah."

The father studied his son's face for quite a while. Then he lowered his glance and poked with his fork at the pile of pits in his plate.

"A giant menorah," he said slowly. "No, David, there is no need for it. I understand your thoughts, my son. But the beauty of a menorah is in its small lights. They fill the whole house with a warm glow and they remind every single family of the wonderful Hanukkah story. Best of all is lighting them with your own hands so that you can see their little flames flicker."

"Father, tell me," David interrupted, "what kind of menorah will you buy?"

"Wait and see," answered his father with a steady voice.

David was on edge all day. He kept glancing at the clock on the dresser. When it began to grow dark and the Hanukkah lights started to flicker in the neighboring homes, David's father arose and said: "Bring a stout plank of wood, David, and nine potatoes from the pantry." Then he reached into his pocket and opened a penknife.

David soon returned with the board and potatoes.

"Take the knife," said his father, "and split each potato in half. In each half carve a hole big enough to set a candle into. We'll place the halves on the board and we will have a menorah."

David didn't know whether to laugh or cry. He took the knife and started to cut and carve. As he worked with the first potato, it seemed silly to him. With the second one, he tried to cut evenly and smoothly and with the third he enjoyed the idea. A potato menorah! Who ever heard of such a remarkable menorah!

The *shammash* candle stood firm in its holder.

The first candle stood upright too. And when his father started to sing "*Maoz Tzur*," the two flames danced and so did their images in the windowpanes.

A few minutes later, David ran toward his friends in the street. Before they could say a word, he cried out: "What a menorah we've got! You never saw anything like it! It's made of potatoes and it's homemade and—"

"Potatoes?" said Reuben. "I never heard of a potato menorah."

"Potatoes?" snickered Joseph. "What will you do with your menorah after Hanukkah? Eat it?" He burst into laughter.

David's spirits refused to be dampened.

"Look at the lights," he pointed to his window. In the back of the menorah he saw the blurry image of his father standing behind the lights.

"My father created that menorah," said David proudly. "It shines with a bright and beautiful light. To me, it's the most beautiful menorah in the whole world."

His voice trembled and his wide eyes glistened. Joseph and Reuben looked at him as though they were seeing him for the first time. Then they gazed long and hard at the potato menorah and at the shadow of David's father.

"You know," whispered Reuben, "when you think of it, it is a beautiful menorah."

And Joseph nodded his head in agreement.[15]

17 CHILDREN'S POEMS FOR HANUKKAH

iiiiiiii
=

Blessings for Hanukkah
JESSIE E. SAMPTER

an American poet who settled in an Israeli kibbutz, where she wrote about the life she lived (1883–1938)

Blessed art Thou, O God our Lord,
Who made us holy with His Word,
And told us on this feast of light
To light one candle more each night.

(Because when foes about us pressed
To crush us all with death or shame,
The Lord His priests with courage blest

359

To strike and give His people rest
And in the House that he loved best
Relight our everlasting flame.)

Blessed art Thou, the whole world's King,
Who did so wonderful a thing
For our own fathers true and bold,
At this same time in days of old![1]

iiiiiii
=

Eight Little Candles
JESSIE E. SAMPTER

I thought of all the wondrous things the Maccabees had done;
I lit a little candle—
 And then there was one.

I thought of all the wondrous things that I myself might do;
And lit another candle—
 And then there were two.

I thought of Eretz Yisrael, the Maccabees, and me;
I lit another candle—
 And then there were three.

I thought of Jewish heroes that fell in peace and war;
And lit another candle—
 And then there were four.

I thought of Young Judeans all pledged to serve and strive;
I lit another candle—
 And then there were five.

I thought of Jewish pioneers with shovels, rakes, and picks;
And lit another candle—
 And then there were six.

I thought of white as white as stars, of blue as blue as heaven;
I lit another candle—
 And then there were seven.

I thought of the great Lord our God who guides us early and
late;
And lit another candle—
And then there were eight.[2]

iiiiiii
=

My Trendle
SADIE ROSE WEILERSTEIN

See my little trendle spin,
Whirling, whirling out and in;
You had better watch it well,
There's a tale it has to tell.

Spin! Spin! Fall!
Nun is first of all!
Whirl, whirl, spin!
Now the *gimel*'s in.

Whirl, twirl; away!
See, it's on the *he*!
Again, spin, spin!
It's fallen on the *shin*!

NES GADOL HAYAH SHAM
—Hear my little trendle hum—
A great wonder happened there.
Read the tale and you'll know where.[3]

‖‖‖‖‖
=

What's in My Pocket?
SADIE ROSE WEILERSTEIN

Clinkety, clinkety, clinkety, clink!
  What's in my pocket? What do you think?
Pennies! A nickel! A quarter! A dime!
  Didn't you know it was Hanukkah time?
Nickels, a quarter, a dime, and a penny!
  Hanukkah *gelt*! Have *you* gotten any?[4]

‖‖‖‖‖
=

For Hanukkah
HAYYIM NAHMAN BIALIK

*the most eminent of modern Hebrew poets and leader of the Hebrew literary
renaissance; also wrote verse for children (1873–1934)*

Father lighted candles for me;
  Like a torch the *shammash* shone.
In whose honor, for whose glory?
  For Hanukkah alone.

Teacher brought a big top for me,
  Solid lead, the finest known.
In whose honor, for whose glory?
  For Hanukkah alone.

Mother made a pancake for me,
  Hot and sweet and sugar-strewn.
In whose honor, for whose glory?
  For Hanukkah alone.

Uncle had a present for me,
  An old penny, for my own.
In whose honor, for whose glory?
  For Hanukkah alone.

Translated by Jessie E. Sampter[5]

ÏÏÏÏÏÏÏ
=

My Dreidel
HAYYIM NAHMAN BIALIK

Come, my dreidel, my dreidel of tin,
Dance about merrily, dance and spin!
    Go swift, go far,
    And shining bright,
    Find the star
    Of my delight.

Spin to India, Afric-land,
Spin away over desert sand.
    No toil or lack
    Will spoil my pleasure,
    When you come back
    Bringing treasure.

Come, my dreidel, merrily scale
The towering hill, and span the vale.
    Over the prairie
    Dance and reel,
    Light and airy,
    Like a spinning wheel.

Make way for my dreidel, his whirl and sweep,
One step is a league, and a mile his leap.
    He's off with a bound
    Like a stallion bold.
    Hurrah! He has found
    A mountain of gold!

Rush to the mountain! Make way, make way!
Seize the treasure without delay!
    Win it, O
    My dreidel of tin,
    Before my foe
    Can say, *I win*!

The dreidel swayed and shuddered once,
And then went backwards—oh, oh, you dunce!

It wavered, strained,
No longer bold.
It had not gained
The mountain of gold.

Tipsy, it staggered, backed, until
Down it went—my heart stood still . . .
   Gimel! Oh, joy!
   Come all and see
   How my spinning toy
   Has won for me.

                    Translated by Deborah Pessin[6]

iiiiiii
=

Eight Are the Lights
ILO ORLEANS

lawyer and prolific poet whose verses have been included in anthologies, text-books, and music collections

Eight are the lights
  Of Hanukkah
We light for a week
  And a day.
We kindle the lights,
  And bless the Lord,
And sing a song,
  And pray.

Eight are the lights
  Of Hanukkah
For *justice* and *mercy*
  And *love*,
For *charity, courage*
  And *honor* and *peace*,
And *faith* in heaven
  Above.

Eight are the lights
  Of Hanukkah
To keep ever bright
  Memories
Of the valiant soul
  And the fighting heart
And the hope of the
  Maccabees![7]

iiiiiii
=

The Miracle
PHILIP M. RASKIN

lifelong Zionist and prolific poet who wrote in English, Hebrew, and Yiddish
(1878–1944)

The *rebbe* tells his old, old tale,
  The pupils seated round,
". . . And thus, my boys, no holy oil
  In the Temple could be found.

"The heathens left no oil to light
  The Lord's eternal lamp;
At last one jar, one single jar,
  Was found with the high priest's stamp.

"Its oil could only last one day—
  But God hath wondrous ways;
For lo! a miracle occurred:
  It burned for eight whole days."

The tale was ended, but the boys,
  All open-eyed and dumb,
Sat listening still as though aware
  Of stranger things to come.

"Just wait, my boys, permit me, pray,
  The liberty to take;

Your *rebbe*—may he pardon me—
  Has made a slight mistake.

"Not eight days, but two thousand years
  That jar of oil did last;
To quell its wondrous flames availed
  No storm, no flood, no blast.

"But this is not yet all, my boys:
  The miracle just starts;
This flame is kindling light and hope
  In exile-saddened hearts.

"And in our long and starless night,
  Lest we should go astray,
It beaconlike sheds floods of rays,
  And eastwards points the way,

"Where Zion's hill again will shine,
  And we in peace shall dwell;
The miracle of light, my boys,
  Your *rebbe* failed to tell."[8]

iiiiiiii

Hanukkah Lights
PHILIP M. RASKIN

I kindle my eight little candles,
  My Hanukkah candles, and lo!
Visions and dreams half-forgotten
  Come back of the dim long ago . . .

I musingly gaze at my candles,
  And see in their quivering flames,
Written in fiery letters,
  Immortal indelible names.

The names of valorous Hebrews
  Whose soul no sword could subdue;

A battlefield stretches before me,
  Where many are conquered by few.

Defeated lies Syria's army,
  Judea's proud foe, in the field;
And Judah, the great Maccabeus,
  I see in his helmet and shield.

His eyes are like stars in the desert,
  Like music each resonant word:
"We fought and we conquered the tyrant,
  'For People and Towns of the Lord!' "

50. V-Mail Hanukkah greeting. Italy. 1944.

He speaks, and the hills are repeating,
  "For People and Towns of the Lord,"
The groves and the towers reecho,
  "For People and Towns of the Lord."

Swiftly the message is spreading,
  Judea, Judea is free!
The lamp in the Temple rekindled,
  And banished idolatry!

My eight little candles expire,
  Around me spreads darkness of night,
But deep in my soul is still burning
  The ages-old miracle light. . . .[9]

iiiiiii
=

Judah Maccabeus to His Soldiers
ELMA EHRLICH LEVINGER

*author of twenty-five books for Jewish children, including stories, poems, texts,
and plays (1887–1958)*

O brothers, who have laid aside
  The plowshare for the sword,
Who gather from the hills and plains
  To battle for the Lord:
If ye have hopes of honor,
  Or to reap wealth are fain,
Serve not the cause of Israel,
  But seek your homes again.

I have no golden gifts to give,
  Our land is stripped and bare;
Nor Grecian gauds and raiment rich—
  Behold the rags I wear!
They sleep on ivory couches,
  The rocks must be your bed;
Their tables groan with plenty,
  My men eat bitter bread.

No glories crown my faithful men,
  Who know the traitor's shame,
Until they meet in Syrian courts
  The death I dare not name.
My fighting hands are empty;
  My promises are grim;
Yet ye who honor Israel's God
  Will pledge your swords to Him.[10]

The Tale of Hanukkah Retold by This Gay Minstrel's Pen of Gold
ABRAHAM BURSTEIN

rabbi, author, and editor who penned a book of Jewish verse for children (1893–1966)

An ancient king is known to us,
Who bore the name Antiochus.
Of all the knaves and fools of yore
Who e'er that lofty title bore,
Who loved to strut and kill and quarrel,
He took the palm, the wreath, the laurel.
(You'll hear of this unpleasant creature
Some Sunday from your Hebrew teacher.)

Now first the king was proven foolish
When in his regal way and mulish
He loudly called himself a god,
For worship by the common clod.
And all the courtiers bowed low
Before his braggadocio—
A profitable, harmless thing
It is to please one's doting king.

He set his statues everywhere,
And ordered men to worship there.
To busts of metal and of stone

The zealous populace fell prone,
While in the squares the soldiers stood—
A cheery, joyous brotherhood—
To pierce with pike the luckless gent
Who failed to hail the monument.

But here and there appeared a Jew,
A member of that stubborn crew
Whom even kings of high degree
Could never force to bend the knee.
"One only God is ours!" they cried—
A God that none of them had spied:
Yet from this Being far and strange
Not threat of death would make them change.

The king was wroth. "I stand supreme
O'er gods and men. These Jews blaspheme!
Go, set my image in the place
Of worship of this willful race.
Defile their sacred objects. Give
Them pork—who eats not shall not live!"
And so they did. Too, in their spite
They dimmed the everlasting light.

In Modin town the news was spread,
Where ancient Mattathias led
His five great sons and all the rest
In homage to the Being Blest.
He smote one treacherous coward down,
And called the men of Modin town
To fight the king and all his men,
And purify their shrine again.

Heading the Maccabean breed,
The mighty Judah took the lead.
Throughout the land the fighters came,
Their arms held high, their hearts aflame.
A handful many thousands slew!
They hacked the Syrian army through,
Until the Maccabean stand
Had saved our altars and our land.

Then, in the Temple's walls they fell
On one day's oil—which, strange to tell,
They saw give holy fire for eight!—
A wonder which we celebrate
As Hanukkah this very day—
Telling the world, and kings, for aye—
No matter what you scheme or do,
You simply cannot crush the Jew![11]

iiiiiii

Hanukkah Candles
ZALMAN SHNEOUR

Hebrew poet and Yiddish novelist considered one of the major figures in Hebrew and Yiddish literature; his novels were translated in many languages (1887– 1959)

We light tiny candles
    And bless them with paeans,
Recalling the deeds of
    The brave Maccabeans.

Both graybeards and children
    Were slain by profaners
Who defiled in the Temple
    Oil flasks and containers.

But one cruse of oil
    Was found which they slighted;
A miracle happened,
    It burned and it lighted.

Eight days in succession
    It fed the menorah,
And lit up our fane and
    The ark with the Torah.

These eight days of wonder
  Forget them we'll never;
Our hearts they'll illumine
  Forever and ever.

Translated by Harry H. Fein[12]

 iiiiiiii
=

A Hanukkah Top
N A H U M   D.   K A R P I V N E R

educator and author who emigrated from Russia to settle in Israel; he wrote poems, stories, and legends for the press of both countries (1890–1937)

Turn, my top, around, around,
Past the bush and pit and mound,
Past the vineyards, brook, and rill,
Past the valley and the hill,
On to Kishon, as you veer,
When you meet a pioneer,
Tell your legend, bring him cheer:
"Miracles have happened here!"

Once this land was swampy, friend,
Now to that has come an end.
Conquered were the waste and mud
In a battle void of blood;
Not with swords was won the soil,
But with ceaseless, endless toil.

Unto Modin swiftly fly,
And your tidings shout and cry:
"Maccabeans, rest in peace,
Lo, your valiant heirs increase.
In the vanguard they wage war,
Planting vineyards by the score,
Swinging hammers, hauling loads,
Building houses, paving roads . . ."

Tell your legend, bring him cheer:
"Miracles are happening here!"

Translated by Harry H. Fein[13]

iiiiiii
≡

It Happened on Hanukkah
NATAN ALTERMAN

Israeli exponent of the imagist idiom in Hebrew poetry; author of several volumes of poetry, plays, and children's books; and translator of Shakespeare and other noted writers

It happened on Hanukkah, so it is said,
When all of the children had gone up to bed,
The classroom was empty, and everything still,
The first candle flickered alone on the sill.

Silence and darkness and no one around,
Just household utensils alone on the ground.
They trembled together, a little from cold,
And a little from fear, so the story is told.

And each one was thinking: "What's that? Did you hear?
The wind whispered something, just now, in my ear.
Why does the floor seem to crackle and spark?
And what's crawling toward me from out of the dark?

"Who whistled? It wasn't a cricket, I know.
The sound was so strange, and it frightened me so.
A terrible something will happen tonight . . .
You'll see before sunrise, I'm perfectly right."

The table was shaking—it really was scared.
The chair would have yelled out for help if it dared.
An old, wornout broom standing up at the wall
Was even afraid to be frightened at all.
The puppy among them, too small yet to growl,
Almost fainted each time that he heard the wind howl.

It ended when suddenly, out of the gloom,
In a voice made of iron and sounding like doom,
The clock on the shelf gathered courage and spoke,
"What's going on? Is this some kind of joke?

This one is trembling and that one is tense,
The third one is moody—it doesn't make sense.
What are you anyway? Honored utensils
Or tatters and dishrags and old pointless pencils?"

The utensils awoke, as it seemed, from a dream
And with one voice, together they let out a scream,
"Shut up, stupid ticker, up there on the shelf.
You're only a dirty old dishrag yourself.

"Look here! Pay attention! No cowards are we.
We haven't forgotten what fun 'fun' can be.
Come on, let's get started. We'll set up a game
Just to put that old tick-tocking timepiece to shame."

When all the utensils were quiet at last
The broom in the corner gave out with a blast,
"The Hanukkah game—we know every rule.
Let's play it and shut up that tock-ticking fool.

"Let's start with me, with my beard I'll admit it,
It's made out of straw, but it's really exquisite.
So with your permission, without any bother,
I'll be Mattathias, the Maccabees' father.

"And you, little potbellied stove over there,
You will be Judah, my son and my heir.
So get up—there's a war and you've got to take part
With the hot burning flame of the Lord for your heart.

"What we need now are some brothers for you,
And for these parts, I think that the cacti will do.
Into battle we're going, you brave fighting flowers
Your spikes must be sharpened for hours and hours."

The broom kept on giving out parts to his men
Till he came to the Syrian soldiers. And then
He grew quiet. Nobody grabbed for the part
And each of them wanted to cry in his heart.

For they knew very well, and it wasn't a mystery,
Syria lost in the pages of history.

The chairs got together and quickly decided
And then, to the rest, their decision confided,
"We'll be the Syrians, worry no more.
We're twice the men you are, our legs number four.
Shall we be afraid of the Maccabees' force?
We'll beat them on foot and we'll beat them on horse."

The teapots came marching in milital rows,
And each one was waving his long crooked nose.

51. V-Mail Hanukkah greeting. Persian Gulf. 1943.

The chairs gaily thundered, "Our elephants, they—
We'll murder the Maccabees. . . . Hip, hip, hurray.
From this time and forward, we are all can be sure
That under our king we'll be safe and secure."

"Our king," cried a chair, "Who's the king?" . . . no one spoke,
For no one was willing to carry that yoke.
They all shook their heads and gave out with a sigh,
"I'm not Antiochus the Madman . . . not I."

The game was in danger of falling apart
For, lacking a ruler, the play had no heart.
An elephant wandered around like a mourner
Until he bumped into the pup in the corner,
When lifting him up in the air with his nose
He trumpeted, "Here he is. Anything goes."

The poor little puppy, he cried and he whined,
He squirmed and he twisted—went out of his mind,
He scratched and he bit, oh, how bravely he fought
But nothing could help him . . . the puppy was caught.

When they saw his reluctance, the elephant said,
"Shut up and be king. You're our chief and our head.
If you try to escape—and you'd better not dare—
If you do, you'll be captured and tied to a chair."

With everything ready the game could begin
And Judah yelled loudly, his face in a grin,
"Take care, Antiochus, watch out what you're doing,
My anger is boiling and cooking and stewing.

"My city, Jerusalem, leave it alone,
Or I'll beat you so hard that I break every bone.
When I've finished, your moldy old corpse I'll bequeath
To the birds of the sky and the beasts underneath."

The puppy cried out to his mother in fright,
"Mommy, why does this potbellied stove want to fight?
I'm not the king of the Syrian host.
I'm just a poor puppy who'll soon be a ghost."

The little pup's cries didn't help anymore,
For suddenly—whack—the beginning of war,

And before he could find a dark corner to hide in,
A big chair fell over and half crushed his side in.

The sounds of the battle rose up from the floor
From cellar to rafters and on out the door,
The shouts of the brave and the cries of the weak,
The laugh of the mighty, the moans of the meek.

The brave Judah Maccabee lowered his sword,
And swung it with joy at the Syrian horde,
His flying locks burned as the sword rose and fell,
And he looked like a devil come straight out of hell.

The broom, Mattathias, yelled out from the side,
"You're a warrior, Son, full of courage and pride.
Let's go forward, you Maccabees, let your swords ring
Till we capture the Madman, the Syrian king.

"That's the way, that's the way—forward we go."
Then in charge the elephants, straight in a row.
"Come on, wake up, boys, we're really in trouble.
The elephants must be turned back—on the double."

And chaos arose, and a dreadful confusion,
It looked like a terrible nightmare illusion.
Head against head and chest against chest,
And hand against hand, without any rest.

The dreidel alone, being calm and serene,
Whirled forward and backward, surveying the scene.
Being brilliant and clever, he's making a test,
To discover which army will come out the best.

For, being quite clever, and being quite wise,
And wanting to know who would take home the prize,
"I'll wait till the end of the battle," he thought,
"And I'll know how to choose once the battle's been fought."

But wait just a moment! The Syrian men
Are retreating. . . . The Maccabees conquer again.
And Judah cries, "Yippee! Hurrah! . . . Look and see,
We've won freedom and light with our great victory."

The dreidel stopped spinning and fell on his side.
He stretched out on the floor and he happily cried,
"Victory, victory, do you all hear?
A wonderful miracle happened right here."

Translated by Steve Friedman[14]

18 HOME SERVICE FOR HANUKKAH

iiiiiii
=

The Blessings on Kindling the Lights*

The major ritual for Hanukkah is the kindling of the lights. This is performed soon after nightfall. On Friday it precedes the kindling of the Sabbath candles.

The *shammash* candle is lit and used to kindle the other candles. One candle, set in the extreme right candle-holder, is lit on the first night of Hanukkah. On each succeeding night another candle is added to the left until eight candles are lit on the eighth night. The kindling is from left to right. The same procedure is followed if oil and wicks are used.

The following two blessings are chanted each night before kindling the lights:

*Music for the service will be found in the chapter "Music for Hanukkah."

379 ·

בָּרוּךְ אַתָּה יְיָ אֱלֹהֵינוּ מֶלֶךְ הָעוֹלָם, אֲשֶׁר קִדְּשָׁנוּ בְּמִצְוֹתָיו וְצִוָּנוּ לְהַדְלִיק נֵר שֶׁל חֲנֻכָּה.

בָּרוּךְ אַתָּה יְיָ אֱלֹהֵינוּ מֶלֶךְ הָעוֹלָם, שֶׁעָשָׂה נִסִּים לַאֲבוֹתֵינוּ בַּיָּמִים הָהֵם בַּזְּמַן הַזֶּה.

"Blessed art Thou, Lord our God, King of the universe, who hast sanctified us with Thy commandments and hast commanded us to kindle the Hanukkah light.

"Blessed art Thou, Lord our God, King of the universe, who didst perform miracles for our fathers in those days at this season."

The following blessing is chanted only on the first night:

בָּרוּךְ אַתָּה יְיָ אֱלֹהֵינוּ מֶלֶךְ הָעוֹלָם, שֶׁהֶחֱיָנוּ וְקִיְּמָנוּ וְהִגִּיעָנוּ לַזְּמַן הַזֶּה.

"Blessed art Thou, Lord our God, King of the universe, who hast granted us life, and sustained us, and brought us to this season."[1]

"Hanerot Hallalu"—*These Lights*

After kindling the first light, the following passage is read or chanted:

הַנֵּרוֹת הַלָּלוּ אֲנַחְנוּ מַדְלִיקִים עַל הַנִּסִּים וְעַל הַנִּפְלָאוֹת וְעַל הַתְּשׁוּעוֹת וְעַל הַמִּלְחָמוֹת שֶׁעָשִׂיתָ לַאֲבוֹתֵינוּ בַּיָּמִים הָהֵם, בַּזְּמַן הַזֶּה, עַל יְדֵי כֹּהֲנֶיךָ הַקְּדוֹשִׁים. וְכָל שְׁמוֹנַת יְמֵי חֲנֻכָּה, הַנֵּרוֹת הַלָּלוּ קֹדֶשׁ הֵם וְאֵין לָנוּ רְשׁוּת לְהִשְׁתַּמֵּשׁ בָּהֶם אֶלָּא לִרְאוֹתָם בִּלְבָד, כְּדֵי לְהוֹדוֹת וּלְהַלֵּל לְשִׁמְךָ הַגָּדוֹל עַל נִסֶּיךָ וְעַל יְשׁוּעָתֶךָ וְעַל נִפְלְאוֹתֶיךָ.

"We kindle these lights to commemorate the miracles and the wonders, and the victorious battles that Thou achieved for our fathers in those days, at this season, through Thy holy priests. During all the eight days of Hanukkah these lights are sacred, and we are not permitted to make use of them; but we are only to look at them, in order to give thanks and to praise Thy Name for Thy miracles, Thy wonders, and Thy salvations."[2]

iiiiiii

"Maoz Tzur"—*Rock of Ages*

"*Maoz Tzur*" (Rock of Ages) is one of the most popular hymns sung by Ashkenazic Jews. It is generally accepted that it was written in the thirteenth century by someone named Mordecai. We derive his name from an acrostic of the first letters of the first five stanzas. This hymn praises God for Israel's redemption from Egyptian slavery and from the Babylonian exile; for saving the Persian Jews from Haman's plot of extermination, and for the triumph over Antiochus Epiphanes. Finally, it expresses the hope that those nations guilty of persecuting Jews will be avenged and Israel will be redeemed from exile. The last stanza, attributed to another author, was frequently omitted from prayer books "for the sake of peace" with the nations among whom Jews dwelt. The origin of the melody is a medieval German folk song; however, the stirring tune underwent changes in the course of time.[3] The singing of this hymn concludes the candlelighting ceremony.

The English version by Solomon Solis-Cohen is a free translation that attempts to adhere to the rhyme scheme and spirit of the original Hebrew while retaining the basic ideas. Another singable English translation will be found in the chapter "Music of Hanukkah."

מָעוֹז צוּר יְשׁוּעָתִי　לְךָ נָאֶה לְשַׁבֵּחַ
תִּכּוֹן בֵּית תְּפִלָּתִי　וְשָׁם תּוֹדָה נְזַבֵּחַ
לְעֵת תָּכִין מַטְבֵּחַ　מִצָּר הַמְנַבֵּחַ
אָז אֶגְמֹר בְּשִׁיר מִזְמוֹר　חֲנֻכַּת הַמִּזְבֵּחַ.

רָעוֹת שָׂבְעָה נַפְשִׁי　בְּיָגוֹן כֹּחִי כָלָה
חַיַּי מֵרְרוּ בְקֹשִׁי　בְּשִׁעְבּוּד מַלְכוּת עֶגְלָה
וּבְיָדוֹ הַגְּדֹלָה　הוֹצִיא אֶת־הַסְּגֻלָּה
חֵיל פַּרְעֹה וְכָל־זַרְעוֹ　יָרְדוּ כְאֶבֶן מְצוּלָה.

דְּבִיר קָדְשׁוֹ הֱבִיאַנִי　וְגַם שָׁם לֹא שָׁקַטְתִּי
וּבָא נוֹגֵשׂ וְהִגְלַנִי　כִּי זָרִים עָבַדְתִּי
וְיֵין רַעַל מָסַכְתִּי　כִּמְעַט שֶׁעָבַרְתִּי
קֵץ בָּבֶל זְרֻבָּבֶל　לְקֵץ שִׁבְעִים נוֹשַׁעְתִּי.

כְּרֹת קוֹמַת בְּרוֹשׁ בִּקֵּשׁ　אֲגָגִי בֶּן הַמְּדָתָא
וְנִהְיְתָה לוֹ לְפַח וּלְמוֹקֵשׁ　וְגַאֲוָתוֹ נִשְׁבָּתָה

רֹאשׁ יְמִינִי נִשֵּׂאתָ   וְאוֹיֵב שְׁמוֹ מָחִיתָ
רֹב בָּנָיו וְקִנְיָנָיו   עַל־הָעֵץ תָּלִיתָ.

יְוָנִים נִקְבְּצוּ עָלַי   אֲזַי בִּימֵי חַשְׁמַנִּים
וּפָרְצוּ חוֹמוֹת מִגְדָּלַי   וְטִמְּאוּ כָּל הַשְּׁמָנִים
וּמִנּוֹתַר קַנְקַנִּים   נַעֲשָׂה נֵס לְשׁוֹשַׁנִּים
בְּנֵי בִינָה יְמֵי שְׁמֹנָה   קָבְעוּ שִׁיר וּרְנָנִים.

חֲשׂוֹף זְרוֹעַ קָדְשֶׁךָ   וְקָרֵב יוֹם הַיְשׁוּעָה
נְקֹם נִקְמַת עֲבָדֶיךָ   מִמַּלְכוּת הָרְשָׁעָה
כִּי אָרְכָה הַשָּׁעָה   וְאֵין קֵץ לִימֵי רָעָה
דְּחֵה אַדְמוֹן בְּצֵל צַלְמוֹן   הָקֵם לָנוּ רוֹעִים שִׁבְעָה.

Mighty, praised beyond compare,
  Rock of my salvation,
Build again my house of prayer,
  For Thy habitation!
Offering and libation, shall a ransomed nation
  Joyful bring
  There, and sing
Psalms of dedication!

Woe was mine in Egypt-land,
  (Tyrant kings enslaved me);
Till Thy mighty, outstretched hand
  From oppression saved me.
Pharaoh, rash pursuing, vowed my swift undoing;
  Soon, his host
  That proud boast
'Neath the waves was ruing!

To Thy holy hill, the way
  Madest Thou clear before me;
With false gods I went astray—
  Foes to exile bore me.
Torn from all I cherished, almost had I perished;
  Babylon fell,
  Ze-rub-ba-bel
Badest Thou restore me!

Then the vengeful Haman wrought
  Subtly, to betray me;

In his snare himself he caught—
  He that plann'd to slay me.
(Haled from Esther's palace; hanged on his own gallows!)
  Seal and ring
  Persia's king
Gave Thy servant zealous.

When the brave Asmonéans broke
  Javan's chain in sunder,
Through the holy oil Thy folk
  Didst Thou show a wonder.
Ever full remainèd the vessel unprofanèd;
  These eight days.
  Light and praise,
Therefore were ordained.

Lord, Thy holy arm make bare,
  Speed my restoration;
Be my martyr's blood Thy care—
  Judge each guilty nation.
Long is my probation; sore my tribulation—
  Bid, from heaven,
  Thy shepherds seven
Haste to my salvation!

                     Translated by Solomon Solis-Cohen[4]

iiiiiiii
=

Al ha-Nissim—*For the Miracles*

In the Grace after Meals as well as in the *Amidah* (the Eighteen Benedictions, recited silently while standing) an additional prayer is recited throughout the eight days of Hanukkah.[5] It is a paean of thanksgiving for divine intervention and deliverance from the enemy. Epitomizing the Maccabean struggle, it emphasizes the spiritual over the military aspect. While an abbreviated text of *Al ha-Nissim* is in the Talmud,[6] the current version is first found in the prayer book of Rav Amram Gaon, head of the academy in Sura, Babylonia, in the ninth century.

עַל הַנִּסִּים וְעַל הַפֻּרְקָן וְעַל הַגְּבוּרוֹת וְעַל הַתְּשׁוּעוֹת וְעַל הַמִּלְחָמוֹת שֶׁעָשִׂיתָ
לַאֲבוֹתֵינוּ בַּיָּמִים הָהֵם בַּזְּמַן הַזֶּה.

בִּימֵי מַתִּתְיָהוּ בֶּן יוֹחָנָן כֹּהֵן גָּדוֹל חַשְׁמוֹנַאי וּבָנָיו כְּשֶׁעָמְדָה מַלְכוּת יָוָן הָרְשָׁעָה
עַל עַמְּךָ יִשְׂרָאֵל לְהַשְׁכִּיחָם תּוֹרָתֶךָ וּלְהַעֲבִירָם מֵחֻקֵּי רְצוֹנֶךָ. וְאַתָּה בְּרַחֲמֶיךָ
הָרַבִּים עָמַדְתָּ לָהֶם בְּעֵת צָרָתָם. רַבְתָּ אֶת רִיבָם, דַּנְתָּ אֶת דִּינָם, נָקַמְתָּ אֶת
נִקְמָתָם, מָסַרְתָּ גִּבּוֹרִים בְּיַד חַלָּשִׁים וְרַבִּים בְּיַד מְעַטִּים וּטְמֵאִים בְּיַד טְהוֹרִים
וּרְשָׁעִים בְּיַד צַדִּיקִים וְזֵדִים בְּיַד עוֹסְקֵי תוֹרָתֶךָ. וּלְךָ עָשִׂיתָ שֵׁם גָּדוֹל וְקָדוֹשׁ
בְּעוֹלָמֶךָ וּלְעַמְּךָ יִשְׂרָאֵל עָשִׂיתָ תְּשׁוּעָה גְדוֹלָה וּפֻרְקָן כְּהַיּוֹם הַזֶּה. וְאַחַר כֵּן בָּאוּ
בָנֶיךָ לִדְבִיר בֵּיתֶךָ וּפִנּוּ אֶת הֵיכָלֶךָ וְטִהֲרוּ אֶת מִקְדָּשֶׁךָ וְהִדְלִיקוּ נֵרוֹת בְּחַצְרוֹת
קָדְשֶׁךָ. וְקָבְעוּ שְׁמוֹנַת יְמֵי חֲנֻכָּה אֵלּוּ לְהוֹדוֹת וּלְהַלֵּל לְשִׁמְךָ הַגָּדוֹל.

We thank Thee for the miracles, the redemptions, the mighty deeds and the victorious battles that Thou achieved for our fathers in those days at this season.

It was in the days of Mattathias, son of Johanan, the Hasmonean high priest, and his sons, when the wicked Greek government rose up against Thy people Israel to force them to forsake Thy Torah and to transgress the laws of Thy will. Thou in Thy abundant mercy didst stand up for them in their time of travail, defended their cause, judged their suit, and avenged their wrong. Thou didst deliver the strong into the hands of the weak, the many into the hands of the few, the impure into the hands of the pure, the wicked ones into the hands of the righteous, and the insolent ones into the hands of those occupied with Thy Torah. Thou didst make for Thyself a great and holy name in Thy universe. For Thy people Israel Thou didst create a great deliverance and relief as at this day. Then Thy children came to the holy of holies of Thy house, cleansed Thy Temple and purified Thy sanctuary. They kindled lights in the courtyards of Thy sanctuary and established these eight days of Hanukkah to give thanks and praise to Thy great Name.

19 HANUKKAH PROGRAMS AND ACTIVITIES

HANUKKAH INSTITUTE

The purpose of the institute is to prepare parents for full participation with their children in a meaningful and joyous celebration of Hanukkah, both at home and in the synagogue, through an understanding of its background and by learning the practical ways and skills required. Planning for the workshop should start early in the program season. Several sessions of two to three hours each may be required; these may be held once a week or concentrated within a weekend. This book serves as the source for the contents of the program.

The institute might attempt to cover as many of the following aspects as feasible:

Lecture, followed by discussion, on the history and meaning of Hanukkah

Study of the laws and customs

Chanting of the blessings for kindling the lights and singing of
  songs
Display and reviews of books and stories on the festival
Demonstration of cooking Hanukkah dishes
Presentation of a film or filmstrip
Demonstration of arts and crafts projects
Playing of dreidel and other games
Planning of a latke party
Quiz program
Participatory experience integrating the above elements at the
  conclusion of the institute

STUDY SESSIONS

Some adults and young people may be interested in studying basic
Jewish texts relevant to Hanukkah that are not generally included
in study programs. Special groups for this purpose can be organized, and ongoing classes in Jewish history and related subjects
might devote a number of sessions to such material. The Apocryphal books of Maccabees and Judith give the background of the
festival. The *Shulhan Arukh* and Maimonides's *Mishneh Torah* present
the laws and traditions. Selections from the Talmud and midrashim
provide a variety of interesting details and folklore.

LECTURE AND DISCUSSION THEMES

The rich historical background of Hanukkah and the relevance and
timeliness of its message for this generation provide many subjects
for lectures, forums, and discussions. There are a number of perti-
nent themes:
  The Rebellion of Mattathias: Its Causes and Consequences
  Judaism versus Hellenism
  The Maccabean Defense of Civil Rights
  The Maccabean Struggle: The First Fight for Religious Liberty
  The Significance of the Temple Rededication
  Jewish Warriors as Defenders of the Spirit
  The Role of Women in the History of Hanukkah
  The Spirit of Martyrdom in Jewish Life
  The Maccabean Revolution and the American Revolution:
    Similarities and Contrasts

52. *"In the days of Mattathias"* from the Al ha-Nissim *prayer
for Hanukkah. Illuminated by Sol Nodel.*

Wars of Independence: Maccabean, American, and Israeli
The Maccabees of Yesterday and Today
Ancient Hellenism and Modern Assimilation
The Jewish View of Hanukkah-Christmas Programs in Public
  Schools
Hanukkah Observances in Many Lands
The Hanukkah Lamp: A Beacon of Freedom
The Feast of Dedication: An Annual Rededication
The Significance of Lights on Hanukkah and All Jewish Festi-
  vals
Some of the above subjects may be used for an essay contest.

Awards to the writers of the best essays may be menorahs or books on Hanukkah.

CANDLELIGHTING CEREMONY

As the major observance of Hanukkah is in the home, a festive atmosphere should be created with a variety of appropriate decorations. A beautiful menorah should be the center of attraction; some households provide Hanukkah lamps for each member of the family and for the guests invited to share in the holiday joy. For those guests who may not know the blessings or songs, these should be made available in Hebrew and English. The candlelighting ceremony should be dignified and impressive. All or most of the lights in the room can be lowered or turned off. Following the kindling of the lights and the singing of "*Hanerot Hallalu*" and "*Maoz Tzur*" (see "Home Service for Hanukkah," pages 379–84), gifts can be distributed and dreidel games played. A festive meal should be served on at least one evening.

LATKE PARTY

The setting of the latke party should be decorated in the spirit of Hanukkah. Parties can be held for children, youth, adults, and entire families. The program may include a variety of elements: kindling the lights, singing songs, playing dreidel and other games, storytelling, readings or short dramatizations, listening to recordings, folk dancing, quiz programs, distribution of gifts and Hanukkah *gelt*, and, of course, serving latkes.

The latke theme can be expressed in the decor: the use of place cards in the shape of latkes, latke-eating contests, and an impromptu humorous debate on "The Latke versus the Hamantash." "Latke Ladies" can serve as the hostess and waitresses. The pièce de résistance will be a variety of latkes that are served (see "The Hanukkah Cuisine," pages 290–97).

MUSICAL EVENTS

Hanukkah concerts are conducted in many communities with performances by cantors and choirs, guest soloists, and instrumentalists. Appropriate for such an occasion is the well-known oratorio

"Judah Maccabee" by George F. Handel, which may be performed in whole or in part.

Small groups can have a songfest featuring community singing and the playing of Hanukkah recordings. For sources, see the Bibliography, pages 462–65.

DRAMATICS

Amateur groups can select from a variety of dramatic media the type of performance to be staged. "Eternal Light" radio scripts can be performed with simple staging. Dramatized readings from the books of the Maccabees can also be arranged. Puppet and marionette shows have a special appeal to children. Where a number of groups are available, a one-act play contest, preferably with original scripts, can be planned. A classic drama is *Judah Maccabeus* by Henry Wadsworth Longfellow (see pages 132–50), which can be undertaken by an experienced cast. For other available Hanukkah dramatizations, see the Bibliography, pages 456–60.

SPECIAL PUBLICATIONS

A souvenir booklet entitled *The Book of the Maccabees* or a newspaper named *The Modin Times* can be edited and published by a group interested in journalism. The booklet might include original articles, poems, and stories built around Hanukkah themes, timely editorials, illustrations, programs of local festival events, Hanukkah candlelighting time, the method of kindling the menorah, and advertisements.

The Modin Times can be produced separately or as an insert in the souvenir book. Using the dateline of Kislev 26, 165 B.C.E., the newspaper can feature stories on the triumph of the Maccabees and the rededication of the Temple as current news items. The lead articles can be headlined "MACCABEES REDEDICATE TEMPLE" and "OIL FOR ONE DAY FOUND." A front-page feature could be an interview with Judah Maccabee. The subject of the editorial might be "The Triumph of Right over Might." Other articles can portray the death of Mattathias, the martyrdom of Hannah and her sons, and the bravery of Judith.

Source material will be found in the chapters "Hanukkah in Postbiblical Writings," pages 32–65, and "Hanukkah in Talmud and Midrash," pages 66–79.

SERVICES FOR THE ILL AND AGED

Young people and adults can be encouraged to organize a group of volunteers to serve as "Maccabean Messengers" to visit those that are shut-ins or otherwise incapacitated, patients in hospitals and veterans' facilities, and residents of homes for the aged. Arrangement for each visit should be made in advance. At each place the Maccabean Messengers will kindle the menorah, sing the traditional songs, and distribute token Hanukkah *gelt*.

PHOTOGRAPHY

Amateur photographers can be encouraged to take motion pictures and still photographs of all local Hanukkah events, both in private homes and at community affairs. They can start before the festival by photographing rehearsals of dramatic performances, the sales of Hanukkah supplies, and class and group sessions. Prizes can be presented for the best films and the best photographs.

EXHIBITS

Sundry exhibits of subjects related to Hanukkah can be attractively arranged. A fairly comprehensive display might feature lamps, books, Israeli commemorative coins and stamps for Hanukkah, a selection of artistic greeting cards, dreidels, recordings, art, and photographs. Three-dimensional dioramas, maps, and friezes depicting the story of the Maccabees, and other items created with arts and crafts media can enhance the exhibit.

A major attraction might be a collection of Hanukkah lamps borrowed from private homes. Such menorahs, solicited through the use of all available local publicity media, may include family heirlooms or modern ones. Awards in the form of certificates or ribbons can be offered for the oldest, most valuable, most beautiful, and most original menorahs. A card with information about the lamp and the name of the owner should be placed alongside each one. Adequate security arrangements can be provided by displaying the lamps in locked showcases or by having volunteers serve as guards.

FESTIVAL BOOK AND GIFT SHOP

If there is no available local Jewish book and gift shop, one can be opened that will feature Hanukkah items, including books, recordings, menorahs, candles, dreidels, games, gift-wrapping paper, decorations, and greeting cards. Supplies should be ordered from dealers about two months in advance of the holiday so that the stock will be available at least a month prior to Hanukkah.

TORCH RELAY

In Israel a torch relay is an annual happening during the days of Hanukkah. The starting point is at the traditional catacombs of the Maccabees in Modin, where their revolt was initiated. Following an impressive torchlighting ceremony, torches are carried by relay runners to Jerusalem and other historical places in Israel. Such relays can be simulated in Jewish communities.

Relay runners holding aloft lit torches may start at different Jewish institutions in the community and converge at an arranged destination. If the torchbearers start at a central staging area, then a brief initial ceremony can be held there. With police authorization and escort, the course of the relay can be through the main streets. The relay teams can also be escorted by other runners, bicycle riders and a motorcade with the vehicles decorated with bunting, crepe paper, and flags. The torches can be handed from runner to runner of each team at set intervals, depending on the number of participants and the distance to be covered. The final destination may be the city hall, a synagogue, a Jewish community center, or a Jewish school where a large outdoor menorah is prominently displayed. The concluding ceremony can include the kindling of the Hanukkah lights by members of the winning relay team, the presentation of greetings by officials, and the singing of songs and folk dancing by the audience.

MACCABEAN LIBERATION CELEBRATION

This day-long community-wide celebration, held on the Sunday during Hanukkah, can start in the morning with assembly programs for children. The afternoon can be devoted to a Maccabiah with sports events and tournaments for youth. The evening program might be preceded by a torchlight parade that will proceed to the auditorium where the main event will take place. At the head of the march, winners of Maccabiah events can carry a large menorah carved from wood or beaver board with flashlights attached with wire in place of candles. Contingents from the participating organizations, bearing torches or flashlights and signs with slogans like THE TORAH OF LIBERTY, THE TORCH OF FREEDOM, and HAPPY HANUKKAH, would sing Hanukkah songs as they march.

The Maccabean liberation celebration is climaxed with a mass program of drama, music, and dance.

GAMES

The distinctive Hanukkah games are played with a four-sided or four-winged spinning top, known as a dreidel, trendel, or teetotum; in Hebrew, it is called *sevivon*. It has four letters, one on each side or wing—*nun, gimel, he, shin*—which are the initials of *Nes gadol hayah sham* (A great miracle happened there). In Israel, the dreidel has a *pe* for *po* (here) instead of a *shin* for *sham* (there), recalling that the miracle happened in Palestine.

A story is told about the days of the Maccabees when Jews were forbidden by the Syrians to study the Torah. When schoolchildren were warned by a lookout that Syrians were approaching, they quickly hid their books and played with a dreidel in an effort to prove that they were not studying.

While games of chance and gambling were generally frowned upon by Jewish communal leaders, many generations ago European Jews introduced the dreidel as part of the Hanukkah celebration, the way similar spinning tops had been in use in several European countries. Probably because of the prohibition of doing any work by the light of the Hanukkah lamp, it became customary to indulge in riddles, games, and other pastimes. Thus cardplaying and dreidel games were generally tolerated, and sometimes even encouraged, to enhance the joyousness of the festival.

Dreidel Game: While any number of players can join the game, it is best to limit the number to four or five to provide for more active participation. The game opens with each player placing an equal number of pennies, nuts, or Hanukkah *gelt* (specially prepared scrip) in a common pot or a kitty. Each in turn spins the dreidel, and when it stops the letter on top determines the action to be taken. If it is a *nun*, the initial for *nisht* (nothing), the player gives and takes

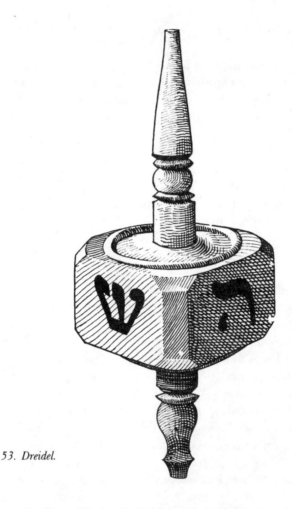

53. *Dreidel.*

nothing from the kitty; if a *he*, the initial of *halb* (half), he takes half of the pot; if a *shin*, that is, *shtel* (put), he puts in the kitty a stipulated amount; if a *gimel*, meaning *gantz* (all), he takes the entire pot. When the kitty is empty, each player again contributes to it. The game is terminated by one of the following methods: the elimination of players who have nothing left to add to the pot; at a predetermined time; or after a set number of rounds.

A variation of the game, as was played by Jewish children in Europe, may be made by drawing a large Hebrew letter *pe* or a circle about two feet in diameter. If the dreidel when spun falls outside the *pe* or circle, the spinner loses his turn.

Numerical Dreidel Game: The letters on the dreidel are given their numerical Hebrew values; that is, *nun* equals 50, *gimel* equals 3, *he* equals 5, and *shin* equals 300. Each player has one spin in turn and receives the number of points equivalent to the letter on top when the dreidel stops spinning. The winner is the first to reach a score of 1,000 points or any other goal agreed upon in advance, or the player who has the highest score following a stipulated number of rounds.

The Longest Spin: Each player at a given signal spins a dreidel. The one whose dreidel spins the longest is the winner.

A variation of this game entails the use of a stopwatch. Each player is given a specified number of chances—three or four—to spin a dreidel. The winner is the one whose cumulative time is longest.

Jumbled Letters: Distribute to each participant a list of words pertaining to Hanukkah with the letters jumbled so that they are not immediately recognizable. Allow a given number of minutes for the players to untangle the letters and write the correct spelling of the words. The following are examples that can be used: ranhoem (menorah), Hatcousin (Antiochus), Hadju (Judah), phelanet (elephant), Becamaces (Maccabees), Shemannoa (Hasmonean), Tamiatasht (Mattathias), Donim (Modin), Dijhut (Judith), stalek (latkes), claned (candle), Esheltlin (Hellenist), Khukanah (Hanukkah), Lempet (Temple), Krege (Greek), riddele (dreidel), remham (hammer).

The Last Word: Each player draws a number from a box. The players are lined up or seated in numerical order. The player with number one starts by saying a word usually associated with Hanukkah—for example, menorah, lamp, oil, Judah, etc. The next player repeats that word and adds another. The third one must repeat in the same order what the others have said and add another word. Any participant who fails to repeat in the same order the words said previously or to add another word is eliminated. The game continues until only one player remains.

Hanukkah Gelt Treasure Hunt: Pennies or nickels are hidden in various parts of the room, apartment, or building in which the treasure hunt takes place. The treasure may also include a cruse (small bottle) of oil, a dreidel, menorah, and box of candles. A limited time is allowed for the participants to search for the Hanukkah *gelt*. Each one keeps whatever treasure he finds.

The Hidden Dreidel: One player leaves the room while the others conceal a dreidel. Then the player reenters the room. While he searches for the dreidel, the others sing a Hanukkah song. If the searcher is coming close to the hidden dreidel, the singing grows louder; when he moves away the volume of the singing decreases.

Mattathias and Antiochus Issue Orders: The leader issues orders to the participants standing in a row. He commands them to perform various acts, such as, "Kneel before me," "Follow me," "At ease," "Stand at attention." Each order is prefaced with either "Mattathias says" or "Antiochus says." The orders of Mattathias are to be obeyed while those of Antiochus are ignored. Whoever fails to respond correctly and promptly is eliminated from the game.

Inserting the Shammash on the Menorah: Prepare a large Hanukkah menorah drawn on cardboard or shelving paper and hang it on a wall. Give each player a candle cut from construction paper and a straight pin. One at a time, blindfold the players, spin them around, and allow them to try to pin the candle on the *shammash*-holder. The one who inserts his candle on the *shammash*-holder or comes closest to it is the winner.

Hanukkah Pantomimes: Players are divided into two or more groups of about three to six actors. Each cast leaves the room and prepares a pantomime within a stipulated number of minutes. Players are limited to the depiction of scenes related to the history of Hanukkah and its celebration, such as Mattathias calling to the Jews to follow him; Antiochus ordering Hannah's sons to bow before an idol; the search for a cruse of oil in the Temple, and kindling the Hanukkah lights. As the pantomimists enact the scene, the others try to guess what is being presented.

Yes or No: After one player leaves the room, the others decide on a Hanukkah object or character. Then the player who was outside reenters and asks questions to ascertain the object or name selected. Only yes or no answers are permitted. He may ask such questions as "Is it animate or inanimate?," "Is it made of lead?," "Is he a brave person?," "Does it turn?" When he guesses the name or object chosen, he selects the next player to be the questioner.

Eight Days of Hanukkah: Players are seated in a circle. The first player starts to count, saying: "One," and each player continues the count. Whenever the count is eight, a multiple of eight (16, 24, 32, etc.), or includes eight (18, 28, 38, etc.), the player whose turn it is does not count but he stands up and says "Hanukkah." A player who errs is eliminated from the game.

Candle Relay: Form a relay race between two or more teams. Each team has a lit candle which is passed from runner to runner. At the final destination is a Hanukkah lamp with candles. The winner is the team whose last runner is the first to reach the lamp and kindle the candles with the lit candle he holds. If a candle is extinguished, the runner holding it must relight it and start again.

Latke-eating Contest: Teams of two players participate. Each team sits across an oblong table facing each other. Between them in the center of the table is a plate of four latkes. Each player is given a twenty-four-inch fork (a regular fork tied tightly to a stick). At a given signal, each player must pick up a latke with his fork and feed his teammate. Players are not permitted to rise from their seats. The pair that consumes the four latkes first is the winner.

Another latke-eating contest may be conducted in the following manner. A plate of two latkes is placed on a table in front of each contestant while he holds his hands behind his back. The latkes may be covered with applesauce or jam. The contestants must eat the latkes without using their hands.

ARTS AND CRAFTS

Clay Menorah: Knead and pound about one pound of self-hardening clay while it is moist. Roll out the clay with a rolling pin, a round stick, or a bottle, eliminating any cracks, until the clay is soft and malleable and about ¾" thick. If the clay becomes dry in the process, add some water. Cut the clay into an oblong, semicircle, or other shape for the base of the menorah. Punch holes, evenly spaced, in the base with a pencil or another round instrument so that the candles will fit snugly; test the holes with a candle to make sure they are not too large or too small. If a back is desired, use another batch of clay and mold into shape about ¾" thick. Attach the base, filling in all the seams with wet clay. The back and base should be one solid piece. Allow the clay to harden a bit and then scratch lettering and a design with a nail or any pointed tool. When the menorah is thoroughly dry, which may take one or more days, paint with poster paints or enamel; if poster paints are used, cover with a coat of shellac when the paint is dry.

Wood Menorah: Use a strip of lumber 3" wide, ½" to ¾" thick, and at least 25" long. Saw the wood into five blocks of the following dimensions: 1" × 1", 1½" × 3", 2" × 5", 2½" × 7", 3" × 9". Place the largest piece, 3" × 9", on the bottom and glue or nail on the other pieces in ascending order of size so that the 1" × 1" block of wood is on top. Each block should be centered on the one under it. Figure I A shows how the blocks should be positioned. The dots indicate the position for the candle-holders. From tin or any pliable metal, make nine small candle-holders with bottoms using the actual pattern in Figure I B; bend on the dotted line. Before shaping the candle-holders, nail the bottoms where the dots are on the pattern on the two ends of each block, with the *shammash*-holder centered on the top. Curve the ends around a candle. Paint the menorah as desired.

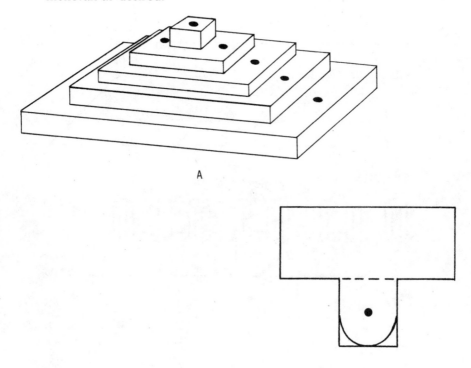

A

B

Figure I

Tin Menorah: With heavy scissors, cut down the side of a large tin can and then cut from it a 4″ × 8″ sheet of tin. On one 8″-side measure eight 1″ parts and make seven cuts, each ¾″ deep. With a pliers bend up each 1″ part; cut along the bend about one-third of the way on each side, leaving the middle third attached, as shown in Figure II A. Using a dowel stick, a pencil, or a candle, curve each bent piece to form a candle-holder, as shown in Figure II B. The *shammash*-holder should be in the center of the opposite side of the tin. Make 2 cuts, each ¾″ deep and 1″ apart on the edge, as in Figure II A. Cut away the excess tin on both sides of the *shammash*-holder as indicated by the broken line. With a pliers bend up the projecting piece of tin; cut along the bend about one-third of the way on each side, leaving the middle third attached; form the *sham-mash*-holder in the same way as the other candle-holders with the open slit over the tin base, as in Figure II B.

A menorah with a base and a back can be made by using a 6″ × 8″ sheet of tin; bend the tin over a table edge until it forms a right angle, so that both the base and back will each be 3″ × 8″. The back may be trimmed to an arc shape. The *shammash*-holder can be made in the top edge of the back.

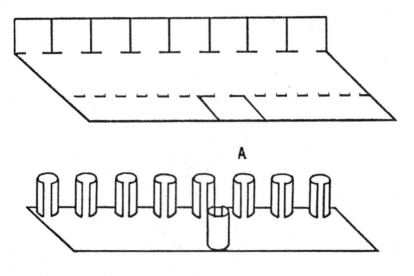

A

B

Figure II

Potato Menorah: Cut four potatoes in half. Place the flat sides down and bore a hole in the tops to hold candles. For the *shammash-holder*, cut off about ¼ " from a whole potato so that it will have a flat surface on which to stand; bore in it a hole for the *shammash*. Line the holes with aluminum foil. The potato candle-holders can be arranged variously on a board or a tray. Apples may be substituted for potatoes.

Lamp with Oil: Remove the top and bottom from a one-pound coffee can, cutting with a heavy tinsmith shears. The top rim and bottom can be removed by cutting with an electric or hand rotary can opener. Flatten the sides of the can. With a nail, mark eight circles on the flattened tin where bottle caps will be placed to serve as the oil containers. The tin can be decorated with enamel. Spread some solder from a tube of liquid solder within the circles and press down the bottle caps until they are firmly set. Insert wicks and pour olive oil in the bottle caps that will be lit each night. Wicks can be made from absorbent cotton twisted into strings.

A similar menorah for use with oil can be made with a piece of lumber, about 4" × 16" as the base. If a back is desired, carve another piece of wood and nail to the base. Paint the lumber as desired. Cement or nail bottle caps on the base.

Menorah Transparency: Draw the outline of a Hanukkah lamp on gold or silver transparent paper. Cut out the menorah on the outline. Mark spaces where candles will be pasted. Cut out strips of yellow or orange paper for the candles and small pieces of red paper for the flames. Paste the candles on the menorah and the flames on the tops of the candles. Hang in a window.

Another type of transparency may be made by drawing the outline of a menorah with candles on a sheet of heavy construction paper. With an x-acto knife or a razor, cut out the menorah. On the back of the frame paste colored cellophane or tissue paper to cover the cut-out spaces.

A shadow box of wood can be made with an electric socket at bottom and the transparency placed over the open end.

Wood Dreidel: Use a square soft pine stick, ¾ " × ¾ " and 12 or more inches in length. Sandpaper the stick to eliminate splinters. Draw two diagonal lines from corner to corner on the top of the stick; the lines will meet at the center (a) (see Figure III A). One inch below the top draw a line around the four sides (line b); this top 1″ will become the handle; ¾″ below line b, draw another line around the four sides (line c). This cube will be the body of the dreidel. About ⅜″ below line c, draw a third line around the four sides (line d); this will be the point or bottom of the dreidel. With a sharp knife, cut or whittle from line b to the top center (a), leaving about ⅛″ or 3/16″ in diameter on top of the handle; continue cutting until the handle is carved (see Figure III B). Cut or whittle down from line c to line d to carve the dreidel point; it can be shaped like a reverse pyramid. Continue cutting until the dreidel is separated from the balance of the stick, making certain that the point is in the center (see Figure III C). Paint with ink a different one of the four Hebrew letters—*nun, gimel, he, shin*—on each side. If desired the letters can be incised. The dreidel handle can now be cut to about ½″ in length.

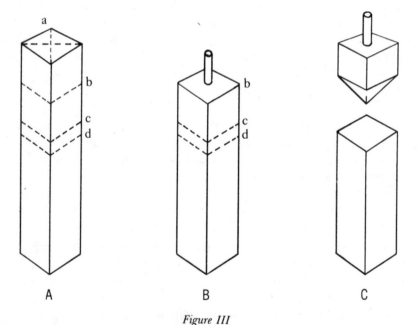

Figure III

Lead Dreidel: Take a dowel stick or a small tree branch about 1½″ in diameter. Saw off a 3″ length. With a sharp knife make two longitudinal cuts to divide the wood into four equal parts so that they fit together again at right angles, as shown in Figure IV A. On each of these four pieces, starting 1″ below the top, cut out a section approximately ½″ deep, ⅝″ straight down, and, then, slanting down to the front (inner edge) about ¼″. The wood that is cut out can be discarded. Above the cut-out section, slice off a small piece of the front (inner edge) as shown in Figure IV B. The shaded portion represents the part that is cut out. At the top a conical piece is cut out which will become the funnel for pouring the lead into the mold. This process must be repeated on the other three pieces of wood. In each piece of wood where the sections have been cut out, carve one of the four Hebrew letters reversed—*nun, gimel, he, shin*. To carve the letters in reverse, print them on onionskin paper, turn over the paper, and copy.

Tie together the four pieces of wood tightly with cord or masking tape, as shown in Figure IV C. Set the entire wooden mold in a can of sand to hold it upright. Heat lead in a tablespoon until it is liquefied. Slowly pour the molten lead into the funnel-shaped hole at the top, filling the entire cavity. Allow the lead to cool and then remove the four pieces of wood. With a hacksaw, cut off the "funnel" above the handle of the dreidel, as shown in Figure IV D. If necessary, file any rough edges of the dreidel.

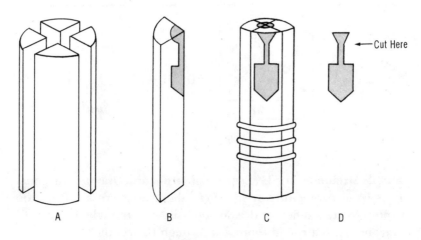

A   B   C   D

Figure IV

Cardboard Dreidel: Cut out of cardboard a design similar to the pattern in Figure V. Each of the six squares should be 1″ × 1″ with the flaps about ⅜″ wide. Print in Hebrew one of the four letters—*nun, gimel, he, shin*—on each of the four sides. These four dreidel sides and the top can be colored with crayons or paints. Punch holes in the center of the top and bottom. Fold the four sides and paste the flap on the inside. Then fold the top and bottom to complete the cube and paste the flaps on the inside. Sharpen a 3″ dowel stick to a dull point with a pencil sharpener. Insert the dowel stick through the top and bottom holes so that it fits snugly. If necessary, use transparent tape to hold the stick in place.

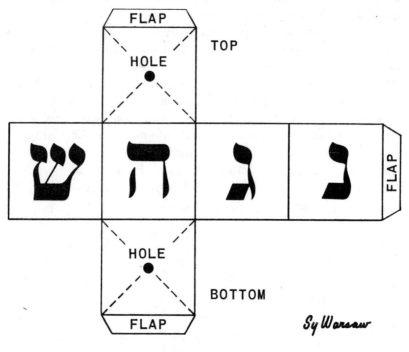

Figure V

Simple Dreidel: Cut a 1½″ square of cardboard. Draw two diagonal lines from corner to corner; where these lines cross will be the center. Write a different dreidel letter in each triangle. Color with crayons. Push a round toothpick through the center.

Decorative Dreidel: On heavy construction paper draw a pattern for a 2″ × 2″ cube: four 2″ × 2″ sides should be contiguous; adjacent to both the top and bottom of the second 2″ × 2″ square, draw a 2″ × 2″ square for the top and another for the bottom of the dreidel; add a ½″ flap to the top and bottom squares and to the sides of the first and fourth squares. Print one of the four letters— *nun, gimel, he, shin*—on each side. With sharp scissors or a knife cut out the letters and paste colored cellophane or crepe paper on the back to cover the spaces of the letters. Draw two diagonal lines from opposite ends of the top and bottom squares to find the center. Punch small holes through the two centers. Decorate the dreidel with crayons. Cut around the outside of the pattern. Fold into a cube and paste the flaps in place with rubber cement or glue. Sharpen a thin dowel stick 4″ long to a dull point with a pencil sharpener. Insert the dowel stick through the top and bottom holes, with the pointed end below. If necessary, use transparent tape to hold the dowel stick in place.

This dreidel can be made into a decorative lantern in the following manner: make each square about 5″ × 5″; omit the top square and the dowel stick; attach string or wire to each side and hang under an electric bulb or insert a small flashlight.

Hanukkah Mobiles: Cut pieces of cardboard or aluminum foil into shapes of menorahs, candles, dreidels, hammers, shields, latkes, or other items related to Hanukkah. Punch holes near the top center of each object and attach them with string or wire to a clothes hanger to form a mobile. Make sure that the mobile is balanced and that each item hangs freely.

A Hanukkah *gelt* mobile can be made by attaching (with transparent tape) metal dreidels and coins to wire strands.

Shield of Judah: On a 9″ × 12″ cardboard, outline a shield and color it with yellow, gold, or silver paint. Cut out the shield. On blue or dark green construction paper print JUDAH in English or Hebrew and draw a picture of a hammer. Cut out the letters and hammer and paste them on the shield. For the handle, cut a 2″ × 7″ strip of cardboard. Bend the strip about 1″ from each end. Paste or staple the 1″ ends of the strip to the back of the shield, allowing enough room to grasp the handle.

Decorations: A festive atmosphere during Hanukkah can be created in the home, school, synagogue, and community center by the use of appropriate symbolic decorations. The color scheme may be orange and its harmonizing colors. Large paper or cardboard cutouts of menorahs, dreidels, hammers, candles, cruses of oil, *gelt,* latkes, shields, elephants, and the characters of the Hanukkah story can adorn the walls or be strung around the room. Murals depicting episodes of the Maccabean War can be drawn on shelving paper or large sheets of wrapping paper. A mosaic of colored paper cutouts of the Hanukkah objects in different sizes and shapes can be mounted on a beaverboard.

Posters can be designed with apt slogans such as: HAPPY HANUK-KAH; "Who is unto the Lord, follow me"—Mattathias; "Not by might, nor by power, but by My spirit, saith the Lord of hosts"—Zechariah 4.6; "The Maccabees will rise again"—Theodor Herzl; A GREAT MIRACLE HAPPENED THERE; SALUTE THE NEW MACCABEES IN ISRAEL.

Party Invitations: Draw an outline of two dreidels adjacent to each other; the total width should not exceed 7″. Trace this outline on a mimeograph stencil. Type, or write with a stylus, the invitation wording within the outline. After the stencil is mimeographed, cut the paper along the outside outline, leaving the common side of the two dreidels. Fold in half on the common side.

Place Cards: Draw an outline of a menorah or a candle on construction paper, adding a 1″ flap on each side. Cut on the outline with the flaps. Decorate and insert the guest's name. Fold back the side flaps so that the place card will stand up.

As an alternative take a piece of construction paper, 4″ × 5″, and fold it in half to 2″ × 5″. On one side make a design and write the name of the guest.

Greeting Cards: Take 8½″ × 11″ sheets of construction paper and cut them in half to 5½ × 8½″. Fold each sheet in half to 4¼″ × 5½″. Draw an appropriate Hanukkah design or illustration on the outside and write a greeting on the inside.

20 DANCES FOR HANUKKAH

iiiiiiii
=

Oy Hanukkah, Oy Hanukkah: *Circle Dance*
SARA LEVI

Music and words for "Oy Hanukkah, Oy Hanukkah" *will be found in the chapter* "Music for Hanukkah."
    This little dance is suitable for kindergarten and first- and second-grade children. Part II may describe a dreidel turning. Part IV may interpret the turning on and off of lights.

Formation: Single circle, hands joined.

PART I. Facing clockwise, take sixteen steps in line of direction.

PART II. Release hands and make right turn in place (like a dreidel) pivoting with eight pivot steps* and eight claps. (There are two complete turns to fill the music.)

PART III.

Phrase 1. Facing center of circle and joining hands, take three steps toward the center, gradually lifting hands forward and up, accentuating the third step with a stamp of the foot. Then hold one count.

Phrase 2. Lowering hands gradually, take three steps backward, accentuating the third step with a stamp of the foot. Then hold one count.

Repeat movements of Part III, Phrases 1 and 2.

PART IV.

Phrase 1. Releasing hands and raising right hand overhead, make a right turn in place with eight pivot steps, accentuating each pivot step by extending fingers of hands slightly, then quickly bringing fingers together.

Phrase 2. On the repeat of the music of Part IV, do the same movements of Part IV, Phrase 1, making a left turn in place with left hand held overhead.[1]

iiiiiiii
=

Oy Hanukkah, Oy Hanukkah: *Couple Dance*
D V O R A   L A P S O N

Music and words for "Oy Hanukkah, Oy Hanukkah" will be found in the chapter "Music for Hanukkah."
This gay Yiddish song has inspired a simple couple dance in folk style.

Formation: Group is divided, with one half on one side of the room and the other half on the other side of the room, arranged in two lines following leaders.

*Pivot step = turn body in place by stepping on one foot and progressing with the other foot, accentuating with a knee-bend the foot around which you are turning.

PART I.

Phrase 1. The leaders of each line walk toward each other, followed by the rest of the group. When they meet, each one becomes a partner of the person coming toward him. They face the front and come down the center aisle holding each other's inside hands.

As couples reach the front of the room, they turn alternately right and left and run toward the rear.

All form a circle.

Phrase 2. Holding hands in circle formation, all take four running steps toward the center of the circle, lifting hands gradually; four running steps backward, lowering hands gradually; then repeat four steps toward center and four steps backward.

Phrase 3. All take fourteen steps to the right, by placing right foot to the right side (step 1), left foot in back of it (step 2), for fourteen counts. On the repeat of the music of Phrase 3, fourteen steps are taken to the left in the same manner (left foot to the left side, then right foot in back of it).

PART II. Repeat music.

Phrase 1. Partners cross hands and promenade around the room.

Phrase 2. Facing each other, partners take four tiny steps toward each other, lifting hands; four steps backward, lowering hands; then repeat, four steps toward each other and four steps backward.

Phrase 3. Still facing each other, hands clasped and crossed, partners spin each other around, feet sliding fourteen steps to the right.

On the repeat of music of Phrase 3, partners spin each other fourteen slide steps to the left.[2]

ïïïïïïï
=
Maoz Tzur: *Hanukkah Candles Processional*
DVORA LAPSON

Music and words for "Maoz Tzur" will be found in the chapter "Music for Hanukkah."

The festive lights of the Hanukkah lamp lend themselves beautifully to a dance in which each child represents one of the nine traditional candles.

Formation: The nine, representing the candles of the Hanukkah lamp, stand abreast.

PART I.

Phrase 1. All stand in place holding before them in right hand, chest high, lighted candles or decorated flashlights.

No. 5 represents the *shammash*.

Figure 1:   1 2 3 4 5 6 7 8 9

Phrase 2. No. 1 and No. 9 walk forward seven steps.

Phrase 3. No. 2 and No. 8 walk forward seven steps, while 1 and 9 return to their original places.

Phrase 4. No. 3 and No. 7 walk forward seven steps, while 2 and 8 return to their original places.

Phrase 5. No. 4 and No. 6 walk forward seven steps, while 3 and 7 return to their original places.

Phrase 6. No. 5 (the *shammash*) walks forward and the rest arrange themselves in a semicircle.

Figure 2:

```
        4   6
       3     7
      2       8
     1    5    9
```

Phrase 7. Partners step toward each other with right feet, lifting candles high and toward each other. Left foot joins the right. Partners step back, away from each other with left foot, right foot joining the left.

Phrase 8. Partners take seven steps around each other, circling the upstretched candles.

Phrases 9 and 10. Repeat music and steps of Phrases 7 and 8.

PART II. Music starts from beginning.

Phrases 1–6. No. 5 walks in and out among the other candles, touching each one's candle as he passes in order to light them.

Phrases 7 and 8. Same as Part I, Phrases 7 and 8.

Phrases 9 and 10. Repeat movement of Phrases 7 and 8, ending in original menorah formation with lit candles held high.[3]

iiiiiiii

My Dreidel: Spinning Top Game
DVORA LAPSON

Music and words for "My Dreidel" will be found in the chapter "Music for Hanukkah."

The Hanukkah dreidel dance, a favorite with young and old alike, is a circle game.

Formation: Children arrange themselves in a circle, hands joined and facing the center. One child, placed in the middle, is the dreidel.

PART I. Children in the circle go around clockwise sixteen steps, singing the first part of the song.

The dreidel in the center, meanwhile, turns in place in the opposite direction.

On the last few counts, the dreidel chooses a partner and pulls him into the center.

PART II. The chorus of the song is now sung.

The children of the circle face the center, and clap hands sixteen times as the two children inside the circle whirl each other around, each one getting a chance to be the dreidel. On the last few counts the child who was originally in the center becomes part of the circle while the child of his choice remains in the middle of the circle, as the new dreidel.

The music is sung over and over again, and each time a new child is given a chance to be the dreidel.[4]

iiiiiiii
=

Mi Yemalel?: *Victory Dance*
DVORA LAPSON

Music and words for "Mi Yemalel?" will be found in the chapter "Music for Hanukkah."

In biblical times it was customary for victory dancers to go forth with tambourines and cymbals to welcome the returning heroes. The victorious Maccabees were probably greeted in this manner when they arrived in Jerusalem to rededicate the Temple.

Formation: Girls are arranged in two lines with a solo girl in front. Each holds a tambourine in her right hand, with left hand on left hip.

PART I.

Phrases 1 and 2. All take sixteen polka steps,* shaking tambourine alternately to right and left, and ending with the following formation:

Figure 1.

<pre>
              4   5
   Row A   3   6   Row B
             2   7
             1   8
                 9
</pre>

Chorus

Phrase 3. Each one makes a right turn in place with pivot steps for eight counts, beating tambourine on the eighth count and changing it to the left hand.

Phrase 4. Same as Phrase 3, but pivoting to the left with tambourine in the left hand.

*Polka step=three steps in one direction, then hop.

Phrase 5. Same as Phrase 3.
Phrase 6. Same as Phrase 4.
Repeat music and steps of chorus.

PART II.

Phrases 1 and 2. On first count beat tambourine. On second count
cross right foot and right hand to left side in front, left
hand over head. On count 3 same as count 1. On count
4 cross left foot and left hand to right side in front and
right hand overhead.

This is done alternately right and left eight times altogether.

Chorus
Phrases 3, 4, 5, 6. Same as in Part I.

PART III.

Phrase 1. Rows A and B (see Figure 1) face each other and take
eight polka steps across the stage, changing places. As
they polka with right foot leading, the right hand is forward. As they polka with left foot leading, the left hand
is forward.

Phrase 2. Eight polka steps back to place in the same manner.

Chorus
Phrases 3, 4, 5, 6. Same as in Part I.[5]

MUSIC FOR HANUKKAH

COMPILED AND EDITED
BY PAUL KAVON

Blessings on Kindling the Hanukkah Lights

We thank God for having commanded us to kindle the Hanukkah lights; for the miracles that He performed, and for having brought us to this day.

Liturgy

Traditional
Arr. by A. W. Binder

Ba - rukh A-tah A - do - nai, E - lo - he - nu Me-lekh ha-o - lam,___ a -
sher kid-sha-nu be-mitz-vo - tav, ve-tzi-va - nu le-had-lik___ ner
shel___ Ḥa-nu - kah. Ba - rukh A-tah A - do - nai E - lo -
he - nu Me-lekh ha-o - lam,___ she - a-sah ni-sim la-a-vo-te -
nu, ba-ya - mim___ ha - hem ba - ze-man ha-zeh. Ba -
rukh A-tah A - do - nai E - lo-he - nu Me-lekh ha-o - lam,___ she -
he-ḥe-ya - nu, ve-ki-ye-ma - nu ve - hi - gi-ya - nu la - ze-man ha-zeh.

Hanerot Hallalu

We kindle these sacred lights in remembrance of the miracles, the wonders, and salvations wrought by God.

Liturgy   **Harry Coopersmith**

Maoz Tzur: *Rock of Ages*

This famous anthem celebrates the end of tyranny and the emergence of freedom.

Hebrew verse: Mordecai Ben Isaac   Traditional
English verse: Gustav Gottheil and M. Jastrow

2. Ye-va-nim nik-be-tzu a-lai
   A-zai bi-me Hash-ma-nim,
   U-far-tzu ho-mot mig-da-lai
   Ve-tim-u kal hash-ma-nim.

   U-mi-no-tar kan-ka-nim,
   Na-a-sah nes le-sho-sha-nim.
   Bene vi-nah ye-me
   she-mo-nah
   Kav-u shir ur-na-nim.

2. Kindling new the holy lamps,
   Priest approved in suffering,
   Purified the nation's shrine,
   Brought to God their
   offering.
   And His courts surrounding
   Hear, in joy abounding,
   Happy throngs
   Singing songs,
   With a mighty sounding.

3. Children of the martyr-race,
   Whether free or fettered,
   Wake the echoes of the
   songs,
   Where ye may be scattered.
   Yours the message cheering
   That the time is nearing
   Which will see
   All men free,
   Tyrants disappearing.

Al ha-Nissim

A paean of thanksgiving for divine intervention and deliverance from the enemy.

Liturgy

Folk song
Arr. by Harry Coopersmith

Al ha-ni-sim ve - al ha-pur-kan, ve - al hag-vu-rot, ve - al hat'-shu-ot she - a - si - ta la-a-vo - te - nu, la-a-vo-te-nu ba - ya - mim ha-hem ba - ze-man_ ha - ze. Bi'ye - me___ Ma - tit - ya - hu, Ma-tit-ya - hu ben Yo-ḥa - nan___ ko - hen ga - dol___ Hash-mo-na - i u - va-nav,___ ke-she - am - dah mal - khut_ Ya - van al am-kha Yis-ra - el, al am-kha Yis-ra-el,___ le - hash - ki - ḥam To-ra-te - kha, ul-ha'a-vi - ram me - ḥu-ke_ re-tzo - ne - kha. Ve-a - tah be - ra-ḥa - me-kha, be - ra-ḥa - me-kha ha-ra - bim___ a-ma-de-ta la-hem be-et tza-ra - tam,___ be - ra - ḥa - me-kha ha-ra - bim.

Mi Yemalel?*: *Who Can Retell?*

Hebrew verse: Menashe Ravina   Folk song
English verse: Ben M. Edidin   Adapted by Menashe Ravina

Mi ye-ma-lel g'vu-rot Yis-ra-el? O - tan mi yim - neh?
Who can re-tell the things that be-fell us? Who can count them?

Hen be-khol dor ya - kum ha-gi-bor go - el ha - am.
In ev-'ry age, a he - ro or sage came to our aid!

Sh'ma! Ba - ya - mim ha-hem ba-z'man ha - zeh, Brave
Hark! In days of yore, in Is-rael's an - cient land,

Ma - ka - bi mo - shi - a u - fo - deh, But
Mac - ca - be - us led the faith - ful band. But

u - v'ya - me - nu kol am Yis - ra - el, Re -
now all Is - rael must as one a - rise, Re -

D.C. al Fine

yit - a - ḥed ya - kum le - hi - ga - el,
deem it - self thru deed and sac - ri - fice.

* This may be sung as a round. Second voice starts at [II] from the beginning.

*Hanukkah**

Hanukkah is a beautiful holiday: light is all around, the dreidel spins, and there are latkes in every home—so sing and dance.

Levin Kipnis

Folk song
Arr. by Samuel E. Goldfarb

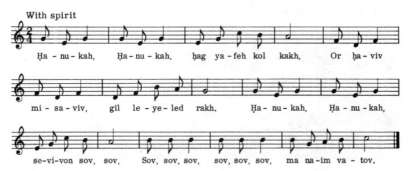

With spirit

Ḥa - nu - kah, Ḥa - nu - kah, ḥag ya - feh kol kakh, Or ḥa - viv mi - sa - viv, gil le - ye - led rakh. Ḥa - nu - kah, Ḥa - nu - kah, se-vi-von sov, sov, Sov, sov, sov, sov, sov, sov, ma na-im va - tov.

2. Ha-nu-kah, Ha-nu-kah, en ha-lon be'li esh,
Le-vi-vot, mig-da-not, be-khol ba-yit yesh.
Ha-nu-kah, Ha-nu-kah, hag ha-viv me-od.
Shi-ru na, zam-ru na, u-tze-u lir-kod.

Oy Hanukkah, Oy Hanukkah: *O Hanukkah, O Hanukkah:* Ha-Erev Hanukkah

There is nothing to compare with the lovely holiday of Hanukkah.

Yiddish verse: M. Riversman
English verse: F. Minkoff
Hebrew verse: E. Indelman

Folk song

Moderately

Oy Ḥa-nu-kah, Oy Ḥa-nu-kah, a yom-tov a she-ner, A
O Ḥa-nu-kah, O Ḥa-nu-kah, a time to re-mem-ber A
Ha - e-rev Ḥa-nu-kah__ sim-ḥat ḥag la-en ge-mer,__

lus-ti-ker, a fre-le-kher, ni-to nokh a zoi-ner,
jol-ly, jol-ly ho-li-day that comes in De-cem-ber.
A-ba ner yad-lik__ ve-yan-im kol be-ze-mer.

Al-le nakht in dreid-lekh sh'pi-len__ mir,
Ev-'ry day for eight days drei-del to spin,
Gam ha-ye-la-dim man-i-mim shir be'kol,

1.
Zi-dik he-se lat-kes est on a shir.
Crisp-y lit-tle lat-kes, tast-y and thin.
Ve-i-ma o-fah le'vi-vot ḥag la-kol.

2.
est on a shir. Ge-
tast-y and thin. And
vot ḥag la-kol. A-

Chorus

shvin-der, tzindt kin-der, Di di-nin-ke likh-te-lekh ohn.
night-ly, so bright-ly, The can-dles of Ḥa-nu-kah glow!
leh na, ha-la-hav, A-leh na, o-ri, u-ge-dal!

Zingt "Al ha-ni-sim," loibt Gott far di ni-sim, Un
Shin-ing with glo-ry, re-tell-ing the sto-ry, The
Saper na, ha-ner,__ al yom shel ge'vu-rot,__ Al

1.
kumt gi-kher tan-tzen in kohn.
won-ders of long, long a-go.
lel shel u-rim ba-he-khal.

2.
kumt gi-kher tan-tzen in kohn.
won-ders of long, long a-go.
lel shel u-rim ba-he-khal.

Yiddish:

2. Ye-hu-dah hot far-tri-ben dem soi-ne dem ro-tze-ah,
   Und hot in bes ha-mik-dash ge-zungen lam-na-tze-ah,
   Die shtot Ye-ru-sho-la-yim, hot vie-der oif-ge-lebt,
   Un tzu a nai-em le-ben hot ye-der ge-shtrebt.
   Dar-i-ber, dem gi-bor,
   Ye-hu-dah ha-mak-bi liobt hoich,
   Zol ye-der ba-zun-der, ba-zin-gen dos vun-der,
   Und lie-ben dos folk zolt ir oich.

Hebrew:

2. Ha-erev Ha-nu-kah, nit-a-sef po ba-he-der,
   Na-gil un-sa-hek be-rov ta-am va-se-der.
   U'khmo ne-rot Ha-nu-kah ha-me'i-rim,
   Al yom ge'vu-rot ne'sa-per be'shi-rim.
      (chorus)

Oy Ir Kleine Likhtelekh

The little Hanukkah candles tell us the ancient story of our ancestors' heroism.

Morris Rosenfeld   Sonia Cheifetz

Andante con moto

Oy   ir klei - ne likh - te-lekh!   Ir der-tzelt_ ge - shikh - te-lekh,
Ir   der-tzelt fun blu - ti-keit   ber - ye-shaft_ un mu - ti-keit

1. mai - se - lekh on__ a tzol; *2.* mohl. Ven ikh ze eikh
vun - der fun__ a -

rit.
shmink - len - dik kumt a ho - lem fink - len-dik redt an al - ter troim.

f
Yid, du host_ ge - krigt a - mol, Yid, du host_ ge - zigt a - mol,
Siz bei dir__ a folk ge - ven, Bist a - mol__ a folk ge - ven

rit.
Got, es gleibt_ zikh koim. Oy ir klei - ne likh - te-lekh
Ach, vi tif___ dos rirt! Tif in hartz__ ba - vegt es zikh

1. ai - e - re__ ge - shikh - te - lekh vek - en oif__ mein pein.
2. un mit tre - ren fregt es zikh vos__ vet itz - ter zain?

My Dreidel

Samuel S. Grossman   Samuel E. Goldfarb

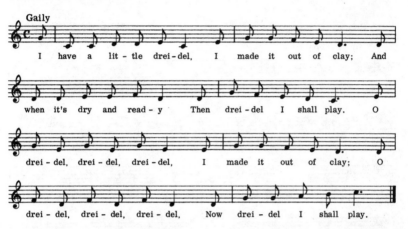

Gaily

I have a lit - tle drei - del, I made it out of clay; And

when it's dry and read - y Then drei - del I shall play. O

drei - del, drei - del, drei - del, I made it out of clay; O

drei - del, drei - del, drei - del, Now drei - del I shall play.

2. It has a lovely body
   With leg so short and thin;
   And when it is all tired,
   It drops and then I win.

   O dreidel, dreidel, dreidel,
   With leg so short and thin;
   O dreidel, dreidel, dreidel,
   It drops and then I win.

3. My dreidel is always playful,
   It loves to dance and spin;
   A happy game of dreidel
   Come play, now let's begin.

   O dreidel, dreidel, dreidel,
   It loves to dance and spin;
   O dreidel, dreidel, dreidel,
   Come play, now let's begin.

Hear the Voice of Israel's Elders

This anthem lauds the Maccabees as exemplars for all Jews.

Samuel S. Grossman   Samuel E. Goldfarb

March tempo

Hear the voice of Is - rael's el - ders, Call - ing on Ju - de - a's sons,

Who will be the fu - ture lead-ers When the— el - der— men are gone.

Who will do what we have start - ed, Bring the Jew to an - cient sta - tion,

Who will urge the wea- ry heart-ed, fight for— right and— live a na - tion?

2. Hear the brave and youthful heroes,
   Coming onward with the call,
   When we're one, oppressors fear us.
   Courage, courage, brothers all.
   Israel's patriots and sages
   Taught us how to live like men.
   Israel's youth with hearts courageous,
   Live for God and race again.

3. Ev'ry Jew is each man's brother,
   Fighting on for God and right;
   Fearless, cheering one another,
   Aiding all with main and might.
   Hopeful hearted, helpful handed,
   Join in union ev'ry Jew.
   God will help us when we're banded,
   Build the nation up anew.

Kindle the Taper

The American Jewish poetess pays tribute to the heroic Maccabees.

Emma Lazarus   Jacob Singer

Kin - dle the ta - per like the stead - fast star A -
blaze on___ eve - ning's fore-head o'er_the earth; Send thro' the night its
lus-ter till a-far, An eight - fold splen-dor shine a - bove thy hearth.

2. Clash, Israel, the cymbals, touch the lyre,
   Blow the loud trumpet and harsh-tongued horn;
   Chant psalms of victory till the heart take fire,
   The Maccabean spirit leaps newborn.

3. Still ours the dance, the feast, the glorious psalm,
   The mystic lights of emblem and the word.
   Where is our Judah? Where our five-branch'd palm?
   Where are the lion warriors of the Lord?

See, the Conqu'ring Hero Comes

In mid-eighteenth century the famed composer celebrated the triumph of the Maccabean hero in this chorus from the oratorio "Judah Maccabeus."

Thomas Morell   George F. Handel

See, the___ con - qu'ring he - ro comes! Sound___ the

trum - pets, beat___ the___ drums. Sports___ pre - pare,___ the

lau - rels bring, Songs___ of tri - umph to___ him___

sing, Sports pre - pare, the lau - rels bring,

Songs___ of tri - umph to___ him___ sing. See, the___

god - like youth___ ad - vance! Breathe___ the flutes, and

lead___ the___ dance; Myr - tle wreaths and ros - es

twine, To deck___ the he - ro's brow___ di - vine;

Myr - tle___ wreaths and ros - es twine, to___ deck___ the

he - ro's brow___ di - vine. See, the___ con - qu'ring

he - ro comes! Sound___ the trum - pets,

beat___ the drums. Sports___ pre - pare, the lau - rels

bring, Songs___ of tri - umph to___ him

sing. See, the___ con - qu'ring he - ro comes!

Sound___ the trum - pets, beat___ the___ drums.

ŊOTES

iiiiiiii
=

1 Hanukkah and Its History

_ 1. Solomon Grayzel, "Hanukkah and Its History," *Hanukkah: The Feast of Lights*, ed. Emily Solis-Cohen, Jr. (Philadelphia: Jewish Publication Society of America, 1937, 1965), pp. 17–47. Reprinted with slight modifications by the author.

2 Hanukkah in the Bible

1. Baba Batra 14b.
2. *Daniel, Ezra and Nehemiah* . . . , introduction and commentary by Judah J. Slotki (London: Soncino Press, 1951), pp. xi–xiv.
3. *The Psalms* . . . , ed. A. Cohen (London: Soncino Press, 1945), p. 85.
4. *The Holy Scriptures according to the Masoretic Text* . . . (Philadelphia: Jewish Publication Society of America, 1917), pp. 1144–45. The bracketed inserts are based on *Daniel, Ezra Nehemiah*, Slotki, 1951 ed., pp. 91–98.

429

5. *The Book of Psalms: A New Translation according to the Traditional Hebrew Text* (Philadelphia: Jewish Publication Society of America, 1972), pp. 27–28.

3 Hanukkah in Postbiblical Literature

1. Solomon Zeitlin, ed., *The Second Book of Maccabees*, trans. Sidney Tedesche (New York: Harper & Brothers, 1954), pp. 131–35.
2. Solomon Zeitlin, ed., *The First Book of Maccabees.* Translated by Sidney Tedesche (New York: Harper & Brothers, 1950), pp. 69–79.
3. Ibid., pp. 79–89.
4. Ibid., pp. 89–99.
5. Ibid., pp. 99–105.
6. Ibid., pp. 105–9.
7. *Josephus.* . . , trans. Ralph Marcus. 9 vols. *Jewish Antiquities*, Books 12–14, vol. 7 (Cambridge, Mass.: Harvard University Press, 1943), pp. 165–69.
8. Zeitlin, ed., *Second Book of Maccabees*, pp. 189–91.
9. Ibid., pp. 155–59.
10. Ibid., pp. 159–69.
11. Solomon Zeitlin, ed., *The Book of Judith*, trans. Morton S. Enslin (Leiden: E. J. Brill, 1972), pp. 77–79, 107–27.
12. Ibid., pp. 127–55.
13. Ibid., pp. 155–57, 165–67.

4 Hanukkah in Talmud and Midrash

1. Selections from *The Babylonian Talmud* are from the translation under the editorship of Isidor Epstein (London: Soncino Press, 1935–50).
2. *Midrash Rabbah*: vol. 7: *Lamentations*, trans. A. Cohen (London: Soncino Press, 1939), pp. 130–33.
3. William G. Braude, trans., *Pesikta Rabbati: Discourses for Feasts, Fasts and Special Sabbaths* (New Haven: Yale University Press, 1968), 1:50.
4. Ibid., p. 60.
5. Ibid., pp. 145–46.
6. Ibid., pp. 50–51.
7. Ibid., p. 83.
8. Louis Ginzberg, *The Legends of the Jews* (Philadelphia: Jewish Publication Society of America, 1911), 3: 218.
9. Braude, trans., *Pesikta Rabbati*, p. 58.

5 The Medieval Scroll of the Hasmoneans

1. Louis Ginzberg, "Scroll of Antiochus." *Jewish Encyclopedia*, 1: 637–38; Moses Gaster, "The Scroll of the Hasmoneans," *Transactions of the*

International Congress of Orientalists: *9th Congress*, *1892* (London, 1893)
2: 3–32; N. Fried, "*Inyanut Megillat Antiochus*," *Areshet* 3: 166–75.
2. *Ha-Siddur ha-Shalem*: *Daily Prayer Book*. Translated and annotated by
Philip Birnbaum (New York: Hebrew Publishing Co., 1949), pp. 714–
26.

6 Hanukkah in Jewish Law

1. *The Code of Maimonides*, book 3, *The Book of Seasons*, trans. Solomon
Gandz and Hyman Klein (New Haven: Yale University Press, 1961),
pp. 463–65.
2. Ibid., pp. 468–71.

7 Hanukkah in Modern Prose

1. A. Alan Steinbach, *Spiritual Cameos: Reflections and Meditations on the Holy
Days and Festivals* (New York: Gertz Bros., n.d.), p. 15.
2. Leo Jung, *Crumbs and Character* (New York: Night and Day Press, 1942),
p. 215.
3. Theodor Herzl Gaster, *Festivals of the Jewish Year: A Modern Interpretation
and Guide* (New York: William Sloane Associates, 1953), pp. 244–46.
4. Samson Raphael Hirsch, *Judaism Eternal: Selected Essays . . .* , trans.
Isidor Grunfeld (London: Soncino Press, 1956), 1: 26–27.
5. Judah L. Magnes, *What Is Hanukkah?* (New York: American Friends of
the Hebrew University, 1946), unpaged.
6. Abram Leon Sachar, *A History of the Jews*, 2d rev. ed. (New York: Alfred
A. Knopf, 1940), pp. 100–102.
7. Yehezkel Kaufmann, "The Biblical Age," *Great Ages and Ideas of the
Jewish People*, ed. Leo W. Schwarz (New York: Random House, 1956),
pp. 91–92.
8. Morris Joseph, *Judaism as Creed and Life* (London: George Routledge
and Sons, 1903), pp. 284–85.
9. Grace Aguilar, *The Women of Israel: Characters and Sketches from the Holy
Scriptures and Jewish History* (London: Groombridge and Sons, 1872),
pp. 403–5, 409.
10. Alex Bein, *Theodor Herzl: A Biography*, trans. Maurice Samuel (Philadelphia: Jewish Publication Society of America, 1940), pp. 248–51. "The
Menorah," by Herzl, originally appeared in *Die Welt* (Hanukkah,
1897), a publication of the Zionist organization.
11. *Hanucah Program* (Jerusalem: Jewish National Fund, 1935), p. 5; reprinted in *Chanukah Highlights: A Handbook for Teachers and Youth Leaders*,
ed. Misha Louvish (Jerusalem: Jewish National Fund, Youth Department, 1959), p. 29.
12. *The Jewish Spectator* 17, no. 11 (December 1952): 15.
13. Yaacov Herzog, *A People that Dwells Alone* (New York: Sandhedrin Press,
1975), pp. 155–58.
14. *Jewish Life* 14, no. 2 (December 1946): 26–28.

15. Herman Wouk, *This Is My God: The Jewish Way of Life* (Garden City, N.Y.: Doubleday & Co., 1959), pp. 103–8.
16. Bernard Postal and David H. White, eds., *The Best of Ten Years in "The Jewish Digest"* (Houston: D. H. White & Co., 1965), pp. 201–3.
17. *American Examiner-Jewish Week* 181, no. 30 (December 9, 1971): 15.

9 A Hanukkah Drama

1. Henry Wadsworth Longfellow, *Judas Maccabaeus* (Cambridge, Mass.: Riverside Press, 1886), pp. 11–17, 25–34, 37–44.

10 Hanukkah in Many Lands

1. Leo W. Schwarz, ed., *A Golden Treasury of Jewish Literature* (New York: Farrar & Rinehart, Inc., 1937), pp. 187–91.
2. Devora and Menahem Hacohen, *One People: The Story of the Eastern Jews*, trans. Israel I. Taslitt (New York: Sabra Books, 1969), pp. 35, 89, 167.
3. Tovia Preschel, "*Ha-Ner ha-Nosaf ve-Nerot ha-Nesiim ba-Hanukkah shel Haleb*," *Hadoar* 46, no. 6 (Kislev 26, 5627): 86; Yehudah Levi Nahum, *Mi-Tzefunot Yehude Teman*, ed. Shimon Garidi (Tel Aviv: author, 1962), pp. 131–32; Daniel Persky, *Likhvod ha-Regel* (New York: author, 1947), pp. 96–98; Mehalel ha-Adeni, "*Hag ha-Urim le-Yalde Yisrael be-Aden*," Menasheh Mani, "*Hag ha-Hanukkah be-Hevron*," "*Hag ha-Banot le-Or ha-Ner ha-Shevii shel Hanukkah*," *Sefer ha-Moadim*, ed. Yom Tov Lewinski (Tel Aviv: Oneg Shabbat and Dvir, 1954), 8: 250, 251–53, 286–87.
4. Israel Tabak, *Judaic Lore in Heine* (Baltimore: Johns Hopkins Press, 1948), p. 162.
5. A. B. Levy, *East End Story* (London: Vallentine, Mitchell & Co., n.d.), pp. 53–54.
6. A. S. Sachs, *Worlds That Passed*, trans. Harold Berman (Philadelphia: Jewish Publication Society of America, 1928), pp. 215–21.
7. Shmarya Levin, *Childhood in Exile*, trans. Maurice Samuel (New York: Harcourt, Brace and Co., 1929), pp. 120–21.
8. Bella Chagall, *Burning Lights*, trans. Norbert Guterman (New York: Schocken Books, 1946), pp. 122–25.
9. Esther J. Ruskay, *Hearth and Home Essays* (Philadelphia: Jewish Publication Society of America, 1902), pp. 42–46.
10. [Zelda Popkin], *GI Holy Days: Jewish Holidays and Festival Observances among the Armed Forces throughout the World* (New York: National Jewish Welfare Board, 1944), pp. 35–41.
11. *McCall's* 100, no. 3 (December 1972): 36.
12. *American Judaism* 13, no. 2 (Winter 1963–64): 16, 57.
13. Chaim A. Kaplan, *Scroll of Agony: The Warsaw Diary of Chaim A. Kaplan*, trans. and ed. Abraham I. Katsh (New York: Macmillan Co., 1965), pp. 234–36.
14. Herman Kruk, "Diary of the Vilna Ghetto," *YIVO Annual of Jewish Social Science* (New York: YIVO Institute for Jewish Research, 1965), 13: 46.

15. Moshe Flinker, *Young Moshe's Diary: The Spiritual Torment of a Jewish Boy in Nazi Europe* (Jerusalem: Yad Vashem; New York: Board of Jewish Education, 1971), pp. 34–35, 39–40.
16. *American Examiner-Jewish Week*, November 30–December 6, 1972, p. 21.
17. Moshe Prager, *Sparks of Glory*, trans. Mordecai Schreiber (New York: Shengold Publishers, 1974), pp. 76–80.
18. Joshua Rothenberg, *The Jewish Religion in the Soviet Union* (New York: Ktav Publishing House; Waltham: Philip W. Lown Center for Contemporary Jewish Studies, Brandeis University, 1971), pp. 93–94.
19. Alla Rusinek, *Like a Song, Like a Dream: A Soviet Girl's Quest for Freedom* (New York: Charles Scribner's Sons, 1973), pp. 78–82.
20. Ben Ami [Arie L. Eliav], *Between Hammer and Sickle* (Philadelphia: Jewish Publication Society of America, 1967), pp. 302–6.
21. Joseph J. Rivlin, "*Hagigat Yeladim be-Hanukkah*," *Tziyyon* 2, nos. 8–10 (1931): 1–7.
22. Shirley Lashner and Yehuda Fogellewitz, eds., *Hamekasher Anthology* (Tel Aviv: World Habonim, 1956), pp. 126–27.

11 Hanukkah in Poetry

1. Israel Abrahams, *Jewish Life in the Middle Ages* (London: Edward Goldston, 1932), p. 151.
2. Emma Lazarus, *The Poems of Emma Lazarus in Two Volumes: Jewish Poems: Translations* (Boston: Houghton Mifflin Co., 1888), 2: 10–12.
3. Ibid., pp. 18–20.
4. Ruth F. Brin, *Interpretations for the Weekly Torah Reading* (Minneapolis: Lerner Publications Co., 1965), p. 141.
5. Michael I. Hecht, *The Fire Waits: Prayers and Poems for the Sabbath and Festivals* (Bridgeport: Hartmore House, 1972), pp. 137–38.
6. *CCAR* (Central Conference of American Rabbis) *Journal* 19, no. 4 (Autumn 1972): 42.
7. Moshe Davis and Victor Ratner, *The Birthday of the World* (New York: Farrar, Straus & Cudahy, 1959), pp. 27–29.
8. Charles Reznikoff, *By the Waters of Manhattan* (New York: New Directions and San Francisco Review, 1962), pp. 91–92.
9. *The Jewish Guardian* (London) 5th year, no. 218 (November 30, 1923), p. 13.
10. Chaim Lewis, *Shadow in the Sun* (Cape Town, S.A.: Juta & Co., 1972), pp. 81–82.
11. *The Collected Poems of A. M. Klein*, compiled by Miriam Waddington (Toronto and New York: McGraw-Hill Ryerson Limited, 1974), p. 12.
12. Ibid., p. 13.

12 Hanukkah in the Short Story

1. Howard Fast, *My Glorious Brothers* (Boston: Little, Brown and Co., 1948), pp. 86–87, 89–94, 96–97.

2. Ibid., pp. 135–38.
3. *The Judaean* 2, no. 3 (December 1928): 7–8 (Federation of Young Judea of Canada).
4. *The Jewish Spectator* 12, no. 2 (December 1946): 10–11.
5. Sholom Aleichem, *The Old Country*, trans. Julius and Frances Butwin (New York: Crown Publishers, 1946), pp. 183–200.
6. Nathan Ausubel, ed., *A Treasury of Jewish Humor* (Garden City, N.Y.: Doubleday & Co., 1951), pp. 73–77.
7. *The Reconstructionist* 22, no. 15 (November 30, 1956): 14–16.

13 Hanukkah Oddities

1. In the preparation of this essay the author made use of articles he had written previously: "Hanukkah Anagrams," *The Orthodox Union* 4, no. 3 (December 1936): 1–2; "Hanukkah in the Bible," *The Orthodox Union* 5, no. 3 (November–December 1937): 2, 4–5; "The Dreidel: A Novel Spin," *West Side Institutional Review* 7, no. 15 (December 15, 1944): 1; "Quips and Quirks for Hanukkah," *Hanukkah: The Feast of Lights*, ed. Emily Solis-Cohen, Jr. (Philadelphia: Jewish Publication Society of America, 1937, 1965), pp. 107–16.

14 Hanukkah Sidelights

1. *Jewish Antiquities* 12.7.7.
2. Solomon Zeitlin, "Hanukkah," *Jewish Quarterly Review* 29, no. 1 (1938): 9.
3. Nahman Tzelnik, "*Hanukkah: Shemotav ve-Kinuyav*," *Bitzaron* 53 (1966): 86–88.
4. Solomon Zeitlin, *The Rise and Fall of the Judaean State* (Philadelphia: Jewish Publication Society of America, 1964), 1:96.
5. *Jewish Antiquities* 12.6.1.
6. Tzelnik, "*Hanukkah: Shemotav ve-Kinuyav*," pp. 86–88.
7. *The First Book of Maccabees*. English translation by Sidney Tedesche. Introduction and commentary by Solomon Zeitlin (New York: Harper & Brothers, 1950), pp. 249–50.
8. Ibid., p. 28.
9. Eliyahu Kitov, *The Book of Our Heritage: The Jewish Year and Its Days of Significance* (Jerusalem–New York: "A" Publishers, 1968), 1:286–88.
10. Jacob Glis, ed., *Minhage Eretz Yisrael* (Jerusalem: Mosad Harav Kook, 1968), p. 205.
11. Shmuel Hakohen and Eliyahu Shragai, eds., *Ha-Nerot Hallalu: Perakim le-Hanukkah* (Israel: Chief Military Rabbinate, Israel Defense Force, 1950), p. 6.
12. J. David Bleich, "Survey of Recent Halakhic Periodical Literature," *Tradition: A Journal of Orthodox Thought* 13, no. 2 (Fall 1972): 136–38.
13. Marshall Sklare and Joseph Greenblum, *Jewish Identity on the Suburban Frontier* (New York: Basic Books, 1967), pp. 50–56.

14. Israel Abrahams, *Festival Studies: Being Thoughts on the Jewish Year* (Philadelphia: Julius H. Greenstone, 1906), p. 146.
15. James G. Heller, *Isaac M. Wise: His Life, Work and Thought* (New York: Union of American Hebrew Congregations, 1965), p. 564.
16. David Philipson, *The Reform Movement in Judaism* (New York: Macmillan Co., 1931), pp. 321–22; W. Gunter Plaut, *The Rise of Reform Judaism: A Sourcebook of Its European Origins* (New York: World Union for Progressive Judaism, 1963), pp. 204–5.
17. Yosef Hayim Yerushalmi, *From Spanish Court to Italian Ghetto: Isaac Cardoso: A Study in Marranism and Jewish Apologetics* (New York: Columbia University Press, 1971), pp. 141–43.
18. Ibid., pp. 143–44, note 14.
19. *The First Book of Maccabees*. Commentary by Neil J. McEleney (New York: Paulist Press, 1973), p. 8.
20. Barbara W. Tuchman, *Bible and Sword: England and Palestine from the Bronze Age to Balfour* (New York: Funk & Wagnalls, 1956), pp. 89–90, 199.
21. Yom-Tov Lewinski, ed., *Sefer ha-Moadim*: vol. 8: *Yeme Moed ve-Zikkaron: Rosh Hodesh—Hanukkah—Hamishah Asar be-Shevat* (Tel Aviv: Dvir Co., 1954), pp. 155–56; *The Catholic Encyclopedia* (New York, 1908), 3: 163; Thomas Kelly Cheyne, *The Origin and Religious Contents of the Psalter* (London: Kegan Paul, Trench, Trübner & Co., 1891), p. 29.
22. Lewinski, *Sefer ha-Moadim*, p. 275.
23. Zeitlin, "Hanukkah," pp. 19–25.
24. Zev Vilnay, *Yerushalayim—Birat Yisrael: Ha-Ir ha-Hadashah* (Jerusalem: Ahiever, 1960), pp. 106–7.
25. *The Maccabean*, January 1918, pp. 3, 8.
26. George Putnam Upton, *The Standard Oratorios: Their Stories, Their Music, and Their Composers* (Chicago: A.C. McClurg & Co., 1909), pp. 149–51.
27. Abraham W. Binder, "Hanukkah in Music," *Hanukkah: The Feast of Lights*, ed. Emily Solis-Cohen, Jr. (Philadelphia: Jewish Publication Society of America, 1937, 1965), pp. 64–65.

15 The Hanukkah Cuisine

1. Rama citing *Kol Bo* and Ran (Nissim b. Reuben Gerondi, c. 1340–80), *Shulhan Arukh, Orah Hayyim* 670.2; *Hayye Adam* 154.3.
2. Hanna Goodman, *Jewish Cooking around the World: Gourmet and Holiday Recipes* (Philadelphia: Jewish Publication Society of America, 1973), pp. 167–68.
3. Ibid., p. 56.
4. Ibid., p. 42.
5. Ibid., p. 183.
6. Ibid., pp. 23–24.
7. Ibid., pp. 171–72.
8. Ibid., p. 172.
9. Ibid.
10. Ibid., pp. 172–73.
11. Ibid., p. 175.

16 Children's Stories For Hanukkah

1. Sadie Rose Weilerstein, *What the Moon Brought* (Philadelphia: Jewish Publication Society of America, 1942), pp. 68–75.
2. Lillian S. Abramson, *Join Us for the Holidays* (New York: National Women's League of the United Synagogue of America, 1958), pp. 23–24.
3. Morris Epstein, *My Holiday Story Book* (New York: Ktav Publishing House, 1958), pp. 20–24.
4. Leonard Jaffe, *The Pitzel Holiday Book* (New York: Ktav Publishing House, 1962), pp. 7–18.
5. Judah Steinberg, *The Breakfast of the Birds and Other Stories*, trans. Emily Solis-Cohen, Jr. (Philadelphia: Jewish Publication Society of America, 1917), pp. 42–50.
6. Ben M. Edidin, ed., *Jewish Life and Customs: Unit Four: Hanukkah* (New York: Jewish Education Committee, 1942), pp. 1–8.
7. Ezekiel Schloss and Morris Epstein, eds., *More World Over Stories: An Illustrated Anthology for Jewish Youth* (New York: Bloch Publishing Co., 1968), pp. 65–69.
8. *World Over* 22, no. 5 (December 2, 1960): 6–7.
9. Itche Goldberg, ed., *Yiddish Stories for Young People* (New York: Kinderbuch Publishers, 1966), pp. 137–41.
10. *World Over* 8, no. 4 (December 13, 1946): 10–11.
11. Joseph Gaer, *The Unconquered: Adapted Folklore Legends* (Cincinnati: Sinai Press, 1932), pp. 135–47.
12. Arthur Saul Super and Joseph Halpern, *Storytime: A Jewish Children's Story-Book* (London: Edward Goldston, 1946), pp. 55–60.
13. *World Over* 14, no. 3 (November 28, 1952): 6–7.
14. Barton's Candy Corporation, New York.
15. Ezekiel Schloss and Morris Epstein, eds., *The New World Over Story Book: An Illustrated Anthology for Jewish Youth* (New York: Bloch Publishing Co., 1968), pp. 51–57; originally published in *World Over* 17, no. 3 (November 25, 1955): 6–7.

17 Children's Poems for Hanukkah

1. *The Jewish Child* 4, no. 36 (December 22, 1916): 2.
2. *The Young Judaean* 9, no. 3 (November 1918): 79.
3. Sadie Rose Weilerstein, *The Singing Way: Poems for Jewish Children* (New York: Women's League of the United Synagogue, 1946), p. 24.
4. Ibid., p. 25.
5. Hayyim Nahman Bialik, *Far Over the Sea: Poems and Jingles for Children*, trans. Jessie E. Sampter (Cincinnati: Union of American Hebrew Congregations, 1939), pp. 50–51.
6. Ben M. Edidin, ed., *Jewish Life and Customs: Unit Four: Hanukkah* (New York: Jewish Education Committee, 1942), pp. 9–10.
7. Ilo Orleans, *Within Thy Hand: My Poem Book of Prayers* (New York: Union of American Hebrew Congregations, 1961), p. 63.
8. Philip M. Raskin, *Poems for Young Israel* (New York: Behrman's Jewish Book Shop, 1925), pp. 67–68.

9. Philip M. Raskin, *Collected Poems of Philip M. Raskin: 1878–1944* (New York: Bloch Publishing Co., 1951), pp. 78–79.
10. Elma Ehrlich Levinger, *Jewish Festivals in the Religious School* (Cincinnati: Union of American Hebrew Congregations, 1923), p. 96.
11. Abraham Burstein, *A Jewish Child's Garden of Verses* (New York: Bloch Publishing Co., 1940), pp. 38–41.
12. Harry H. Fein, trans., *Gems of Hebrew Verse: Poems for Young People* (Boston: Bruce Humphries, 1940), p. 25.
13. Ibid., p. 26.
14. *The Young Judaean* 49, no. 30 (December 1960): 3–6.

18 Home Service for Hanukkah

1. Shabbat 23a; Sukkah 46a; Soferim 20.6; *Shulhan Arukh, Orah Hayyim* 676.
2. Soferim 20.6; *Shulhan Arukh, Orah Hayyim* 676.
3. *Jewish Encyclopedia* 8: 315–16.
4. Solomon Solis-Cohen, *When Love Passed By and Other Verses* (Philadelphia: The Rosenbach Co., 1929), pp. 94–95.
5. *Shulhan Arukh, Orah Hayyim* 682.
6. Soferim 20.8; also mentioned in Shabbat 24a.

20 Dances for Hanukkah

1. Dvora Lapson, *Folk Dances for Jewish Festivals* (New York: Jewish Education Committee Press, 1961), pp. 21–22.
2. Dvora Lapson, *Jewish Dances the Year Round* (New York: Jewish Education Committee Press, 1957), pp. 21–22.
3. Ibid., pp. 18–19.
4. Ibid., pp. 23–24.
5. Ibid., pp. 26–27.

GLOSSARY OF HANUKKAH TERMS

AL HA-NISSIM (For the Miracles). A prayer of thanksgiving briefly summarizing the background of the festival, which is inserted in the Eighteen Benedictions and the Grace after Meals throughout the eight days of Hanukkah.

ANTIOCHUS IV EPIPHANES. The Syrian king (175–163 B.C.E.) who plundered the Temple, forbade the Jews to observe their religious practices, and forcefully tried to hellenize Judea, leading to the Maccabean uprising. Sometimes called Antiochus Epimanes—"the Madman."

APOCRYPHA (hidden, not recognized). The Greek name for the non-canonical Jewish books, that is, those works not included in the Bible. These Apocryphal books, written during the period of the Second Temple and for a time following its destruction, include the books of the Maccabees and Judith.

DREIDEL (trendel). A four-sided spinning top used in Hanukkah games; on each side is one of the Hebrew letters *nun, gimel, he, shin*, the initials of *Nes gadol hayah sham* (A great miracle happened there).

FEAST OF DEDICATION. See HANUKKAH.

FEAST OF THE LIGHTS. See HANUKKAH.

FEAST OF THE MACCABEES. See HANUKKAH.

GELT, HANUKKAH (Hanukkah money). Gifts of money given during the festival.

HAG HA-MAKKABIM (Feast of the Maccabees). See HANUKKAH.

HAG HA-URIM (Feast of the Lights). See HANUKKAH.

HALLEL (praise). A prayer of praise to God consisting of Psalms 113–18, which is recited daily during Hanukkah.

HAMMER. According to some authorities Judah was called Maccabee, meaning "hammer," signifying that he was as strong as a hammer and hammered away at the Syrian foe.

HANEROT HALLALU (These Lights). A prayer recited after kindling the Hanukkah lights.

HANNAH. The mother whose seven sons were slain for refusing to bow before an idol; they are considered the earliest martyrs for religious freedom.

HANUKKAH (dedication, inauguration, consecration). The eight-day Festival or Feast of Dedication, commencing on Kislev 25 and continuing to Tevet 2, in commemoration of the rededication of the Temple and altar by the Maccabees in 165 B.C.E. following its desecration under Antiochus IV; also called Feast of the Lights and Feast of the Maccabees.

HANUKKIAH. The modern Hebrew name of the special candelabrum used on Hanukkah.

HASMONEAN. The family cognomen of the dynasty founded by Mattathias.

HELLENISM. The Greek civilization that spread throughout the Near East at the end of the fourth century B.C.E. The Greek belief in many gods and Hellenistic sensuality was in diametric opposition to Jewish monotheism and morality.

HELLENISTS. Followers, including some Jews, of ancient Greek culture, customs, and ideas.

JUDAH MACCABEE. One of the five sons of Mattathias; victorious leader of the revolt against the Syrians under Antiochus IV Epiphanes.

KISLEV. The ninth month of the Jewish calendar. Hanukkah commences on Kislev 25.

LATKES (pancakes). A dish traditionally associated with Hanukkah.

LEVIVOT (pancakes). See LATKES.

MACCABEE. The surname given to Judah and later to his kinsmen and followers. Its derivation is uncertain. See HAMMER.

MAOZ TZUR (Fortress Rock). A well-known Hanukkah hymn, popularly known in English as "Rock of Ages," which is sung by Ashkenazic Jews at the conclusion of the kindling of the lights.

MATTATHIAS. Father of the five Hasmonean brothers who initiated and led the revolt against the Syrians. He was succeeded by his son Judah.

MENORAH (lamp, candelabrum, candlestick). The Hanukkah lamp consisting of nine branches or light-holders, including one for the *shammash*.

MODIN. A village north of Jerusalem, the hometown of Mattathias and his family where the rebellion started.

SEVIVON (trendel, spinning top). See DREIDEL.

SHAMMASH (attendant). The auxiliary light provided to kindle the other Hanukkah lights, as it is not permitted to ignite one from another.

BIBLIOGRAPHY

General References

Abrahams, Israel. *Festival Studies: Being Thoughts on the Jewish Year*. Philadelphia: Julius H. Greenstone, 1906, pp. 145–55.

Agnon, S. Y., and Herrmann, H., eds. *Moaus Zur: Ein Chanukkahbuch*. Berlin: Jüdischer Verlag, 1918.

Amorai, Y., and Ariel, Z., eds. *Moreshet Avot (Entziklopediah "Mayan")*. Tel Aviv: Joseph Sreberk, n.d., pp. 90–102.

Amsel, Jacob Chaim. *Sefer Nahlat Yaakov: Helek Rishon: Ner Hadash le-Hanukkah*. Brooklyn, N.Y., 1973.

Ariel, Z., ed. *Sefer ha-Hag veha-Moed*. Tel Aviv: Am Oved, 1962, pp. 127–66.

Ayali, Meir, ed. *Haggim u-Zemanim: Mahzore Keriah le-Moade Yisrael*. Tel Aviv: Gazit, 1955, 2: 377–496.

Bamberger, Bernard J. *The Story of Judaism*. New York: Union of American Hebrew Congregations, 1957, pp. 65–69.

Beker, Hayyim S., ed. *Yalkut le-Moadim: Hanukkah*. Jerusalem, 1970.

Ben-Ezra, Akiba. *Minhage Haggim*. Tel Aviv: M. Newman, 1963, pp. 131–41.

Ben Gurion, Aryeh, ed. *Hanukkah*. Tel Aviv: Ha-Vaadah ha-Benkibbutzit le-Hivui u-Moed, 1966.

Birnbaum, Philip. *A Book of Jewish Concepts*. New York: Hebrew Publishing Co., 1964, pp. 226–30.

Bugatch, Simon; Esterson, Sidney I.; and Kaplan, Louis L., eds. *Spotlight on Hanukkah*. Baltimore: Board of Jewish Education, 1950.

Cornfeld, Gaalyahu, ed. *Pictorial Biblical Encyclopedia*. New York: Macmillan Co., 1964, pp. 370–76.

Ehrmann, Elieser L. *Chanukka: Ein Quellenheft*. Berlin: Schocken Verlag, 1937.

Eisenstein, Ira. *What We Mean by Religion: A Modern Interpretation of the Sabbath and Festivals*. New York: Reconstructionist Press, 1958, pp. 124–35.

Encyclopaedia Judaica. 16 vols. Jerusalem: Keter Publishing House, 1971. See vol. 1, index.

Farber, Walter C. *Jewish Holidays*. Detroit: Jewish Heritage Publishing House, 1967, pp. 35–43.

Fishman (Maimon), Judah Leb. *Haggim u-Moadim*. 2d ed. Jerusalem: Mosad Harav Kook, 1944, pp. 81–116.

Freehof, Lillian S., and Bandman, Lottie C. *Flowers and Festivals of the Jewish Year*. New York: Hearthside Press, 1964, pp. 86–98.

Frishman, Isaiah, ed. *Hanukkah: Hag ha-Urim: Homer Hadrakhah le-Morim be-Bate ha-Sefer ha-Memlakhtiim*. Jerusalem: Tarbut Vehinukh, 1967.

Gaster, Moses. "The Scroll of the Hasmoneans." *Studies and Texts in Folklore, Magic, Mediaeval Romance, Hebrew Apocrypha and Samaritan Archaeology*. 3 vols. New York: Ktav Publishing House, 1971, 1: 165–83.

Gaster, Theodor H. *Festivals of the Jewish Year: A Modern Interpretation and Guide*. New York: William Sloane Associates, 1953, pp. 233–53.

————. *Purim and Hanukkah in Custom and Tradition*. New York: Henry Schuman, 1950, pp. 85–118.

Goldin, Hyman E. *The Jewish Woman and Her Home*. Brooklyn, N.Y.: Jewish Culture Publishing Co., 1941, pp. 219–31.

————. *A Treasury of Jewish Holidays: History, Legends, Traditions*. New York: Twayne Publishers, 1952, pp. 52–92.

Goldman, Alex J. *A Handbook for the Jewish Family: Understanding and Enjoying the Sabbath and Holidays*. New York: Bloch Publishing Co., 1958, pp. 91–124.

Goodman, Philip. *Rejoice in Thy Festival: A Treasury of Wisdom, Wit and Humor for the Sabbath and Jewish Holidays*. New York: Bloch Publishing Co., 1956, pp. 139–49.

Gordon, Albert I., ed. *How to Celebrate Hanukkah at Home*. New York: United Synagogue of America, n.d.

Goren, Shelomoh. *Torat ha-Moadim: Mehkerim u-Maamarim Al Moade Yisrael le-Or ha-Halakhah*. Tel Aviv: Avraham Tzioni, 1964, pp. 150–215.

Greenberg, David, and Bernards, Solomon. *The Living Heritage of Hanukkah*. New York: Anti-Defamation League of B'nai B'rith, 1964.

Greenstone, Julius H. *Jewish Feasts and Fasts*. Philadelphia, 1945, pp. 83–122.

————. *The Jewish Religion*. Philadelphia: Jewish Chautauqua Society, 1929, pp. 101–9.

Greenwald, Asher Anshil, ed. *Sefer Ner Mitzvah: Kolel Kal Inyane Hanukkah*. Ungvar, 1928. Reprinted New York: Yehezkel Shraga Vagshal, n.d.

Hakohen, Menahem, ed. *Mahanaim: Masseket le-Hayal le-Hanukkah*. Israel: Tzava Haganah le-Yisrael, no. 34 (1958), no. 41 (1960), no. 52 (1961).

Hakohen, Shmuel, and Shragai, Eliyahu, eds. *Ha-Nerot Hallalu: Perakim le-Hanukkah*. Israel: Tzava Haganah le-Yisrael, 1949.

Hanuka Programme. Jerusalem: Overseas Youth Department, Jewish National Fund, 1942.

Hanukkah: Yalkut le-Moreh. Jerusalem: Department of Torah Education and Culture in the Diaspora, World Zionist Organization, 1968.

Harari, Hayyim, ed. *Moadim: Sefer ha-Hanukkah*. Tel Aviv: Jewish National Fund and Omanut, 1938.

Hirsch, Samson Raphael. *Be-Maagle Shanah: Sefer Rishon*. Translated by Aviezer Wolf. Bnai Brak: Netzah, 1965, pp. 183–247.

The Jewish Encyclopedia. 12 vols. New York: Ktav Publishing House. See Hanukkah, Hasmoneans, Judas Maccabeus, Maccabees, Ma'oz Zur, Mattathias Maccabeus.

Joseph, Morris. *Judaism as Creed and Life*. London: George Routledge and Sons, 1903, pp. 277–86.

Jospe, Alfred, ed. *Hanukkah in the Hillel Foundation: A Guide to Hanukkah Programs and Resources*. Washington, D.C.: B'nai B'rith Hillel Foundation, 1965.

Kaplan, Mordecai M. *The Meaning of God in Modern Jewish Religion*. New York: Jewish Reconstructionist Foundation, 1947, pp. 330–60.

Kariv, Abraham, ed. *Shabbat u-Moed be-Derush uve-Hasidut*. Tel Aviv: Dvir, 1966, pp. 333–66.

Kitov, Eliyahu. *The Book of Our Heritage: The Jewish Year and Its Days of Significance*. Vol. 1, *Tishrey-Shevat*. Translated by Nathan Bulman. Jerusalem–New York: 'A' Publishers, 1968, pp. 269–314.

———. *Sefer ha-Todaah: Ladaat Huke ha-Elokim u-Mitzvotav Hagge Yisrael u-Moadav*. Jerusalem: Alef Makhon le-Hotzaat Sefarim, 1964, 1: 165–89.

Lavia, Eliezer Lipman, ed. *Otzar Maamarim: Shabbatot Haggim u-Zemanim ve-Yeme de-Pagra*. Jerusalem: Rubin Mass, 1962, pp. 121–28.

Lehrman, S. M. *A Guide to Hanukkah and Purim*. London: Jewish Chronicle Publications, 1958, pp. 7–49.

———. *The Jewish Festivals*. London: Shapiro, Vallentine & Co., 1938, pp. 125–36.

Leshem, Haim. *Shabbat u-Moade Yisrael be-Halakhah, be-Aggadah, be-Historiah, uve-Folklor*. Tel Aviv: Niv, 1965, 1: 269–92.

Levi, Shonie B., and Kaplan, Sylvia R. *Guide for the Jewish Homemaker*. New York: Schocken Books, 1964, pp. 125–30.

Lewinski, Yom-Tov. *Eleh Moade Yisrael*. Tel Aviv: Ahiasaf, 1971, pp. 99–120.

———. *Entziklopediah Shel Hivui u-Mesoret be-Yahadut*. Tel Aviv: Dvir, 1970, pp. 202–6.

———. *Sefer ha-Moadim*. Vol. 5, *Yeme Moed ve-Zikkaron:Rosh Hodesh, Hanukkah, Hamishah Asar bi-Shevat*. Tel Aviv: Oneg Shabbat and Dvir, 1954, pp. 91–314.

Mahanaim: Massekhet le-Hayale Tzahal le-Hag ha-Hanukkah. Israel: Tzava Haganah le-Yisrael, no. 63, 1962.

Markowitz, S. H. *Leading a Jewish Life in the Modern World*. Rev. ed. New York: Union of American Hebrew Congregations, 1958, pp. 199–224, 300–303.

443 · Bibliography

Menes, Abraham. *Shabes un Yom-Tov: Sotziale Gerechtikeit, Heshbon Hanefesh, Geula, inem Gang fun Yidishn Yar.* Tel Aviv: Hamenorah, 1973, pp. 143–70.
Mervis, Leonard J. *We Celebrate Chanuka.* New York: Union of American Hebrew Congregations, 1952.
Persky, Daniel. *Matamim le-Hag.* New York: Pardes, 1939, pp. 73–122.
Picker, Shlomoh. *Shabbat u-Moadim ba-Aretz.* Tel Aviv: M. Newman, 1968, pp. 307–25.
Pougatch, I., ed. *Hanoucca: Historique Célébration à Travers les Âges.* Paris: Editions O.P.E.J., 1950.
Rabinowitz, Esther, ed. *Haggim u-Moadim be-Hinukh: Le-Mehankhim be-Gan uve-Kitot ha-Nemukhot.* Tel Aviv: Urim, 1954, pp. 122–55, 365–69.
Rivkin, B. *Yidishe Yom-Tovim.* New York: Morris S. Sklarsky, 1950, pp. 67–85.
Rosenblum, William F., and Rosenblum, Robert J. *Eight Lights: The Story of Chanukah.* Illustrated by Shraga Weil. Garden City, N.Y.: Doubleday & Co., 1967.
Roth, Cecil, ed. *The Standard Jewish Encyclopedia.* Garden City, N.Y.: Doubleday & Co., 1959, cols. 839–40, 854–57, 1077, 1240–41.
Schauss, Hayyim. *Dos Yom-Tov Buch.* New York: author, 1933, pp. 163–89.
————. *The Jewish Festivals from Their Beginnings to Our Own Day.* Translated by Samuel Jaffe. Cincinnati: Union of American Hebrew Congregations, 1938, pp. 208–36.
Seidman, Hillel. *The Glory of the Jewish Holidays.* Edited by Moses Zalesky. New York: Shengold Publishers, 1969, pp. 124–32.
Sidrat Moadim: Hanukkah. Jerusalem: Ministry of Education and Culture, Torah Culture Department, 1966.
Solis-Cohen, Emily, Jr., ed. *Hanukkah: The Feast of Lights.* Philadelphia: Jewish Publication Society of America, 1937.
Soltes, Mordecai. *The Jewish Holidays: A Guide to Their Origin, Significance and Observance.* Rev. ed. New York: National Jewish Welfare Board, 1968, pp. 9–11, 28–30.
The Story of Chanuko: As Told in the First Book of Maccabees, in the Talmud & in the Liturgy. Illustrated by Nelson Ronsheim. Cincinnati: Union of American Hebrew Congregations, 1950.
Thieberger, Friedrich, ed. *Jüdisches Fest: Jüdischer Brauch: Ein Sammelwerk.* Berlin: Jüdischer Verlag, 1936, pp. 343–63.
Tverski, Shimon, ed. *Maoz: Yalkut Hanukkah.* Israel: Tzava Haganah le-Yisrael, 1951.
Tzur, Mikhael; Kuvarsky, Hayyim; and Rakovsky, Eliyahu, eds. *Hanukkah: Yalkut le-Hag ha-Urim.* Israel: Tzava Haganah le-Yisrael, (1948 ?).
Unger, Menashe. *Hasidus un Yom-Tov.* New York: Farlag Hasidus, 1958, pp. 185–205.
The Universal Jewish Encyclopedia. 10 vols. New York: Ktav Publishing House, 1968. See Al Hanissim, Antiochus, Hanukkah, Hasmoneans, Maccabees.
Unterman, Isaac. *The Jewish Holidays.* 2d ed. New York: Bloch Publishing Co., 1950, pp. 103–37.
Wahrmann, Nahum. *Hagge Yisrael u-Moadav: Minhagehem ve-Semalehem.* Jerusalem: Ahiasaf, 1959, pp. 91–105.
————, ed. *Moadim: Pirke Halakhah, Aggadah, ve-Tefillah le-Khol Moade ha-*

Shanah. Jerusalem: Kiryat Sefer, 1957, pp. 71–85, 183–85, 216–18, 236–37.

Zobel, Moritz. *Das Jahr des Juden in Brauch und Liturgie.* Berlin: Schocken Verlag, 1936, pp. 131–39.

Hanukkah and Its History

Bentwich, Norman. *Hellenism.* Philadelphia: Jewish Publication Society of America, 1919.

Bevan, E. R. "Hellenistic Judaism." *The Legacy of Israel.* Edited by E. R. Bevan and C. Singer. Oxford: Clarendon Press, 1927, pp. 29–67.

Bickerman, Elias. *From Ezra to the Last of the Maccabees: Foundations of Post-Biblical Judaism.* New York: Schocken Books, 1962.

———. "The Maccabean Uprising: An Interpretation." *The Jewish Expression.* Edited by Judah Goldin. New York: Bantam Books, 1970, pp. 66–86.

Brodsky, Alyn. *The Kings Depart.* New York: Harper & Row, 1974.

Conder, Claude Reignier. *Judas Maccabaeus and the Jewish War of Independence.* New York: G. P. Putnam's Sons, 1889.

Ehrmann, Eliezer L. *Readings in Jewish History: Unit on the Conflict with Hellenism.* Chicago: Board of Jewish Education, 1944.

Goldberg, Israel, and Benderly, Samson. *An Outline of Jewish Knowledge.* New York: Bureau of Jewish Education, 1931, 3:249–90, 325–67.

Graetz, Heinrich. *History of the Jews.* Philadelphia: Jewish Publication Society of America, 1891, 1:420–502.

Grayzel, Solomon. *A History of the Jews: From the Babylonian Exile to the End of World War II.* Philadelphia: Jewish Publication Society of America, 1947, pp. 52–68.

Hengel, Martin. *Judaism and Hellenism.* 2 vols. Philadelphia: Fortress Press, 1974.

Lieberman, Saul. *Hellenism in Jewish Palestine: Studies in the Literary Transmission, Beliefs and Manners of Palestine in the I Century B.C.E.—IV Century C.E.* New York: Jewish Theological Seminary of America, 1950.

Marcus, Ralph. "The Hellenistic Age." In *Great Ages and Ideas of the Jewish People.* Edited by Leo W. Schwarz. New York: Random House, 1956, pp. 93–139.

Mindlin, Valerie, and Cornfeld, Gaalyahu. *The Epic of the Maccabees.* New York: Macmillan Co., 1962.

Morgenstern, Julian. "The Chanukkah Festival and the Calendar of Ancient Israel." *Hebrew Union College Annual* 20 (1947): 1–136; 21 (1948): 365–496.

Orlinsky, Harry M. "The Story of Hanukkah—What Really Happened." *Essays in Biblical Culture and Bible Translation.* New York: Ktav Publishing House, 1974, pp. 239–44.

Pearlman, Moshe. *The Maccabees.* Jerusalem: Weidenfeld and Nicolson, 1973.

Rankin, Oliver Shaw. "The Festival of Hanukkah." In *The Labyrinth.* Edited by S. H. Hooke. London: 1935, pp. 159–209.

———. *The Origins of the Festival of Hanukkah: The Jewish New-Age Festival.* Edinburgh: T. & T. Clark, 1930.

Schalit, Abraham, ed. *The Hellenistic Age*. Vol. 6 of *World History of the Jewish People*. New Brunswick: Rutgers University Press, 1972.

Stern, Menahem. "The Hasmonean Revolt and Its Place in the History of Jewish Society and Religion." In *Jewish Society Through the Ages*. Edited by H. H. Ben-Sasson and S. Ettinger. New York: Schocken Books, 1971, pp. 92–106.

Tcherikover, Victor. *Hellenistic Civilization and the Jews*. Translated by S. Applebaum. Philadelphia: Jewish Publication Society of America, 1959.

Zeitlin, Solomon. "Hanukkah." *Jewish Quarterly Review* 29, no. 1 (1938): 1–36.

———. *The History of the Second Jewish Commonwealth*. Philadelphia: Dropsie College, 1933.

———. *The Rise and Fall of the Judaean State*. Philadelphia: Jewish Publication Society of America, 1962, 1:37–117.

Postbiblical Writings

The Book of Maccabees. Translated by Sidney Tedesche. Illustrated by Jacob Shacham. Hartford: Prayer Book Press, n.d.

The Books of the Maccabees. London: East and West Library, 1949.

Charles, R. H., ed. *Apocrypha and Pseudepigrapha of the Old Testament*. Oxford: Clarendon Press, 1913.

Cohen, Gershon. "*Maaseh Hannah ve-Shivat Baneha be-Sifrut ha-Ivrit.*" In *Sefer ha-Yovel Likhvod Mordecai Menahem Kaplan Limlot Lo Shivim Shanah*. New York: Jewish Theological Seminary of America, 1953, pp. 109–22.

The First Book of Maccabees. Commentary by H. A. Fischel. New York: Schocken Books, 1948.

Goodspeed, Edgar J. *The Apocrypha: An American Translation*. Chicago: University of Chicago Press, 1938.

Hadas, Moses, ed. and trans. *The Third and Fourth Books of Maccabees*. New York: Harper & Brothers for Dropsie College for Hebrew and Cognate Learning, 1953.

Zeitlin, Solomon, ed. *The Book of Judith*. Translated by Morton S. Enslin. Leiden: E. J. Brill for Dropsie University, 1972.

———. *The First Book of Maccabees*. Translated by Sidney Tedesche. New York: Harper & Brothers for Dropsie College for Hebrew and Cognate Learning, 1950.

———. *The Second Book of Maccabees*. Translated by Sidney Tedesche. New York: Harper & Brothers for Dropsie College for Hebrew and Cognate Learning, 1954.

Jewish Law

The Code of Maimonides. Book 3, *The Book of Seasons*. Translated by Solomon Gandz and Hyman Klein. New Haven: Yale University Press, 1961, pp. 463–71.

Galis, Yaakov. *Minhage Eretz Yisrael*. Jerusalem: Mosad Harav Kook, 1968, pp. 203–6.

Ganzfried, Solomon. *Code of Jewish Law*. Translated by Hyman E. Goldin. New York: Hebrew Publishing Co., 1927, 3: 108–14.

Karo, Joseph. *Shulhan Arukh, Orah Hayyim: "Hilkhot Hanukkah,"* 670–85.

Laws and Customs of Israel. Translated by Gerald Friedlander. London: Shapiro, Vallentine and Co., 1934, 3: 389–94.

Moses Ben Maimon. *"Sefer Zemanim." Mishneh Torah*. Amsterdam, 1702.

Sperling, Abraham Isaac. *Reasons for Jewish Customs and Traditions*. Translated by Abraham Matts. New York: Bloch Publishing Co., 1968, pp. 258–62.

_____. *Sefer Taame ha-Minhagim u-Mekore ha-Dinim*. Jerusalem: Eshkol, 1961, pp. 363–70.

Zevin, Shlomoh Yosef. *Ha-Moadim be-Halakhah*. Tel Aviv: Betan Hasefer, 1949, pp. 156–81.

Hanukkah in Art

Dawidowitz, David. "Menorat Hanukkah le-Merutzat ha-Dorot." *Mahanaim* 52 (1961): 94–99.

_____. "Semalim Zarim u-Muzarim be-Menorat Hanukkah." *Mahanaim* 63 (1962): 162–67.

Godwin, F. "The Judith Illustration of the *Hortus Deliciarum.*" *Gazette des Beaux-Arts* 36 (1949): 25–46.

Golnitzki, Heshil. *Be-Mahzor ha-Yamim* (Haifa: Jewish Folklore-lovers' Circle, 1963), pp. 47–51.

Gutmann, Joseph, ed. *Beauty in Holiness: Studies in Jewish Customs and Ceremonial Art* (New York: Ktav Publishing House, 1970).

Kanof, Abram. *Jewish Ceremonial Art and Religious Observances* (New York: Harry N. Abrams, n.d.), pp. 158–74.

Katz, Karl; Kahane, P. P., and Broshi, Magen. *From the Beginning: Archaeology and Art in the Israel Museum, Jerusalem* (New York: Reynal & Co., 1968), pp. 174–82.

Kayser, Stephen S., ed. *Jewish Ceremonial Art* (Philadelphia: Jewish Publication Society of America, 1955), pp. 120–38.

Landsberger, Franz. "Old Hanukkah Lamps." *Hebrew Union College Annual* (Cincinnati: 1954) 25: 347–67; reprinted in *Beauty in Holiness: Studies in Jewish Customs and Ceremonial Art*. Edited by Joseph Gutmann (New York: Ktav Publishing House, 1970), pp. 283–309.

Mayer, L. A. *Bibliography of Jewish Art*. Edited by Otto Kunz (Jerusalem: Magnes Press, The Hebrew University, 1966). See Hanukkah in index.

Narkiss, M. *Menorot ha-Hanukkah: The Hanukkah Lamp*. (Jerusalem: Bney Bezalel Publishing Co., 1939). Hebrew with English summary.

Romanoff, Paul. "Hanukkah and the Menorah." In *Hanukkah: The Feast of Lights*. Edited by Emily Solis-Cohen, Jr. (Philadelphia: Jewish Publication Society of America, 1931), pp. 83–92.

Roth, Cecil. "The Cardinals' Hanukkah Lamps." *The Jewish Monthly* 3 (1949), Supplement, i–iv.

Shahar, Yeshayahu. *Osef Feuchtwanger: Mesoret ve-Omanut Yehudit* (Jerusalem: Israel Museum, 1971), pp. 133–49.

Stern, Henri. "Quelques problèmes d'iconographie paléochrétienne et juive." *Cahiers Archéologiques* 12 (1962): 99–113.

Strauss, H. "Goralah ve-Tzuratah Shel Menorat ha-Hashmonaim." *Eretz-Yisrael: Mehkarim be-Yediot ha-Aretz ve-Atikotehah: Sefer Shishi* (Jerusalem: Israel Exploration Society and Bezalel National Museum, 1960), pp. 122–29.

Wischnitzer, Rachel. "Origine de la lampe de Hanouka." *Revue des Études Juives* 89 (1930): 135–46.

Hanukkah in the Novel and Short Story

A. L. O. E. *Hebrew Heroes: A Tale Founded on Jewish History*. London: T. Nelson and Sons, 1869.

Church, Alfred J., and Seeley, Richmond. *The Hammer: A Story of the Maccabean Times*. London: Seeley and Co., 1890.

Fast, Howard. *My Glorious Brothers*. Boston: Little, Brown and Co., 1948.

Fineman, Irving. "How Many Angels. . . ." In *The Menorah Treasury: Harvest of Half a Century*. Edited by Leo W. Schwarz. Philadelphia: Jewish Publication Society of America, 1964, pp. 385–94; also in *A Golden Treasury of Jewish Literature*. Edited by Leo W. Schwarz. New York: Farrar & Rinehart, 1937, pp. 12–20.

Peretz, Isaac Loeb. "The Chanukah Light." *Stories and Pictures*. Translated by Helena Frank. Philadelphia: Jewish Publication Society of America, 1906, pp. 391–98.

———. "Chanukah Lights." *The Book of Fire*. Translated by Joseph Leftwich. New York: Thomas Yoseloff, [1959], pp. 431–32.

———. "The Little Hanukkah Lamp." Translated by Nathan Ausubel. In *A Treasury of Jewish Humor*. Edited by Nathan Ausubel. Garden City, N.Y.: Doubleday & Co., 1951, pp. 73–77.

Schott, Ann. "The Little Boy Who Didn't Believe." In *The Best of Ten Years in "The Jewish Digest."* Edited by Bernard Postal and David H. White. Houston: D.H. White & Co., 1965, pp. 365–69.

Sholom Aleichem. "The Spinning Top." *Jewish Children*. Translated by Hannah Berman. New York: Bloch Publishing Co., 1937, pp. 153–77.

———. "Cnards," "Hanukkah Money." *The Old Country*. Translated by Julius and Frances Butwin. New York: Crown Publishers, 1946, pp. 412–28, 183–200; *Selected Stories of Sholom Aleichem*. Introduction by Alfred Kazin. New York: Modern Library, 1956, pp. 410–25, 196–212.

———. "Hanukkah Money." Translated by Leonard Wolf. In *Yiddish Stories: Old and New*. Edited by Irving Howe and Eliezer Greenberg. New York: Holiday House, 1974, pp. 11–17.

Wise, Isaac Mayer. *The First of the Maccabees: A Historical Novel*. Cincinnati: Bloch Publishing and Printing Co., n.d.

Children's Stories and Descriptions of Hanukkah

Abramson, Lillian. *Hanukkah ABC*. Illustrated by Gabe Josephson. New York: Shulsinger Brothers, 1968.

_____. "Hanukkah in Old Venice." *Join Us for the Holidays*. Illustrated by Jessie B. Robinson. New York: National Women's League of the United Synagogue of America, 1958, pp. 23–24.

Bami. "The Great Hanukkah Strike." In *More World Over Stories: An Illustrated Anthology for Jewish Youth*. Edited by Ezekiel Schloss and Morris Epstein. New York: Bloch Publishing Co., 1968, pp. 65–69.

Bearman, Jane. *Happy Chanuko*. Cincinnati: Union of American Hebrew Congregations, 1943.

Ben-Asher, Shlomo, ed., *The Maccabean Times: A Freedom Newspaper*. New York: Ktav Publishing House, 1974.

Bial, Morrison David. *The Hanukkah Story*. Illustrated by Stephen Kraft. New York: Behrman House, 1952.

Bloch, Charles E. *The First Hanukah*. Illustrated by Aralee. New York: Bloch Publishing Co., 1957.

Bronstein, Charlotte. *Tales of the Jewish Holidays as Told by the Light of the Moon*. Illustrated by Art Seiden. New York: Behrman House, 1959, pp. 20–25.

Cedarbaum, Sophia N. *Chanuko*. Illustrated by Clare and John Ross. New York: Union of American Hebrew Congregations, 1960.

Chanover, Hyman, and Chanover, Alice. *Happy Hanukah Everybody*. Illustrated by Maurice Sendak. New York: United Synagogue Commission on Jewish Education, 1954.

Chaver Paver. "The Pan of Oil." Translated by Benjamin Efron. In *Yiddish Stories for Young People*. Edited by Itche Goldberg. Illustrated by Herb Kruckman. New York: Kinderbuch Publishers, 1966, pp. 137–41.

Chiel, Kinneret. *The Complete Book of Hanukkah*. Illustrated by Arnold Lobel. New York: Friendly House, 1959.

Chomsky, William, ed. *Haggenu u-Moadenu*. New York: Histadruth Ivrith, 1945, pp. 185–214.

Cohen, Lenore. *Came Liberty beyond Our Hope: A Story of Hanukkah*. Illustrated by Georges Gaal. Los Angeles: Ward Ritchie Press, 1963.

Cone, Molly. *Stories of Jewish Symbols*. Illustrated by Siegmund Forst. New York: Bloch Publishing Co., 1963, pp. 58–64.

Covich, Edith S. *The Jewish Child Every Day*. Illustrated by Mary Ida Jones. New York: Union of American Hebrew Congregations, 1955, pp. 22–29.

Doniach, A. S. "What the Candles Say: A Hanucah Vision." In *Apples & Honey: A Gift-Book for Jewish Boys and Girls*. Edited by Nina Salaman. New York: Bernard G. Richards Co., 1927, pp. 98–103.

Edidin, Ben M. *Jewish Holidays and Festivals*. Illustrated by Kyra Markham. New York: Hebrew Publishing Co., 1940, pp. 87–103.

_____. *Jewish Life and Customs: Unit Four: Hanukkah*. New York: Jewish Education Committee, 1942.

Einhorn, David. "The Miracle of the Chanukah Candles." *The Seventh Candle and Other Folk Tales of Eastern Europe*. Translated by Gertrude Pashin. Illustrated by Ezekiel Schloss. New York: Ktav Publishing House, 1968, pp. 50–52.

Epstein, Morris. *All about Jewish Holidays and Customs*. Rev. ed. Illustrated by Arnold Lobel. New York: Ktav Publishing House, 1970, pp. 34–41.
————. "Eight Little Candles." *Tell Me about God and Prayer*. Illustrated by Lawrence Dresser. New York: Ktav Publishing House, 1953, pp. 49–52.
————. "The Old Dreidel." *My Holiday Story Book*. Illustrated by Arnold Lobel. New York: Ktav Publishing House, 1958, pp. 20–24.
————. *A Pictorial Treasury of Jewish Holidays and Customs*. New York: Ktav Publishing House, 1959, pp. 48–61.
Fine, Helen. "Plans for Chanuko," "The First Candle," "Latkes! Latkes! Latkes." *G'dee*. Illustrated by Hal Just. New York: Union of American Hebrew Congregations, 1958, pp. 54–79.
Fishko, B. "These Candles We Light. . . ." Translated by Deborah Pessin. In *Jewish Life and Customs: Unit Four: Hanukkah*. Edited by Ben M. Edidin. New York: Jewish Education Committee, 1942, pp. 17–19.
Freehof, Lillian S. *Candle Light Stories: Eight Little Tales for Chanuko*. Illustrated by Jane Bearman. New York: Bloch Publishing Co., 1951.
————. *The Carrot Candle*. Illustrated by Hal Just. New York: Union of American Hebrew Congregations, 1954.
————. *The Grumpy Television*. Illustrated by Hal Bachemin. New York: Union of American Hebrew Congregations, 1951.
————. *The Littlest Chime*. Illustrated by Hal Bachemin. New York: Union of American Hebrew Congregations, 1950.
————. *The Lost Menorah*. Illustrated by Hal Bachemin. New York: Union of American Hebrew Congregations, 1951.
————. *The Runaway Candle*. Illustrated by Hal Bachemin. New York: Union of American Hebrew Congregations, 1950.
Gaer, Joseph. "Seven Sacrifices," "Judas the Maccabee," "A Knave's End." *The Unconquered: Adapted Folklore Legends*. Illustrated by Aaron J. Goodman. Cincinnati: Sinai Press, 1932, pp. 135–66.
Gamoran, Mamie G. *Days and Ways: The Story of Jewish Holidays and Customs*. Illustrated by Bernard Segal. Cincinnati: Union of American Hebrew Congregations, 1941, pp. 69–85.
————. "A Different Chanuko," "A Night to Remember." *Hillel's Calendar*. Illustrated by Ida Libby Dengrove. New York: Union of American Hebrew Congregations, 1960, pp. 76–86.
————. *Hillel's Happy Holidays*. Illustrated by Temima N. Gezari. Cincinnati: Union of American Hebrew Congregations, 1939, pp. 87–104.
————. *The New Jewish History: Book One: From Abraham to the Maccabees*. Illustrated by Bruno Frost. New York: Union of American Hebrew Congregations, 1953, pp. 217–40.
Garvey, Robert. "The Amazing Adventures of Solly." *Happy Holiday!* Illustrated by Ezekiel Schloss. New York: Ktav Publishing House, 1953, pp. 29–38.
————. "Eleazar the Maccabee." In *The New World Over Story Book: An Illustrated Anthology for Jewish Youth*. Edited by Ezekiel Schloss and Morris Epstein. New York: Bloch Publishing Co., 1968, pp. 46–51.
————. *A First Chanukah Word Book*. Illustrated by Ezekiel Schloss. New York: Ktav Publishing House, 1952.
————. "The Freedom Puppet." *In The World Over Story Book: An Illustrated Anthology for Jewish Youth*. Edited by Norton Belth. New York: Bloch Publishing Co., 1952, pp. 267–72.

————. *Holidays Are Nice: Around the Year with the Jewish Child*. Illustrated by Ezekiel Schloss and Arnold Lobel. New York: Ktav Publishing House, 1960, pp. 19–28.

Gaster, Moses. *The Story of Chanucah*. London: M. L. Cailingold, 1939.

Gersh, Harry, et al. *When a Jew Celebrates*. Illustrated by Erika Weihs. New York: Behrman House, 1971, pp. 171–81.

Gold, Doris B. "Uncle Ed, Chanukah 'Inventor.' " *Stories for Jewish Juniors*. Illustrated by Irene M. Burstein. New York: Jonathan David, 1967, pp. 150–54.

Gold, Sharlya. *The Potter's Four Sons*. Illustrated by Jules Maidoff. Garden City, N. Y.: Doubleday & Co. 1970.

Goldberg, David. *Holidays for American Judaism*. Explanatory notes by Samuel Halevi Baron. Illustrated by Patricia Passloff. New York: Bookman Associates, 1954, pp. 146–56.

Goldin, Hyman E. *Holiday Tales: Jewish Holidays and Their Legends*. New York: Hebrew Publishing Co., 1929, pp. 167–81.

Goldman, Edith B. "A New Kind of Draydel." In *A Handbook for the Jewish Family: Understanding and Enjoying the Sabbath and Festivals*. By Alex J. Goldman. New York: Bloch Publishing Co., 1958, pp. 117–20.

Golomb, Morris. *Know Your Festivals and Enjoy Them: The How and Why of the Jewish Festivals*. New York: Shengold Publishers, 1973, pp. 67–80.

Golub, Rose W. "The Dreidel That Ran Away," "Fighting the Elephants." *Down Holiday Lane*. Illustrated by Louis Kabrin. Cincinnati: Union of American Hebrew Congregations, 1947, pp. 69–84.

Grand, Tamar. *Chanukah Make Believe*. Illustrated by Irv Sher. New York: Ktav Publishing House, 1961.

Halpern, Joseph. "A Syrian Diary." *Storytime: A Jewish Children's Story-Book*. By Arthur Saul Super and Joseph Halpern. London: Edward Goldston, 1946, pp. 55–60.

Ish-Kishor, Judith. "Banner of Judah." In *The World Over Story Book: An Illustrated Anthology for Jewish Youth*. Edited by Norton Belth. New York: Bloch Publishing Co., 1952, pp. 33–68.

————. "Catching Up." *Holiday Storybook*. Compiled by the Child Study Association of America. Illustrated by Phoebe Erickson. New York: Thomas Y. Crowell Co., 1952, pp. 315–28.

Ish-Kishor, Sulamith. *Pathways through the Jewish Holidays*. Edited by Benjamin Efron. New York: Ktav Publishing House, 1967, pp. 37–52.

Jaffe, Leonard. "Bee-utiful Candles." *The Pitzel Holiday Book*. Illustrated by Bill Giacalone. New York: Ktav Publishing House, 1962, pp. 7–18.

————. *A Pitzel Chanukah*. Illustrated by Bill Giacalone. New York: Ktav Publishing House, 1962.

Kipnis, Levin. "The Little Jug of Oil," "The War between Light and Darkness," "The Parade of the Flames." *My Holidays: Holiday Stories for Children*. Translated by Israel M. Goodelman. Illustrated by Isa. Tel Aviv: N. Tversky, 1961, pp. 37–53.

————. "Matti Lights the Menorah." Translated by Deborah Pessin. In *Jewish Life and Customs: Unit Four: Hanukkah*. Edited by Ben M. Edidin. New York: Jewish Education Committee, 1942, pp. 14–16.

————, and Tchernowitz, Yemima. "Grandfather Tells a Story." *Gan-Gani:*

Let Us Play in Israel. Translated by Leslie Daiken. Illustrated by Isa Hershkovitz. Tel Aviv: N. Tversky Publishing House, 1957, pp. 43–46.

Klaperman, Gilbert, and Klaperman, Libby M. *The Story of the Jewish People*. New York: Behrman House, 1957, 2: 61–75.

Klaperman, Libby M. *The Dreidel Who Wouldn't Spin*. Illustrated by Laszlo Matulay. New York: Behrman House, 1950.

_____. *The Five Brothers Maccabee: A Novel.* New York: Sabra Books, 1969.

Kolatch, Alfred J. *Chanukah Gelt Storybook*. Illustrated by Betty Hebard. New York: Jonathan David, 1955.

Kranzler, Gershon. "The Missing Chanukah Light," "After Chanukah." *Jewish Youth Companion*. Brooklyn, N. Y.: Merkos L'Inyonei Chinuch, 1957, pp. 94–99, 100–102.

Kripke, Dorothy K. *Let's Talk about the Jewish Holidays*. Illustrated by Naama Kitov. New York: Jonathan David, 1970, pp. 19–22.

_____. "The World Gets a Gift." *Debbie in Dreamland: Her Holiday Adventures*. Illustrated by Bill Giacalone. New York: National Women's League of the United Synagogue of America, 1960, pp. 27–30.

Learsi, Rufus. "Scars of Battle," "Severed Menorah." *Kasriel the Watchman and Other Stories*. Philadelphia: Jewish Publication Society of America, 1936, pp. 258–66, 296–311.

_____. "Shimmele Would a Hero Be." *Shimmele and His Friends*. New York: Behrman House, 1940, pp. 21–42.

Levinger, Elma Ehrlich. "Hannah, the Mother of the Seven Martyrs." *Great Jewish Women*. New York: Behrman's Jewish Book House, 1940, pp. 75–78.

_____. "In the Court of Antiochus," "The Heathen," "The Cruse of Oil," "When the Lights Burned Low." *Tales Old and New*. New York: Bloch Publishing Co., 1926, pp. 59–86.

_____. "The Light That Never Failed." *Jewish Holiday Stories: Modern Tales of the American Jewish Youth*. New York: Bloch Publishing Co., 1918, pp. 79–90.

_____. "The Menorah of Remembrance." *In Many Lands*. New York: Bloch Publishing Co., 1923, pp. 59–68.

_____. "The Time-Edged Sword." *The Tower of David*. New York: Bloch Publishing Co., 1924, pp. 49–56.

Lurie, Rose G. "Fight for Right." *The Great March: Post-Biblical Jewish Stories*. Illustrated by Todros Geller. New York: Union of American Hebrew Congregations, 1931, 1: 22–29.

Marenof, Martha. "A Runaway Dreidel," "A Hanukkah Gift," "Young Maccabees." *Stories Round the Year*. Illustrated by Frances H. Quint. Detroit: Dot Publications, 1967, pp. 67–82.

Margolis, Isidor, and Markowitz, Sidney L. *Jewish Holidays and Festivals*. Illustrated by John Teppich. New York: Citadel Press, 1962, pp. 53–61.

Maximon, Saadyah. *The Book of Hanukkah*. Illustrated by Siegmund Forst. New York: Shulsinger Brothers, 1958.

Mazer, Sonia. *Yossele's Holiday and the Brave Maccabees*. Illustrated by author. New York: Behrman's Jewish Book House, 1939.

Mikhal, B., ed. *Haggim u-Moadim le-Yisrael: Aggadot Shirim ve-Sippurim*. Tel Aviv: M. Biram, 1954, pp. 105–17.

Mindel, Nissan. *Complete Story of Chanukah*. Brooklyn, N. Y.: Merkos L'Inyonei Chinuch, 1965.

Morrow, Betty. *A Great Miracle: The Story of Hanukkah*. Illustrated by Howard Simon. Irvington-on-Hudson, N.Y.: Harvey House, 1968.

Peretz, I. L. "The Little Chanukah Lamp." In *Yiddish Stories for Young People*. Edited by Itche Goldberg. Illustrated by Herb Kruckman. New York: Kinderbuch Publishers, 1966, pp. 142–48.

Pessin, Deborah. *The Jewish People*. Illustrated by Ruth Levin. New York: United Synagogue Commission on Jewish Education, 1952, 2:74–88.

_____. "The Story of Hanukkah." In *Jewish Life and Customs: Unit Four: Hanukkah*. Edited by Ben M. Edidin. New York: Jewish Education Committee, 1942, pp. 1–8.

Ross, Sharon L. *The Dreidel Hero and How He Earned His Letters*. Illustrated by author. New York: Bloch Publishing Co., 1952.

Samuels, Ruth. *The Gelt That Grew* and *The Singing Shammos*. Illustrated by Ezekiel Schloss. New York: Ktav Publishing House, 1961.

_____. *The Happy Draydel*. Illustrated by Ezekiel Schloss. New York: Ktav Publishing House, 1960.

Sanders, James. *The Glory of Chanukah*. Illustrated by Lil Goldstein. New York: Jonathan David, 1968.

Scharfstein, Bernard, ed. *Chanukah Fun and Story Book*. Illustrated by Lili Cassel. New York: Ktav Publishing House, 1952.

Scharfstein, Edyth, and Scharfstein, Sol. *The Book of Chanukah*. Illustrated by Siegmund Forst. New York: Ktav Publishing House, 1950.

_____. *Chanukah Surprise!* Illustrated by Ezekiel Schloss and Cyla London. New York: Ktav Publishing House, 1958.

_____. *Chanukah Treasure Chest*. Illustrated by Ezekiel Schloss and Cyla London. New York: Ktav Publishing House, 1958.

Scharfstein, Sol. *Draydel Draydel Draydel*. Illustrated by Bill Giacalone. New York: Ktav Publishing House, 1969.

_____. *The Picture Story of Hanukkah*. Illustrated by Arie Haas. New York: Ktav Publishing House, 1974.

Silberman, Althea O. "*Hazak Ve-ematz*—Be Strong and of Good Courage." *Habibi's Adventures in the Land of Israel*. Illustrated by Jessie B. Robinson. New York: Bloch Publishing Co., 1951, pp. 53–68.

_____. "How Yow Got into Trouble Just before Hanukkah," "Habibi and Yow Have a Hanukkah Party." *Habibi and Yow: A Little Boy and His Dog*. Illustrated by Jessie B. Robinson. New York: Bloch Publishing Co., 1946, pp. 39–49.

Simon, Norma. *Hanukah in My House*. Illustrated by Ayala Gordon. New York: United Synagogue Commission of Jewish Education, 1960.

_____. *Hanukkah*. Illustrated by Symeon Shimin. New York: Thomas Y. Crowell Co., 1966.

Simon, Shirley. "The Lost Hanukah Top." In *Once upon a Jewish Holiday*. By Bea Stadtler. Illustrated by Bill Giacalone. New York: Ktav Publishing House, 1965, pp. 48–53.

Singer, Isaac Bashevis. "Grandmother's Tale," "The Devil's Trick," "Zlateh the Goat." *Zlateh the Goat and Other Stories*. Translated by author and Elizabeth Shub. Illustrated by Maurice Sendak. New York: Harper & Row, 1966, pp. 21–23, 71–90.

Smith, Harold P. *A Treasure Hunt in Judaism*. New York: Hebrew Publishing Co., 1950, pp. 91–98.

Sokolow, Helena. "Festival of the Maccabees." *Bible Rhapsodies*. Translated by E. W. Shanahan. Tel Aviv: Massada, 1956, pp. 43–48.

Sol, Robert. *All about Chanukah*. Illustrated by Gabe Josephson. New York: Ktav Publishing House, 1954.

_____. *Chanukah Is Coming* and *Chanukah Is Fun*. Illustrated by Gabe Josephson. New York: Ktav Publishing House, 1957.

_____. *Chanukah Is Here*. Illustrated by Gabe Josephson. New York: Ktav Publishing House, 1953.

_____. *The First Book of Chanukah*. Illustrated by Laszlo Matulay. New York: Ktav Publishing House, 1956.

Solis-Cohen, Emily, Jr. "Hanukah Memories," "The Sacrifice at Modin." *David the Giant Killer and Other Tales of Grandma Lopez*. Illustrated by Alfred Feinberg. Philadelphia: Jewish Publication Society of America, 1908, pp. 43–47, 77–90.

_____. "Hanukkah at Valley Forge." In *Hanukkah: The Feast of Lights*. Edited by Emily Solis-Cohen, Jr. Philadelphia: Jewish Publication Society of America, 1965, pp. 329–34.

Spiro, Saul S., and Spiro, Rena M. *The Joy of Jewish Living: Jewish Holidays and Practices at Home and in the Synagogue*. Cleveland: Bureau of Jewish Education, 1965, pp. 93–101.

Steinberg, Judah. "The Magic Top." *The Breakfast of the Birds and Other Stories*. Translated by Emily Solis-Cohen, Jr. Philadelphia: Jewish Publication Society of America, 1917, pp. 42–50.

Taylor, Sydney. "Festival of Lights." *More All-of-a-kind Family*. Illustrated by Mary Stevens. Chicago: Wilcox and Follett, 1954, pp. 55–71.

Teitelbaum, Edith. *Judah and the Brave Maccabees*. New York: Union of American Hebrew Congregations, 1952.

Trager, Hannah. "The Chanuka." *Festival Stories of Child Life in a Jewish Colony in Palestine*. New York: E. P. Dutton & Co., 1920, pp. 149–65.

Vered, Ben. *Why Is Hanukkah?* Illustrated by Siegmund Forst. New York: Shulsinger Brothers, 1961.

Weilerstein, Sadie Rose. "The Chanukah Lights." *What Danny Did: Stories for the Wee Jewish Child*. Illustrated by Jessie B. Robinson. New York: Bloch Publishing Co., 1944, pp. 55–57.

_____. "The Dolls' Hanukkah." *What the Moon Brought*. Illustrated by Mathilda Keller. Philadelphia: Jewish Publication Society of America, 1942, pp. 68–75.

_____. "K'tonton Takes a Ride on a Runaway Trendel." *The Adventures of K'tonton: A Little Jewish Tom Thumb*. Illustrated by Jeannette Berkowitz. New York: National Women's League of the United Synagogue, 1935, pp. 27–31.

_____. "Ruth Shines the Menorah," "How Ruth Counted the Hanukkah Candles," "How Ruth Went Out at Night—on Hanukkah," "A Hanukkah Story," "The Ever-Burning Light That Went Out and Was Lit Again." In *Hanukkah: The Feast of Lights*. Edited by Emily Solis-Cohen, Jr. Philadelphia: Jewish Publication Society of America, 1965, pp. 314–15, 317, 318–22, 324–28.

Welcher, Rosalind. *The Magic Top*. Illustrated by author. New York: Panda Prints, 1965.

Wengrov, Charles. *Hanukkah in Song and Story*. Illustrated by Emanuel
    Schary. Music edited by Samuel Bugatch. New York: Shulsinger
    Brothers, 1960.
Ya'akov. "A Menorah in Tel Aviv." In *The New World Over Story Book: An
    Illustrated Anthology for Jewish Youth*. Edited by Ezekiel Schloss and
    Morris Epstein. New York: Bloch Publishing Co., 1968, pp. 51–57.
Zeligs, Dorothy F. *The Story of Jewish Holidays and Customs for Young People*.
    Illustrated by Emery I. Gondor. New York: Bloch Publishing Co.,
    1942, pp. 95–109.

Activity Books and Related Materials

Abramson, Lillian S., and Leiderman, Lillian T. *Jewish Holiday Party Book: A
    Practical Guide to Parties Planned for Children Ages 5 to 12*. New York:
    Bloch Publishing Co., 1966, pp. 29–36.
Beckerman, Solomon, ed. *Teaching Hanukkah: Resource and Enrichment Materials*. Los Angeles: Bureau of Jewish Education, 1974.
Brevis, Anne Bear, ed. *"Judaism in-the-Home" Project: Hanukkah*. New York:
    National Women's League of the United Synagogue of America,
    1950.
Brody, Roxane, ed. *United Synagogue Program Notebook: Hanukkah*. New York:
    United Synagogue of America, 1957.
Campeas, Hyman. *Workbook: All about Jewish Holidays and Customs*. New York:
    Ktav Publishing House, 1959, pp. 29–34.
Carlebach, Esther. *A Chanukah Manual for Kindergarten and Primary Grades*.
    Illustrated by Hy Gershon. New York: Torah Umesorah, 1948.
Edidin, Ben M., ed. *Jewish Child Home Library: Chanukah*. Chicago: Board of
    Jewish Education, n.d.
Eisenberg, Azriel, and Robinson, Jessie B. *My Jewish Holidays*. New York:
    United Synagogue Commission of Jewish Education, 1958,
    pp. 88–105.
Fine, Helen. *G'dee's Book of Holiday Fun*. Illustrated by Hal Just. New York:
    Union of American Hebrew Congregations, 1961, pp. 24–37.
Garvey, Robert. *Chanukah Activity Funbook*. Illustrated by Gabe Josephson.
    New York: Ktav Publishing House, 1954.
Golub, Rose W. *Down Holiday Lane: Teacher's Book: Projects and Programs for
    the Holidays*. New York: Union of American Hebrew Congregations, 1952, pp. 59–92.
_____. *Hillel's Happy Holidays Teacher's Book*. New York: Union of American
    Hebrew Congregations, 1944, pp. 25–37.
Goodman, Hannah Grad. *Pupils' Activity Book for Days and Ways*. New York:
    Union of American Hebrew Congregations, 1964, pp. 37–47.
Goodman, Philip, ed. *Habanoth Manual: A Guide for Jewish Girls Clubs*. New
    York: Women's Branch, Union of Orthodox Jewish Congregations, [1937], pp. 31–39.
_____. *Hanukkah: Program Material for Young Adults and Adults*. New York:
    National Jewish Welfare Board, 1948.
Grand, Tamar. *Happy Times with Hanukah Rhymes*. Illustrated by Arnold
    Lobel. New York: Ktav Publishing House, 1959.

Hanukkah Manual. New York: National Women's League of the United Synagogue of America, 1972.

Heckelman, Dvorah. *Hanukkah and the Young Child*. New York: Jewish Education Committee Press, 1969.

Kabakoff, Jacob, ed. *Hag ha-Hanukkah*. New York: Jewish Education Committee, n.d.

Kessler, Aharon, ed. *Hanukkah: A Manual for Junior Clubs*. New York: National Young Judea, 1942.

Koppman, Lionel, ed. *Hanukkah for All Ages*. New York: National Jewish Welfare Board, 1970.

Levinger, Elma Ehrlich. *Jewish Festivals in the Religious School: A Handbook for Entertainments*. Cincinnati: Union of American Hebrew Congregations, 1923, pp. 53–107, 305–49.

Lister, Louis, ed. *The Religious School Assembly Handbook*. New York: Union of American Hebrew Congregations, 1963, pp. 45–47, 59–63, 65–66, 86–87, 139–44, 153–54, 190–92.

Loewy, M., ed. *Programme Material and Suggested Activities for the Hannukah Festival*. Jerusalem: Youth and Hechalutz Department, World Zionist Organization, [1973].

Louvish, Misha, ed. *Chanukah Highlights: A Handbook for Teachers and Youth Leaders*. Jerusalem: Youth Department, Jewish National Fund, 1959.

Nadelmann, Ludwig, and Edelman, Lily. *Hanukkah: Three Programs*. Washington D.C.: B'nai B'rith Department of Adult Jewish Education, n.d.

Nulman, Louis. *What Is Chanukah? A Programmed Text*. New York: Torah Umesorah, 1962.

Perry, Mrs. M. Milton. *Hanukkah Mini-Institute*. New York: Women's League for Conservative Judaism, n.d.

Pessin, Deborah, and Gezari, Temima. *The Jewish Kindergarten: A Manual for Teachers*. Cincinnati: Union of American Hebrew Congregations, 1944, pp. 115–73.

Purdy, Susan Gold. *Jewish Holidays: Facts, Activities, and Crafts*. Philadelphia: J. B. Lippincott Co., 1969, pp. 31–39.

Sanders, James. *Fun-in-Learning about Chanukah*. Illustrated by Gabe Josephson. Middle Village, N. Y.: Jonathan David, 1972.

Schary, Dore. *Hanukkah Home Service*. New York: United Synagogue of America, 1959.

Siegel, Richard; Strassfeld, Michael; and Strassfeld, Sharon, eds. *The Jewish Catalog: A Do-It-Yourself Kit*. Philadelphia: Jewish Publication Society of America, 1973, pp. 44–48, 130–34.

Silbermintz, Joshua, ed. *Chanukah Leaders Guide*. New York: Zeirei Agudath Israel of America, 1963.

Silverstein, Ruth. *Teacher's Syllabus for the Kindergarten*. New York: Union of American Hebrew Congregations, 1960, pp. 49–64.

Stiskin, Hershel, and Magaliff, Millicent. *Chanukah: A Special Reader-Activity Book* [for retarded pupils]. New York: Board of Jewish Education, 1963.

Stolper, Pinchas, ed. *Chanukah*. New York: National Conference of Synagogue Youth, 1960.

Sussman, Samuel, and Segal, Abraham. *Fifty Assembly Programs for the Jewish*

School. New York: United Synagogue Commission on Jewish Education, 1948, pp. 53–58.

Hanukkah games, decorations, greeting cards, wrapping paper are produced by Ktav Publishing House, Shulsinger Bros., and Hebrew Publishing Co., among others.

Arts and Crafts

Berland, Helen, and Levy, Della. *Chanuko Decoration Workbook*. New York: National Federation of Temple Sisterhoods, 1957.

Chanukah Coloring Book. Illustrated by Siegmund Forst. New York: Ktav Publishing House, 1949.

Comins, Harry L., and Leaf, Reuben. *Arts-Crafts for the Jewish Club*. Cincinnati: Union of American Hebrew Congregation, 1934, pp. 29–33, 119–25, 184.

Gezari, Temima N. *Jewish Festival Crafts*. New York: National Jewish Welfare Board, 1968, pp. 14–19.

My Dreidel Coloring Book. Illustrated by Joseph Bloch. New York: Ktav Publishing House, 1955.

My First Chanukah Coloring Book. New York: Ktav Publishing House, 1960.

Robinson, Jessie B. *Holidays Are Fun*. New York: Bloch Publishing Co., 1950, pp. 27–31.

Scharfstein, Edythe, and Scharfstein, Sol. *Chanukah Paste and Play*. Illustrated by Cyla London. New York: Ktav Publishing House, 1956.

Sharon, Ruth. *Arts and Crafts the Year Round*. New York: United Synagogue Commission on Jewish Education, 1965, 1:129–75.

Dramatizations

(min.=minutes; m=male; f=female; figures in parenthesis indicate age level)

Amarant, Avraham. "For My Fighting Brothers." In Louvish, *Chanukah Highlights*, pp. 60–66. 1 act, 20 min., 6 m, 2 f, extras (10–14). An adventure of children during the Maccabean revolt.

Barzel, Istar. "A Marionette Mutiny." In Citron, *Dramatics the Year Round*, pp. 157–69. 1 act, 30 min., 11 m, 2 f, extras (9–15). Marionettes, in the absence of the marionette-maker, try to enact a Hanukkah play.

Bayer, Jerome. "Eightfold Splendor." In *Hanukkah in the Hillel Foundation*. Edited by Alfred Jospe. Washington, D.C.: B'nai B'rith Hillel Foundations, n.d., pp. 89–110. 2 acts, 40 min., 5 m, 4 f, extras (young adults and adults). A dramatic candlelighting ceremony, including a scene from Longfellow's *Judah Maccabeus*.

Becker, Charles S. *Another Year—Another Hanukah*. Cincinnati: Bureau of Jewish Education. 1 act, 30 min., 20 to 35 m and f (10–14). An amusing play in which the cast create an original Hanukkah dramatization.

_____. *Eight Candles in Search of a Shammas*. Cincinnati: Bureau of Jewish Education. 1 act, 18 min., 8 m, 8 f (10–14). A comedy skit.

_____. *The Hanukkah Story*. Cincinnati: Bureau of Jewish Education. 1 act, 30 min., 9 m, 7 f, extras (11–15). The historic struggle of the Maccabees.

_____. *Nes Gadol Haya Sham* (A Great Miracle Happened There). Cincinnati: Bureau of Jewish Education. 1 act, 25 min., 7 or more m, 3–5 f (9–13). A comedy set in an Israeli army camp.

_____. *'Twas the Night before Hanukkah*. Cincinnati: Bureau of Jewish Education. Also in Citron, *Dramatics the Year Round*, pp. 103–6. 1 act, 10 min., 4 m, 2 f, 10 m or f (7–11). Animated objects prepare to celebrate the festival.

Bial, Morrison D., and Binder, A. W. *Hanukkah of the Maccabees*. New York: Transcontinental Music Publications, 1955. 60 min., 5 m, 2 f, chorus and audience (adults). A musical narrative.

Citron, Samuel J. "The Call to Freedom: An Operetta." Music by Harry Coopersmith. In Citron, *Dramatics the Year Round*, pp. 137–57. 1 act, 30 min., 12 m, 6 f, extras (9–15). The revolt of Mattathias and his sons in Modin.

_____. "The Jug of Oil." In Citron, *Dramatics the Year Round*, pp. 97–99. 1 scene, 5 min., 3 m, extras (8–12). A young lad finds oil for the menorah at the Temple rededication.

Citron, Samuel J., ed. *Dramatics the Year Round*. New York: United Synagogue Commission on Jewish Education, 1956. Includes 10 Hanukkah plays listed separately by author in this bibliography.

Cohen, Mortimer J. *By These Lights We Walk*. New York: National Jewish Welfare Board. 1 act, 30–60 min., 8 m, 5 f, extras (adults).—A dramatic pageant depicting the spiritual lights of Judaism—the Eternal Light, Sabbath and Hanukkah candles, memorial lamp.

_____. *The Light-Bringers*. New York: National Jewish Welfare Board. 20 min., 10 m, 4 f, choral group (youth and adults). A Hanukkah candlelighting ceremony illustrating the relevance for today of the Maccabean ideals.

Cook, Ray M. *Mattathias Comes to Chelm*. New York: Union of American Hebrew Congregations. 3 acts, 50 min., 18 roles and chorus (10–14). A musical comedy.

Epstein, Marian. *Tyrants Disappearing*. New York: Union of American Hebrew Congregations. 1 act, 20 min., 9 m, 13 f (11–14). A pageant with incidental music about tyrants who oppressed the Jews throughout history.

Fast, Howard. *The Legate*. "Eternal Light" television script no. T-121. New York: Department of Radio and Television, Jewish Theological Seminary of America. 30 min. (adults). An episode from the author's novel on the Maccabeans, *My Glorious Brothers*.

Festival on Trial. New York: National Program Department, Hadassah. 1 act, 20 min., 5 m or f (adults). Hanukkah is tried in a courtroom setting.

Fine, Helen. *A Miracle for Chanuko*. Music by Moses J. Eisenberg. New York: Union of American Hebrew Congregations. 2 acts, 35 min., 16 roles (6–11). A rag doll goes to a special Hanukkah party.

Franklin, Harold. "Freedom Hall." In Citron, *Dramatics the Year Round*, pp. 118–29. 1 act, 30 min., 10 m, 7 f (9 and up). Children visit "Freedom Hall" in a museum where they see busts of freedom-fighters, including George Washington, Joan of Arc, and Judah Maccabee.

Freed, Clarence I. *The Maccabee*. New York: National Jewish Welfare Board. 1 act, 40 min., 4 m, 2 f (12–16). A fictionalized version of the Hanukkah drama.

Freehof, Lillian S. *The Chanuko Parade*. New York: Union of American Hebrew Congregations. 1 act, 15 min., 7 m, 3 f, choir (12–14). Children dream that their Hanukkah gifts come alive.

———. *The Hanukkah Mystery*. New York: National Jewish Welfare Board. 3 acts, 40 min., 8 m, 4 f (11–15). A Hanukkah menorah has the secret formula for the "oxide bomb."

Gersh, Harry. *The Top That Ran Away*. "Eternal Light" radio script no. 1031. New York: Department of Radio and Television, Jewish Theological Seminary of America. 30 min. (youth and adults). A Hanukkah fantasy about a mother who sacrifices her bread money to buy her sons a dreidel.

Haezrahi, Yehuda. *The Young Hero*. Jerusalem: Youth and Education Department, Jewish National Fund. 1 act, 30 min., 11 m, 1 f (10–15). A ten-year-old boy dreams of joining the Maccabean band.

Handel, George Frederick, composer. *Judas Maccabaeus: An Oratorio*. Words by Thomas Morell. New York: G. Schirmer, Inc. 3 parts, 90 min., 5 m, 2 f, chorus (adults). The famous oratorio.

Haniford, Beatrice G. *Alice in Chanukoland*. New York: Union of American Hebrew Congregations. 1 act, 20 min., 1 m, 2 f, 4 m or f (6–12). A parody on Lewis Carroll's *Alice in Wonderland* with songs and dances.

Hillel, Malkah. "The Festival of Heroism." In Louvish, *Chanukah Highlights*, pp. 41–52. 1 act, 25 min., 3 m or f, choir (youth and adults). A narration of Jewish heroism from the Maccabees to the establishment of the state of Israel.

Hyman, Frieda Clark. "The Little Candle That Wouldn't." In Citron, *Dramatics the Year Round*, pp. 99–103. 1 scene, 12 min., 3 m, 1 f, 10 m or f (8–14). On the last night of Hanukkah the eighth candle insists on being the *shammash*.

Kauffman, Gladys D. *The Secret Chanukah*. New York: Union of American Hebrew Congregations. 1 act, 25 min., 6 m, 5 f, extras (13–16). A family behind the iron curtain attempts to observe the festival.

Kessler, Harry. "A Modern Modin." In Citron, *Dramatics the Year Round*, pp. 130–37. 5 scenes, 20 min., 13 f (10–14). A group of young Israeli girls are attacked by another group of girls who pretend to be Syrians.

Kripke, Mrs. Myer S., and Guss, Mrs. Joseph. *Judaism Illumines the Path*. New York: Women's League for Conservative Judaism. 1 act, 10 min., 9 f (adults). A candlelighting program.

Kroeger, Cathie. *Light unto All the House*. New York: Union of American Hebrew Congregations. 1 act, 20 min., 6 m, 3 f (8–14). A "miracle of oil" occurs in the first century C.E.

Levinger, Elma Ehrlich. "The Unlighted Menorah." In Citron, *Dramatics the Year Round*, pp. 179–85. 1 act, 20 min., 3 m, 1 f (14 and up). Moses

Mendelssohn's son Abraham, who deserted Judaism, is aroused to return to his faith when he hears a Hanukkah melody.

Louvish, Misha, ed. *Chanukah Highlights: A Handbook for Teachers and Youth Leaders*. Jerusalem: Youth Department, Jewish National Fund, 1959. Includes 3 plays listed separately by author in this bibliography.

————. "Chanukah in Israel." In Louvish, *Chanukah Highlights*, pp. 67–71. 1 act, 15 min., 4 m or f (youth and adults). A narration depicting Hanukkah celebrations in Israel.

Marion, Ira. "A Light to Live By." In Citron, *Dramatics the Year Round*, pp. 172–79. 1 act, 15 min., 10 m or f (youth and adults). A prose poem for speaking chorus depicting the principles for which the Maccabees fought.

Mindel, Joseph. *The Unvanquished*. "Eternal Light" television script no. T-157. New York: Department of Radio and Television, Jewish Theological Seminary of America. 30 min. (youth and adults). A Hanukkah program featuring the martyrdom at Masada in the year 73 C.E.

Mindel, Nissan. *Candles in the Night*. Brooklyn, N. Y.: Merkos L'Inyonei Chinuch. 3 scenes, 20 min., 9 m, 1 f (9–12). Three historical episodes in rhyme.

————. *The Miracle of the Dreidel*. Brooklyn, N. Y.: Merkos L'Inyonei Chinuch. 1 act, 20 min., 10 m, 2 f, 8 extras (10–14). A humorous adventure.

Orentlicher, Mrs. William. *The Sparkling Menorah*. New York: Women's League for Conservative Judaism. 1 act, 30 min., 3 f, choral group (adults). A dramatized short story with action in silhouette form and songs.

Pinkerfeld, Anda. *Hanukkah Candles*. Translated by Alexander M. Dushkin. Music by Harry Coopersmith. Dances by Dvora Lapson. New York: Board of Jewish Education. 8 min. (7–10). Dramatized song in Hebrew and English.

Pitlik, Samuel. "At this Season." In Solis-Cohen, Jr. *Hanukkah: The Feast of Lights*, pp. 217–42. Prologue, 6 scenes and epilogue, 45 min., 12 m, 3 f, extras (children and adults). The origin of Hanukkah and its observance throughout the centuries.

Sampter, Jessie E. "Candle Drill for Hanukkah." In Solis-Cohen, Jr., *Hanukkah: The Feast of Lights*, pp. 381–88. 1 scene, 10 min., 9 f (10–13). A candlelighting ceremony with dancing.

Savin, Isadore. *The Miraculous Flame*. New York: Women's League for Conservative Judaism. 1 act, 25 min., 5 m, 1 f, extras (youth and adults). A narration of the Maccabean epic with tableaus.

Siegel, Marc. *Oil for but One Day*. "Eternal Light" television script no. T-190. New York: Department of Radio and Television, Jewish Theological Seminary of America. 30 min. (children and adults). A children's Hanukkah program of drama and song.

Soifer, Margaret K. *Into the Frying Pan*. New York: Board of Jewish Education. 1 act, 25 min., 4 m, 3 f (13 and up). A light operetta in the Gilbert and Sullivan style.

————. *Judas the Strong-Armed*. New York: Board of Jewish Education. 1 act, 20 min., 10 m, extras (11–14). A play in rhyme that retells the Maccabean epic.

———. *The Wonder Trendel*. New York: Board of Jewish Education. 1 act, 40 min., 11 m, 1 f, extras (11–14). A fantasy of modern children within the historical setting of the Maccabean War.

Solis-Cohen, Emily, Jr., ed. *Hanukkah: The Feast of Lights*. Philadelphia: Jewish Publication Society of America, 1965. Includes 4 plays listed separately by author in this bibliography.

Solis-Cohen, Emily, Jr., and Buffano, Remo. "The Valiant Maccabees." In Solis-Cohen, Jr., *Hanukkah: The Feast of Lights*, pp. 189–216. 1 act, 35 min., 10 m, 1 f, extras (10–14). The revolt of the Maccabees; the play can be produced with actors, puppets, or marionettes.

Solis-Cohen, Emily, Jr., and Gerson, Mary. "The Magic Top." In Solis-Cohen, Jr., *Hanukkah: The Feast of Lights*, pp. 159–86. Also in Citron, *Dramatics the Year Round*, pp. 107–17. 1 act, 35 min., 9 m, 1 f, extras (8–12). A puppet play in four scenes; two boys chase a magic dreidel.

Stoller, Minna L. *The Chanuko Play*. New York: Union of American Hebrew Congregations. 3 acts, 20 min., 4 m, 4 f (12–14). A lesson in religious freedom.

The Story of Hanukkah: A Dance Pageant with Music. Choreography by Eleanor Goff. Music by Harry Anik. New York: Anti-Defamation League of B'nai B'rith. 3 acts, 60 min., large cast (youth and adults). The historical account depicted with narration, dance, and music.

To Light a Candle. New York: Women's League for Conservative Judaism. 1 act, 12 min., 2–7 f, extras (adults). A ceremony depicting the kindling of Sabbath and Hanukkah candles and a memorial lamp.

Wishengrad, Morton. *The Lantern in the Inferno*. "Eternal Light" radio script no. 1063. New York: Department of Radio and Television, Jewish Theological Seminary of America. 30 min. (youth and adults). The story of a modern Maccabee, Hanna Senesh, and her efforts to save children during World War II.

———. *The Maccabees*. "Eternal Light" radio script no. 991. New York: Department of Radio and Television, Jewish Theological Seminary of America. 30 min. (youth and adults). The classic story of Judah and the restoration of the Temple.

Woolf, Henry. *The Dreambook*. New York: Union of American Hebrew Congregations. 1 act, 30 min., 6 m, 3 f, 4 extras (7–13). The characters of the Hanukkah story step out of a book to reenact the historic account.

Wyenn, Than. *Brighter! Brighter! Brighter!* Los Angeles: Bureau of Jewish Education. 1 act, 10 min., 2 m, 10 extras (5–8). Judah and Mattathias teach the Hanukkah candles about their important role.

Authentic Costumes for Jewish School Plays: Hanukkah. Edited by Samuel J. Citron. 12 patterns. New York: Board of Jewish Education.

Films

Cry a Warning. By Morton Wishengrad. New York: National Academy for Adult Jewish Studies, United Synagogue of America. 16 mm, black and white, sound, 28 minutes. A hellenized Jewish lad joins the Maccabees in their fight for freedom.

A Cup of Light. By David Mark. New York: National Academy for Adult
Jewish Studies, United Synagogue of America. 16 mm, black and
white, sound, 28 minutes. Features the history of several Hanukkah lamps and songs by Yaffa Yarkoni.

The Five Sons. By Howard Fast. New York: National Academy for Adult
Studies, United Synagogue of America. 16 mm, black and white,
sound, 28 minutes. A rehearsal of a traditional Hanukkah play to
dramatize the eternal values of the festival.

Hanukkah. By Yehoshua Brandstatter. Brooklyn, N.Y.: Alden Films. 16 mm,
color, sound, 14½ minutes. How the festival is celebrated in Israel.

The Legate. By Howard Fast. New York: National Academy for Adult
Jewish Studies, United Synagogue of America. 16 mm, black
and white, sound, 28 minutes. Based on the writer's *My Glorious
Brothers.*

The Liberation. By Elihu Winer. New York: National Academy for Adult
Jewish Studies, United Synagogue of America. 16 mm, black and
white, sound, 28 minutes. A blending of narration and choral and
solo music of Hanukkah.

A Light in Darkness. By Joseph Mindel. New York: National Academy for
Adult Jewish Studies, United Synagogue of America. 16 mm, black
and white, sound, 28 minutes. A contemporary retelling of the
Hanukkah story.

Oil for but One Day. By Marc Siegel. New York: National Academy for Adult
Jewish Studies, United Synagogue of America. 16 mm, black and
white, sound, 28 minutes. A program of drama and songs featuring Theodore Bikel.

A Time for Valor. New York: Jewish Chautauqua Society. 16 mm, black and
white, sound, 13½ minutes. The universal values of Hanukkah are
interpreted while a flashback depicts the struggle of the Maccabees.

A Visit with Roberta Peters. New York: National Academy for Adult Jewish
Studies, United Synagogue of America. 16 mm, black and white,
sound, 28 minutes. Miss Peters reminisces about her travels in
Israel and sings the Hanukkah blessings and hymns.

Filmstrips

Chanukah: Festival of Lights. By Mel Alpern. Photography by Shirley Flug.
Produced by Samuel Grand. New York: Union of American Hebrew Congregations. 41 frames, color, teacher's guide. Children
prepare for the festival observance.

Hanukkah and Tu Bi-Shevat. Photography by Fritz Cohen. Produced by Samuel Grand. New York: Publications Department, World Zionist
Organization. 53 frames, color, teacher's guide. The unique ways
in which the holidays are celebrated in Israel.

Our Festival of Hanukkah. By Harold Friedman and Morton Barman. Produced by Alexander Arkatov. Los Angeles: Alexander and Norsim.
35 frames, color, teacher's guide. A comparison between the
American and Maccabean revolutions.

Shlumimi and the Spinning Top. Edited by Moses Singer. Tel Aviv: Or and Kol, 40 Ibn-Gabirol St. 32 frames, color. Hebrew captions.

A Songstrip for Chanuka. Edited by Emanuel Gamoran. Produced by Samuel Grand. New York: Union of American Hebrew Congregations. 44 frames, black and white, teacher's guide. 12 Hebrew and English songs.

The Story of Hanukkah. By Samuel Grand. Art by William L. Steinel. New York: Board of Jewish Education. 42 frames, black and white, narration. The background and observances.

Dances

Lapson, Dvora. *Folk Dances for Jewish Festivals.* New York: Jewish Education Press, 1961, pp. 10–23.

_____. *Jewish Dances the Year Round.* New York: Jewish Education Press, 1957, pp. 18–20.

Solis-Cohen, Emily, Jr. *Hanukkah: The Feast of Lights.* Philadelphia: Jewish Publication Society of America, 1937, 1965, pp. 360–66.

Music

Adler, Hugo Ch. *The Joy of Dedication: A Chanukkah Poem* (mixed chorus, unison children's chorus, or solo voice with organ or piano accompaniment). Text by Alexander M. Schindler. New York: Transcontinental Music Corp., 1954.

_____. *The Lights We Have Kindled (Haneros Halalu).* New York: Transcontinental Music Corp., 1958.

Aronin, Ben. *Latkeh Ditties.* Piano arrangments by Max Janowski. Chicago: Board of Jewish Education, 1951.

Barukh, Tzefirah, ed. *Zemirot 6: Shirim le-Hanukkah.* Jerusalem: World Zionist Organization, Department of Education and Culture in the Diaspora, n.d.

Cook, Ray M. *Sing for Fun: The Complete Collection of Original Melodies and Lyrics.* New York: Union of American Hebrew Congregations, 1974, pp. 75–105, 311–45.

Coopersmith, Harry, ed. *Companion Volume to "The Songs We Sing."* New York: United Synagogue Commission on Jewish Education, 1950, pp. 37–49.

_____. *Hanukkah Songster for Choral Groups.* New York: Jewish Education Committee, 1940.

_____. *Hebrew Songster for Kindergarten and Primary Grades.* New York: Jewish Education Committee, 1948, pp. 34–38.

_____. *More of the Songs We Sing.* New York: United Synagogue Commission on Jewish Education, 1971, pp. 46–67.

_____. *The New Jewish Song Book.* New York: Behrman House, 1965, pp. 21–35.

————. *The Songs We Sing*. New York: United Synagogue Commission on Jewish Education, 1950, pp. 108–37.

Eisenstein, Judith Kaplan. *Festival Songs*. New York: Bloch Publishing Co., 1943, pp. 16–26.

————. *The Gateway to Jewish Song*. New York: Behrman House, 1939, pp. 79–92.

————, and Prensky, Frieda, eds. *Songs of Childhood*. New York: United Synagogue Commission on Jewish Education, 1955, pp. 218–32.

Engel, Rose, and Berman, Judith. *My Hanukkah Song Book*. Cincinnati: Willis Music Co., n.d.

Ephros, Gershon, ed. *Cantorial Anthology of Traditional and Modern Music*. Vol. 5. New York: Bloch Publishing Co., 1957, pp. 132–69.

Fromm, Herbert. *Hanukkah Madrigal: Mi Y'mallel: Who Can Retell*. New York: Transcontinental Music Corp., 1951.

Goldfarb, Israel, and Goldfarb, Samuel E., eds. *The Jewish Songster: Music for Voice and Piano*. Part 1. Brooklyn, N.Y., 1925, pp. 8–31.

Hanukkah Song: Mi Y'malel: Who Can Retell. Transcribed for mixed voices by Julius Chayes. New York: Transcontinental Music Corp., 1945.

Indelman, Elhanan. *Hag Li—Shir Li*. Music by Harry Coopersmith. New York: Jewish Education Committee, 1956, pp. 10–17.

Kariv, Yosef, and Miron, Issachar, eds. *Zemirot 28: The Feast of Lights*. Jerusalem: World Zionist Organization, Department for Education and Culture in the Diaspora, n.d.

————. *Zemirot 38: Milhemet Hamakabim Bayevanim: An Opera for Youth*. By Nissan Cohen Melamed. Jerusalem: World Zionist Organization, Department for Education and Culture in the Diaspora, 1961.

Krawitz, Myron J. *Four Songs for Chanukah for Two Part Chorus*. New York: Mills Music, Inc., 1956.

Levy, Sara C., and Deutsch, Beatrice L., *So We Sing: Holiday and Bible Songs for Young Jewish Children*. New York: Bloch Publishing Co., 1950, pp. 24–29.

Lomir Kinder Zingen: Let's Sing a Yiddish Song. New York: Kinderbuch Publications, 1970, pp. 64–71.

Luskin, Samuel. *The Feast of Lights: Mixed Voices*. Words by Philip M. Raskin. New York: Transcontinental Music Corp., 1941.

Mlotek, Chane, and Gottlieb, Malke, eds. *Yontefdike Teg: Song Book for the Jewish Holidays*. New York: Board of Jewish Education, 1972, pp. 24–35.

Nathanson, Moshe. *Manginoth Shireynu*. New York: Hebrew Publishing Co., 1939, pp. 72–76.

Newman, Louis I. *Ein Bereirah: No Alternative: A Maccabean Cantata*. New York: Bloch Publishing Co., 1950.

Rubin, Ruth, ed. *A Treasury of Jewish Folksong*. New York: Schocken Books, 1950, pp. 152–57.

Secunda, Sholom. *Brochos Shel Chanukoh and Haneros Halolu* (cantor and mixed voices with organ or piano accompaniment). Melville, N.Y.: Belwin Mills Publishing Co., 1964.

Union Hymnal: Songs and Prayers for Jewish Worship. 3d ed. New York: Central Conference of American Rabbis. Part 1 (1940), pp. 230–38.

Union Songster: Songs and Prayers for Jewish Youth. New York: Central Conference of American Rabbis, 1960, pp. 241–51, 257–72.

Wengrov, Charles. *Hanukkah in Song and Story*. New York: Shulsinger Brothers, 1960, pp. 61–80.

Wernick, Richard. *Chanukah Festival Overture* (unison–two part–mixed with piano accompaniment). Melville, N.Y.: Belwin Mills Publishing Co., 1962.

Recordings

Chanukah Festival of Songs. Sung by Sidor Belarsky. Artistic Enterprises B111.

Chanukah Music Box. Sung by Shirley R. Cohen. Narrated by Eli Gamliel. Kinor Records 1231.

The Chanukah Party: A Child Participation Record. Sung by Jesse Silverstein. Narrated by Fred Vogel. Ktav R 318.

Chanukah Song Parade. Sung by Gladys Gewirtz. Narrated by Eve Lippman. Menorah Men LP 206.

Chanukah Songs for Children. Sung by Shimon and Ilana. Elite ELS 404.

Chanuka: Sing with Seymour. Sung by Seymour Silbermintz. Rotona RTN-100.

Chanuka Songs for All the Family. Sung by Cilla Dagan, Yaffa Yarkoni et al., and male chorus. CBS International S 64465. Available from Peters International, New York.

Children Sing on Hanukah. Narrated by Joachim Prinz. Tikva T-88.

Hanukah: The Feast of Lights. Sung by Emanuel Rosenberg. Directed by Judith K. Eisenstein. Ktav 102.

Hanukah Songs. Sung by Dahlia Amihud. Hed Arzi AN 14059. Available from Peters International, New York.

Hanukkah at Home. Sung by Robert Segal. Script by Marc Siegel. Women's League for Conservative Judaism, New York.

Hanukkah Melodies. Sung by Claire Gordon and Dora Brenner with chamber ensemble conducted by Maurice Goldman. Bureau of Jewish Education, Los Angeles.

Hanukkah: Story of Light. Sung by Balfouria Gilad. Century 41073.

Happy Chanukah: Little Yomo: A Chanukah Story: Mother Goose Rhymes for Chanukah. Narrated by Fred Vogel. Ktav.

Judas Maccabaeus. By George F. Handel. Soloists, University of Utah Chorus, and Utah Symphony. Westminster XWL-3310.

Judas Maccabaeus: An Oratorio. By George F. Handel. Performed in Hebrew by Kol Israel Youth Choir, Tel Aviv Philharmonic Choir, and Kol Israel Orchestra. CBS-Israel 72599.

Judas Maccabeus (excerpts). By George F. Handel. British Light Orchestra. Columbia 333M.

Judas Maccabeus (excerpts). By George F. Handel. Mixed choir with organ and orchestra. Decca 25337.

More Songs for Hanukkah. By Emanuel Rosenberg. Directed by Judith K. Eisenstein. Ktav 109.

Songs for Hanukkah. Arranged by Harry Coopersmith. Board of Jewish Education. JEC 1003.

Songs for Hanukkah. Sung by Maurice Goldman. Script by Irwin Soref. Narrated by Than Wyenn. Bureau of Jewish Education, Los Angeles.

Tell Me about Chanukah. Sung by Victoria Yousha. Narrated by Edward Gold. Ktav R 302.

Tape

Judas Maccabeus. Excerpts from Handel's oratorio. New York: Commission on Interfaith Activities, Union of American Hebrew Congregations. 7-inch reel, 30 minutes.

וּקְרָאתֶם

דְּרוֹר

Proclaim liberty through-
out the land unto all the
inhabitants thereof Leviticus 25:10

Published in Philadelphia in the two-hun-
dredth year of American Independence by
The Jewish Publication Society of America

בְּאֶרֶץ לְכָל

יֹשְׁבֶיהָ

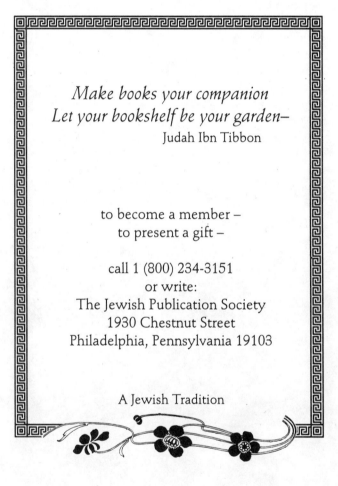

Make books your companion
Let your bookshelf be your garden—
Judah Ibn Tibbon

to become a member –
to present a gift –

call 1 (800) 234-3151
or write:
The Jewish Publication Society
1930 Chestnut Street
Philadelphia, Pennsylvania 19103

A Jewish Tradition